CHOCTAW CONFEDERATES

CHOCTAW CONFEDERATES

The American Civil War in Indian Country

Fay A. Yarbrough

THE UNIVERSITY OF NORTH CAROLINA PRESS

CHAPEL HILL

Published with the assistance of the Fred W. Morrison Fund
of the University of North Carolina Press.

© 2021 The University of North Carolina Press
All rights reserved

Designed by April Leidig
Set in Arnhem by Copperline Book Services, Inc.

Some material from chapter 1 previously appeared as "Women, Labor, and Power in the Nineteenth-Century Choctaw Nation," in *Gender and Sexuality in Indigenous North America*, edited by Sandra Slater and Fay A. Yarbrough, 123–45 (Columbia: University of South Carolina Press, 2011).

A version of chapter 6 originally appeared as "'Dis Land Which Jines Dat of Ole Master's': The Meaning of Citizenship for the Choctaw Freedpeople," in *Civil War Wests: Testing the Limits of the United States*, edited by Adam Arenson and Andrew R. Graybill, 224–41 (Oakland: University of California Press, 2015).

Front cover, top: Photograph of Hleohtambi, a Choctaw man born in Mississippi in 1825 who served as a Confederate soldier in a Choctaw regiment. Reprinted by permission of the Oklahoma Historical Society.
Front cover, bottom: Choctaw sash, ca. 1790, Metropolitan Museum of Art.
Back cover, top: Flag of the Choctaw Brigade (1st Choctaw Battalion Cavalry) during the Civil War. Back cover, background: "The War in Arkansas—The Battle of Honey Springs, July 17. Defeat of the Rebels under General Cooper by the U.S. troops under Major-General James G. Blunt," from a sketch by James R. O'Neill, *Frank Leslie's Illustrated Newspaper*, August 29, 1863.

Library of Congress Cataloging-in-Publication Data
Names: Yarbrough, Fay A., author.
Title: Choctaw Confederates : the American Civil War in Indian Country / Fay A. Yarbrough.
Description: Chapel Hill : The University of North Carolina Press, 2021. | Includes bibliographical references and index.
Identifiers: LCCN 2021015303 | ISBN 9781469665115 (cloth ; alk. paper) | ISBN 9781469688336 (pbk. ; alk. paper) | ISBN 9781469665122 (ebook) | ISBN 9798890861535 (pdf)
Subjects: LCSH: Treaty of friendship & alliance (1861 July 12) | Choctaw Indians—Indian Territory—History. | Slavery—Indian Territory—History. | Choctaw Indians—Government relations—History—19th century. | United States—History—Civil War, 1861-1865—Participation, Indian. | Indian Territory—Race relations—History.
Classification: LCC E540.I3 Y37 2021 | DDC 976.004/97387—dc23
LC record available at https://lccn.loc.gov/2021015303

For Arthur, Wilson, and Rivers

Contents

List of Maps and Figures ix

Introduction
1

1
Before the White People Came in Large
Numbers and Brought Their Customs:
Choctaws in the Southeast
13

2
Even If the Master Was Good the Slaves Was Bad Off:
Slavery and Racial Ideology
in the Choctaw Nation
47

3
The Choctaws and Chickasaws Are Entirely Southern
and Are Determined to Adhere to the Fortunes of the South:
Choosing Sides in the Conflict
75

4
We Know Dey Is Indians:
Red Soldiers in Gray
115

5
Earning One's Name:
Warfare and Choctaw Masculinity
151

6
Dis Land Which Jines Dat of Ole Master's:
Reconstruction in the Choctaw Nation
177

Conclusion
203

Acknowledgments 209

Notes 211

Bibliography 243

Index 259

Maps and Figures

MAPS

Choctaw land cessions and acquisitions 4

Choctaw and Chickasaw Nations, 1830 5

Indian Territory after removal 6

Removal of southeastern Natives 37

Physical features of Indian Territory 49

Indian Territory, 1860 77

District map of the Choctaw Nation 79

Choctaw and Chickasaw Nations, 1860 125

Civil War battle sites in Indian Territory 125

Indian Territory, 1866 183

FIGURES

Enlistment record of Private Fullumini 118

Opothle Yahola 126

Choctaw battle flag 131

Battle of Honey Springs 133

CHOCTAW
CONFEDERATES

Introduction

In the fall of 1864, Peter P. Pitchlynn, the newly elected principal chief of the Choctaw Nation, addressed his people with grim determination. He described the "rivers of blood" that had already been shed and a "land filled with widows and orphans" as a consequence of an American civil war that raged on "with unabated fury and vindictiveness on the part of the foe." In the face of an uncertain outcome, he proclaimed that Choctaws' destiny was "indissolubly involved in that of the South. By the side of our Confederate friends we must stand or we must fall." Pitchlynn juxtaposed the thousands of southern white men who had "deserted the flag of their country and become traitors and thieves" with the Choctaw soldiers who "stood as firm as their eternal mountains with their honor unsullied and their integrity unaffected." He urged his fellow Choctaws to remain committed to the Confederate cause and ended by again praising "the gallant officers and brave men of the allied army of the District of the Indian Territory."[1] Pitchlynn's words paint a picture of an Indian nation more committed to the Confederate cause than white southerners were; why and how this came to be is the subject of this book.

Each year hundreds of thousands of people, from both America and abroad, participate in reenactments of American Civil War battles, visit battle sites, and devour literature about the people, places, and events that made up the Civil War. Seldom do they encounter Native history there. And each year authors produce numerous books on the subject in treatments ranging from biographies of military leaders to exegeses on the causes of the war to the fictionalized adventures of Abraham Lincoln, "vampire hunter."[2] While centennial or sesquicentennial anniversary years of the war may further concentrate interest, resulting in special journal issues devoted to the war, newspaper editorials about battles, university lecture series on the subject, and special programs designed to encourage visitors to explore important Civil War locations at state and national parks, the war never really fades from the public imagination. And why should it? The Civil War is a defining moment in American history.

What many overlook, however, is that the Civil War was not just a rupture between northern and southern states and Americans over the issue of slavery; other groups were drawn into the fray. Though we now sometimes acknowledge the participation of Black soldiers in the Union army, the war evokes images of white men clashing in blue and gray uniforms on familiar battlegrounds: Antietam, Gettysburg, Chickamauga. But there were other battlefields out west, such as Honey Springs and Locust Grove, and other people for whom this war was a watershed.

Several American Indian nations, including the Choctaw Nation, officially sided with the Confederacy during the Civil War. Choctaw legislative documents from the era reveal that Choctaw lawmakers spent a great deal of time talking about their commitment to the Confederate States of America. Choctaw legal authorities even passed a measure demanding that all whites living in the Choctaw Nation swear allegiance to the Confederate cause. They then adjudged any criticism of the Confederacy or of the Confederate army to be a form of treason against the Choctaw Nation punishable by death. Lawmakers raised an infantry force, and later a cavalry, to fight with the Confederate forces.[3] This book explores the reasons for this level of commitment to the Confederate cause among the Choctaw and examines aspects of Confederate ideology that appealed to Choctaw authorities.

Choctaw Indians and other Native groups were deeply concerned about issues of states' rights and sovereignty. The attempts by the states of Mississippi and Georgia to unilaterally extinguish Native sovereignty rights in the decade prior to the forced removal of Native groups from the southeastern United States in the 1830s represented only the most recent in a long history of assaults on Native self-government and territorial claims. Removal policy itself starkly demonstrated that the federal government would do little to protect Native rights to land. Thus, precisely what Confederate states meant when they claimed states' rights could have profound consequences for Native nations. Choctaw leaders hoped that a strong commitment to states' rights would translate into respecting Native sovereignty rights as well, which would permit the Choctaw Nation to maintain rights to land and self-government.

The Choctaw also had a vested interest in the paramount issue for the Confederate South—maintaining the institution of slavery. European traders and settlers had introduced the Choctaw to enslaved Africans as early as the 1720s.[4] Some Choctaws participated in the capture and sale of fugitive enslaved people in the eighteenth century or retained enslaved people for their own use. Actively trading in chattel slaves was the next logical step. And by the end of the eighteenth century, Choctaws were apt to consider enslaved Africans as property to be accumulated for personal wealth rather than primarily as objects in transactions with white Americans.[5] In 1831, a federal census conducted in preparation for removing Choctaw Indians to Indian Territory enumerated 17,963 Indians, 151 white persons, and 521 enslaved people.[6] By 1860, enslaved people of African descent made up 14 percent of the population in the Choctaw Nation.[7] Enslaved people in the nation performed agricultural labor and, when fluent in both English and Choctaw languages, frequently served as interpreters for their Choctaw enslavers.[8] Like their counterparts in the American South, Choctaw enslavers carefully circumscribed the behavior of their chattel by passing legislation that prevented enslaved people from owning property or carrying guns without permission from their enslavers and prohibited the education of enslaved people.[9]

The Confederate states' argument for secession, then, addressed two concerns for the Choctaw: protecting their right to own human property and buttressing their claims to sovereignty, which Choctaws understood as vital to maintaining their polity. Surely the newly formed Confederate government could not profess to respect the sovereignty of each member state while denying the sovereignty of Indian nations. And the constitution of the newly formed Confederate States of America included clear and inviolable protections for the institution of slavery.[10]

The Choctaw Nation also shared a common geography with southerners, though the Mississippian peoples who would become the Choctaw had been there first. Prior to European immigration to the New World, Mississippian Mound Builders lived in the southeast of what would become the United States. As these societies declined, sometimes on their own and at other times due to the introduction of European diseases, groups combined to form the Choctaw and other southeastern Native groups.[11] The Choctaw people who emerged through this process lived in the Mississippi River valley until the forced relocation of Natives from the southeastern United States to Indian Territory. The boundaries of the Choctaw Nation included much of the present-day state of Mississippi, as well as western parts of Alabama. To the west, Choctaw lands ended at the Mississippi River and to the north at the boundary of Chickasaw territory.

During the first three decades of the nineteenth century, however, the Choctaw Nation ceded portions of this territory to the United States through a series of treaties advocated by federal and state governments as a part of a larger American settler colonial project.[12] For land-hungry white Americans, the Choctaws and other southeastern groups appeared to be in possession of large tracts of territory that could support, according

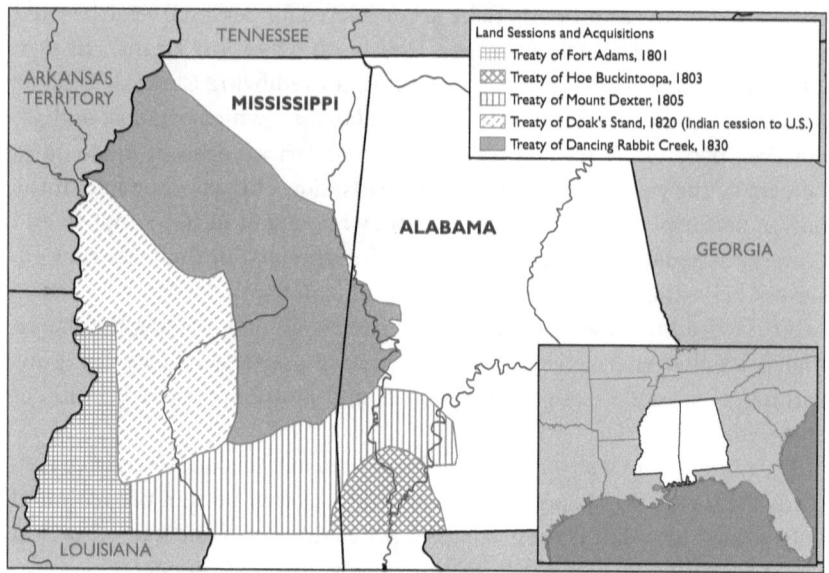

Choctaw land cessions and acquisitions.
(Map by Rice University GIS/Data Center)

to then-president Andrew Jackson, "cities, towns, and prosperous farms" rather than be "ranged by a few thousand savages."[13] In this view, Indian nations had far more land than was needed to sustain their small populations, and a much more appropriate and efficient use of this land could be cotton cultivation. Of course, many Choctaws were in fact farmers who cultivated corn and cotton, and some would even join the ranks of enslavers. Nevertheless, by the time of removal, the Choctaw territory had shrunk to a diagonal swath of land that stretched from the northwestern corner of the present-day state of Mississippi to southeastern Mississippi, and white Americans had moved into the ceded territory.

The new Choctaw lands west of the Mississippi River remained within the larger geographic confines of the South. The 1830 Treaty of Dancing Rabbit Creek stipulated that the Choctaw would cede to the United States over 10 million acres of land in the Mississippi River valley in exchange for land in Indian Territory. In other words, the treaty provided for the removal of the Choctaw Nation from the Southeast, which opened up more territory for white settlement, increased cotton cultivation, and, in turn, fed the demand for enslaved labor. The combined Choctaw and Chickasaw Nations in Indian Territory extended across approximately the southern third of

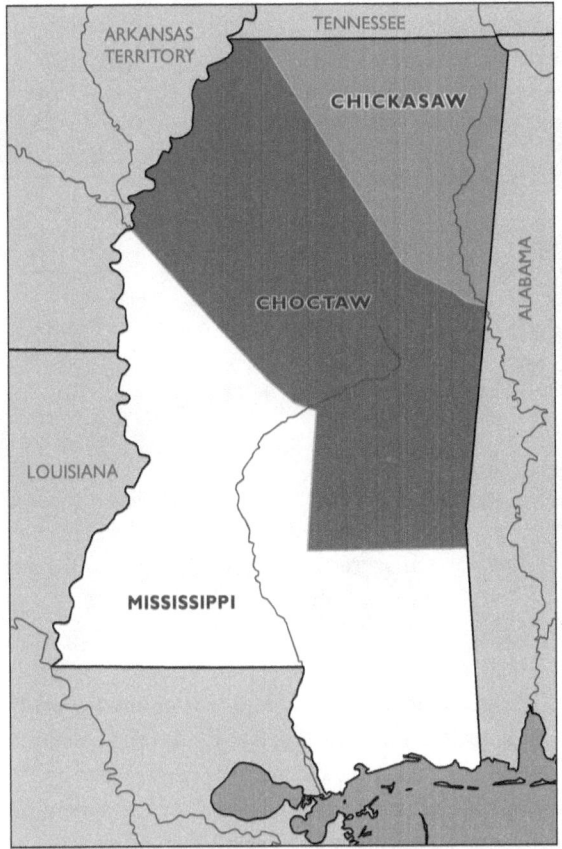

Choctaw and Chickasaw Nations, 1830.
(Map by Rice University GIS/Data Center)

the present-day state of Oklahoma. Chickasaws' desire to assert more political autonomy led to the dissolution of the special relationship between the Choctaw and Chickasaw Nations in 1855, which meant that by the eve of the Civil War, the Choctaw Nation held territory only in the southeastern corner of Indian Territory.

Despite the massive geographic upheaval that Choctaws experienced in the first half of the nineteenth century, a constant was their contact with white southerners: they often conducted business with white southerners, their neighbors were southerners both white and Black, and they had adopted the enslavement of people of African descent, an institution that was increasingly concentrated in the South geographically, though the entire

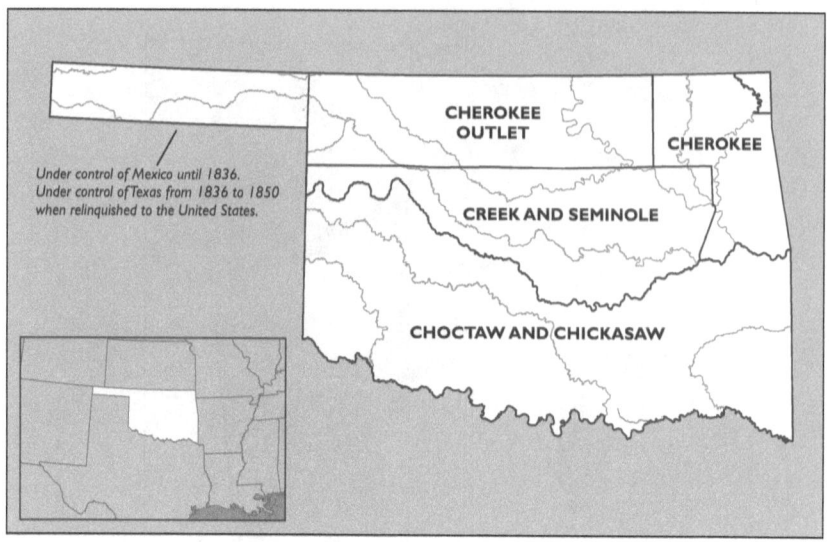

Indian Territory after removal.
(Map by Rice University GIS/Data Center)

United States benefited economically and was shaped socially by its practice. Slavery was a national institution, but living with enslaved people was largely a southern phenomenon by the antebellum period.[14] Moreover, if one drew a latitudinal line east along the northern border of the 1860 Choctaw Nation, southern states such as Texas, Mississippi, Alabama, Georgia, and South Carolina would fall below it, and Tennessee, North Carolina, and Virginia above it. The Choctaw experience, then, was a southern experience.

When the American Civil War ended, the Choctaw were subject to federal authority like their southern Confederate allies. And, as with the American South, the federal government attempted to reestablish friendly relations with the Choctaw Nation and create a new position within Choctaw society for freedpeople formerly held as slaves by members of the Choctaw Nation. Federal authorities negotiated a treaty with the Choctaw Nation that included provisions for granting the Choctaw freedpeople Choctaw citizenship, civil rights, and access to land (something that the federal government neglected to do for its own formerly enslaved population), but the Choctaw Nation circumvented these measures. In a move that bears some striking similarities to events in the post–Civil War American South, Choctaw lawmakers created a separate class of citizenship for people of African descent in the Choctaw Nation. Ironically, given the history of removal, nineteenth-century Choctaws were far more "southern" than their white contemporaries realized. This book will consider Choctaws' perspective in their decision to ally with the Confederacy during the American Civil War and Choctaw efforts to limit the legal rights of formerly enslaved people in the Reconstruction era.

In the wealth of scholarship produced about the Civil War, Native groups, when they are discussed, tend to appear as a footnote or perhaps a chapter, often about military tactics or land loss, or as part of a larger effort to consider who constituted the southern population. For instance, Scott Nelson and Carol Sheriff discuss Native populations largely in reference to changes in Union military tactics and the Lieber Code—instructions regarding the conduct of warfare that seemed to draw in part on the military's interactions with Indians out west.[15] In James M. McPherson's magisterial *Battle Cry of Freedom*, Native populations appear briefly as they lose land to American expansion and send regiments to fight in the war.[16] In Anne J. Bailey's work, Native populations represent one chapter in a consideration of the ethnic and racial variety of southerners.[17] Bailey describes the prejudice Native troops faced in the Confederate army and the variety of positions Native groups took regarding the war. Similarly, in Susannah J. Ural's edited volume, William McKee Evans posits that Natives served largely for financial incentives or because of "pressure from some powerful patron or protector" in his chapter on western and eastern Cherokees and Lumbees in North Carolina in the Civil War.[18] None of this is to suggest that there are shortcomings in these and other scholarly works; rather, these comments demonstrate that even with the plethora of books produced about the American Civil War, there is still fresh territory to be explored and stories that remain untold.

In general, there is a dearth of historiographical material that studies Native participation in the American Civil War from the perspective of Native peoples. Mark Lause, for instance, argues that the Union army in the western theater of the Civil War offered positive potential for American race relations but pays little attention to Native attitudes toward people of African descent.[19] Laurence M. Hauptman focuses on specific Native groups in particular regions and how each participated in the American Civil War. Thus, Hauptman examines Delaware Union scouts and home guards and Ottawa sharpshooters and suggests that Native groups entered the war to push back against American expansion and because "it seemed imperative for their own and/or their Indian community's survival."[20]

Scholars have devoted a few volumes to the participation of Cherokee Indians in the war, but the Choctaw Nation has not yet been a focus of study.[21]

Recent works by Mary Jane Warde and Bradley R. Clampitt look at the war's impact in Indian Territory as a whole.[22] In classic studies that remain valuable a century after their publication, Annie Heloise Abel explored the ties between the Confederacy and various Indigenous groups, but Abel placed the onus for the alliance on the Confederate South.[23] While white southerners worked in the Indian agencies, sought Indian allies, and influenced Indian attitudes, the Indian nations had their own reasons for pursuing alliances with the Confederacy, and these reasons explain the strength of Choctaw support for the South. I explore the ways Choctaw Indians saw the American Civil War as connected to their own survival as a separate, sovereign nation—that is, what common cause Choctaw Indians found with the Confederate South.

One goal of this work is to capture Choctaw voices by using sources produced by the Choctaw Indians themselves whenever possible. Fortunately, the Choctaw produced a wide variety of documents, including legislative and legal records, for historians to consider. Figures such as Peter P. Pitchlynn, whose comments as chief open this volume, left behind journals and correspondence that provide valuable insight into life in Indian Territory during the nineteenth century. Pitchlynn's papers are especially useful because he played such an important role in Choctaw affairs: he helped draft several Choctaw constitutions; he "was architect of the educational system" for the Choctaw; and he traveled to Washington, DC, to represent Choctaw financial interests to the federal government.[24] While written sources tend to capture the experiences of literate and often wealthier individuals, the Indian Pioneer History (IPH) Collection includes a rich store of anecdotal material about the nineteenth-century Choctaw Nation from a wider variety of informants. The Works Progress Administration (WPA) created the IPH Collection during the 1930s, in an initiative similar to the one that led to the collection of the narratives of formerly enslaved people. Workers interviewed people who had lived in Indian Territory during the nineteenth century and recorded the responses. The IPH Collection includes interviews from men and women; from people of African descent, whites, and Natives; from people of all ages; and from people of varying levels of literacy and wealth. Interviewees talked about a variety of subjects, including the food they ate, the habits of the Indigenous populations, education, the functioning of the government, daily life, the landscape, sensational crimes, and, most importantly for my purposes, the Civil War. The service records for the First Choctaw and Chickasaw Mounted Rifles provide enlistment information about Choctaw troops and occasional insights into the experiences of individual soldiers. And when all of these sources fell short, I have turned to the methodology of "'side-streaming,' or the use of general (often regional) models, to conceptualize histories of a specific Native society and apply that model to the available written evidence from other geographic or historical contexts."[25] In other words, information about other Native groups in the region can shed light on the Choctaw experience.

I also draw on the WPA slave narratives collected from informants living in the state of Oklahoma, which capture the experiences of both enslaved people owned by members of Indian nations and enslaved people owned by American citizens. Scholars have questioned these narratives for a number of reasons: the uncertain reliability of sources dependent on fallible memory, the biases of those recording the interviews, and the possible impact of the race of the interviewers on the respondents.[26] Moreover, the interviewees were quite elderly, and the experience of enslaved children is overrepresented because freedpeople who survived until the 1930s were likely small children at the time of emancipation. The interviews are also not a random sample that reflects the distribution of slavery in the South: for instance, Louisiana did not participate in the collection of these narratives, while Arkansas furnished 33 percent of the freedpeople interviewed, though the state never had more than 3.5 percent of the enslaved population.[27]

In chapters 2 and 6, which focus on slavery and Reconstruction respectively, I rely on the Oklahoma WPA narratives to give voice to enslaved people. Not all of these individuals experienced slavery in Indian Territory, nor were they all owned by members of Indian nations. In fact, only 28 of the 130 narratives collected in the Oklahoma Slave Narrative Project capture the experiences of enslaved people held by American Indians.[28] Some informants arrived in the territory or its vicinity as the Civil War erupted and their enslavers hoped to keep human property out of Union hands. Others came after emancipation in search of opportunities, as we will see, and still others followed family members to settle in the state. That said, the Oklahoma slave narratives do offer one of the few inside glimpses of slavery among the so-called Civilized Tribes. I supplement these narratives with IPH interviews of residents of Indian Territory. In spite of the problems of the WPA slave narratives, they still offer one of the few windows to the interior lives of enslaved people.[29]

Perhaps most troubling to modern readers of the WPA slave narratives are the informants who insisted that they fared better as slaves than as freedpeople. As historian Stephanie J. Shaw has argued, such comments suggest that the interviews reveal more about the conditions of the Great Depression, particularly the grinding poverty and real hunger faced by many African Americans, than about the lives of enslaved people.[30] Interestingly, similar questions have not materialized about the use of the IPH Collection. Sometimes the informants used language that readers may find racially insensitive. Rather than censor the sources, I have left quoted material as it appears. Moreover, the use of these terms reveals how pervasive such language and attendant ideas about race were in the 1930s. In the WPA and IPH sources, the informants' voices have already been mediated through interviewers. I do not want to add myself as another layer filtering those informants; thus, I attempt to preserve their voices whenever possible, often through extensive quotes. To be sure, the WPA slave narratives have their problems, as do all sources, but they remain one of the few connections to an otherwise almost silent mass of people, a population legally prohibited from accessing literacy to record their own experiences. If one follows the suggestions of historian Elizabeth Fox-Genovese to approach the narratives carefully, to check them against other accounts of slavery, to compare the narratives to each other for consistency, and to put them in context, the narratives can be a fruitful and invaluable source about slavery, the Civil War, and emancipation.[31]

This work follows a largely chronological organization. I begin with a summary of the origins of the Choctaw Nation; traditional practices, particularly regarding gender; and the nation's removal to Indian Territory. Chapter 2 provides an overview of slavery as implemented by Choctaws and the growth of racial thinking in the Choctaw Nation. These two chapters demonstrate that Choctaw people attempted to preserve some traditional practices or adapt new institutions to older beliefs in the face of relentless pressure from the federal government, state officials, and white settlers. The third chapter traces Choctaw lawmakers' political calculus in siding with the Confederate states, paying special attention to the treaty language that forged the alliance. Choctaw officials negotiated terms that protected Native sovereignty. I turn to the mechanics of war in chapter 4 and mine enlistment records for what they reveal about Confederate Choctaw soldiers' martial experiences. The Civil War offered Choctaw men an opportunity to recover their identities as warriors, an essential component of traditional understandings of Choctaw masculinity, which is the subject of chapter 5. Reconstruction and the efforts to establish the terms for incorporating people of African descent into the Choctaw polity are the focus of the final chapter. Again, I demonstrate that Choctaw legislators' decisions about the place of people of African descent in the Choctaw Nation took traditional practices and the protection of sovereignty and Choctaw identity into account.

In sum, the chapters that follow examine slavery, emancipation, the Civil War era, and Reconstruction from the less familiar vantage point of the Choctaw Nation and Indian Territory. I ask readers to redefine what we mean by "southern"; shift our perspective to see beyond the traditional binary of the Union and the Confederacy; and interrogate what we think we know about the historical relationship between Native populations and slavery. The perspective of Choctaw Indians on the conflict was at times startlingly similar to that of other white southerners, given the part played by Confederate states such as Georgia, Mississippi, and Alabama in Indian removal. I argue that Choctaw officials were driven by a desire to protect Native sovereignty and Choctaw identity and believed the Confederate States of America offered the best path to do so. Contemporary debates within Native groups about the inclusion or exclusion of the descendants of their formerly enslaved people as tribal citizens and recent controversies about the meaning of the Confederate flag and Confederate monuments demonstrate that the issues that cleaved Indian Territory and the United States during the Civil War have yet to be resolved and continue to have repercussions for people today.

Chapter 1

Before the White People Came in Large Numbers and Brought Their Customs

CHOCTAWS IN THE SOUTHEAST

Even before fighting from the American Civil War arrived on the doorstep of Indian Territory in 1861, the nineteenth century had already proven to be a time of tremendous change for the people of the Choctaw Nation. In the first three decades of the century, the Choctaw people shifted from governing individual behavior through traditional practices and understandings of clan obligation and responsibility to writing down laws to control behavior and punish criminality in the nation. This shift reflected the Choctaw Nation's efforts to make itself legible to federal and state governments as independent and sovereign, with a distinct culture and identity, a move made simultaneously by its Native neighbors in the Southeast, including the Chickasaw Nation, the Cherokee Nation, and the Creek Nation. But such action did not stem white southerners' demands for Native territory or prevent the federal government from pushing Natives out of the southeastern United States.

For Choctaws, clans were a central component of identity that shaped family and marriage structure. Within these Choctaw families, labor was gendered, with men and women performing different, complementary tasks for the household. But when Choctaws moved to formalize practices through written laws, they began to turn away from traditional labor arrangements. The newly formalized Choctaw government negotiated land cessions that resulted in the relocation of the Choctaw Nation to Indian Territory. Thousands of people migrated from the Mississippi River valley to new lands west of the Mississippi River and then reestablished their newly formed government. The Choctaw movement west was a part of the larger removal of Native people from the southeastern United States that "undoubtedly contributed to the growth of slavery and the conditions that caused the Civil War" and embroiled Native nations.[1] In this chapter I will outline the basic social organization of traditional Choctaw society, describe the contours of the new Choctaw constitution, and provide a brief summary of the Choctaw removal to Indian Territory. This exploration of Choctaws' traditional values, motivations for institutionalizing their form of governance, and negotiation of the process of removal sheds light on how Choctaws would later approach their decision to join the Confederacy in the Civil War: Choctaws prioritized protecting their legitimacy as a nation and their coherence as a community with a shared identity.

Traditionally, the Choctaw organized themselves into two groups, the Imoklasha and the Iholahata, each consisting of several clans.[2] Choctaw Indians determined clan membership, which was a key part of Choctaw identity, matrilineally; that is, children became members of their mother's, not their father's, clan.[3] Thus, within a household, a mother and her children were kin, while the husband was "a guest rather than a relative."[4] Elizabeth Kemp Mead may have been referencing the practice of assigning clan membership matrilineally when she remarked, "In old time the Choctaw children took the mother's housename instead of taking the father's name."[5] Given the traditional lack of the use of surnames among the Choctaw, this description of how one traditionally received a "housename" may have served as a kind of shorthand for clan membership or a nineteenth-century interpretation of what clan membership meant.[6] Matrilineal kinship arrangements also meant that the family sought the advice of the oldest maternal uncle or oldest maternal male relative in important decisions regarding children. The maternal family took responsibility for raising children who lost their mother through death. And the woman's children, not her husband, inherited her property. A Choctaw man's siblings or other members of his clan took possession of his property if he died: "His children, being looked on as members of another *ogla*, since they belonged to their mother's family, were not considered as entitled to any of this property."[7]

Clan membership had been so vital as a form of social organization because of the traditional practice of blood revenge among the Choctaw Indians: "*Iksa* [clan] members were obligated to aid each other and to obtain blood revenge for the killing of one of their members." It was the "right, but also the imperative duty of the nearest relative on the male side of the slain, to kill the slayer wherever and whenever a favorable opportunity was presented."[8] If the guilty party fled, which was an unusual occurrence, a male relative might volunteer or be chosen as a substitute whose death would fulfill the debt. The victim's family would never choose a female relative of the perpetrator to serve as a substitute, though a female relative could choose to volunteer.[9] Once the debt was paid, there was no further retribution. In other words, the perpetrator's (or substitute's) clan did not feel obliged to avenge his or her death in turn. Scholar Michelene E. Pesantubbee argues that the term "blood revenge" is a mischaracterization of the practice and that clan members were not actually obliged to kill the murderer of a kinsperson but rather to "restore balance to their world" or to "seek restitution for a life."[10] Thus, a Choctaw family or clan could seek the death of the person responsible for the death of their kinsperson or adopt the responsible party into the family's clan. In rare instances, the family might accept some form of payment as restitution.[11] The recognition by all Choctaws, as well as other Native peoples, of the clan obligations in the event of a member's death served to curb warfare and personal violence.[12] When Choctaws chose to go to war with another group that shared a similar perspective about clan obligations, they recognized that not only warriors would be put in jeopardy. Any Choctaw could be the target of retribution. This practice may, in part, explain the Choctaw's avoidance of offensive wars.[13] Similarly, one would tread carefully in daily personal exchanges because a misstep could obligate kinsmen in complicated ways.

While children were born into the clans of their mothers, both Choctaw men and women were responsible for the care and nurture of children, the difference being that Choctaw men were not the primary decision makers regarding their own biological children but instead played an important role in the lives of their nieces and nephews. Historians suggest the practice of infanticide existed among the Choctaw, which prompts the question of who made decisions about the practice given these understandings about who was responsible for childcare among the Choctaw. Richard White, for instance, notes, "Infanticide was widespread in the nation, but it was a practice about which little is known. Which children the Choctaws killed and why remains unclear."[14] In such cases, the burden for these decisions may have been shared between parents or between mothers and their male relatives. That is, the child's maternal uncle may have been a part of the decision-making process, as one would expect given the operation of matrilineal clans, or the child's parents may have made this decision alone. H. B. Cushman, the son of missionaries who lived among the Choctaw during the nineteenth century, offers a quote from Chief Aboha Kulla Humma of the Okla Hunnali, who claimed that "the Choctaw women sometimes killed their infants, when they did not want to provide for them," which, if taken at face value, suggests that Choctaw women in particular practiced infanticide.[15] Given the concept of blood vengeance, the death of one member of a Choctaw clan at the hands of another member of the same clan could circumvent the need for external retribution, perhaps lending further weight to the role of Choctaw women in the practice of infanticide. That is, because the death of the infant was perpetrated by someone from the same clan, other clan members would not be obligated to seek revenge as they would if the perpetrator were from outside of the clan. And Chief Aboha Kulla Humma's reference to the inability to provide for infants as the cause for infanticide might indicate that food shortages account for the practice.

Choctaw households were not only matrilineal but also matrilocal: husbands joined their wives' households upon marriage.[16] These two facts, that Choctaws assigned clan membership matrilineally and that Choctaw men joined their wives' households, may explain the ease with which marital unions could be dissolved, though separations seldom occurred, according to early descriptions of Choctaw marriages.[17] By the nineteenth century, according to Chief Aboha Kulla Humma, separations between Choctaw husbands and wives may have been more common. In 1822, the Choctaw of Six Towns enacted a law punishing men who ran away with other men's wives with whippings of thirty-nine lashes.[18] Runaway wives received the same punishment. Chief Aboha Kulla Humma did not mention punishments for runaway husbands; perhaps Choctaws did not find errant husbands as threatening because such men could not produce individuals with clan membership. In any case, when a couple separated, there were no questions about who would be responsible for raising the children: the wife and her family would maintain any children. The husband remained a member of his own clan and could return to his mother's or some other female relative's household. Such social factors may also explain the traditional Choctaw acceptance of polygamous unions, although polygamy was not widespread among the Choctaw and tended to occur when the plural wives were sisters.[19] These women may have shared a household anyway, and adding one husband rather than two may have lessened labor burdens for the women.[20] By 1849, the General Council outlawed polygamy and penalized those individuals found guilty of polygamy with a fine of ten to twenty-five dollars for each count.[21]

Within these matrilocal households, men and women performed different kinds of labor.[22] Choctaw men provided meat for their families through hunting.[23] Men also served as warriors in the larger Choctaw society. While men might help with the planting and harvesting of crops, women were primarily responsible for maintaining the crop and might even ridicule men who performed too much agricultural labor.[24] Such men were stepping outside of the prescribed gendered division of labor, and Choctaw women tried to push these men back into their accepted roles through public shame.

William Edward Baker, a Cherokee resident of Indian Territory familiar with his Choctaw neighbors, described Native labor practices more generally, but his depiction could easily have applied to the Choctaw: "The Indian women did all the work unless they hired it done. The men hunted and fished and sat around eating and drinking sofkey."[25] Knowledge of the traditional division of labor among the Choctaw Indians even filtered down to their enslaved property. Jefferson L. Cole, enslaved by a Choctaw family, recalled that Choctaw women had initially farmed while men hunted until "after the white people came in large numbers and brought their customs." Then Indian men also helped with farming.[26] The traditional division of labor between Choctaw husbands and wives may best be encapsulated by the Choctaw marriage practice in which "the man offers meat and the woman corn to seal the relationship."[27]

These gendered labor divisions were not entirely rigid. Another group about whom historians know less is two-spirit people, individuals with mixed gender roles or queer sexuality and sometimes a combination of both.[28] Two spirits might assume the dress or mannerisms of the other gender, including the performance of labor. While the written record is sparse, some evidence suggests that two-spirit people were members of southeastern tribes, including the Choctaw.[29] Historian Roger Carpenter finds some regional variation: some two spirits moved between gender roles multiple times in their lives, while for others the change was more permanent, and many Native peoples believed "that two-spirit people could wield considerable supernatural power" to both positive and negative effect.[30]

Women controlled the home and communally owned farmlands and performed the bulk of agricultural labor. In fact, Cushman stated that Choctaw women performed all of the "drudgery work about the house and hunting camp."[31] Cushman's characterization of the labor as "drudgery work" reflects his attitude rather than that of Choctaw Indians regarding this important work performed by Choctaw women. Nineteenth-century Indian Territory resident Lucy Case, who described both of her parents as "full-blood" Choctaw Indians, stated, "I remember that my mother did most of the work. She always did the breaking of the land."[32] In particular, Choctaw women were responsible for growing corn, a staple of the Choctaw diet.[33] Anna McClendon Smallwood, a Choctaw woman, recalled, "The only crops raised by the Indians of early territory days were small patches of squaw corn, called Tom Fuller corn and later named squaw corn because the squaws, or women, did all the raising of this particular crop."[34] Emmaline Terrell also related that squaw corn was so named because women did all of the work to cultivate it.[35] Women also seemed to be responsible for the preparation of corn into other food products.[36] Rodolphus Gardner remembered his mother beating corn in a mortar.[37] Many different traditional Choctaw dishes began with pounded corn as their base.[38]

Women's management of corn production was a source of influence in Choctaw society.[39] Corn provided important sustenance for Choctaw families; historian Richard White extrapolates that corn and other cultivated crops could have provided roughly two-thirds of the daily caloric intake for Choctaws. Choctaw women, then, provided the bulk of a family's food supply. Corn was also a gift for a daughter's wedding. A feast was generally a part of the marriage ritual, and corn would have figured prominently in such a meal.[40] Friendly diplomatic negotiations often included an exchange of corn, and corn was at the center of hospitality more generally because many dishes that Choctaws would offer to their guests included corn as an ingredient.[41] Corn also could serve as a form of medicine that "drew on the power of all three worlds to bring health."[42] For warriors, corn sustained expeditions by providing important nutrition when using rifles to shoot game would have alerted enemies of their presence.[43] Finally, corn was an important part of ceremonial life. The appearance of green corn indicated that the end of the Choctaw year was near.[44] The Choctaw also held most of their feasts at this time, including a Green Corn Dance.[45] This celebration of green corn may also have served as an acknowledgment of Choctaw women and the important agricultural work they did.[46]

During the first third of the nineteenth century, the Choctaw began an uneven process of formalizing their practices in written laws. Rather than respond to American pressure to cede more land, adopt Christian religion, or abandon Choctaw cultural practices by creating a national and unified polity, the three districts that made up the Choctaw Nation each, at least initially, continued to behave more like independent nations. The districts did meet in a national council, which required unanimity for a decision to be binding; however, the districts sometimes had antagonistic relationships that made such consensus difficult to achieve. Moreover, individual districts sometimes acted against the wishes of the others. For instance, in 1803 the southern district independently ceded 853,000 acres to the United States without the consent of the other two districts. The districts did sometimes agree on policy, as when they officially abandoned the practice of blood revenge in murders involving American perpetrators and Choctaw victims in 1812. As scholar Duane Champagne notes, however, this change says more about the pressure exerted by American officials who objected to the practice of blood revenge than about the effectiveness of the council as a national political unit; the Choctaw continued the practice among themselves—that is, in murders in which both the perpetrator and victim were Choctaws—until the late 1820s.[47]

So while the Cherokee, for instance, were drafting a constitution and creating a bicameral legislative body to enact national laws, the Choctaw continued to address legal change at the district level. In the 1820s, the northeastern district created a lighthorse patrol that aided in the collection of debts and the protection of private property. The lighthorsemen—the Choctaw equivalent of law enforcement officers—also upheld other local ordinances passed by the northeastern district council regarding infanticide, the sale of liquor, and the theft of livestock. In the southern district, the council banned the trade of whiskey and polygamy and ordered the destruction of crops of corn produced by men rather than women because such agricultural activity violated social norms.[48] By 1826, however, the Choctaw aimed to form a more centralized government through a constitution. The chiefs of the three districts composed the executive branch, with unanimity required for any decision to be binding, and were elected to four-year terms. The legislative branch consisted of a National Council and a National Committee.[49] Rather than meeting on an ad hoc basis, the National Council, whose members were selected by the district chiefs, would meet twice per year. Each district still had the ability to pass its own laws; however, those laws now also required the approval of the larger legislature. Each district also maintained a "standing eight-man committee" that was required to meet four times per year.[50] The three standing committees met in combination as the National Committee. Many members of the National Committee came from English-speaking families who owned people of African descent, which may account for the early enactment of laws regarding inheritance and the protection of property by this Choctaw legislature. Indeed, the overrepresentation of slave-holding, English-speaking families among Choctaw legislators would continue throughout the antebellum period.[51] The National Committee was also responsible for assisting in any treaty negotiations with the federal government.[52]

From 1826 until removal in 1830, this new Choctaw government enacted a variety of laws. One of the first orders of business was to prohibit the sale of land by any district unless the other two districts consented to the sale.[53] Clearly, one motivating factor for the creation of this centralized polity was the belief that it would better protect the Choctaw land base. In a system with clearly designated lines of authority and procedures for enacting legislation in a form recognizable to federal officials, the Choctaw hoped Americans and individual Choctaws would cease land cessions for the settling of private debts, for instance.

Other new legislation addressed crimes against individuals. Perpetrators of infanticide and rape would receive lashes with a switch.[54] In 1828, the legislature outlined the various categories of homicide and their penalties. Accidental deaths and deaths due to someone acting in self-defense were not punishable. The penalty for murder was incarceration, but where "a group of two or more men gets out of control, if even one, or all, is killed, all of them shall be executed." The lawmakers also addressed blood vengeance when they prohibited the family members of a murderer from being harmed in the event that the murderer fled the authorities.[55] In effect, this law enlarged the ban on blood vengeance from 1812 to include murders in which both the victim and perpetrator were Choctaws, a departure from traditional practice that reveals the influence of multiple factors: Americans' continued objections to the practice, the presence of Christian missionaries within Choctaw territory, and the growing influence of legislators who adopted Christian religion.[56]

Around the same time that the new Choctaw government was forming and passing legislation, Christian missionaries also focused their attention on southeastern Natives, in part because they thought the population of Indigenous people in New England was disappearing. For instance, the Society for Propagating the Gospel among the Indians and Others in North America, which officially formed in Massachusetts in 1787, sent Presbyterian minister John Schermerhorn in 1813 to visit remote areas where Natives resided, including the southeastern United States, to report back on what he observed. Schermerhorn thought the Choctaw, along with the Cherokee and Chickasaw, would be particularly receptive to the establishment of a mission in their territory.[57] A similar group called the American Board of Commissioners for Foreign Missions formed in 1810 and sent representatives such as Cyrus Kingsbury among Indian nations to ascertain the living conditions there to determine whether the population was ready for Christianity.[58] It seemed that different denominations, including Presbyterians, Methodists, and Baptists, were willing to compete for the privilege of converting Choctaw souls.[59] And some of these missionaries would serve as valuable allies who advocated for Native nations' land rights and sovereignty to members of Congress and federal officials.[60]

Choctaw legislation passed in 1828 reveals changes in Choctaw thinking about clan obligations and gender roles that suggest the influence of Christian missionaries. A new law stated that "when a man dies without having made a will, his wife and his children shall come to inherit all his lifestock [*sic*] and estate." The husband's estate was to be divided into three portions, with the widow receiving one-third and any children the remaining two-thirds. If the husband died without children, his relatives could inherit his property.[61] In the past, the widow and her children would not have received any of the deceased man's property. Rather, she would have relied on support from her clan as she raised her children, and his clan members would have received his estate. The lawmakers then reiterated this division of property in cases where an individual died intestate, but in more inclusive language, so that either the husband or the wife could inherit one-third of the deceased spouse's estate if the couple had been "living together compatibly for four months." The other two-thirds of the estate was designated for relatives.[62] If one passed away with a properly prepared will, the terms of the will would be fulfilled; however, "every individual's will must provide for his wife and children, both of them; if the will is insufficient for his children, it shall not be upheld." The surviving child and parent would then receive half of the estate. If the union had not produced children, the surviving spouse would receive one-third of the estate.[63] Again, this insistence that wives and children had a claim on husbands' and fathers' property after death was not a traditional Choctaw practice. The new inheritance patterns indicate a newer expectation that fathers rather than clans were responsible for the well-being of individuals, reflecting a change in thinking about men's roles and the importance of clan membership. This change also likely reflects the reality of an increasing number of white men marrying into Choctaw society who wanted to leave property to their Choctaw children and brought their own ideas about the roles that fathers should play in families into the nation.

The rise in marriages between white men and Choctaw women spurred other Choctaw legislation to regulate the practice and its consequences. In 1828, the Choctaw legislature required "an officer of the particular district" to be present and a marriage license for such unions. Marriages could be validated by a religious ceremony or recognition from an official, and the white husband would "be included with us and be counted with us."[64] Based on the language of this law, it is unclear whether licenses and the presence of a district officer were required for marriages between white women and Choctaw men or in marriages in which both partners were Choctaws. Later legislation, which I will discuss, suggests that these latter categories of marriage did not have to adhere to these conditions to achieve official recognition. Moreover, as discussed previously, marriages in the Choctaw Nation had traditionally involved an exchange of meat and corn, not the presence of district officers or the issuance of a license. This 1828 law, then, represents a dramatic shift in thinking about what constituted the act of marriage when the parties were a white man and a Choctaw woman.

These unions could precipitate other questions in which Choctaw and American practices collided. The legislature also stipulated that "if a white man and Choctaw woman are married, the woman has a right to their property" and that "if a white man is married to a Choctaw woman, if that woman is deceased, the woman's possessions cannot be taken out of the Choctaw nation and taken away."[65] Both of these laws addressed the differences in the property rights of Choctaw women and white American women: Choctaw women had traditionally been agriculturalists with a vested interest in communally owned lands and had property rights that did not terminate upon marriage, while white women legally lost control of their property upon marriage. These legal statutes recognized and affirmed Choctaw women's property rights even in the face of their marriages to white men, who were likely unfamiliar with Choctaw gender norms. Choctaw lawmakers may also have been suspicious that some white men were choosing Choctaw wives in order to gain access to the women's property. Unscrupulous intermarried white men might attempt to sell Choctaw land to whites, for instance. And perhaps preventing the removal of property from the nation by white widowers was lawmakers' attempt to acknowledge that a woman's clan members had an interest in that property.

That Choctaw lawmakers were particularly concerned about the marital choices of Choctaw women is clear from their omission of laws regulating unions between Choctaw men and outsiders, particularly given the events at the Foreign Mission School in Cornwall, Connecticut, just a few years prior. The American Board of Commissioners for Foreign Missions had established the school to educate Indigenous young men from abroad and eventually from Indigenous nations closer to home. Elite Native families such as the Choctaw Folsoms and the Cherokee Ridges sometimes sent their sons to attend the school.[66] In 1824, when Sarah Northrup, a local young white woman, and John Ridge, son of a wealthy Cherokee planter, announced their engagement, members of the public threatened to lynch Ridge. And local newspapers printed articles denouncing the school's supporters. The Northrup family relented in their opposition to the union, though, after Ridge returned to the community in a coach driven by an enslaved and liveried driver. Perhaps this demonstration of wealth softened the Northrups' attitude.[67] Still, when news of the impending marriage between Harriet Gold, a young woman from Cornwall, and Elias Boudinot, a Cherokee student at the Foreign Mission School and cousin of John Ridge, was announced the following year, community tempers had not cooled. Harriet's brother and her friends from the choir in which she sang burned Harriet in effigy as she watched.[68] News of these events surely reached the Choctaw Nation. Thus, the possibility of Choctaw men marrying white women was clear to legislators, but they did not pass laws to address these unions, despite the potential of such intermarriages to disrupt the operation of clan membership.

The introduction of written legal statutes that deviated from traditional Choctaw practices regarding property distribution and marriage demonstrates that ideas about clan and gender were in the midst of transformation; so, too, were ideas about what constituted property more broadly. Previously, individual districts had passed laws about private property and fences, but in 1828 these laws took on a national character. The national law mandated that fences surrounding livestock be five feet high and fences around fields be two to three feet high with a spacing of four inches between the logs. Livestock owners were liable for damage caused by their animals to others' property.[69] This new interest in fencing livestock and fields ran counter to older practices that relied on hunting game rather than raising livestock for meat. Richard White describes this transition from game to livestock as part of a "larger economic and social breakdown" that was a move away from the traditional Choctaw economy and older settlement patterns.[70] Choctaws had also farmed communally on large tracts of land that surrounded the village. In part, the practice of communal landownership meant that individual Choctaws could not sell land to others, especially outsiders, thereby protecting the tribal land base. By the nineteenth century, however, families controlled specific fields fenced off within the communal field.[71] Enclosing the fields with fences further punctuated the idea of these family fields being private property. While the Choctaw would continue to hold land communally for much of the nineteenth century, these laws about fencing signal, first, that some Choctaws were thinking about the land as a form of property and, second, that this property in land could be owned by individuals. As Claudio Saunt lucidly remarks in his study of Creek Indians and their relationship to property, "Fences testified visibly to [one's] sense of ownership."[72]

Once Choctaws began to think in terms of private property, they also had to create protections for that private property and penalties for its damage.[73] The Choctaw legislature determined that those who destroyed property had to compensate the owner.[74] Livestock was private property, and punishment for stealing livestock varied based on the animal: for instance, horse theft warranted 100 lashes, cows 50 lashes, and pigs 30 lashes.[75] The lighthorsemen administered these penalties. The differences in the penalties demonstrated the value and availability of these forms of livestock. Stray livestock also required maintenance, and officials charged owners for the cost and made provisions for selling unclaimed livestock.[76] Again, these provisions indicated that this form of property had value. Petty theft of small items was also punishable by the lash at the judge's discretion.[77] These penalties would also vary in severity based on the perceived value of the stolen items. Choctaw lawmakers also concluded that those who induced others to steal property were as culpable as the thief, and the penalty was to compensate the victim for the value of the stolen items.[78] All of these bits of legislation together reveal a society experiencing a profound shift in thinking about the concept and importance of things as property. And this shift was not limited solely to Choctaws during this period; southeastern Native peoples more broadly were confronting an American legal and cultural system that valued property and were adjusting some of their own practices to accommodate the Americans.[79]

Notably, these early laws regulating property in the Choctaw Nation did not include discussion of enslaved people as property. Rather, Choctaw lawmakers were concerned about the prospect of marriages between enslaved people and Choctaws or whites, which I will discuss in detail in chapter 2. Thus, while Choctaws had been familiar with enslaved Africans as property since the eighteenth century and engaged in the practices of capturing, selling, and owning enslaved Africans themselves, they were still formulating ideas about what constituted property and how to address the realities of human property in particular.

This version of a partially centralized Choctaw government was short-lived, crumbling in the face of American pressure for the removal of southeastern tribes. The rumblings of dissension started even before the Choctaw statesmen met to create the constitution. Amid allegations of alcohol abuse during a treaty negotiation with federal authorities in 1825, a slaveholding leadership eventually prevailed in all three Choctaw districts. This cadre of men was able to maintain power because of their fierce opposition to removal and land cessions. They argued that the Choctaw needed bicultural leadership, that is, leaders who were bilingual in English and Choctaw and had some familiarity with American culture in order to be effective negotiators with federal authorities. These leaders encouraged a more thorough program of "civilization," of which the new constitution was a part, that targeted the entire Choctaw population rather than just the leadership.[80] The law eliminated allegedly barbaric practices and protected property while mission schools became an important center for general literacy and temperance groups urged sobriety. The religious revivals of 1828 that swept through Choctaw country and were embraced by many district chiefs and lawmakers, however, raised some alarms among non-Christian Choctaws and those disenchanted with the current leadership.[81] These disaffected individuals sought a justification to push pro-civilization leadership out, and that came when those leaders relented on the absolute refusal to relocate to Indian Territory.

In 1829, an American official warned the Choctaw that the state of Mississippi would soon extend its jurisdiction over the Choctaw Nation and that newly elected president Andrew Jackson would do little to protect them. When the Mississippi legislature did just that in January 1830 and the US Congress shortly thereafter passed the Indian Removal Act, Choctaw leaders reversed their stance on removal. These actions left no doubt as to the viability of Indian groups remaining in the southeastern United States as sovereign nations; it was time to move and to negotiate the best terms possible for this removal. District Chief Greenwood LeFlore argued that a negotiated removal was the best way to protect the Choctaw people. In a National Council meeting to discuss removal dominated by representatives from LeFlore's western district, the members elected LeFlore principal chief. The council then worked with Methodist ministers, who had joined the meeting in large numbers, as did American Board of Commissioners for Foreign Missions missionary Cyrus Kingsbury, to draw up favorable terms for removal. LeFlore himself was a Methodist convert, which explains in part his willingness to work with Methodist ministers.[82] But Methodist missionaries had also been full-throated in their support of the right of Natives such as the Choctaw to remain in the Southeast. An 1829 letter printed in a Methodist newspaper asked, "What account will our people render to God, if, through their neglect, this people, now ripe for the gospel, should be forced into the boundless wilds beyond the Mississippi in their present state of ignorance?"[83] Thus, LeFlore and some other Choctaws thought the missionaries could help them negotiate the best possible terms for the seemingly inevitable move west of the Mississippi River.

LeFlore and his compatriots also sought to further centralize Choctaw governance by eliminating the autonomy of the districts in order to streamline decision-making and create policy coherence. Unsurprisingly, all of this was met with sharp opposition. Supporters of the older district system and opponents of removal accused LeFlore and missionaries of conspiring to alienate Choctaws from their lands. Others disputed the legality of the treaty when two of the three districts were not well represented at the council meeting. Some saw LeFlore's ascendancy to principal chief as a usurpation of authority. Ultimately, the factions almost came to civil war as LeFlore struggled to command the authority to hold the new government together and those among the opposition expressed their willingness to fight to preserve district autonomy.[84]

Though the Indian Removal Act of 1830 did not demand the ejection of southeastern Native groups from southern states, for many Choctaws, the act's passage eliminated any doubts about their ability to remain. In the act, Congress authorized the president to exchange territory west of the Mississippi River for Indian lands within a US state or territory. The president could guarantee possession of those new western lands to the various Native groups forever. Moreover, Congress permitted the president to compensate individuals for improvements made to land ceded to the federal government and to pay for the migration of Natives—the physical movement of people and property—to the western territory. The president could also offer protection or administration to those groups who accepted territory out west and extinguished their land claims in the Southeast.[85] Of course, these provisions ignored previous treaty agreements that already guaranteed territory in the Southeast to Native nations in perpetuity by creating the fiction of choice: the Choctaw Nation could choose to migrate and give up title territory in exchange for land and money. Moreover, the American Congress discounted the sovereignty of Native peoples who already resided west of the Mississippi by offering their territory to southeastern nations.

Prior to 1830, Native groups might have hoped that Congress would honor treaty agreements made between federal officials and individual Indian nations and prevent southern states from unilaterally seizing Native territory. The passage of the Indian Removal Act, however, signaled a real shift in federal policy: the act "made it official American policy to remove all eastern Indian nations." While white Americans' seemingly insatiable demand for more land was certainly an impetus for the adoption of the act, so too were questions about federal versus state power, particularly in matters involving Native groups but also in relation to states' rights more generally.[86] Moreover, the question of what to do with land acquired by removing Indians to western territories could also magnify sectional tensions about the spread of slavery. Further, Samuel J. Wells argues that an important but rarely considered incentive for the federal government to pursue removal policy was national defense. Initially, federal authorities in the new United States were concerned about both the threat Native groups such as the Choctaw or Cherokee represented on their own and the foreign powers with whom Native groups might ally.[87]

In some ways, the Mississippi state legislature's action was more draconian than the Indian Removal Act. The legislature's act abolished all the "rights, privileges, immunities and franchises, held, or claimed or enjoyed, by those persons called Indians, and their descendants." Instead, Indians were entitled to the same benefits enjoyed by free white people in the state. In other words, Mississippi state law now applied equally to all persons in the state, excluding enslaved persons, of course, though it is unclear just what status was held by free people of color, given the language of this law. And Clara Sue Kidwell suggests that the act did not give Choctaws suffrage in the state.[88] The act also recognized marriages that had been deemed valid by the Indians within their own nations. In effect, this law dissolved the Indian nations within the state of Mississippi. By extending state authority over citizens of Indian nations, Mississippi lawmakers were denying the legitimacy of the Choctaw and Chickasaw governments and disregarding any claims to sovereignty made by these groups. In fact, the act of exercising sovereignty was illegal: "Any person or persons who shall assume on him or themselves, and exercise in any manner whatever the office of chief, mingo, head-man, or other post of power, established by the tribal statutes, ordinances or customs, of the said Indians, and not particularly recognized by the laws of this state," faced a fine of up to $1,000 and up to twelve months in prison.[89] Arthur H. DeRosier Jr. contends, however, that the state government lacked the will to enforce the provisions of this act because to do so would have led to bloodshed, and perhaps an all-out war, between Indian and white residents of the state. Rather, the aggressive stance of the legislature was an effort to convince Natives to accept plans to voluntarily remove. In any case, the actions of the state legislature sparked debate, within the state but also nationally, about the ethics of removal.[90]

The ensuing debate played out largely in the newspapers and took for granted that the real aim of the law was not the extension of state jurisdiction over Indian peoples but the removal of Indian peoples from Mississippi, or in the language of anthropologist Patrick Wolfe, the *elimination* of Indian peoples from Mississippi.[91] Some opponents of the legislation argued for the sovereignty of the Indian nations and pointed out that the federal government had also recognized this sovereignty in various treaties. Thus, as sovereign nations, the Choctaw and Chickasaw could not be forcibly removed against their will. Other arguments against the legislation highlighted the material well-being of the Indian nations: the western lands were inferior to the ones that would be ceded in the east; the physical act of removing the population was dangerous because of inadequate transportation lines; and placing the various Indian nations together in the western territory would lead to conflict and fighting among them. Still another line of argument against the act's extension of state law over the Indian population was more philosophical. How could the Indians hope to "improve" if they were cut off from contact with whites and segregated onto some Indian territory? Further, the Native population had no guarantee that the state governments would not again seek to push into Native territory and claim more land for white settlement.[92]

Those who saw Indian removal as a necessity supported the law and marshaled their own arguments in favor of removal. Perhaps most importantly, white Mississippians wanted more land to cultivate themselves and to attract eastern immigrants. Choctaw and Chickasaw lands were within the state's boundaries and should, therefore, be controlled by the state. In this logic, the wishes of the Indian peoples were immaterial. Implicit in this disregard of Indian will was the notion that Indian people were not deserving of consideration because of their alleged inferiority and lack of civilization. Another line of reasoning focused on the undesirability of the Indian population in the state: they imposed a financial burden on the state because of their tax-exempt status; Indian nations served as a haven for fugitive enslaved people and white criminals; and Indians did not use the land "properly" because they hunted rather than farmed.[93] Proponents of these arguments ignored the fact that the Choctaw and Chickasaw received funds from their land cessions and generated funds through fees and taxes to operate their own government and provide services to Indian citizens. Moreover, both the Choctaw and the Chickasaw had adopted the practice of enslaving people of African descent and passing legislation to circumscribe their behavior. Finally, these groups had a long history of agricultural production and had increasingly turned to raising livestock rather than hunting for meat.

The Mississippi state legislature's unilateral extension of jurisdiction to include Native peoples and the federal government's passage of the Indian Removal Act focused national attention on the question of what place Native people should occupy with respect to American society. For many Choctaws, the answer was clear: white Mississippians would not allow the Choctaw people to remain in the state as a separate, sovereign nation, and the federal government would do nothing to protect the Choctaw Nation. If they did not emigrate voluntarily, they might be forced to do so. Even before the passage of the Indian Removal Act in May 1830, many Choctaws had been prepared to negotiate a voluntary removal to territory west of the Mississippi River. So now, and in spite of a great deal of internal dissent, the Choctaw put forward a plan with very favorable terms: every head of household would receive 640 acres of land to be sold to the state of Mississippi, and single men received half this amount. It is unclear whether this proposal would have given each head of household the equivalent price of 640 acres of land or if the Choctaw legislature would have divided the territory into 640-acre sections and granted them to heads of household to be sold individually to the state of Mississippi in this proposal. Additionally, some members of the political leadership would also receive clothing, a sword, and $200 over the course of four years; every adult male Choctaw would receive a rifle and farming implements; every adult female Choctaw would receive a spinning wheel and a loom; and the government would pay to transport the Choctaw and their possessions and furnish them with food and clothing for the first year after their migration. Finally, the government would pay the Choctaw Nation $50,000 annually forever.[94]

This preliminary overture by the Choctaw, or at least a faction of Choctaws, to set advantageous terms for their removal demonstrates the shrewdness of the Choctaw leadership, as well as some dramatic changes in Choctaw notions of property and gender roles. The leadership proposed that the Americans pay for every facet of the migration: the land the Choctaw would vacate, the transportation costs to move people and property west of the Mississippi River, and then an additional annual fee. In other words, if the federal government wanted the consent of the Choctaw to remove to the west, they would have to pay dearly for it. One estimate was that the federal government would be paying $50 million "to induce some forty thousand Indians to move to the new country."[95] Even allies of the Choctaw such as Cyrus Kingsbury worried that the proposal asked for too much and would therefore net the Choctaw very little.[96] The plan also called for the sectioning off of land into parcels held by families or single men, a departure from the traditional Choctaw idea of communal landownership and from the practice of women making decisions about the land in their role as agriculturalists. On the one hand, this was an implicit adoption of the "principles of private property that the state was forcing on them."[97] As discussed, Choctaw understandings of private property were in flux, and that might be especially true for members of the Choctaw leadership. On the other, it can also be read as an attempt to speak in terms that Americans would recognize. In a similar vein, the drafters of this plan asked for farm implements for the men and weaving tools for the women, another indication that gender roles were undergoing transformation. Men would receive farming equipment because they would be the agriculturalists, not the women. Women, instead, would produce cloth. American officials and missionaries had long encouraged the Choctaw to adopt these practices. Again, the proposal reveals both a people in the midst of change and Choctaw efforts to conform, at least outwardly, to Euro-Americans' expectations.

The terms set forth by the Choctaw in their plan for voluntary removal were so steep that President Jackson forwarded the plan to the Senate with the recommendation that the Senate reject it. The Choctaw plan was expensive, but perhaps of more concern was the potential for it to serve as a model for other Indian nations in future treaty negotiations for southeastern, or other, land cessions. The Senate concurred with Jackson and declined to pass the treaty. This episode must have been confusing for the Choctaw. The creation of the treaty, and the issue of removal itself, had brought the Choctaw to the brink of a civil war. People who had come to political power based on their staunch opposition to removal were now advocating removal as the only way for the nation to survive. The Choctaw leadership had managed, just barely, to stitch together a treaty that some could tolerate. Yet the Americans rejected the treaty, despite their continual clamor for the Choctaw to extinguish their land claims in Mississippi and exhortations about the benefits of removal for Indian peoples. Conceding to American demands seemed to offer little payoff, and some Choctaws hardened their opposition to migrating under any conditions and threatened death to any Choctaws who negotiated the sale of more territory to the federal government. For American officials such as Andrew Jackson and Secretary of War John Eaton, the terms of the Choctaw proposal were less important than the very existence of the proposal itself: the proposal signaled that the Choctaw were willing to migrate.[98] The Americans were quite aware of the internal dissension among the Choctaw over this issue and sought to exploit it to create a treaty with more favorable terms for the United States.[99]

In September 1830, Choctaws met with Secretary Eaton and John Coffee, acting as commissioners from the federal government, near Dancing Rabbit Creek in Choctaw territory. As many as 5,000–6,000 Choctaws may have gathered for the meeting, which included the three district chiefs, their advisors, and any other Choctaws who wished to attend. The numbers swelled as Choctaws engaged in the traditional practice of gathering when the district chiefs assembled. In the past, "the common people made it a holiday and engaged in ball playing or dancing" when the National Council met.[100] The large number of Choctaws who converged at Dancing Rabbit Creek also demonstrates the importance of the subject of the meeting for many Choctaws: further land cessions and removal to the west, and the deep divisions within the tribe. Even at the meeting site, the political factions segregated themselves from each other geographically, using a branch of the creek as a natural dividing line between LeFlore's followers and those of Mushulatubbee and Nitakechi, the chiefs of the northeastern and southern districts who opposed LeFlore's leadership.[101] Those in attendance did not merely want to observe the discussions; they wanted to express their political allegiances as well as their desired outcomes.

The federal government actively excluded missionaries from the negotiations, despite the fact that Cyrus Kingsbury from the American Board of Commissioners for Foreign Missions asked to be there. A few missionaries managed to attend anyway. They may have been surprised to hear Commissioners Coffee and Eaton advise the Choctaw to disregard any counsel offered by the missionaries.[102] Missionaries were often harsh critics of federal policy regarding Natives and supported Native sovereignty and the protection of Native claims to land.[103] Perhaps the lack of religious influence at the treaty negotiations also contributed to the carnival-like atmosphere described by one observer. Apparently, the large number of Choctaws who attended attracted the notice of entrepreneurs such as "gamblers, saloonkeepers, frontier rowdies, and prostitutes, all interested in separating the Indians from their meager possessions." The federal officials apparently did little to curb this activity.[104] Thus, Coffee and Eaton's ban on the missionaries' attendance may also be read another way: the commissioners may have seen the benefit of encouraging Choctaws to drink alcohol and partake in other amusements rather than pay close attention to the treaty discussions.

Initially, the Choctaw were nearly unanimous in their adamant refusal to cede more land to the federal government. The commissioners offered bribes to Choctaw political leaders in the form of extra land and the opportunity for those individuals to choose specific parcels of land in Mississippi or in Indian Territory, and still they said no.[105] Hence, many Choctaws withdrew from Dancing Rabbit Creek thinking that the opposition to ceding land and moving west was firm. Their departure roughly two weeks into the negotiations signaled their rejection of continued negotiations about the matter. Only about 500 Choctaws remained, including district chiefs LeFlore, Mushulatubbee, and Nitakechi.[106] Coffee and Eaton then turned to threats: the Choctaw could cede their lands in Mississippi or remain in the state and be subject to Mississippi laws. If the Choctaw refused to accept the state of Mississippi's authority, the federal government would bring its military power to bear on them. The Choctaw could also lose their territory west of the Mississippi and any annuity funds.[107] Given these alternatives, accepting some kind of treaty for land cessions made sense to the remaining Choctaws.

Comprising more than twenty articles, the Treaty of Dancing Rabbit Creek attempted to manage every aspect of removal. The central purpose of the document was to effect a land exchange: the Choctaw extinguished their land claims in Mississippi in return for land west of the Mississippi River.[108] The federal government assured the Choctaw "that no part of the land granted them shall ever be embraced in any territory or state." Moreover, the Choctaw Nation would not be subject to any laws except those passed by its own national councils or occasionally Congress.[109] The intent of these provisions was to secure the new territory to the Choctaw in perpetuity and to protect their sovereignty. No state would again be permitted to extend its legal jurisdiction over the Choctaw population. Given that the preamble of this treaty admitted that the president could not protect the Choctaw from the state of Mississippi's actions in this regard, perhaps the Choctaw should not have put much faith in this language. Related to the issue of sovereignty were questions about jurisdiction in legal matters that involved both Choctaws and non-Choctaws. In this treaty the federal government reserved the authority to adjudicate matters in which one party was not Choctaw, meaning the federal government consented only to Choctaws adjudicating legal matters wherein all parties were Choctaw. In other words, Choctaws who committed crimes against American citizens or members of other groups were to "be delivered up to an officer of the United States," as were whites and members of other Native groups who committed crimes against Choctaws.[110]

The treaty stipulated that the move would take place over the course of three years—1831, 1832, and 1833—so that "a better opportunity in the manner will be afforded the Government, to extend to them the facilities and comforts which it is desirable should be extended in conveying them to their new homes."[111] The treaty negotiators recognized that the movement of 20,000 people and their property over a distance of some 550 miles was no small undertaking and would be better managed over a long period of time. The federal government agreed to pay for the expense of providing wagons and steamboats to transport the Choctaw and their property to their new homes. The treaty also specified that the federal government would supply corn and meat to the Choctaw for twelve months after their arrival west.[112]

In addition to exchanging land in the west for Choctaw territory in Mississippi and paying for the physical relocation of the population, the federal government also agreed to pay the Choctaw directly. The United States would provide an annual annuity of $20,000 for twenty years and continue to pay any annuities due based on previous treaties.[113] The United States also would pay for other items that had value both monetarily and in terms of larger plans to "civilize" the Choctaw. For the next twenty years, the federal government would pay for forty Choctaw children to attend boarding schools annually. Federal funds would also pay for several construction projects: a council house, houses for each district chief, and a church for each district that could also be used as a school. The treaty provided for the salaries of three teachers for twenty years, as well as three blacksmiths for sixteen years and a millwright for five years. Federal authorities would supply blankets, rifles, axes, plows, hoes, and looms, as well.[114] These items may be read as the accoutrements of civilization: an American-style education for the children; a more centralized government with which American officials would find it easier to negotiate; churches to encourage the spread of Christianity; tools to engage in agriculture, presumably in the mode of American small farmers; and looms for the women to use to make cloth. It is uncertain how much the inclusion of these items was about Coffee and Eaton's efforts to change the Choctaw, the Choctaws' own desires to have churches and schools in their new territory, or a shrewd understanding on the part of the Choctaw about what kinds of requests would be met favorably.

The treaty negotiators also acknowledged that there were Choctaws, perhaps more than they wanted to admit, who would not agree to move west under any terms. Those who wished to remain in Mississippi could do so if they informed the Indian agent within six months of the treaty's ratification. Heads of household, who could be men or women according to the treaty's language, would receive 640 acres of land, also referred to as one section. Their unmarried children over age ten would receive 320 acres of adjoining land, and those under age ten would receive 160 acres of adjoining land. After five years of residence upon the land, these Choctaws would gain title to the land in fee simple. Interestingly, individuals who remained in Mississippi would not necessarily lose their Choctaw citizenship; rather, they could choose to become US citizens or to maintain all of the "privileges of a Choctaw citizen." One wonders what privileges of Choctaw citizenship an individual could retain at such great distance from the rest of the polity. Could one vote? Would the Choctaw authorities intercede on one's behalf in matters involving the state of Mississippi or the federal government? If the individuals who initially chose to remain in Mississippi should decide later to join the rest of the Choctaw in their new territory, they would not be entitled to receive any of the Choctaw annuity funds.[115]

The Choctaw also requested "the privilege of a Delegate on the floor of the House of Representatives extended to them." They felt that the Choctaw people were "in a state of rapid advancement in education and refinement" that warranted having a person who represented their own interests present in Congress. Commissioners Coffee and Eaton did not think they had the authority to grant such a request but offered to present it to Congress.[116] It is unclear precisely what role the Choctaws hoped this delegate would play; would he have voting privileges, serve as an observer, or be able to able to take the floor and address other representatives? What is clear is that the Choctaw understood the need to have representation at American legislative proceedings. Even if this delegate had no voting or speaking privileges, at the very least he could report back to the Choctaw Nation about topics of importance being discussed in Congress and legislation that was being proposed. Moreover, the Choctaw were savvy enough to couch this request in terms that might please American lawmakers: the Choctaw had earned a delegate because of their "rapid advancement in education and refinement," in other words, their degree of "civilization."

Another important part of the Treaty of Dancing Rabbit Creek outlined compensation for officials in the Choctaw Nation. The treaty granted each district chief four sections—that is, 2,560 acres—of land. The chiefs and their successors also would receive $250 annually while they held office. If the Choctaw chose to elect a principal chief, he would receive $500 annually. The treaty also specified the pay for other Choctaw officials, including district speakers, district secretaries, and captains. Once removal started, the ninety-nine captains would receive $50 annually for four years "for the trouble of keeping their people at order in settling" as well as "a good suit of clothes, and a broad sword."[117] Similarly, the treaty included many special land grants to officials of the Choctaw Nation.[118] While some might have construed the extra land grants and salary for the chiefs as payment for their hard work, others saw the extra land and salary as bribes to gain the chiefs' agreement. Why else would the federal government so generously compensate these Choctaw leaders? The Choctaw, after all, would receive annuity funds that they could use to reimburse district officials for the travel and expenses incurred in the performance of their duties. These funds could also be used to pay salaries for officials. For those who had left the meeting at Dancing Rabbit Creek confident that the Choctaw were fairly united in their opposition to migrating, these land grants provided an explanation for the unexpected change of heart.

There are conflicting reports about the response of rank-and-file Choctaws to the Treaty of Dancing Rabbit Creek. Clearly, many Choctaws opposed the treaty, and the district chiefs faced some public wrath. All three, LeFlore, Mushulatubbee, and Nitakechi, were pushed out of office. George Harkins replaced LeFlore. Mushulatubbee resigned in order for his nephew

Peter P. Pitchlynn to replace him, but another faction in the northeastern district attempted to elect David Folsom as chief. The district council in the southern district claimed that Nitakechi had never been duly elected by the district captains and thus had held office illegally; it then elected Joe Nail in his place. The new chiefs sent protests to Washington in opposition to the Treaty of Dancing Rabbit Creek, but federal officials refused to recognize the new chiefs and insisted that the chiefs who had negotiated the treaty were the legitimate leaders of the Choctaw. These new leaders ultimately had to resign and relinquish their positions.[119] Stories circulated that some Choctaws were so opposed to the treaty that they were willing to take up arms against the federal government or that Choctaws had been forced to sign the treaty by American soldiers. Some American observers in the nation remarked that the majority of the Choctaw Indians opposed the treaty. On the other hand, Choctaw interpreter M. Mackey claimed that most Choctaws saw the treaty as fair. In any case, the feared physical violence toward American officials did not materialize.[120] Perhaps the larger Choctaw population understood all too clearly at whom they could direct their ire. Engaging in physical resistance to removal would have had disastrous consequences, but removing people from office who supported the treaty and sending petitions to Washington were far less dangerous.

On the eve of removal, the Choctaw population numbered nearly 20,000 people. Though the first group of migrants was not supposed to leave for Indian Territory until 1831, some 400 Choctaws left in December 1830, hoping that their early arrival would permit them to choose the best lands prior the influx of a larger population. Other early migrants feared that the value of the land that individual Choctaws were selling in Mississippi might also decline as more people migrated and more land became available for purchase. Secretary of War Eaton appointed Lieutenant J. R. Stephenson to plan their journey, offering tacit approval of the plan to claim land preemptively despite the fact that the Treaty of Dancing Rabbit Creek was not yet ratified.[121]

By February 1831, the census taker enumerated 17,693 Indians, 151 whites, and 521 enslaved people in the Choctaw Nation. Officials from the War Department hoped to transport one-third of the Choctaw population to Indian Territory in 1831 and made plans based on these census figures.[122] Roughly 1,000 Choctaws chose to emigrate without the supervision of the federal government in 1831, with another 4,000 traveling under the direction of Colonel George S. Gaines.[123] Francis Desales Taaffe's family was among this first migration of Choctaws who "moved their stocks, slaves, and cattle over the Government Military trail from Mississippi."[124] During their five-month journey, the Choctaw faced trying conditions. Heavy summer and fall rains had made overland travel almost impossible, forcing the travelers to use steamboats as much as possible, a far more expensive proposition than traveling by wagon. The winter that followed was one of the harshest recorded for the region, and the migrants were not well provisioned to face it. Ice in the waterways slowed down some of the Choctaw, as did overflowing swamps and fallen timber. By the spring of 1832, American officials reported providing rations for a total of 4,285 Choctaws.[125]

Given the dismal experience of the first group of Choctaw migrants to Indian Territory, it should come as no surprise that some Choctaws in Mississippi balked when the military called for the second group to sign muster rolls in 1832. Government officials anticipated that between 8,000 and 10,000 Choctaws would travel in this second group, but in the end only 5,317 Choctaws assembled. Particularly disappointing were the numbers from LeFlore's western district: only 617 of an expected 3,000 people emigrated at this time. On this journey, cholera rather than bad weather plagued the travelers. A number of self-emigrating parties also made their way to Indian Territory, perhaps thinking that their chances traveling alone could be no worse than for those accompanied by the army, given the previous group's experiences. In total, roughly 6,000 Choctaws traveled west of the Mississippi River in this second wave of migrants.[126]

By the fall of 1833, more than 6,000 Choctaws remained in Mississippi, most of whom refused to leave. The last party of Choctaws to emigrate numbered only about 900 people, in addition to smaller self-emigrating parties that traveled without supervision by the American army.[127] Upon the completion of removal according to the terms of the Treaty of Dancing Rabbit Creek, about 12,500 Choctaws had migrated and 2,500 had perished. And still some 5,000 other Choctaws continued to reside in Mississippi, a fact made possible by article 14 of the treaty. These numbers raise some questions about the success of the Choctaw removal, since nearly one-third of the population remained in Mississippi. If the goal of the Treaty of Dancing Rabbit Creek was solely the federal acquisition of Choctaw lands, then the treaty was a success. If, however, the goal was also to erase the Choctaw presence in Mississippi, to physically remove all Choctaw people from the state, the treaty fell short. Later efforts in the 1840s to induce those remaining Choctaws to leave for Indian Territory suggest that land acquisition was not the only target of the treaty negotiators.[128] Moreover, there is the question of whether to describe the Choctaw removal as a forced removal, as scholar Valerie Lambert does, or as a voluntary act on the part of the Choctaw.[129] The treaty provision permitting Choctaws to choose to remain

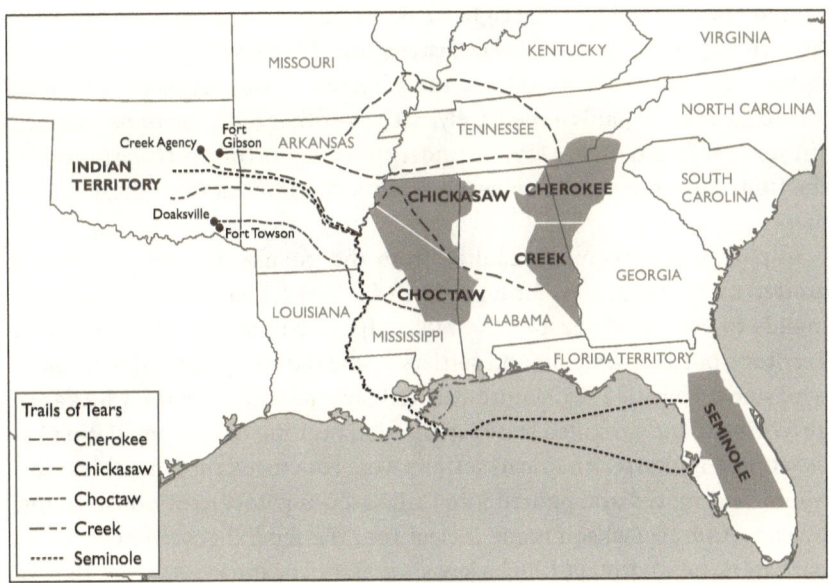

Removal of southeastern Natives.
(Map by Rice University GIS/Data Center)

in Mississippi and the number of Choctaws who mustered for enrollment give the patina of consent to removal; however, the reality is that the actions and threats of the federal government and whites in Mississippi virtually compelled Choctaws to accept a removal treaty. A choice between removal and annihilation is not a choice.

The efforts to remove other southeastern tribes to Indian Territory in the 1830s also precipitated an unusual arrangement between the Choctaw and Chickasaw Nations in the Treaty of Doaksville. The Choctaw agreed "that the Chickasaws shall have the privilege of forming a district within the limits of their country, to be held on the same terms that the Choctaws now hold it, except the right of disposing of it, (which is held in common with the Choctaws and Chickasaws) to be called the Chickasaw district of the Choctaw Nation." The Chickasaw Indians would receive the same legal and political rights as Choctaw Indians, including representation in the Choctaw General Council, which was the new name for the Choctaw legislative branch by 1838, for the Chickasaw district.[130] The only exception was that the Chickasaw would not be entitled to any annuity funds, that is, moneys received for previous or future land cessions. Likewise, the Chickasaw reserved the right to control their own funds gained in treaties with the

United States, as well as the right to elect officers to manage the funds.[131] In exchange for this Chickasaw district and Choctaw legal and political rights, the Chickasaw would pay the Choctaw Nation $530,000, of which $30,000 was to be paid immediately, with the other $500,000 to be invested "in some safe and secure stocks, under the direction of the Government of the United States." The Choctaw were to receive interest from these investments annually.[132]

In part, this agreement resulted from the intense pressure Americans exerted on Native groups for land. The Chickasaw had resisted federal demands to cede lands east of the Mississippi River and resettle in Indian Territory, but state officials and settlers from Mississippi proved to be quite persistent. The state legislature enacted laws to eliminate the Chickasaw government and extended state jurisdiction over the Indian population between 1819 and 1829. American settlers were convinced that the Chickasaw would be removed and poured into Chickasaw territory to establish farms. By 1830, Andrew Jackson made it clear that the federal government would not intervene to protect Chickasaw sovereignty or interests. All of this, of course, mirrors what had occurred with the Choctaw Nation. So the Chickasaw agreed to migrate and buy land from the Choctaw on which to settle; however, the Chickasaw and Choctaw could not come to an agreement at first. The Choctaw insisted that the Chickasaw join the Choctaw Nation as a fourth district, but the Chickasaw wanted to maintain their political autonomy and refused. By 1837, however, the Chickasaw were desperate enough to come to terms with the Choctaw Nation: that year they lost another 1.3 million acres of land to the United States through allotment and individual land sales; Chickasaw authorities could not protect their own people from the flood of settlers or enforce laws; and many in their population were now landless and destitute.[133] Thus, the Chickasaw Nation reluctantly came to be incorporated into the Choctaw Nation.

The integration of the Chickasaw population into the Choctaw Nation as a part of removal may have been strategic on the part of the Americans, if a bit disingenuous. American agents Benjamin F. Reynolds and George S. Gaines argued that "combined the two nations could make one of the strongest, wealthiest and most respectable communities of aborigines on the continent of America with the means in their own hands of soon becoming civilized, educated, independent American citizens."[134] To the Choctaw and Chickasaw peoples, American agents suggested that such a union would benefit both populations. Of course, it likely did not escape the agents' notice that if the Chickasaw settled on Choctaw territory, the United States would not have to provide more land for a Chickasaw homeland, and that a combined Chickasaw/Choctaw Nation with one governing body might lessen the number of Native groups the federal government would need to consider in treaty negotiations. This perspective, however, did not take into account the Chickasaw people's desire to remain an independent and sovereign nation in control of its own affairs or the understandable Choctaw refusal to part with any more land after decades of land cessions. Moreover, many in both the Chickasaw and Choctaw Nations had no aspiration to become American citizens; rather, they wanted to remain citizens of their respective nations.

The fusion of the two groups also had some basis in historical relationships and the origins of the Choctaw and Chickasaw peoples. A common thread in some of the origin stories of both nations was a relationship between two brothers, Chahtah and Chikasah. H. B. Cushman related an origin story in which the ancestors of the Chickasaw and Choctaw, led by two brave and skillful warriors who were also brothers, emigrated east to escape a conquering population. At the instruction of their chief medicine man, the brothers used a *fabussa*, or pole, to determine the direction in which the group should travel. Each evening they placed the *fabussa* in the center of their camp and in the morning marched in the direction that the *fabussa* leaned. They traveled in this way many months until one morning the *fabussa* remained erect. To commemorate this event, the ancestors built a large mound thirty feet high, which they called Nunih Waiyah, on three acres of land. Some years later, the two brothers disagreed on some "national question," and they again used a pole to determine their course of action. They each held the pole and then let it drop. The direction in which the pole fell would determine where Chikasah and his followers would settle. And so the two factions separated, each taking on the name of its chief and forming a new community: Chikasah and his followers moved to the north, and Chahtah and his followers remained in the south.[135] In Choctaw Nation member Israel Folsom's rendering of the Choctaw origin story, the cause of the migration from the west was a food shortage, and a great storm separated the two brothers and their followers.[136] Still another nineteenth-century version presented by Dr. Gordon Lincecum describes a friendly connection between the Choctaw and Chickasaw peoples that was eventually replaced by suspicion. In Lincecum's telling, Nunih Waiyah mound was not only a monument to the end of a long journey but also the base of a rampart added by the Choctaw as a defense against Chickasaw attacks.[137]

Of course, one must exercise caution when approaching these origin and migration stories. Recorded in the nineteenth century, often by white missionaries or travelers in Indian country, these accounts were shaped by the events of the era, the introduction of Christianity, and the prejudices of the writers. It is possible that these stories conveniently explain a contemporary phenomenon rather than recount historic events. They could be either discrete pieces of evidence about past events or iterations of the same story circulated because of the wider spread of literacy. Even if the latter is true, the fact that one story could gain currency and spread speaks to the value those nineteenth-century re-tellers placed on its significance and usefulness. Scholar Patricia Galloway notes, "Because they were collected well after the tribes had passed through such demographic upheaval that most detailed prehistoric tradition had to have been lost, and because the individuals who collected them had very big axes to grind, migration legends may be nearly useless for telling us how the historic tribes originated in the depths of prehistory."[138] For my purposes, I am less interested in what these stories tell us about the prehistoric period or the geographic origins of the tribe; rather, I think the various stories' shared assertion of a relationship between the Choctaw and Chickasaw peoples is important and holds some element of truth, particularly when paired with other evidence.

While these accounts may differ in the precise nature of the historical relationship between the Chickasaw and Choctaw peoples, linguistic evidence does indicate that there are some similarities between these groups. Linguists may revise the relationships between Eastern and Western Muskogean language groups, Northern and Southern Muskogean groups, or the place of Old Alabama speakers in such renderings; however, the connection between Chickasaw and Choctaw language groups is clear.[139] Historian Arrell M. Gibson stated that Chickasaws shared the "closest cultural affinity" with Choctaws, including the Muskogean language with only "mild dialectal differences."[140] Both Choctaw and Chickasaw peoples also shared some commonalities in terms of social and political organization. Both societies were divided into two moieties and then further divided into matrilineal clans. Both groups lived in matrilocal households and permitted polygamy.[141] Thus, imagining that these two nations could coexist in one geographic area in Indian Territory was not a radical proposition in 1837. While both groups may have been reluctant to sign the treaty at Doaksville, each did ultimately accept the existence of a Chickasaw district within the Choctaw Nation.

By 1838, the Choctaw Nation had established a government that bore a strong resemblance to that of the United States.[142] The Choctaw government included four branches that shared power: the legislative, executive, judiciary, and military branches. The General Council, composed of forty annually elected representatives who debated and created legislation, formed the legislative branch. Only male Choctaw citizens could vote in elections or serve as representatives. The executive branch consisted of four district chiefs, who were responsible for approving or rejecting legislation, notifying the council about the affairs of each district, and enforcing laws in each district. The supreme and district courts oversaw civil and criminal matters, serving as the judiciary branch. Finally, each district elected a general who served in the military department and commanded the district military force in the event of an invasion or a war.[143] The Choctaw Constitution also included a Declaration of Rights similar to the American Bill of Rights.[144]

The new Choctaw Constitution did not grant Choctaw women the legal rights to govern that one might expect, given women's traditional importance as corn producers. The Choctaw Constitution did not include women in the electorate or permit them to serve as representatives in the General Council.[145] The language of the constitution also assumed that the four district chiefs were male: "Each Chief shall from time to time give the General Council information respecting the affairs of *his* own district, and recommend to their consideration such measures as *he* may think expedient."[146] The constitution did not make any clear statement about the gender of judges but, again, did assume that jurors and lighthorsemen would be men.[147] Finally, the authors of the constitution also referred to the generals in the Military Department with the male pronoun.[148] Thus, while the constitution did not explicitly bar women from holding offices in the Choctaw government, it did adopt language that reflected the assumption that all elected officials would be men. The constitution's authors apparently saw Choctaw women as capable of social deviance and criminal behavior, though not of civic responsibility and governance.

This linguistic practice of using male pronouns to describe officeholders in the Choctaw Constitution was even more purposeful given the careful way in which the legislators did use gender-neutral language in other legislation prohibiting persons of African descent from holding office in the government or in establishing penalties for crimes.[149] It seems, then, that Choctaw lawmakers wanted to avoid any confusion about whether any people of African descent could hold office. In other words, legally all people of African descent, men and women, were potentially deviant and criminal and ineligible to hold office in the Choctaw polity. The language of constitutional provisions and legal statutes implies a full-blown anti-Black ideology in operation by this time.

During the larger process of formalizing Choctaw laws, women lost some control over reproduction. Chief Aboha Kulla Humma enacted a law by 1822 to punish with whipping those women who committed infanticide. In one case, the woman's "husband also received the same punishment for not restraining his wife in the destruction of the child," suggesting that men were beginning to be involved in the decision-making and thus might bear some responsibility.[150] The punishment for the crime of infanticide seemed to target the unseemliness of the practice to outsiders: Chief Aboha Kulla Humma stated, "We have made the above laws because we wish to follow the ways of the white people. We hope they will assist us in getting our children educated."[151] By conforming to what Euro-Americans saw as acceptable behavior, the chief thought he might in turn gain access to education for his people. A dozen years later, the Choctaw General Council set the punishment for conviction of committing infanticide at sixty lashes without distinction as to the gender of the perpetrator.[152] Interestingly, while infanticide fell into the category of a "willful murder" because it was not an act of self-defense or an accidental death, infanticide did not receive the same punishment meted out for willful murder per se, that is, death.[153] Thus, Choctaws must not have understood infanticide as murder. This distinction lends further credence to the idea that infanticide was an accepted practice in traditional Choctaw society. The council, then, in the interests of "civilization," outlawed an established practice in which Choctaw women had played an important part.

Choctaw authorities also sought to protect women from sexual predators. By October 1836, those convicted of the crime of rape or ravishment received sixty lashes on their bare backs regardless of race. Crimes of attempted rape or ravishment warranted half of this penalty—no more than thirty lashes.[154] Ten years later, the Choctaw legislature passed a much harsher law. Authorities increased the punishment for a man convicted of "committing rape or forcibly ravishing a woman or girl" to "one hundred lashes well laid on his bare back." For a second conviction for the same crime, the perpetrator received a death sentence. In the case of attempted rape, the court had some latitude in determining the penalty as long as it did not exceed thirty lashes.[155] The escalation of the punishment for the crime of rape prompts speculation that its occurrence was growing more frequent. At the very least, more non-Choctaw men were coming into contact with Choctaw women, which may have triggered fears about sexual contact between them.

As Choctaw authorities enacted legislation that reduced women's decision-making power in national and family life, they also prescribed a new formula for disposing of property within families: "All property shall, upon the death of the husband, descend to the wife or children of the deceased husband, and in case of the death of the wife, the husband shall inherit the estate."[156] This change, which deviated from the inheritance patterns provided for by clan relationships, suggests larger transformations in Choctaw social organization: the importance of tracing kinship matrilineally was giving way to patrilineal kinship connections; clan kinship more generally may have been losing force as the primary means of social organization; and husbands may have been playing a more active role in decision-making regarding their own children as opposed to the children of their sisters.[157] These changes in property inheritance patterns may also reflect changes in gendered labor practices. For instance, women were performing less agricultural labor and had less control over land use. Choctaw men were replacing hunting with agriculture as their primary labor responsibility. Certainly in the nineteenth century, the Choctaw Indians faced strong pressure to conform their labor and inheritance practices to American patterns, which may explain why two-thirds of the members of the Choctaw General Council approved this law.

In 1848 the General Council offered further clarification of the property rights of married individuals. In a move in keeping with traditional Choctaw practice, the council stipulated that each party in a marriage retained "the right of the property that he or she may bring into the marriage union."[158] Neither party could dispose of the property of his or her spouse without the spouse's consent. Failure to obtain spousal consent could result in a lawsuit. In life, then, the law respected each marriage partner's individual property rights; at the moment of the death of either spouse, however, the law diverged from traditional practice and no longer respected individual property rights: "And be it further enacted, That no will that is made by the husband or wife, conveying property without the consent of the other, shall be valid."[159] In other words, married persons retained control over their property to do with as they wished until they died, but a partner had to obtain the prior consent of his or her spouse to leave that property to someone other than the living spouse. The act also recognized the concept of joint property, that a married couple could accumulate property together and both have some claim of possession. Husbands apparently had greater authority over this joint property, however, as the property was "subject to the disposal of the husband for the mutual support and benefit of the family."[160] The earlier marriage law also remained in effect, which resolved pesky questions about the disposal of joint marital property by stipulating that in the case of the death of one of the partners, the surviving spouse, not members of the deceased spouse's clan, inherited this marital joint property.

The attempts by Choctaw legislators to protect the property rights of married women may indicate that some outsiders unfamiliar with Choctaw marital practices were marrying Choctaw women. At first blush, the traditionally matrilocal and matrilineal households of the Choctaw might make it easier to incorporate male outsiders into society. After all, any children produced in unions between Choctaw women and non-Choctaw men would have kinship ties and clan membership through their mothers, and other Choctaws would view these children as fully Choctaw because of these connections. The male outsider would seamlessly join the household of his Choctaw wife and contribute meat to the family's diet. If the marriage dissolved, he could return to his own "clan" outside the nation. Given the social organization of the Choctaw, members of the Choctaw Nation might have viewed the introduction of male outsiders to the nation as the husbands of Choctaw women with little trepidation. In actuality, however, some Choctaw Indians did respond with alarm to the prospect of Choctaw women marrying non-Choctaw men.

While Choctaw women's marital choices grew increasingly important to national authorities, these women lost some ground in arenas where they once held power. First, the new system of government, formalized in written constitutions and legal statutes, left little official space for Choctaw women to participate in the political process of managing the nation. Second, though legal authorities protected women's traditional property rights even after marriage, they also departed from clan determinations in reconfiguring rules of property inheritance. Third, within families, Choctaw women exercised less control over reproduction. The growing use of enslaved people to perform agricultural labor, discussed in chapter 2, would also challenge another source of Choctaw women's traditional authority.[161]

The Choctaw were not operating in isolation; similar changes were taking place among neighboring southeastern nations. In the first third of the nineteenth century, Chickasaws, Cherokees, and Creeks also created written constitutions and political institutions that were recognizable to federal officials.[162] The Cherokee Nation had a similar trajectory of excluding women from political decision-making, moving toward patrilineal rather than matrilineal property inheritance, and surveilling women's marital choices. And in each of these nations, the population of enslaved people of African descent engaged in agricultural labor grew. In some ways, this Choctaw story reveals a broader regional change.

By the fourth decade of the nineteenth century, the Choctaw had firmly established a system of centralized government. Controversies over land cessions earlier in the century proved that the system of autonomous districts that had prevailed could be exploited by American officials. The structure of this new political system and the legislation it produced reveals that the Choctaw experienced other dramatic transformations over the course of the first third of the nineteenth century, as well. Geographically, the Choctaw now had a new homeland that they shared with the Chickasaw. Sharp Choctaw resistance to relocating the nation west of the Mississippi River was insufficient to withstand the pressure from Andrew Jackson, Congress, and the Mississippi state legislature. White settlers' voracious appetite for more land seemed insatiable, a fact that would have further consequences for the Choctaw by the end of the century. Choctaw ideas about gender, about what men and women should and should not do, were shifting, as were notions of what legal rights Choctaw men and women could exercise. And the importance of matrilineally determined clan affiliations seemed to be waning, with patrilineal connections gaining importance. But through it all, the Choctaw remained a people determined to protect their rights and territory as a sovereign nation. All of these changes, coupled with the growth in the practice of slavery discussed in the next chapter, provide the backdrop for the events that would unfold in 1861 and explain the choice the Choctaw Nation would make to side with the South.

Chapter 2

Even If the Master Was Good the Slaves Was Bad Off

SLAVERY AND RACIAL IDEOLOGY
IN THE CHOCTAW NATION

After the trauma of removal, the Choctaw Nation experienced a brief period of recovery. Within the parameters set out by their newly reinstituted political structure, Choctaw citizens established communities, built schools for their children or sent them elsewhere to be educated, and conducted commerce with each other and residents of nearby states. And King Cotton extended its economic reach to Indian country as well. Choctaws' adoption of the practice of enslaving people of African descent and the concomitant growth of legislation to buttress the institution in multiple ways demonstrate the importance of slavery in the Choctaw Nation, not just economically but as a part of the developing racial order, and help explain the Choctaw decision to ally with the Confederacy.

As early as 1800, Choctaws had been engaged in the production of cotton, evidenced by Choctaw chiefs who requested items such as cotton gins, cards, and wheels from federal officials.[1] Given communal landownership and the ability of individual Choctaws to cultivate as much land as desired, some Choctaws were able to engage in large plantation-style agriculture, which included the labor of enslaved people of African descent. European traders and settlers had exposed Choctaws to enslaved people of African descent in the early decades of the eighteenth century.[2] A pre-removal census conducted by the federal government tallied 521 enslaved people among the Choctaw.[3] In 1839, this number reached some 600 enslaved people of African descent living among the Choctaw.[4] In 1860, on the eve of the American Civil War, enslaved people of African descent made up 14 percent of the population in the Choctaw Nation.[5] The experiences of the enslaved population in the Choctaw Nation, then, were not insignificant. Moreover, the presence of the enslaved population and the institution of slavery itself had consequences for the laws passed by the Choctaw legislature and for the decision that Choctaw officials would make about their citizens' participation in the American Civil War. Other scholars have written in more depth about slavery in the Choctaw Nation recently, so I offer only a brief sketch of some of its contours here.[6]

The institution of racialized slavery looms large in the history of the United States and conjures in particular images of cotton fields ruled by white enslavers and overseers who administered the lash to the laboring backs of Black enslaved people. Historians continually add more nuance to this image by exploring other experiences of enslaved people, such as those in urban settings, those who did not live on large plantations, and those who cultivated rice. This chapter focuses on the experiences of enslaved people among the Choctaw and in Indian Territory more broadly. What emerges from this examination is an institution that shared some similarities with slavery as practiced in the United States, including work patterns and religious life for the enslaved people; however, some sharp differences are also revealed. Choctaws did not just mirror the nearby southern states in their allocation of resources for the market economy or in the legislation they passed regarding their human property. Rather, they devoted resources to economic activities such as corn production that aligned with traditional Choctaw practices, and they passed statutes regarding the behavior of enslaved people and free people of African descent that respected Choctaw notions of descent and the importance of blood relationships. Thus, as the Choctaw adopted the practice of racialized slavery, they did so in a manner that preserved Choctaw identity.

In the Choctaw Nation, the location most compatible with engagement in plantation-style agriculture, particularly the growth of cotton, was along the Red River.[7] The proximity to water and the soil conditions seemed especially conducive to agricultural production. Thus, more than half of the enslaved population lived on farms and plantations clustered in this area.[8] By 1837 two cotton gins were operating in the Choctaw Nation, and eventually ten cotton gins were in use along the Red River.[9] In this area, Choctaws such as Robert M. Jones flourished. Jones owned several plantations and hundreds of enslaved people, making him one of the wealthiest men not just in Indian Territory but also in the larger American South.[10] His plantations contributed to the more than 1,000 bales of cotton produced annually by the Choctaw Nation during the 1830s and 1840s. More generally, after removal, Choctaws who could afford to do so pursued the acquisition of enslaved people. Jones or his agent John Hobart Heald, for instance, frequently purchased enslaved people in New Orleans. Other Choctaws were

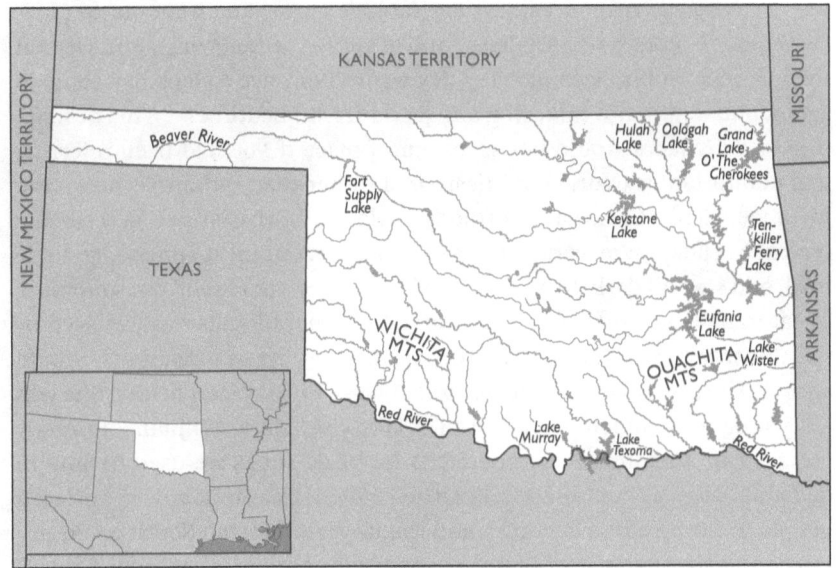

Physical features of Indian Territory.
(Map by Rice University GIS/Data Center)

able to procure enslaved people "from the captive exchange system among western Indian tribes that dominated the Southern plains during the 1830s and 1840s."[11]

Members of the Chickasaw Nation such as Levi Colbert also had large landholdings in this region and utilized the labor of enslaved people of African descent to cultivate cotton. Some contemporary observers referred to the area as "Little Dixie."[12] Reverend William H. Goode, who visited the Choctaw Nation, described Doaksville as "mainly surrounded by large cotton plantations, owned by Choctaws and Chickasaws, mostly half-breeds, and worked by slaves."[13] Of course, holdings the size of Jones's were the exception rather than the rule: farmsteads generally ran between ten and twenty acres, and most small farmers practiced subsistence agriculture, though any surplus might be sold in the market.[14]

Some formerly enslaved people from Indian Territory recalled work patterns that are reminiscent of descriptions of life in the fields on large cotton plantations in the wider South. Matilda Poe's Chickasaw enslaver Isaac Love controlled a workforce of 100 enslaved people. While he did not employ an overseer, his work regimen was fairly standard: "Dey always got up at daylight and de men went out and fed de horses. When de bell rang dey was ready to eat. After breakfast dey took de teams and went out to plow. Dey come in 'bout half past 'leven and at twelve de bell rung agin. Dey eat their dinner and back to plowing dey went. 'Bout five o'clock dey come in again, and den they'd talk, sing and jig dance till bedtime."[15] This description of daily labor would not seem out of place if Poe had been referring to a plantation in Georgia or Mississippi rather than Indian Territory. For instance, Henry Cheatham, formerly enslaved in Mississippi, described a typical workday: "We worked from can to can't. Get up at sunrise, go to de field, and stay till dark. In de middle of de day dey would send out somethin' to eat to de field, with a barrel of water."[16] Frances Banks was enslaved by the Choctaw Wright family and recollected that her grandparents "would pass de time by singing while dey toiled away in de cotton fields." She was too young to do much labor herself.[17] Likewise, Lizzie Williams, formerly enslaved in Alabama, remembered "a lot of de songs we used to sing in de fields" such as "Get on Board, Little Chillen, Get on Board."[18] Enslaved people in both Indian Territory and the larger American South could use music and singing to ameliorate the conditions of their labor in the fields.[19]

The kinds of labor enslaved men and women among the Choctaw performed will not come as a surprise to those who are familiar with the institution of slavery in the American South. Polly Colbert recalled that the enslaved women spun and wove the cloth, "but Miss Betsy cut out all de clothes and helped wid de sewing."[20] Colbert described Miss Betsy, the plantation mistress, as a "half-breed Choctaw." As historian Elizabeth Fox-Genovese noted in her study of women on southern plantations, "To a large extent, American and western European societies have assigned textile production to women, and slaveholding women proved no exception to this rule."[21]

Enslaved women among the Choctaw also performed other domestic and, sometimes, field labor. Former enslaved person Kiziah Love described enslaved women providing care for the children of the master class, and Matilda Poe remembered that her mother sometimes took care of enslaved children as well.[22] Colbert and Love offered detailed, sometimes mouthwatering, descriptions of the food that they prepared, perhaps memories of dietary abundance colored by their contemporary impoverished state.[23] Matilda Poe did not provide a thorough sketch of the food she ate; rather, she merely noted that "the old women done all de cooking in big iron pots that hung over the fire."[24] Enslaved women among the Choctaw also cleaned the homes of their enslavers. And, of course, "enslaved men and women worked together in the cotton fields and performed other labor necessary to ensure the successful operation of commercially oriented farms."[25]

As one might expect, these three accounts of slavery from women held within the Choctaw and Chickasaw Nations reveal more about the labor of women than that of men. Love's narrative offers some sense of enslaved men's labor when she relates the story of Uncle Bill, the defiant enslaved person who dared to run off a white overseer. In her story the overseer ordered Uncle Bill to catch a second plow team in addition to the one Uncle Bill would use for his day's work. Uncle Bill refused because "he had a lot of plowing to git done that morning and besides it was customary for every man to catch his own team." When the overseer attempted to punish Uncle Bill with a stick, Uncle Bill brandished a "single-tree." The overseer quickly turned about face and ran away, never to be seen on the plantation again. Similarly, Poe's description of the work regimen above confirms this pattern of enslaved men preparing teams of horses for plowing and spending the day in the fields.[26]

These accounts should not imply that only enslaved men labored in the fields for Indian enslavers; rather, they reflect the young age of the female informants and the variety of enslaved experiences. Colbert was young, so her labor consisted mostly of running errands for her mistress and "tot[ing] cool water to de field for de hands" with her brother when she was a little older.[27] Poe was only about eight years old when the war ended.[28] Love is the only one of these three women who was an adult by the time of the Civil War, and she did refer to "us" being put under the supervision of a white overseer, suggesting that she performed field labor. Her enslaver also ran a ferry and owned a stage inn, where she cleaned rooms.[29] The enslaver's commercial interests dictated the kinds of labor enslaved women and men performed. The size of the holding also determined the kinds of labor performed by enslaved people; the line between what was "male" versus "female" labor was not sharp. Mary Lindsey's Chickasaw mistress owned just two enslaved people, so Mary did a bit of everything: "water the hosses and slop the hogs and feed the chickens and milk the cows, and then git back to the house and git the breakfast." Lindsey would also plow with oxen and chop and haul wood. As she said so aptly, "That sho' was hard living then!"[30]

The use of male labor in the fields was a marked departure from the traditional gendered division of labor among the Choctaw, where women functioned as the primary agriculturalists, as discussed in chapter 1. The growth of plantation agriculture and use of enslaved people of African descent as field laborers, then, introduced a new paradigm with various implications for gender relations among the Choctaw. If Choctaw women had traditionally derived some authority from their role as agriculturalists, were they ceding some power by turning to enslaved labor to grow corn or other goods for the market? Moreover, was the value of agricultural labor in decline?

After all, enslaved people were outside of clan relationships and held a lower legal status; they surely were not deriving any power or authority from their field labor. Formerly enslaved people offer narratives in which the male enslavers made decisions about hiring an overseer or controlled the labor of the enslaved himself, which suggests that Choctaw women in plantation households did not make the same kinds of decisions about land use as their predecessors had made. Historian Barbara Krauthamer posits that the use of enslaved labor in agricultural work allowed Native men to avoid the stigma attached to taking on roles outside of traditional Choctaw gender norms and permitted such men to own agricultural labor and its products in ways that were not possible when Choctaw women were the agriculturalists. Moreover, Krauthamer suggests that Choctaws were racializing agricultural labor; that is, this labor not only was no longer the province of Choctaw women but became appropriate only for people of African descent.[31]

The outdoors was not solely a place of labor; it could also be a site of religious worship with practices shared by enslaved people in Indian Territory and others in the South. Kiziah Love and Polly Colbert described church meetings under brush arbors and attending church with whites. Meetings included preaching, praying, and singing, much as one would find in any church, though the style in which believers preached, prayed, and sang likely differed.[32] Emily Dixon of Mississippi recalled that enslaved people could attend church with whites "but us wanted ter go whar us could sing all de way through an' hum 'long an' shout, yo' all know, jist turn loose lak." So enslaved people worshipped together in the woods instead.[33] Scholar Albert J. Raboteau discusses the importance of religious services conducted by enslaved people in "hush harbors" or brush arbors, as well as some of the African roots of the religious practices of enslaved people, such as the ring shout and dancing, and how enslaved people's enthusiastic religiosity influenced white worshippers at religious revivals.[34] Of course, not every enslaver thought church was a good influence on bondpeople. Ministers might preach messages about the equality of souls or the sanctity of marriage; it might not always be convenient for enslaved people to refrain from labor on the Sabbath; and congregation members might seek literacy in order to read the Bible for themselves, to name just a few of the potential problems. O. W. Green's enslaver in Arkansas, for example, punished religious enslaved people by burning their hands: "My grandmother said he burnt her hand several times. Masta wouldn't let de cullud folks have meetin', but dey would go out in the woods in secret to pray and preach and shout."[35] Green's grandmother's experience illustrates these multiple truths about enslaved people's religious experiences: sometimes enslaved people worshipped in secret because enslavers disapproved; the outdoors could become a place of worship; and worship could take many, sometimes energetic, forms.

While Choctaw planters had begun to grow cotton for commercial markets, corn production and raising livestock remained important parts of the Choctaw economy. Because corn not only was an important staple of the Choctaw diet but also carried so much symbolic meaning in Choctaw ceremonial life, many Choctaws continued to place particular importance on the cultivation of corn.[36] In contrast, wealthy white southerners often channeled their resources into the production of a cash crop, sometimes to the exclusion of providing enough foodstuffs for their households. In fact, historian Gilbert C. Fite asserted that cotton production was "second only to corn in importance among the Choctaws and Chickasaws on the eve of the Civil War, but to estimate the total production would be sheer speculation."[37] Fite's statement both verifies the persistent importance of corn production to the Choctaw and reveals the growing value of cotton as a crop. Because corn was not, for the most part, a cash crop produced for market consumption, it is difficult to obtain accurate production numbers. Some evidence is available through commissioners' reports. In 1833 the Choctaw produced a surplus of 40,000 bushels of corn, which they sold to the federal government to supply new Choctaw immigrants. By 1836, the corn surplus reached 50,000 bushels.[38] Perhaps the proximity of Indian Territory to Harrison Davis's farm in Sherman, Texas, influenced his decision to focus on corn rather than cotton. Amanda Oliver, a member of Harrison's enslaved workforce, recalled, "Dey didn't raise cotton either; but dey raised a whole lots of corn."[39]

The recollections of formerly enslaved people suggest that both corn and cotton were important crops in Indian Territory. Henry Henderson, formerly enslaved by the prominent Cherokee Vann family, recalled that his enslavers "bought and sold slaves, raised corn and cotton and run the steamboat." The Vanns used the steamboat to transport enslaved people and cotton along the Arkansas River.[40] Patsy Perryman, also enslaved in the Cherokee Nation, described the main crops at the Taylor family holding as "corn and cotton."[41] Kiziah Love remembered that when a white man approached her Choctaw enslaver Frank Colbert for a job as an overseer, he claimed that he could double Colbert's corn and cotton yields.[42] This statement identifies the main crops cultivated at the Colbert farm. Formerly enslaved people were not the only ones to comment on the crops produced in this region. Mrs. Thomas Inge, daughter and wife of missionaries to the

Chickasaw and Choctaw, remarked that "all the well-to-do Indians held slaves and raised stock as well as corn; there was also a small amount of cotton raised."[43]

Polly Colbert, formerly enslaved in the Choctaw Nation, remembered a diet that rested on two important activities: corn production and raising livestock. Colbert lived on a smaller farm of about 100 acres with seven or eight adult enslaved people and a few children. Corn was a part of all of the Indian dishes Colbert described, such as Tom-fuller, pashofa, and Tom-budha. And pork seemed to be the protein source of choice, though she also described eating a lot of game meat such as possum, raccoon, and squirrel. The management of livestock had taken on increasing importance in the Choctaw economy in the late eighteenth century as Choctaw hunters exhausted the population of deer. Individuals turned to horses, cows, and pigs to repopulate forests and prairies. Intermarried whites and traders also recognized the borderlands of the Choctaw territory in the Southeast as particularly valuable as cattle range and initially drove the expansion of livestock raising. For instance, John Pitchlynn, a Scottish immigrant who married Choctaw woman Sophia Folsom and served as an interpreter, built an estate that consisted mostly of livestock by 1805. His son Peter, a future leader in the Choctaw Nation, grew up not as a hunter but as a herdsman.[44] The practice of communal landholding meant that raising livestock could be relatively inexpensive. Animals could be turned loose to graze on communal land and then gathered when ready for market. Polly Colbert's enslaver Holmes Colbert, a "half-breed Choctaw," had "woods full of hogs and cows." No individual needed to own vast tracts of territory for grazing.

Slaveholding Choctaws sometimes turned to their bondpeople to serve as cowboys or herders to manage their livestock.[45] Prominent Choctaw slaveholder Robert M. Jones owned several ranches and used his enslaved workforce, under the management of white overseers, to raise his large number of livestock.[46] One easily imagines Holmes Colbert turning to enslaved people to manage his "woods full of hogs and cows" and perhaps drive them to market for sale. Formerly enslaved by Cherokees, Henry Henderson remembered, "When I got old enough to work around the farm, my job was to care for the sheep."[47] Likewise, Cherokee enslaver Joe Sheppard put Morris Sheppard to work tending cattle. Sheppard maintained a smaller holding of fifty acres, owned only two families of enslaved people, and chose not to grow cotton at all.[48] The practice of raising large livestock grew so widespread that by 1829 a missionary census of the northeastern district of the Choctaw Nation tallied 11,661 cattle, 3,974 horses, 112 oxen, and 22,047 hogs owned by 5,627 people.[49] By the 1840s an observer would predict that

Indian-managed herds might supply most of the southern market.⁵⁰ The raising of livestock had become an important part of the economy in Indian Territory, and those who owned enslaved people used their labor to manage this important resource.

This discussion of the importance of corn and livestock to Native groups in Indian Territory should not suggest that corn was not also cultivated in the cotton belt or that white southerners did not raise livestock. Many people formerly enslaved by white southerners referred to corn shuckings and the food, music, and celebrations that accompanied the activity. Robert Shepherd of Georgia remembered "dem womans cooked for days, and de mens would get de shoats ready to barbecue. Marster would send us out to get de slaves from de farms round about dere. De place was all lit up with light-wood knot torches and bonfires, and dere was 'citement a-plenty when all niggers get to singin' and shoutin' as dey made de shucks fly."⁵¹ White cotton planters in the American South, however, aimed to produce only as much corn as could be consumed by their households and workforce, because there was little market for surplus corn.⁵² Contrast this practice of producing only as much corn as could be consumed by those on the plantation with the Choctaw pattern of harvesting large surpluses of corn; clearly the Choctaw and other Natives in Indian Territory placed a higher value on and devoted more resources to the production of corn than did their counterparts in the southern states.

Several formerly enslaved people from the larger American South recollected labor that included animal husbandry. Doc Daniel Dowdy, formerly of Georgia, described his work as "picking up chips and keeping the calves separate so that the calves wouldn't suck the cows dry."⁵³ Formerly enslaved in Georgia, Morris Hillyer was assigned several tasks as an adolescent, including taking the cows to pasture when he and several friends had spent too much time getting into trouble on the Hillyer plantation.⁵⁴ Another adolescent, Charley Ross, enslaved in Arkansas, had taken care of the livestock because he was too young to work in the fields. His enslavers, the Ross family, used young enslaved boys to "ride the calves to make them gentle for driving, or what folks called 'bridle wise.' Most of the time we didn't ride only just long enough to get tossed off on the ground."⁵⁵ In slavery, youth certainly did not excuse individuals from labor. John Wells, enslaved by Captain R. Campbell Jones, was responsible for 500 head of sheep owned by J. Gardner while refugeeing in Texas.⁵⁶ Scholarly descriptions of daily life for enslaved people on plantations often include some activity related to the care and feeding of livestock.⁵⁷ The propensity to use younger enslaved people for this work, however, suggests that the raising of hogs or cattle or sheep was often not a high priority on these plantations. In fact, scholar of slavery Eugene Genovese argues quite persuasively that white southerners did not pursue the large-scale growth of a livestock industry because of high transportation costs, poor quality stock, and the lack of an urban market. And those planters who did have the capital to be successful were often "prisoners of the plantation myth and scorned pursuits other than cotton growing."[58] In sum, some enslavers in Indian Territory allocated their resources to more diverse economic activities than many slaveholders in the American South.

Choctaw and other Native enslavers had a reputation for being kinder enslavers. Contemporary observer Ethan Allen Hitchcock asserted, "A slave among wild Indians is almost as free as his owner." Hitchcock went on to distinguish between Native slaveholders of varying Native ancestry, claiming that those enslavers of mixed European and Native ancestry were more stringent enslavers.[59] Hitchcock's comments are a part of the long-running trope of the "lazy" Indian man and notions about female "squaw drudges" but also reveal the common perception that Native enslavers demanded less labor from their enslaved workforce and were, therefore, less harsh.[60] Historian Celia E. Naylor contends that enslaved people recognized differences between the behavior of "full-blood" and "mixed blood" enslavers as well.[61] Matilda Poe's assessment of life under a Chickasaw enslaver only affirms Hitchcock's general perception: "I never did know I was a slave, 'cause I couldn't tell I wasn't free."[62] Polly Colbert thought "it was on account of de rich land dat us niggers dat was owned by Indians didn't have to work so hard as dey did in de old states, but I think dat Indian masters was just naturally kinder any way, leastways mine was."[63]

This reputation was due, in part, to the varying work patterns and greater freedoms experienced by people enslaved by Native enslavers, according to formerly enslaved informants. Henry Clay was born in North Carolina but was eventually sold and moved to Louisiana near Texarkana. He observed, "It seem like the slaves in the Creek country had a better time than most of the negroes in Louisiana, too. They played more and had their own church and preachers."[64] Mary Grayson's description of life with her Creek enslaver Mose Perryman supports Clay's observations about Creek enslavers: "We slaves didn't have a hard time at all before the War. I have had people who were slaves of white folks back in the old states tell me that they had to work awfully hard and their masters were cruel to them sometimes, but all the Negroes I knew who belonged to Creeks always had plenty of clothes and lots to eat and we all lived in good log cabins we built." Grayson outlined a work routine that included agricultural labor, tending livestock, and domestic labor for older enslaved women, "but each Negro family looked after a part of the fields and worked the crops like they belonged to us." The implication of Grayson's sketch of life on the Perryman plantation is that enslaved people exercised some control over their daily labor routine, and perhaps over some of the products of that labor. Historian Ira Berlin finds that across the South, some enslaved people were able to "roll back some of the harshest aspects of the plantation revolution" when they exercised some control over when and how they labored.[65]

Some formerly enslaved informants suggested that there was some variation even among Native enslavers: Lucinda Davis, formerly enslaved in the Creek Nation, remembered that her parents were owned by different enslavers who permitted them to live together. Her parents gave most of the product of their labor to the enslavers, but they were also able to keep some of it for themselves: "Dey didn't have to stay on de master's place and work like I hear de slaves of de white people and de Cherokee and Choctaw people say dey do."[66] Davis's statement, as well as those of formerly enslaved people such as Clay and Colbert, is freighted with meaning and provokes questions. The comparison sets up Cherokee and Choctaw enslavers as more like their white counterparts. It also reveals that individuals discussed their experiences in bondage but is vague about when. These comparisons might have been made after emancipation but perhaps during enslavement as well. Enslavers might also have invoked comparisons to convince their human property that their current situation could be worse if not for a beneficent enslaver. And surely enslaved people passed along information about conditions on other plantations when circumstances permitted them to travel. Like the enslavers of Lucinda Davis's parents, Kiziah Love's Choctaw enslaver Frank Colbert and neighboring planter Sam Love also permitted Kiziah and her husband, Isom Love, to live together. Isom and Kiziah both lived on Frank Colbert's property, and Isom traveled to his enslaver's plantation to work. Kiziah Love remarked, "I don't 'spect we could of done that way iffen we hadn't of had Indian masters. They let us do a lot like we pleased jest so we got our work done and didn't run off."[67] Colbert's decision to allow the Loves to live together assuredly colored Kiziah's opinion of Native enslavers.

These descriptions of slavery in Indian Territory as less harsh and of Native enslavers as more lenient have contributed to the notion that Indian slaveholders were kinder than their southern counterparts, but of course not all Indian enslavers behaved in this manner. Kiziah Love juxtaposed her descriptions of the kindness of enslaver Frank Colbert with the behavior of his half brother. Buck Colbert served as a patroller and "was sho' bad to whup niggers." Buck also killed his child's enslaved nurse when he hit her in the head with fire tongs because she could not quiet the baby. When this nurse's replacement was slow to respond to the crying baby, Buck whipped her so badly that she was no longer able to nurse her own child, and Frank Colbert had to intervene.[68] Charlotte Johnson White, enslaved in the Cherokee Nation, blamed her old enslaver Ben Johnson for the death of White's mother. White's mother was sick and slow to get to work in the fields, "so he pushed her in a little ditch dat was by the cabin and whipped her back wid the lash, den he reached down and rolled her over so's he could beat her face and neck. She didn't live long after dat and I guess de whippin's helped to kill her." And White also experienced Johnson's cruelty more directly. When White was twelve years old, she dropped one of her enslaver's children near some burning brush; in response, Johnson pushed White into the fire herself: "See this old drawn, scarred face? Dats what I got from de fire, and inside my lips is burned off, and my back is scarred wid lashings dat'll be wid me when I meet my Jesus." In 1859 another enslaved woman was burned alive after being accused of instigating the murder of her enslaver Choctaw Richard Harkins. Mrs. Harkins demanded the punishment after the enslaved woman's husband confessed to the murder, implicated his wife under torture, and then drowned himself.[69] As scholars such as Claudio Saunt, Rudi Halliburton, Celia Naylor, and Barbara Krauthamer have argued convincingly, Indigenous slaveholders and white slaveholders had much in common, and their treatment of their human property could range from cruel to kind, which is reflected in the comments of formerly enslaved people about their experiences.[70]

Perhaps another factor that contributed to the perception of Choctaws and other Natives as kinder enslavers was their use of their human property as interpreters. Enslaved people who were fluent in both English and Native languages could serve as intermediaries between their Native enslavers and whites. Of course, one would expect enslaved people in Indian Territory to learn the language of their enslavers: Mary Cole claimed to have learned the Choctaw language before she learned to speak English.[71] Lucinda Davis spoke only Creek until after the Civil War.[72] Likewise, Patsy Perryman's mother was raised by her Cherokee enslaver Judy Taylor and was a fluent Cherokee speaker. Some enslaved people in Indian Territory also had English language skills gained from their previous enslavers or had lived in southern states prior to being brought to the territory.[73] In particular, Euro-American missionaries to the Indians sometimes used enslaved people as interpreters.[74] These instances when enslaved persons acted as interpreters represented inversions of the social order: the people with the least status in the group, people who could ordinarily be dismissed as property or an object, became the center of the interaction. A business transaction or the salvation of a soul could depend on the interpreter's language skills. In some ways the interpreter had more knowledge than anyone else, which put him or her in an unusual position of power for an enslaved person.[75] It is conceivable that some Euro-Americans found Natives' reliance on enslaved interpreters to be a sign of weakness; at the very least, Euro-Americans likely saw it as indicative of the Natives' lack of "civilization." And to return to Hitchcock's observations, those less "civilized" Indians, as measured by their degree of European ancestry, exercised less mastery over their enslaved laborers. This also contributed to another common perception held by many whites at that time: Indian planters such as Frank Colbert were not effective managers of their human property or resources. If they had been, the story went, their farms and plantations would have been more productive.

Particularly in the narratives collected by the WPA in the era of the Great Depression, however, one must take into consideration the contemporary circumstances of the formerly enslaved informants when reading descriptions of kind enslavers. As historian Stephanie J. Shaw states, "The Great Depression looms large in these narratives."[76] These elderly informants often were in dire economic circumstances, sometimes unsure of where their next meal was coming from.[77] Hence, some of the interviewees offered rich descriptions of the food they ate while enslaved and expressed a preference for a time when an enslaver provided for all of an enslaved person's material needs. William Walters, who had been enslaved in Tennessee, did not have much patience for such talk: "Those were awful times. Yet I have heard many of the older Negroes say the old days were better. Such talk always seemed to be but an expression of sentiment for some good old master, or else the older Negroes were just too handicapped with ignorance to recognize the benefits of liberty or the opportunities of freedom."[78] And because of Jim Crow segregation and legal efforts to disenfranchise African American voters, many of these formerly enslaved people may not have experienced much tangible benefit from emancipation.

It is quite telling that even formerly enslaved people who described more considerate enslavers often preferred freedom to enslavement. Kiziah Love described her Choctaw enslaver Frank Colbert as fairly kind, yet she reveled in news of her freedom nonetheless: "I was glad to be free. What did I do and say. Well I jest clapped my hands together and said, 'Thank God Almighty, I'se free at last!'"[79] Henry Bibb, author of the famous autobiography that poignantly depicts the impact of slavery on family relationships, described his Cherokee enslaver as humane and stated that Indian enslavers offered adequate food and clothing and better treatment to their enslaved property than did their white counterparts; yet even Bibb, after his enslaver's passing, could only pretend "to be taking on at a great rate about his death," while Bibb was actually more excited about planning his escape.[80] Lucinda Davis's parents, who had been permitted to live together when they were enslaved by different men and who kept some of the fruits of their labor, also eagerly escaped slavery despite their improved situation. Davis was uncertain about whether her parents ran away or purchased themselves; however, she does remember being sold to another enslaver after their departure. Davis's parents likely ran away; given the opportunity to purchase freedom for themselves, one imagines they would purchase their child's freedom also. Lizzie Jackson, formerly enslaved in the Creek Nation, offered a succinct assessment: "I'm glad that slave days is gone. Even if the master was good the slaves was bad off."[81]

The presence of enslaved people and the growing use of their labor in the Choctaw Nation required that authorities create a legal scaffold to support the institution. Choctaw legislators wrote laws to demarcate the status of enslaved people in the nation, to enumerate the legal rights enslaved people could and could not access, and to define their appropriate behavior. One of the earliest pieces of legislation that the Choctaw enacted regarding their human property came in 1828, before the Choctaw were removed to Indian Territory. The act prohibited legal unions with enslaved people: "From this time forward we shall be in agreement that the following shall be prohibited. Choctaw people and the white people who are counted with the Choctaws shall not marry black slaves." Enslavers, Indian or white, were admonished to prevent such occurrences or face a fine of fifty dollars, half of which would be awarded to the witness who reported the crime.[82] Legal unions between enslaved people and free people were dangerous because they could accord the enslaved partner rights to property, access to inheritance, and control over children that Choctaw authorities did not want to grant or recognize. An amendment made clear, however, that legal unions were not the sole target of the legislators: Indian or white men who had sexual relations with a "black female slave" would receive thirty-five lashes as punishment. And Indian or white women would receive twenty-five lashes for participating in sexual relations with enslaved men. The couple would then be separated.[83] That the punishable party was the Indian or the white partner suggests several conclusions about the thinking of the lawmakers: the free person in such relationships was more culpable; enslaved people had an obligation to obey their enslavers and thus were unable to refuse the sexual advances of their enslavers; and perhaps the Indian or white partner's choice of an enslaved sexual partner (legally or otherwise) was particularly unsettling to social norms.

After their removal to Indian Territory, Choctaws reconstituted their governing structures, and Choctaw legislators carefully circumscribed the behavior of enslaved people, as did their counterparts in the American South. In 1836, the General Council prohibited any American citizen, particularly missionaries and preachers, from speaking in favor of or agitating for "the most fatal and destructive doctrine of abolitionism." Those who advocated the end of slavery would be expelled from the Choctaw Nation forever. The language of this act reveals that lawmakers thought abolitionists came from outside of the nation to stir up anxieties within and that such activity was dangerous. Ostensibly, there were no Choctaw abolitionists; that is, none of this thinking originated from Choctaw citizens.

Closely connected to the concern about the spread of abolitionism was the fear of literacy for enslaved people. It was illegal for individuals to teach an enslaved person to read or write, or even to sit at the same table with enslaved people, without the consent of their enslaver. Doing so was sufficient evidence that the offender was an abolitionist and subject to the penalty for espousing abolitionist principles outlined in the first part of the law, namely expulsion.[84] The two parts of this statute expose the relationship Choctaw legislators and slaveholders recognized between education and abolition: a literate enslaved person, in particular, would want freedom. Moreover, literacy could be a tool to gain that freedom by writing passes, by communicating with others without the enslaver's knowledge, or by gaining information from written sources such as newspapers. The extension of this logic was that there were few good reasons for enslavers to permit enslaved people to become literate; however, the statute did allow enslavers to consent to their enslaved laborers' literacy, a recognition of enslavers' ultimate authority over their human property and also of the possibility that an enslaved person's literacy might rarely serve an enslaver's interests.

In 1841, the Cherokee legislature approved a far more restrictive law regarding the literacy of enslaved people than the Choctaw law, one that left an impression on enslaved people that persisted long after emancipation. Cherokee lawmakers made it illegal to teach any free people of African descent as well as enslaved people belonging to Cherokee citizens how to read or write. The punishment was a significant fine ranging between $100 and $500. There was no allowance made for enslavers who might wish to educate their enslaved laborers; however, there was a loophole that exempted individuals of African and Cherokee ancestry from the prohibition.[85] There was some legal benefit, then, to possessing Cherokee ancestry, whereas there was no similar benefit in the Choctaw law.[86] And the statute must have had some bite because it lived on in the memories of formerly enslaved people. Betty Robertson recalled, "But we couldn't learn to read or have a book, and the Cherokee folks was afraid to tell us about the letters and figgers because they have a law you go to jail and a big fine if you show a slave about the letters."[87] Morris Sheppard and Sarah Wilson, each enslaved in the Cherokee Nation, also specifically mentioned Cherokee laws prohibiting the education of enslaved people.[88] Chaney Richardson, formerly enslaved by Cherokee Charley Rogers, remembered that there were no schools for "Negroes" during slavery; hence she could neither read nor write.[89] Richardson did not attribute the lack of schools to a legal statute, but her recollection suggests that the law had a real effect. Here again, the difference between the Choctaw and Cherokee laws regarding the literacy of enslaved people shows the variation even within Indian Territory in terms of the treatment of human property.

Whether in response to the passage of legal restrictions on literacy or because of personal preference, enslavers punished enslaved people who sought the ability to read and write. As early as the colonial period, slaveholders both inside and outside of Indian Territory saw the dangers of literacy for enslaved people and took action in places such as South Carolina and Georgia to repress it. Other locales followed suit to varying degrees.[90] Sam Jordan, who was formerly enslaved in Alabama and claimed a father of Cherokee ancestry, recalled that enslaved people could not obtain an education until after freedom. When his enslaver discovered that a newly purchased enslaved person was literate and dared to teach other enslaved people, the overseers "whipped him giving him 500 lashes and cut off his index finger so that he could not write nor teach the other slaves."[91] Andrew Simms, who had been enslaved in Florida and whose enslaver refugeed his human property in Texas, recalled similarly harsh consequences for enslaved people who pursued literacy. A neighboring enslaver, Elam Bowman, would cut off the finger of enslaved people he caught "toying with the pencil." Such punishments made enslaved people lose interest in seeking an education and focus on field work, in Simms's estimation.[92] And the physical maiming of individuals served as a visible warning to other enslaved people who might attempt to become literate.

Some enslavers did permit enslaved people to achieve literacy despite the legal sanctions or public disapproval. In the Choctaw and Chickasaw Nations, enslaved people could gain access to literacy through missionaries.[93] Sweetie Ivory Wagoner, born around the time of emancipation in Arkansas, stated that her father, through whom she was able to receive a land allotment, was a Creek Indian who had been enslaved by the Cherokee. Her mother had told her that, though many enslaved people never learned to read or write, the mistress of the plantation had taught her to read after her daily work was completed. The mistress also had taken her to church regularly. Perhaps encouraging literacy for Wagoner's mother was related to religious activity.[94] Nelson Denson had been enslaved in Texas and recalled that his parents were taught to read and write on the plantation, which led to Denson becoming a minister of the gospel.[95] Sam Word of Arkansas gained literacy through the help of his young enslaver, who would share knowledge after school, a story similar to that of Frederick Douglass, who "converted into teachers" the young white boys he met in the streets of Baltimore.[96] Douglass also had a mistress, Mrs. Auld, who attempted to teach him to read until her husband forbade her from further instruction.[97] Thus, even in locations where literacy for enslaved people had been prohibited outright, enslavers and enslaved people circumvented the law. Among the Choctaw, enslavers who chose to educate their human property did not have to fear legal repercussions but surely felt the weight of social pressure to refrain. The missionaries among the Choctaw and Chickasaw, for instance, were careful not to encourage an inversion of the social order or empowerment for their enslaved congregants, as Barbara Krauthamer makes clear.[98]

In the same year that they passed the law regarding literacy for enslaved people, Choctaw lawmakers also passed legislation that prevented enslaved people from owning property or carrying guns without permission from their enslavers. Thus, in October 1836, the General Council stipulated that after two months, "no negro slaves shall be in possession of any property, or arms." After that time, any existing property was to be sold to the highest bidder by the lighthorsemen and the proceeds given to the Choctaw Nation.[99] Presumably, the two-month delay for the law's effect was an attempt to give the enslaved people time to dispose of their property, which prompts the question of just how common it was for enslaved people to own property. Given some of the comments of formerly enslaved people in Indian Territory about enslavers who permitted enslaved people to labor for themselves, perhaps many enslaved people were able to accumulate some property. On plantations in rice-growing regions in which enslavers employed the task system, for instance, enslaved people could sometimes carve out time to labor on their own behalf and accrue small amounts of property.[100] And perhaps people enslaved by Choctaws could retain the proceeds of the sale of their property if completed independently and before the two-month deadline. The language of the statute suggests the likelihood of some complicity on the part of enslavers: those who permitted the accumulation of property by their bondpeople were liable for a ten-dollar fine for each offense, and it was likely the enslaver who would share news of the passage of this law and its provisions with the enslaved property owner.[101]

This same legal statute warned enslaved people to behave and to avoid infringing on the rights of Choctaws or else face ten lashes from a lighthorseman "or any other person." Legally, then, any Choctaw citizen had the right to chastise and punish any enslaved person. The final section of this statute permitted "any good honest slave" to carry a gun if he or she had a written pass from his or her enslaver. This last part of the law reinforces why literacy for enslaved people was dangerous: literate enslaved people might write their own passes permitting the carrying of firearms. And armed, the enslaved people might participate in a revolt. Recall that the Choctaw legislature passed these laws in 1836, a short five years after Nat Turner sent the South into convulsions with his attempt to foment an insurrection to overthrow slavery in Southampton County, Virginia. News of Turner's revolt spread like wildfire, and Choctaw enslavers wanted to preempt rebellions by enslaved people if possible. Limiting enslaved people's access to literacy and weapons seemed like a sound prophylactic measure. Note again, though, that enslavers could give permission for their human property to possess a weapon. Choctaw lawmakers were not willing to impinge fully on the authority of enslavers over enslaved people.

The Choctaw statutes aimed at controlling the behavior of enslaved people reflected a larger unwillingness to include people of African descent in the polity and delineated the prescribed place of people of African descent in the nation. For instance, the 1838 Choctaw Constitution stipulated that any "person who is any part negro" could not hold office in the Choctaw government.[102] Moreover, Choctaws did not want people of African descent who were not enslaved to reside in the nation unless they were also of Choctaw or Chickasaw descent: "From and after the adoption of this Constitution, no free negro, or any part negro, unconnected with Choctaw and Chickasaw blood, shall be permitted to come and settle in the Choctaw Nation."[103] Finally, while the General Council had the authority to "naturalize and adopt as citizens of this Nation any Indian or descendant of other Indian tribes," people of African descent could not access Choctaw citizenship in this manner.[104] Thus, the people of African descent who remained in the Choctaw Nation after the passage of this constitution were by default assumed to be enslaved unless they also had a "blood" connection to the tribe. Restrictions on officeholding by people of African descent and on their residence in the nation would persist throughout the nineteenth century in the Choctaw Nation.

By 1840, Choctaw legislators reiterated the prohibition on "free negroes" settling in the nation and made their employers liable for punishment. Moreover, those "free negroes" without Choctaw or Chickasaw blood who remained in the nation were threatened with enslavement for life if they did not leave "and forever keep out of it" by March 1 of the following year. The law directed lighthorsemen to take into custody individuals of unmixed African descent suspected of being free, and the burden of proof fell to the individual and enslavers to "establish the fact of such negro or negroes being, *bona fide*, a slave."[105] Such persons who could not prove they were legally enslaved or who returned after leaving the Choctaw Nation would be sold to the highest bidder. This provision was a strange inversion of presumptions about the legal status of people of African descent in the larger South: rather than assume unknown people of African descent to be enslaved until they presented papers proving their freedom, the Choctaw law supposed unfamiliar people of African descent to be free. Individuals then had to demonstrate their enslaved status in order to remain in the Choctaw Nation. But free status meant expulsion there, as it did periodically in the southern states.

The Choctaw legislature's efforts to keep free people of African descent out of the nation fell in line with similar efforts by other southern states to expel newly manumitted people of African descent, though the Choctaw act made no distinction regarding when and how freedom had been obtained. In other words, the Choctaw lawmakers did not tie expulsion to manumission as those in states such as Virginia and North Carolina did; rather, Choctaws reserved expulsion for free people of African descent who lacked Choctaw or Chickasaw blood, a legacy of traditional kinship affinities and their relation to blood.[106] And the punishment of enslavement for life for those free people of African descent who remained in the Choctaw Nation was far more draconian than the year of servitude proposed in nearby Arkansas in 1859.[107] Given the commercial and personal interactions among slaveholders in Arkansas, Texas, Louisiana, and the Choctaw Nation, members of these state legislatures surely knew of the Choctaw statute. Perhaps some southern states were following the Choctaw Nation's example in considering legislation in the 1850s to remove free people of African descent altogether, rather than solely as a requirement for manumission, especially in light of the increasing prominence of abolitionists and growth in the activity of the Underground Railroad at this time. John Brown's raid on

Harpers Ferry in October 1859 with a company of men that included free people of African descent, for instance, confirmed the prudence of the actions taken by the Arkansas legislature earlier that same year, as well as that of the Choctaw decades prior. At the very least the Choctaw example demonstrates that slaveholding societies shared concerns about the threat represented by a population of free people of African descent.

Despite this fairly clear statute preventing people of African descent from settling in the Choctaw Nation, in 1846 the legislature deemed it necessary to prohibit "negroes" from remaining in the nation "under the pretence of hiring himself or themselves to work, no matter whether they have papers or not." The statute explicitly includes not just "negroes" from the United States but those resident in the neighboring tribes of Indians as well.[108] The statute is brief but tantalizing. It raises the question of whether the law was reactive or preemptive—that is, whether it was addressing an actual increase in the number of free people of African descent in the nation or reflected concerns about the potential future mobility of free people of African descent.

Neither is it clear to what papers the lawmakers were referring. The statute may have been referencing a work permit. An 1836 law had required white men who worked in the Choctaw Nation to obtain a written permit from the chief or federal agent for the nation. Any Choctaw citizen who hired a white man who had not obtained this permit was liable for any property stolen by this employee or for any depredations he might commit.[109] The law was very specific in its reference to "white men," but quite possibly men of African descent were obtaining such permits as well, in spite of this language. If so, why? Perhaps there was a labor shortage in the nation. Or lawmakers may have been referring to the freedom papers of free men of African descent. In this case, Choctaw authorities may have feared the appearance of harboring fugitive enslaved persons or providing such persons with work. After all, the legislature had passed an act to "prevent the harboring of runaway negroes" just three years before with financial penalties for those convicted of aiding a fugitive enslaved person.[110]

The penalty for men of African descent who violated the law and worked in the nation was steep: "not less than one hundred lashes" on the bare back. Moreover, if the violator had accumulated property, it would "be seized and sold at public sale." One-third of the proceeds would go to the lighthorsemen, since they were charged with apprehending violators of the statute. The rest of the proceeds would go to the general funds of the district in which the violation took place. The statute also provided for an exception, however; those "negroes passing through the country, or such as may be hauling for citizens or merchants in the Nation," were exempt from the penalties of this law.[111] Choctaws wanted to benefit from the labor of these individuals but did not want people of African descent settling in the nation permanently and created this mechanism to control the population through the employer.

At this same 1846 legislative session, Choctaw lawmakers also addressed the issue of the manumission of enslaved persons. In order to emancipate an enslaved person, the enslaver had to petition the General Council and verify that he or she had no outstanding debts. Presumably, this measure prevented enslavers from reneging on debts by freeing enslaved property that might be sold to settle those debts. Then the General Council could choose to pass an act for the enslaver effecting the enslaved person's emancipation. Upon the act's passage, the newly emancipated person had thirty days to the leave the nation. Such a provision could be gut-wrenching if the freedperson had family who remained in bondage in the nation. If the freedperson chose to return to the Choctaw Nation at some point, he or she risked apprehension by the lighthorsemen and being sold into indentured servitude for a five-year term. Any proceeds from the sale would be deposited into the national funds.[112] Viewed in conjunction with the laws regulating the behavior of enslaved people, this manumission law again emphasizes the desire of Choctaw officials to ensure that any people of African descent remaining in the nation would be enslaved or, as discussed, individuals with a blood connection to a member of the nation.

Choctaw officials also reaffirmed the 1828 prohibition of relationships between people of African descent and Choctaw citizens but introduced different penalties. In 1838, just two years after the General Council began outlining the proper procedure for white men to marry Choctaw women, the council had also stated that "if any person or persons, citizens of this Nation, shall publicly take up with a negro slave, he or she so offending shall be liable to pay a fine not less than ten dollars nor exceeding twenty five dollars—and shall be separated."[113] A second offense warranted between five and thirty-nine lashes on the bare back as well as separation. Again, the council did not stipulate a punishment for the "negro slave" partner who violated this act. Perhaps the authorities assumed that the enslaver would punish the enslaved person for violating this statute. The council also did not assume the gender of the Choctaw offender. The target of this statute was not fornication or cohabitation; the statute punished only the Choctaw participant in the relationship, not both parties in the relationship, as one generally finds in a fornication or cohabitation statute.[114] Further, in practice the law banned marriage between Choctaw citizens and enslaved people of African descent because of the presumption that married couples "publicly take up" with each other. The language of this act alone does not indicate whether it was the enslaved person's status or race that lawmakers found unacceptable, but the slate of other Choctaw legislation—preventing people of African ancestry from holding political office; prohibiting free people of African descent from residing in the nation unless they were also of Choctaw or Chickasaw descent; and preventing people of African descent from gaining Choctaw citizenship through adoption or naturalization—suggests that Choctaw lawmakers were beginning to think about race and to think about people of African descent negatively.[115]

Despite the legal disapproval for sexual activity between Choctaws and people of African descent, according to formerly enslaved informants such relationships occurred. For instance, freedman Wesley McCoy described his ancestry as "around half Choctaw, or such a matter," because both of his parents were of Choctaw and African ancestry. He was born in 1856; thus, his parents were likely conceived at a time when this prohibition on interracial sex between Choctaws and people of African descent was in place. McCoy himself would marry a "full blood Chickasaw" woman named Parthenia Brown later in life, despite continued legal bans on such unions.[116] Louis Pierce was born at the start of the American Civil War to a Choctaw father and a freedwoman of mixed ancestry.[117] Caroline Pannell was born enslaved in 1853 and claimed her father was of African and Choctaw ancestry and her mother was of African and Creek ancestry.[118] Unfortunately, these descriptions do not offer any detail about the nature of these sexual relationships, for a variety of understandable reasons. Depending on the nature of the relationship, family members may not have discussed them; contemporary taboos about discussing sex during the nineteenth century and during the time of the interviews in the early twentieth century may have served to limit such conversations; and the age of the informants as young children may have inhibited their parents from saying more. The existence of sexual relationships between Choctaw Indians and people of African descent should come as no surprise, however, given human nature and the prerogative of enslavers over human property. Many southern states passed similar kinds of anti-miscegenation statutes, and yet such relationships appear in slave narratives, the complaints of plantation mistresses, and legal records, to name but a few sources.[119]

While marriages between Choctaw women and white men were legally permissible at this time, this had not always been the case. H. B. Cushman, who lived among the Choctaw, and Pete W. Cole, a nineteenth-century resident of Indian Territory, both recounted similar stories about Choctaws' initial reluctance to accept marriages between Choctaw women and white men. In both accounts, the birth of a child provoked a council meeting. Some council members argued successfully that permitting these marriages would allow whites to "become more numerous" and lead to the loss of the nation's characteristics. Thus, the council prohibited "all future marriages between the Choctaws and the White Race," ordered the white husband to leave the nation, and condemned the child to death. The committee appointed to execute the child, however, "felt reluctant" to do so. In the meantime, the mother found out about this decision and hid her baby. The committee blamed the Great Spirit for the child's disappearance and decided that if the baby returned, he would be spared. The mother then reappeared with her son and claimed that the Great Spirit had returned him to her. The boy lived, and others considered the child to be under the protection of the Great Spirit. He later became chief of the Choctaw Nation. The council eventually repealed the ban on intermarriage, recalled the father back to the tribe, and adopted him as a member.[120] Thus, this story also set the precedent for the practice of adopting the white spouses of Choctaw Indians into the nation.

It is difficult to determine the accuracy of this account of the first marriage between a member of the Choctaw Nation and a white person. For instance, record of a legislative ban on intermarriage between Choctaw Indians and whites does not appear in compilations of laws passed by the General Council. And the decision to execute the child of the union seems surprising; given matrilineal clan membership, the boy should have been seen as fully Choctaw and the member of a clan, and some of his clan members should have balked at accepting his death sentence when he had committed no crime. The story also takes on mythical proportions because of its explanatory power: the story provides the origins for the introduction of laws regulating marriages between Choctaws and outsiders, the practice of adopting the white spouses of Choctaws into the tribe, and the presence of Choctaws of European ancestry in positions of authority in the nation. The tidiness of the explanations necessarily provokes questions about when this "accepted fable" emerged.[121] In other words, did some members of the Choctaw Nation develop the story once marriages between Choctaw Indians and whites, along with the procedures governing them, had become common occurrences and well established? It is possible that Cole read Cushman's account and regurgitated it for the Indian Pioneer History Collection. In any case, the story does demonstrate that some parties in the Choctaw Nation viewed marriages between Choctaws and whites with deep suspicion and reservations.

The hostility that some Choctaws felt toward marriages between Choctaws and whites is less surprising if one focuses on the labor that Choctaw women performed rather than on the social organization of matrifocal and matrilineal families. Choctaw women performed important functions in society, so authorities carefully monitored whom they married. In 1836, the General Council passed an act that "any white man, who shall hereafter take a Choctaw woman for a wife, will be required to marry her lawfully by a Minister of the Gospel or other authorized person, after procuring license from any of the Judges or District Clerks for that purpose."[122] In effect, white men would have to register with national authorities before they could marry Choctaw women. And though the act did not state it explicitly, the implication was that a white man's request for such a license could be denied. A white man could not access Choctaw citizenship unless he had followed these procedures. Moreover, Choctaw legislators recognized that within marriages between white men and white women, women often ceded control of their property to their husbands; in order to protect Choctaw women's traditional property rights, legislators included this proviso: "That any white man who shall marry a Choctaw woman, the property of the woman so married shall not be subject to the disposal of her husband contrary to her consent."[123] The law corroborates that Choctaws recognized the value and importance of preserving women's property rights. Finally, this act stated that white men who left their wives without just cause lost their citizenship rights in the Choctaw Nation and would be ordered to pay their wives a sum to be determined by legal officials for breach of marriage.

In 1840 the General Council expanded the law regulating marriage between Choctaw women and white men.[124] This act retained the license requirement for white men seeking to marry Choctaw women; preserved the property rights of Choctaw wives; and continued to impose a financial penalty and a legal penalty—the loss of Choctaw citizenship—on white men who left their Choctaw wives. Choctaw lawmakers also added a residency requirement of two years for white men to marry in the nation, which suggests a desire to know the quality or character of the applicant for the marriage license. Choctaw authorities wanted to know exactly to whom they were granting citizenship. Lastly, this act included a steep penalty in the form of a $100 fine for any person who performed a marriage that did not adhere to the requirements of this act. The fine suggests that not everyone was abiding by the license and residency restrictions. Thus, Choctaw lawmakers, by making collusion expensive, hoped to discourage white men who sought to evade the proper legal course for marriage.

Just nine years later, the General Council addressed another aspect of relationships between white men and Choctaw women when it demanded "that every white man who is living with [an] Indian woman in this Nation without being lawfully married to her, shall be required to marry her lawfully, or be compelled to leave the Nation, and forever stay out of it."[125] Perhaps some couples found the two-year residency requirement for white men onerous and could not wait to establish their households. These couples might also represent an older pattern of traditional Choctaw marriage that did not require governmental sanction to be accepted and respected by community members. The second part of this marriage act suggests that some of these couples were the result of white men being denied licenses to marry Choctaw women: "That no white man who is under a bad character will be allowed to be united to an Indian woman in marriage, in the Nation, under any circumstances whatever."[126] The language is clear: Choctaw authorities wanted to prevent white men of questionable character from accessing Choctaw citizenship specifically and to push those men out of the nation more generally.

The gendered labor arrangements of the Choctaws invite some consideration of how Choctaw men might have viewed the white men who married Choctaw women and functioned as the primary agriculturalists in their households. Choctaw men would likely have been perplexed by the determination of so many white men to farm, just as many white observers found the division of labor among Natives unnatural. Indeed, some white observers thought Native men treated Native women like slaves because Native women performed so many tasks for the sustenance of their families, including hard labor in the fields.[127] H. W. Gay, a Minnesotan who married a Choctaw woman, stated, "In those days when [a] white man married an Indian woman, he was called squaw man and sometimes called galvanized citizen."[128] It is unclear from Gay's statement who was calling him a "squaw man," other whites or Native people; either group might have used this phrase. For many whites the term was a pejorative to indicate discomfort with interracial marriage and the implication that the white husband was choosing to adopt an "Indian" rather than a white lifestyle.[129] In this case, the "squaw" part of the term was distasteful. Native men, on the other hand, might have deployed "squaw man" with the emphasis on "man" to denigrate the white husband for performing agricultural labor, seen as women's work. And for some Natives the term might have indicated that, because he lacked a matrilineally determined clan identity, the intermarried white man's connection to the tribe was through his wife.

The preoccupation of Choctaw legislators with regulating the marriages of Choctaw women and outsiders bears out that the marital choices of

Choctaw women were a matter of national consequence. Choctaw women's marriages were particularly important to legal authorities because of the vital roles that Choctaw women played in society as landowners, as agriculturalists, and as producers of new clan members. Further, in marrying "foreign" men, mostly American, Choctaw women introduced to the nation a new citizen population who had very different perspectives on many aspects of Choctaw life: child custody, the gendered division of labor, governance, property inheritance, and national land policy. Thus, Choctaw officials sought to resolve some of the questions raised by the inclusion of white men in Choctaw society through legislation. Through the intermarriage law, lawmakers sought to control the quality and character of these intermarried white men and affirmed traditional Choctaw values about female property ownership. At the same time, however, the growing population of white husbands who labored in fields and the introduction of enslaved labor encroached on the authority that Choctaw women traditionally held because of their role as agriculturalists.

The expanding number of white men marrying into the Choctaw Nation roughly coincides with the growth of the population of enslaved people of African descent. In many cases intermarried white men brought property in the form of enslaved people with them to the Choctaw Nation. As Choctaw citizens became increasingly comfortable with racialized slavery and as more enslavers turned to plantation-style agriculture, Choctaw lawmakers had to craft legislation to manage this population.

Choctaw legal statutes tended to avoid infringing on the ultimate authority of the enslavers. Hence, enslaved people could carry weapons or gain literacy with the approval of their enslavers, despite the misgivings implied by the statutes. For instance, the statute permitting enslaved people to carry arms with their enslavers' written permission is clear about what kind of enslaved person qualified for this privilege: "good honest" ones. Moreover, the inclusion in the same statute of the admonition that enslaved people should behave themselves or face ten lashes expresses fears about controlling armed enslaved people.[130] Likewise, coupling the law prohibiting individuals from educating enslaved people with penalties for abolitionist activity suggests that lawmakers and the larger Choctaw society had grave concerns about literate enslaved people.[131] And yet, with the enslaver's permission, enslaved people could participate in these so-called dangerous activities. An enslaver's authority was protected under the law.

On the other hand, it was not legally the enslaver's prerogative to enter into sexual relationships with bondpeople; that authority was certainly not confirmed by law. Of course, the testimony of formerly enslaved people attests that sexual relationships did occur between enslavers and the enslaved with few legal repercussions. The anti-miscegenation law and the statutes for enslaved people regarding literacy, property holding, and carrying weapons might suggest it was the status of enslaved people rather than their African ancestry that lawmakers found problematic. Taking these statutes as a whole with other Choctaw legislation limiting access to citizenship for people of African ancestry, preventing their settlement in the nation, and requiring freedpeople to leave the nation upon manumission, however, it becomes clear that lawmakers were targeting people of African ancestry rather than just enslaved people. It just so happens that the majority of people of African ancestry in the Choctaw Nation at this time were also enslaved. The General Council did permit free people of African descent who also had Choctaw and Chickasaw ancestry to live in the nation, an exemption that implies that African ancestry could not entirely displace Choctaw or Chickasaw ancestry. Choctaw or Chickasaw ancestry had real legal benefit.

One might think about the laws regarding interracial marriage and behavior as focusing on the conduct of outsiders—that is, people outside of clan relationships or people who had the status of property, which includes people recognized racially as Black or white. Fairly quickly, though, it becomes clear that the limits Choctaw lawmakers placed on the behavior of people of African descent were far more restrictive than those placed on whites. Moreover, members of the General Council provided ways for white people, specifically white men, to join Choctaw society legally and to exercise some rights, whereas laws regarding people of African descent were increasingly exclusionary. Here is where some of the mechanics of racial ideology creation are revealed: the Choctaw wrote racial difference into law. Stated another way, they treated people differently based on their membership in groups tied to ancestry, and this treatment was enshrined in legal statutes. Further, the Choctaw were clearly associating people of African ancestry with negative characteristics—hence the need to minimize their presence in the nation. Whites were acceptable, but, as one would expect, people of Native ancestry were held in the highest regard and accessed the most rights.

That Choctaws practiced slavery and were developing ideas about race that disadvantaged people of African descent gave them common ground with their Confederate neighbors. Choctaw politicians saw Confederate states as allies in the preservation of a profitable economic practice and the maintenance of a particular racial order. Events such as Nat Turner's insurrection and John Brown's raid on Harpers Ferry sent slaveholders, no matter their national allegiance, into paroxysms of fear. Whereas the Unionists in the border states convinced their fellow state citizens that the Union would preserve slavery, Choctaw lawmakers wagered that the Confederacy would safeguard the practice.[132] More importantly, as we will see in chapter 3, Choctaw leaders also imagined that southern states that proclaimed the supremacy of states' rights over federal authority would respect the sovereign rights of Indian nations. Confederate officials and emissaries from southern states who worked with the Choctaw would only encourage these impressions.

Chapter 3

The Choctaws and Chickasaws Are Entirely Southern and Are Determined to Adhere to the Fortunes of the South

CHOOSING SIDES IN THE CONFLICT

The election of Abraham Lincoln in November 1860 and the wave of southern state secessions that followed made clear to many in the Choctaw Nation that they would have to choose a side. As early as February 1861, the Choctaw legislature passed a resolution stating both their hope for a speedy conclusion to "the present unhappy political disagreement between the Northern and Southern States of the American Union" and their affinity for the southern states.[1] Though some prominent Choctaws such as Principal Chief George Hudson (1860–62) and later Principal Chief Peter P. Pitchlynn (1864–66) expressed support for neutrality months later in May 1861, that February resolution confirmed that the opinions of pro-secession figures such as wealthy slaveholder Robert M. Jones held sway.[2] In fact, Choctaw loyalty to the Confederacy was noteworthy enough that Commissioner S. S. Scott wrote to Confederate secretary of war James A. Seddon in January 1863, "The Choctaws alone, of all the Indian nations, have remained perfectly united in their loyalty to this Government."[3] The strength of Choctaw allegiance to the Confederacy prompts questions: Why did Choctaws ally with states such as Mississippi and Alabama, the very governments that had pushed for the dissolution of Choctaw sovereignty and the acquisition of Choctaw land just three decades prior? What value did the Choctaw see in uniting their fate with the Confederacy? A partial answer to such questions lies in the Choctaw Nation's reliance upon and commitment to using the institution of slavery. But the other part of the answer concerns what the Confederates offered for Choctaw loyalty and what Choctaws themselves hoped to preserve: their sovereignty.

But what did Choctaws themselves say at the war's outset, especially as reflected in the language included in the treaty agreements between the

Choctaw government and the Confederacy? This chapter surveys the internal debate within the Choctaw Nation as a civil war seemed increasingly likely and then as white southerners, particularly from Arkansas and Texas, attempted to coerce and cajole Choctaws and other Native nations in Indian Territory to ally with the Confederacy once southern states seceded. I also compare the Cherokee Nation's extended effort to remain neutral in the war to the Choctaw Nation's relatively swift decision to side with the Confederacy to demonstrate the strength of Choctaws' affinity with the South. Finally, I offer a detailed investigation of the Choctaw alliance treaty with the Confederacy to reveal all of the incentives that Confederate officials offered to secure Native support for their cause. After the defeat of the Confederacy, some Choctaws revised the circumstances of their alliance with the South to frame it as reluctant, which belies their earlier rhetoric. In short, Choctaw officials negotiated for Confederate promises to respect and protect Choctaw sovereignty and to provide financial support in return for Choctaw allegiance.

The Confederate government was eager to gain the support of Native populations in Indian Territory for several reasons: the major travel routes of the Texas and California Roads ran through Indian Territory; the area could serve as a buffer zone between the Union state of Kansas and the Confederate states of Texas and Arkansas; and the territory could provide potentially significant human and supply resources.[4] In fact, on the same day in February 1861 that the provisional government of the Confederate states established the War Department, William P. Chilton of Alabama offered a resolution to direct the Committee on Indian Affairs to open negotiations with the western tribes. Within a week, the provisional government also asked the committee to appoint agents to those tribes. This committee included members from Texas and Arkansas, two states that arguably had the greatest interest in the affairs of the western tribes more broadly and of Indian Territory in particular.[5] By May, L. P. Walker, secretary of war for the Confederate States of America, had written to Major Douglas H. Cooper that "the desire of this Government is to cultivate the most friendly relations & the closest alliance with the Choctaw nation and all the Indian tribes West of Arkansas and South of Kansas."[6] Thus, Confederate agents would offer the Native tribes a number of inducements during treaty negotiations in exchange for their support.

The Choctaw, on the other hand, entered into these negotiations as a sovereign nation aiming to protect that status and preserve Choctaw borders. Choctaw authorities had worried about further American land grabs long before shots were fired at Fort Sumter and recognized that a divided

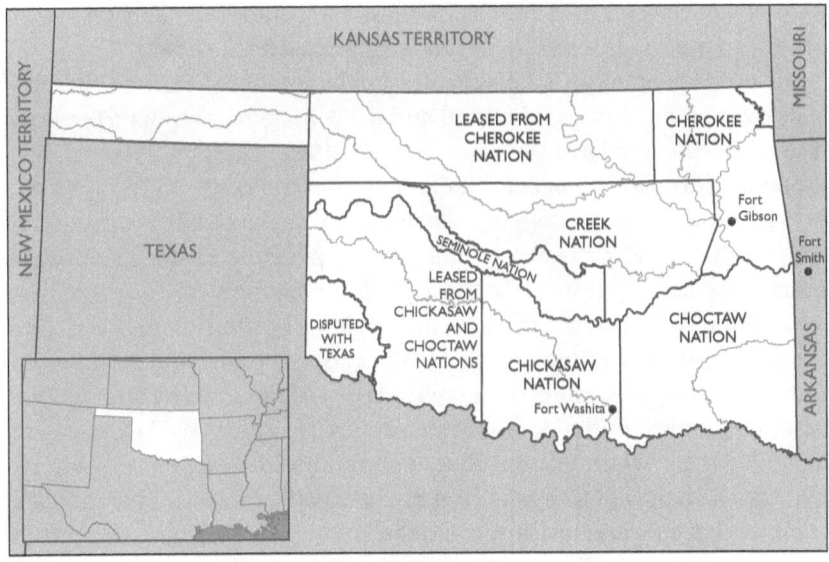

Indian Territory, 1860.
(Map by Rice University GIS/Data Center)

American polity had consequences for Indian nations. In April 1856, for instance, George W. Harkins had written to Peter P. Pitchlynn with concerns over the future of the Choctaw Nation should Kansas become a free state. He asked, "Don't you think the Southern people will like our country anyhow?"[7] News of the violent skirmishes and competing constitutions in the ongoing debate over whether Kansas should be a free or a slave state had reached Indian Territory, and astute observers understood that settlers in Kansas might look at Indian Territory as fertile ground for the continued growth of the institution of slavery or for free-soil rhetoric. In fact, historian Brad Agnew asserts that slavery had been uncontroversial in Indian Territory until the passage of the Kansas-Nebraska Act in 1854 provoked debate over the institution's value. At that point, defenders of slavery had grown more outspoken, which had prompted abolitionist Baptist missionaries such as Evan and John Jones to organize people around antislavery sentiment in the Cherokee Nation. Around this same time, Senator Robert Johnson of Arkansas also had introduced a bill to dissolve the tribal governments in Indian Territory and create the state of Neosho, presumably to expand the number of slave states represented in Congress.[8] With this recent history in mind, it is not surprising, then, that Harkins worried that white southerners in particular would seek to control Indian Territory. And

Kansas's official entrance into the Union as a free state in January 1861 must have been especially alarming for Harkins and other Choctaws.

For many people in the slaveholding Indian nations, fears of the possible connection between abolition and the conversion of Indian Territory into a free state predated the start of the Civil War. Harkins, as noted, had expressed this precise concern in his 1856 letter to Pitchlynn. In 1857, Kansas territorial governor Robert J. Walker had complained in his inaugural address that it was a "grievous injury" to people to be unable to settle on Indian land and suggested that those politicians working to create the new state of Kansas include provisions in the state constitution to "accelerate the extinguishment of Indian title." Walker also proposed that the tribes in Indian Territory be pushed to the western half of the territory and that the eastern half be admitted to the United States as a state.[9] Walker may have imagined this new state as free, but he certainly did not think it should remain in the hands of Natives.[10] And because Walker was the governor of a territory that appeared poised to join the Union as a free state, residents of Indian Territory who knew of his remarks may have connected free states and abolition to the end of Native sovereignty.

Perhaps more importantly, congressional action in the Kansas and Nebraska Territories had demonstrated that Indian land titles would not be respected. In 1853, Congress had authorized negotiations with tribes in Kansas and Nebraska to extinguish their land titles. In the meanwhile, the commissioner of Indian affairs had worked to obtain land cessions that reduced Native landholdings for fourteen tribes from 18 million acres to 1.33 million acres. Some of these tribes were then dispossessed of their reduced landholdings, as the Creek in Alabama had been some two decades before.[11] Newspapers in Arkansas and Texas published articles highlighting Republican senator W. H. Seward's statements from a Chicago election campaign speech: "And Indian Territory south of Kansas must be vacated by the Indian."[12] Lincoln's election only amplified these fears. Under Lincoln's Republican administration, such a plan could come to fruition. White southern sympathizers stoked such anxieties among Natives and urged them to ally with the Confederacy.

A war between the states threatened more than the territorial integrity of the Choctaw Nation; the federal government owed tribal governments annuity funds as a part of land cession agreements, so the tribe's financial well-being was also at stake. Just as Kansas was becoming a free state and southern states were seceding from the Union, Principal Chief Hudson gave a message to the council "relative to the confused state of the United States Government, that some thing should be done to secure our money in the

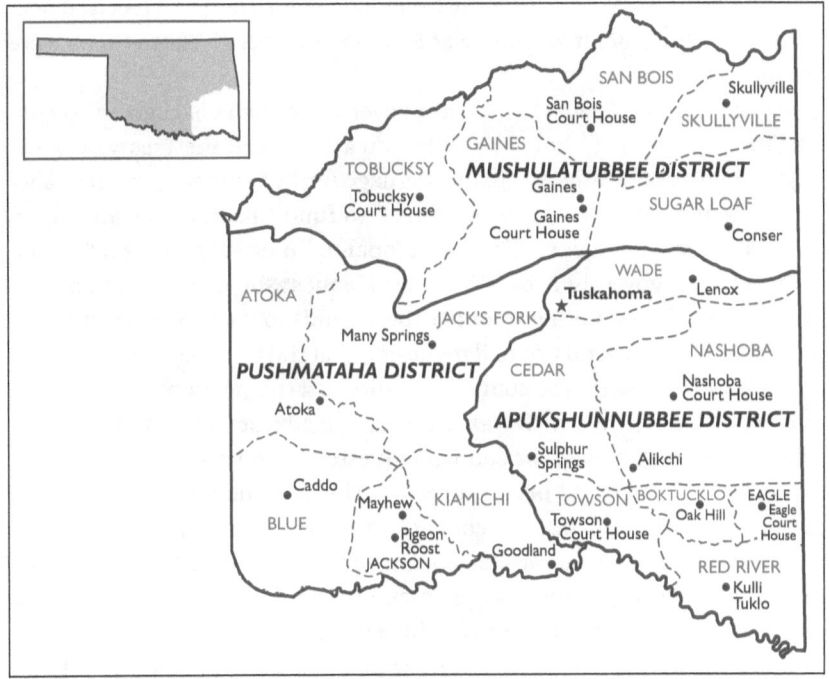

District map of the Choctaw Nation.
(Map by Rice University GIS/Data Center)

hands of the United States Government."[13] Peter Folsom, who had served as the chief of the Mushulatubbee District from 1846 to 1850, also expressed concerns in January 1861 about the threat to the financial well-being of the Choctaw represented by disunion in the United States.[14] He urged Pitchlynn to "obtain a full and accurate descriptive list of all bonds, coupons and other securities belonging to the Choctaws." Folsom worried that if the government of the United States went "to pieces," there would be no trustee to turn to in order to obtain funds due the Choctaw.[15] Article 17 of the Treaty of Dancing Rabbit Creek of 1830 had guaranteed that the Choctaw would continue receiving any annuities "secured under former treaties," as well as a limited annuity of $20,000 for twenty years once the Choctaw removed west.[16] At a minimum, former treaties included a permanent annuity of $3,000 from the 1805 Treaty of Mount Dexter and another permanent $6,000 annuity from the 1825 Treaty of Washington City, in addition to $1,520 in annuities for the employment of blacksmiths and lighthorsemen and for the purchase of iron and steel.[17] The annual report from the commissioner of Indian affairs indicated that the Choctaw general fund had received over $27,000 in 1859 generated from over $450,000 in stock.[18] These funds were not inconsequential.

Beyond annuity funds, the federal government had also agreed to support the education of Choctaw children in article 20 of the Treaty of Dancing Rabbit Creek. While the treaty language limited this support to twenty years, the federal government continued to fund Choctaw educational efforts as a part of a larger civilization campaign. In 1858 the General Council authorized the governor of the Choctaw to request $16,700 for the support of missionary schools. Rather than pay these funds to the superintendents of the schools, the General Council requested that those moneys go directly to the Choctaw Treasury. The council also directed the governor to ask for the interest on $98,391.79, which was to be used to educate Choctaw youth outside of the nation.[19] Last, the council requested a proper accounting of how this interest money had been expended. This specific figure of $98,391.79 appeared on the 1859 annual report from the commissioner of Indian affairs and resulted in an almost $6,000 disbursement for the Choctaw school fund.[20] Federal funds, then, were crucial for supporting the education of Choctaw children. And sometimes this educational support was indirect, as when warriors donated part of their annuity funds for the benefit of a mission school led by missionary Cyrus Kingsbury in 1819.[21] Chief Hudson could see that paying the Indian nations any funds due would not be a priority should war break out. Moreover, Indian nations would have little recourse to claim outstanding debts if the federal government lost the war—hence Hudson's message to secure funds quickly.

Just as Choctaw officials understood that an American civil war would have consequences for Native peoples living in Indian Territory, outside of the United States, white southerners recognized that foreigners could impact the outcome of a war within the United States. White southerners contemplating secession immediately sought alliances with Indian nations. In February 1861, the state of Texas voted on secession and quickly sent three commissioners, James E. Harrison, James Bourland, and Charles Hamilton, to Indian Territory to discuss the possibility of an alliance between the Choctaw, Cherokee, Chickasaw, Creek, and Seminole Nations and the Confederacy.[22] These commissioners traveled through Indian Territory for many weeks, meeting with tribal authorities and the larger public to make their case for the necessity of secession and for "the interest the civilized red man had in this new organization; tendering them [Native peoples] our warmest sympathy and regard." By May 1861, Texas governor Edward Clark forwarded the commissioners' report to Confederate president Jefferson

Davis and described "a general and propitious feeling of sympathy with the Confederate States on the part of those nations." Further, he averred that "the active friendship of these nations is of vital importance to the South." The commissioners asserted that "the Choctaws and Chickasaws are entirely Southern and are determined to adhere to the fortunes of the South." Further, the nations had also passed resolutions authorizing the raising of minute companies for service.[23] Thus, while an official alliance treaty with the Confederacy had not yet emerged, Choctaws were preparing for the possibility of fighting in Indian Territory.

As Texans voted on secession, the Choctaw also made an official statement about their national sympathies in the brewing sectional crisis in a set of "resolutions expressing the feelings and sentiments of the General Council of the Choctaw Nation in reference to the political disagreement existing between the Northern and Southern States of the American Union." The General Council voiced "deep regret and great solicitude" at the "present unhappy political disagreement between the Northern and Southern States" that meant not just a possible dissolution of the United States but also, and more importantly for the Indian nations, "the disturbance of the various important relations existing with that Government by treaty stipulations and international laws, and portending much injury to the Choctaw government and people." The General Council, as it should, focused on how disunion could alter or even nullify any treaty agreements made between the Choctaw Nation and the federal government. The council desired and hoped that the states might come to a solution quickly so that the "fostering care of their General Government, and the many friendly social ties existing with their people, continue for the enlightenment in moral and good government and prosperity in the material concerns of life to our whole population." The references to "fostering care" and "material concerns" were clear allusions to annuity payments, support for the Choctaw educational system, and the stocks held in the Indian Trust Fund.[24] This statement from the Choctaw General Council reveals that officials were carefully considering how best to serve the financial interests of Choctaw people in the conflict between the states.

Should the United States permanently dissolve, Choctaw lawmakers resolved to break ties with the federal government in order "to follow the natural affections, education, institutions, and interests of our people, which indissolubly bind us in every way to the destiny of our neighbors and brethren of the Southern States, upon whom we are confident we can rely for the preservation of our rights of life, liberty, and property, and the continuance of many acts of friendship, general counsel, and material support."[25] This statement deserves some attention because of its full-throated endorsement of the ties between the Choctaw Nation and southern states: "natural affections, education, institutions, and interests." Secession was about dissolving the bonds between the states, but Choctaws were "indissolubly" bound "in every way to the destiny" of southerners. Thus, the Choctaw General Council claimed that the ties between the Choctaw people and southern states were in fact stronger than those between the American states. Finally, the council reminded southern states of their obligations to the Choctaw people to preserve Choctaw "life, liberty, and property" and provide "material support." Council members recognized that an alliance with the southern states could cut them off from financial support and legal protections from the federal government, and this statement nudged southern states to fill that void.

The final two sections of the resolution served as announcements to southern states, especially the Choctaw's immediate neighbors in Arkansas and Texas. The council wanted to "assure" citizens of Arkansas and Texas "of our determination to observe the amicable relations in every way so long existing between us." Moreover, the Choctaw believed that, in spite of conflict with other states, Arkansans and Texans would respect and protect "the rights and feelings so sacred to us." In short, the council was broadcasting to the residents of these states that Choctaws were on their side and reminding them to observe Choctaw rights and laws. The council also directed the principal chief to send these resolutions to the governors of all of the southern states and to request that the document be shared with state conventions and published in state newspapers. Choctaws hoped such public proclamations would prevent any confusion about where Choctaw loyalties lay.

Despite the Choctaw resolution expressing such clear affinity for southern states, at this point the Choctaw Nation officially remained neutral in the dispute between the federal government and Confederate states. Some Choctaws might have agreed with the thinking of Jacob Folsom, who remarked in a January 1861 letter to his uncle Peter Pitchlynn on the news of South Carolina's secession, "I look on, but I am not in the least troubled about it. If they will fight, let them fight it out. I stand neutral and look on."[26] Folsom's comments hark back to the stance taken by some Native peoples during the Revolutionary War: that conflict was a "family affair," in the words of Mohawk chief Little Abraham, that did not involve Natives.[27] In Folsom's view, the Choctaw Nation was a separate, sovereign nation that could choose to remain above the fray of American political fights. Folsom's comments are all the more astonishing because in this same letter he wrote about his hopes to purchase an enslaved boy "if Abe Lincoln and his host of devils don't run over us" while still affirming his belief that Lincoln "will make as good [a] President as any they have had."[28] Folsom assessed a Lincoln presidency positively, even as he thought Lincoln would impede his access to enslaved labor. And note his pronoun: Lincoln will be as good as any president "*they* have had," not "we." Thus, Folsom simultaneously asserted Native autonomy and acknowledged the ability of American political activity to impact his behavior in the Choctaw Nation.

Former district chief Peter Folsom echoed the sentiments of Jacob Folsom in his belief that the Choctaw would best be served by remaining neutral. Peter Folsom urged a policy of "masterly inactivity." He advised against taking "a leap in the dark"; rather, he argued, "we should wait and see what is to be [the] probable result of the present unhappy difficulties among our white friends." Along these same lines, he stated, "It is also thought prudent for the Choctaws to keep quiet, until matters in the U. States assumes a more definite condition, then [sic] at present."[29] These comments highlight the contemporary uncertainty about whether a war was imminent. Modern observers view the events of the years prior to the Civil War with the knowledge that a war took place; thus, all events lead to the war, and it seems inevitable. In the moment, however, people like the Folsoms were not at all certain what secession meant for the future of the United States or that it would result in a war. Moreover, given that uncertainty, choosing a course of neutrality made a great deal of sense. The Choctaw and other Indian nations faced an almost impossible balancing act as they responded to secession and pressure from southern states to commit to the Confederacy.

Choctaw statesman Peter Pitchlynn returned from a trip to Washington, DC, in the spring of 1861 and argued that the Choctaw should remain loyal to the federal government to avoid jeopardizing the payment of funds due the nation. Pitchlynn convinced Principal Chief George Hudson to recommend neutrality at a called-for special session of the council in June.[30] Strictly speaking, this conception of neutrality might better be termed a determination to maintain the status quo. That is, Pitchlynn advocated remaining loyal to the federal government, which in the view of many Americans, especially in the South, likely did not seem neutral at all. Federal officials probably appreciated this kind of neutrality on the part of Indian nations: Choctaws asserted their loyalty to the federal government, and even though they did not offer aid, they were not offering material support to the seceding states, either. Given the Choctaw's February resolution expressing strong affection for their "brethren" in southern states, Pitchlynn and Hudson's avowals to remain neutral may have been a welcome surprise for federal authorities. Those in Lincoln's administration likely read Choctaw neutrality as similar to the position of border states such as Kentucky, Maryland, Delaware, and Missouri, which remained loyal to the Union but were home to sympathizers with the Confederate cause. As for Choctaw officials, from their perspective remaining militarily neutral may have been what mattered.[31]

S. Orlando Lee, who served as a teacher for two years at Spencer Academy, the Choctaw boarding school supervised by Presbyterian missionaries, wrote to Commissioner of Indian Affairs William P. Dole about the efforts of Americans in the area to persuade Choctaws to ally with the seceding states.[32] Lee repeatedly mentioned the influence of Texans on the deliberations. Because Pitchlynn had attempted to convince Chief Hudson to pursue a course of Choctaw neutrality in the war, he was labeled an abolitionist and "visited & threatened by a Texas Vigilance committee." Lee reported that when the Choctaw "Senate and lower house" convened at Doaksville in the summer of 1861 "seven miles from Red River & of course from Texas," the meeting was "largely attended by white men from Texas." The Choctaw legislators could not fail to miss the Confederate leanings of the Texans or their desire for Choctaw support. Lee also claimed that other Choctaws told him, "If the north was here so we could be protected we would stand up for the north but now if we do not go in for the south the Texans will come over here and kill us."[33]

Some Choctaws sorely missed the federal presence in Indian Territory. Unionist missionary Reverend John Edwards remained hidden "from Texan & half blood ruffians for two weeks" because of his political sympathies, and Lee and other missionaries at Spencer Academy received a visit from a Texas committee confiscating weapons.[34] Confederate Texans took advantage of the lack of federal authorities in the area to exert pressure on Choctaws to support the southern war effort.

For many Americans living in Texas and Arkansas, word of the Choctaw intent to remain neutral was quite worrisome. Before the June special session, Texas filibusters entered the Choctaw Nation in order to drive out federal personnel in locales such as Fort Arbuckle and Fort Cobb and attacked missionaries they perceived as antislavery. Sampson Folsom wrote about the activity and noted that the Texans were ignoring "treaty stipulations" between the Choctaw Nation and the United States. He worried that the Texans' plan was to make a *"white settlement"* in the midst of the Choctaw Nation. In other words, white Texans might take advantage of the disruption caused by secession to make inroads on Indian land claims. Folsom was so worried about this that he endorsed the raising of "five thousand Choctaws and Chickasaw troops at once to keep out land *pirates* and abolitionist[s]. To maintain the supremacy of the law of the land. To do this many must be raised." In Folsom's view, white agitators from the South and North, land pirates and abolitionists, were running amok in the Choctaw Nation, and troops might be required to keep them in check. Folsom's comments imply that the Choctaw might resort to military action to maintain a position of neutrality. He concluded that some Choctaws would have to go to Montgomery, presumably to talk to lawmakers from seceding states, and Folsom was preparing to travel to Washington the following month.[35] Again, the decision not to enter the fray was difficult to maintain.

The Cherokee Nation, led by Chief John Ross, initially also attempted to remain neutral in the conflict in the face of a host of southern reminders of shared interests and dire consequences, although the Cherokee did not issue a statement quite so favorable to the seceding states. Ross was quickly bombarded by messages seeking Cherokee support. In January 1861 Henry M. Rector, governor of Arkansas, penned an entreating letter to Ross to gain Cherokee support that highlighted commonalities between the Indian nation and the seceding states. Tellingly, he began by identifying the seceding states as those "having slave property within their borders." Clearly, Rector saw slavery as the first important connection between the seceding states and the Cherokee Nation. He continued, "Your people, in their institutions, productions, latitude, and natural sympathies, are allied to the common brotherhood of the slaveholding States." Again, the term "institutions" is a reference to slavery. Rector described southerners and the Cherokee people as "natural allies in war and friends in peace." He complimented Cherokee land as "salubrious and fertile" and claimed that it would reach its full potential "with the application of slave labor." The implication was that the federal government threatened the continued practice of slavery and, thus, threatened Cherokees' ability to enjoy the full productivity of their lands. Physical proximity between the Cherokee and the seceding states was yet another argument in favor of an alliance.[36] While the Choctaw officially remained neutral, similar conversations must have occurred between white southerners and politicians in the Choctaw Nation.

If positive inducements were not enough to sway Cherokees to the side of the seceding states, Rector invoked the fear of the political unrest the federal government might sow: "It is well established that the Indian country west of Arkansas is looked to by the incoming administration of Mr. Lincoln as fruitful fields, ripe for the harvest of abolitionism, freesoilers, and Northern mountebanks." Unchecked, Lincoln would unleash political radicals in Indian Territory. Rector hoped instead that the Cherokee would aid the South "in defense of her institutions, her honor, and her firesides." Again, the conspicuous reference to southern "institutions" signals the importance of slavery as something to unite over and to protect. In return, the "slaveholding States are willing to share a common future, and to afford protection commensurate with your exposed condition and your subsisting monetary interests with the General Government."[37] Rector was offering security from abolitionists run amok, as well as the promised financial support the federal government was obligated to provide.

Ross tendered a careful response to Governor Rector in February 1861. In language that echoed the Choctaw statement of neutrality just two weeks prior, Ross stated that Cherokees felt "a deep regret and solicitude for the unhappy differences" dividing the states. Rather than take a side, however, Ross hoped that "Divine Power" might intervene to pacify the "discordant elements." In February, it was still early enough to hope that secession might not end in all-out war. He pointed out that the terms of several treaties obligated the United States to protect the Cherokee Nation and its territorial claims as well as the civil and property rights enjoyed by Cherokee peoples. Thus, he concluded, the Cherokee Nation could not take action against the United States. He offered some support for the seceding states by conceding that Cherokee "Institutions, Locality and Natural Sympathies are unequivocally with the Slaveholding States. And the contiguity of our Territory to your State in connection with the daily social and commercial intercourse between our respective citizens forbids the idea that they should ever be otherwise than steadfast friends."[38] Ross did not go as far as the Choctaw resolution, on the other hand, to state explicitly that Cherokees would side with the South in case of a permanent dissolution of the United States, but he did remind white southerners of their many commercial and social ties. Finally, Ross assured Rector that "Cherokee Country" would not welcome abolitionist sentiment.

The correspondence between Cherokee chief John Ross and different representatives of the Confederate government offers some sense of the kinds of arguments white southerners used to gain Indian support. Commanding brigadier general Ben McCulloch, for instance, wrote to Ross in June 1861 that he hoped for Ross's "hearty co-operation in our common cause against a people who are endeavoring to deprive us of our rights." McCulloch invoked inclusive language to connect the fate of the Cherokee and the seceding states: "our common cause" and fears of losing "our rights." Confederate commissioner of Indian affairs David Hubbard claimed that the South was gaining allies in Europe, and if white southerners were successful, "then your lands—your slaves—and your separate nationality are secured and made perpetual; in addition, nearly all your debts are Southern Bonds—and these we will also secure." These assurances must have been sorely tempting to Indian nations, especially perpetual protection of their national sovereignty. On the other hand, if the North was victorious, "you will most certainly lose all. First—your slaves they will take from you—that is one object of the war, to enable them to abolish slavery in such manner and at such time as they choose." Note the prominence that Hubbard gave the question of slavery in the dispute and the threat that a northern victory would mean the end of slavery. Hubbard continued, "Another, and perhaps the chief cause, is to get upon your rich lands, and settle their squatters, who do not like to settle in Slave States." Even the desire for Indian lands was connected to the continuance of slavery. Squatters who did not like slavery, otherwise known as abolitionists, wanted Indian lands and were thus another threat to the institution of slavery.[39]

Hubbard also contrasted the condition of Native peoples in the North with the condition of those in the South to argue that white southerners treated Indians more equitably, with apparent disregard for the recent policy pushed by southern states to remove Native nations from the region. He urged Ross to "join us and preserve your People, their Slaves, their vast possessions in lands and their nationality." Over and over again, Confederate officials highlighted the preservation of slavery as an important benefit of siding with the South. Hubbard also reminded Ross that the federal government had invested Native funds in southern bonds, and therefore the "Government at Washington's" act of war on southern states meant that those states would not make good on any debts owed to the government. If the Cherokee joined the seceding states, however, Hubbard promised to pay any moneys owed them. Hubbard acknowledged that taking sides in this fight held potential danger for the Cherokee but opined that the risk was "tenfold greater" if they opposed the Confederacy. Hubbard also argued against Ross's determination to remain neutral: "Neutrality will scarcely be possible as long as your people retain their National character, your country cannot be abolitionized, and it is our interest, therefore, that you should hold your possessions in perpetuity."[40] To frame neutrality in the Civil War as incompatible with Cherokee national character was a powerful rhetorical move on Hubbard's part.

Despite the flurry of letters, even from average citizens such as "certain Gentlemen of Boonsboro, Arkansas," and visits from Confederate officials, until October 1861 Ross remained firm in his conviction to keep the Cherokee Nation neutral.[41] Ross acknowledged the "pending conflict," reiterated his "purpose to take no part in it whatever," and "admonished the Cherokee people to pursue the same course." He did not see a good reason to choose a side, because doing so would only anger one of the parties; instead, Ross hoped that not giving either side a reason to complain "should cause our rights to be respected by both."[42] He attempted to strike a delicate balance, at once assuring Confederate officials that he believed their promises of fair treatment for the Cherokee but emphasizing that his people did not have sufficient cause to wage war against the United States or to believe that the federal government did not intend to honor its treaty obligations to Native people. Moreover, in response to Commissioner Hubbard's advice that Ross compare his nation's treatment by northerners and southerners, Ross smartly replied that in the past both sections of the country had been quite supportive of policies to acquire Indian lands so that "but few Indians now press their feet upon the banks of either the Ohio or the Tennessee."[43] In other words, Ross had already made the comparison between northern and southern states and found both lacking; he recognized southern states' culpability in removal.

In May 1861, as the Choctaw were wavering about their decision to remain neutral, Ross publicly reminded Cherokee people of their treaty obligations to the United States and urged his fellow citizens to honor those treaties by maintaining "peace and friendship towards the people of all the states." In other words, his stance on neutrality was not confined to official correspondence with Confederate officials or inquiring white southern citizens; he was also waging something of a public relations campaign. He "earnestly" implored other Cherokees to refrain from even discussing the "events transpiring in the States, and from partisan demonstrations in regard to the same." To be sure that everyone understood Ross, this proclamation appeared in English and the Cherokee language.[44] In some important ways, the audience for the message extended beyond the Cherokee Nation to other Indian nations to support their aspirations for neutrality and especially to whites in nearby states. Ross desperately clung to the path of neutrality.

In part, Ross's actions make the point that the Choctaw choice to side with the Confederacy was neither predetermined nor a given. The Cherokee faced some of the same pressures to side with the South immediately when hostilities erupted, but they did not, whereas the Choctaw rushed to ally with the South. Moreover, the continued internal strife within the Cherokee population shows how riven the choice was: after the formal treaty to ally with the Confederacy, a faction of Cherokees sided with the American federal government and rallied troops to the Union cause, while others led by Stand Watie fought alongside soldiers in gray. In many ways, the divisions among the Cherokee fell along old fault lines that had more to do with removal thirty years before and that era's unresolved political disputes than with the current situation.⁴⁵

As Choctaws debated the best course of action and residents of nearby states worked to sway their Indian neighbors, Confederate officials also attempted to entice members of the various Native nations in Indian Territory to leave the sidelines and join the secessionists. On May 21, 1861, the Confederate states approved an act to assume "the duty and obligation of collecting and paying over as trustees to the several Indian tribes now located in the Indian Territory south of Kansas, all sums of money accruing, whether from interest or capital of the bonds of the several States of this Confederacy now held by the Government of the United States as trustees for said Indians." These bonds were to be paid under the same conditions outlined in existing treaties between the Indian nations and the United States.⁴⁶ The Confederate government was broadcasting quite loudly to Indian nations that they had nothing to lose financially should they ally with the South. Confederate states would pay those moneys owed to Indian nations by the federal government under the existing terms. Hence, no new negotiations were required. Further, this act did not include demands for tribal action in order to receive these funds. Instead, the act's title said it all: "An Act for the protection of certain Indian tribes." While the goal of the act was nominally to protect Native peoples, the Confederacy must have imagined this act as the first step in securing Native support for the South.

Pressure to abandon a policy of neutrality came from within the Choctaw Nation as well. Robert M. Jones, a wealthy Choctaw slaveholder, learned of Chief Hudson's plan to call for neutrality at the June special session of the General Council and returned from a self-imposed political exile to argue forcefully against him. Jones met with others sympathetic to secession, including white Texans, before the special session and "made a furious speech in which he declared that 'any one who opposed secession ought to be hung.'" Jones's statement could have been uttered by the most ardent secessionist from South Carolina: opposing secession should be punished by death. While little else from Jones's speech was recorded, he surely presented a thorough case for Choctaw support of the Confederacy.⁴⁷ Jones realized that a conflict between the states could present an opportunity for the Choctaw Nation and other Native peoples to wrest all manner of concessions from the federal government or the Confederate states in order to secure Native interests. Scholar Jeff Fortney describes this as a continuation of the older play-off system that had permitted Native nations to play European powers against each other in order to gain access to favorable trading terms or other agreements. From Jones's perspective, remaining neutral was foolish, a lost opportunity, when choosing a side could be so advantageous in obtaining land protections or overdue funds.[48]

Word of Jones's fiery rhetoric spread, and by the time of the June special session, Chief Hudson was recommending not neutrality but that Choctaws open treaty negotiations with the Confederate government and begin organizing a regiment to fight with the Confederate army.[49] Hudson declared that the United States no longer existed, that the federal government had defaulted on funds due the Choctaw, that the federal government had withdrawn troops from the territory, and that a federal attack was imminent.[50] Hudson may have been swayed by Jones's argument; perhaps he and others interpreted Jones's colorful prose as an actual threat of death to those who opposed secession or even advocated for neutrality; or perhaps it was the presence of white vigilance committee members at the special session and in the nation more generally that pushed Hudson to side with the South. All of these factors played a part in Hudson's change of heart, surely, but given how quickly Choctaws mobilized to volunteer for military service in support of the Confederacy, which I discuss in chapter 4, I would argue that Jones tapped into an existing vein of strong sympathy for the seceding states. Jones did not ignite secessionist fire among the Choctaw; rather, his comments were smoke from an existing blaze. Thus, Hudson recognized that Jones represented a broader sentiment among Choctaws.

Under Hudson's direction, the General Council promptly passed a resolution that carefully laid out its position on secession and a war between the states. The Choctaw understood the union between the states to have been dissolved because southern states had seceded and formed a government. The dissolution of the United States freed the Choctaw of any former treaty obligations. In any case, the resolution contended that the "Government of which Abraham Lincoln claims to be President have utterly refused to abide by solemn covenants and Treaty Stipulations." This statement undermined Lincoln's legitimacy as president with the word "claims" and assessed the federal failure to honor treaty obligations as not accidental or circumstantial but, rather, intentional. The council then listed fresh insults from federal authorities: "Our money has been refused us, the military posts placed in our country for our protection have been abandoned, and we are left to the tender mercies of Kansas cutthroats." Council members identified lawless people from Kansas, not Texas or Arkansas, as the problem, despite stories about vigilance committee members from those states visiting Choctaw officials and missionaries. The Confederate States of America, on the other hand, were far more trustworthy in the Choctaw General Council's own words: "Whereas, we fully believe that all our rights, immunities and privileges will be completely guaranteed to us by the Confederate States of America . . ." Here the resolution's language is quite definite rather than hopeful: "fully believe" and "completely guaranteed to us." The council was confident that the Confederacy would honor obligations to the Choctaw.[51]

The resolution described the war waged upon the Confederacy as "unjust inhuman and without parallel in the annals of history." The Choctaw not only claimed that the Confederate "cause is our cause" but also asserted, "We so far as interest is concerned are identical." This language is extraordinary. Southern state legislatures in Georgia, Mississippi, and Alabama had orchestrated the removal of Native groups such as the Choctaw just three decades prior. It would not have been an overstatement to describe the interests of Indian nations and many southern states as inimical at that time. And yet, by 1861, the Choctaw General Council wrote that its interests were "identical" to those of seceding states. The Choctaw now saw "that the Confederate States are contending for self preservation, the right of self government," fights with which Native nations were quite familiar.

Perhaps some Choctaws believed that southern states finally understood the position of Indian nations seeking to preserve sovereignty and maintain traditional cultures, now that southern institutions were in peril. White southerners had invoked federal power to enforce the Fugitive Slave Act and rebuked states' rights arguments made in Wisconsin and Ohio to justify noncompliance, for instance, but once federal authorities seemed to turn against the spread of slavery, southern states adopted states' rights rhetoric to protect the practice.[52] Instead of seeing the Choctaw Nation as siding with the Confederacy, it may be more accurate to say that the Confederacy proposed principles that were more in line with Choctaw goals than with federal ones. Rather than the Choctaw moving toward the southern position, it was white southerners who moved toward the Native position. And the Choctaw were so firm in their support of southern self-government, and implicitly Native self-government, "that we had rather see a general conflagration sweep over our land or an earthquake sink it than one iota of this right denied."[53] Choctaws would rather see their land destroyed than the principle of self-government obstructed.

With the dissolution of the government of the United States and Choctaws' belief that southern states would guarantee Choctaw rights and protect the principle of self-government, the Choctaw declared themselves "absolutely and unconditionally free and independent people" who could act for themselves. The General Council understood that the Choctaw Nation was relatively weak and "exposed," and because of "the identity of our institutions, etc., we are ready and willing to enter into a Treaty of Alliance and Amity with the Southern Confederacy." The phrase "identity of our institutions" is almost certainly a reference to the institution of slavery. As confirmation of that, the next clause of the resolution discusses the threat of "invasion by the abolition hordes of the North." In an effort to "defend ourselves against their aggressions," the Choctaw proposed to unite with other Indian nations against the shared threat of abolition.[54]

Thus, the Choctaw resolved to send one commissioner from each county in the Choctaw Nation to meet with representatives of the Confederate states and negotiate a "treaty of Alliance and Amity." The commissioners would work toward an agreement for the common defense of the Choctaw and southern states. The General Council directed these same commissioners to attend a convention with delegates from the Cherokee, Creek, Seminole, and Chickasaw Nations set for later in June in Perryville in the Choctaw Nation to create a "league for mutual protection."[55] The creation of this second group is revealing: for all of the earlier language about Choctaws having interests "identical" to those of southern states, they recognized that not all of their interests were, in fact, shared. Rather, the Choctaw had common interests with some of the other Native nations in Indian Territory, and they, too, should meet to discuss how to protect themselves. The speed at which such a meeting was arranged suggests that all of these Indian nations agreed: they had concerns that might not align with those of the Confederacy, and they should meet separately to discuss them.

The meeting of the Indian nations resulted in a compact among the Creek, Seminole, Choctaw, and Chickasaw Nations, signed at North Fork in Creek Nation.[56] The Cherokee Nation was not a party to this compact; John Ross had worked diligently to keep the Cherokee neutral for as long as possible and did not declare their alliance with the Confederacy until October 1861.[57] The agreement reiterated that the dissolution of the American federal government freed Indian nations from any treaty obligations to the United States, so that the Muscogee (or Creek), Seminole, Choctaw, and Chickasaw Nations were "free and independent to form such alliances as may ensure their own safety, promote general welfare, provide for the common defense, establish justice, insure domestic tranquility, as may to them seem best and retain unimpaired their Tribal or National rights, titles and interest in and to the country they now respectively hold."[58] Lifting the list of goals from the preamble of the US Constitution implicitly put the compact of Indian nations on an equal footing with the former (in their view) United States and called attention to the fact that all people, whether Native or white, had the same interests and desires. Moreover, if the founding of the United States had been legitimate, this new confederation of Indian nations must also be legitimate; that is, the rhetorical borrowing lent validity to the new confederation of Indian nations. Last, the treaty authors made clear that all of the member nations retained rights specific to each group and territorial claims.

Thus, the Choctaw Nation entered into a "perpetual union" with each member nation, retaining its "sovereignty, freedom and independence and jurisdiction and constitutional rights not expressly delegated to the Grand Council of the United Nations of the Indian Territory."[59] The language of this clause suggests an attempt to avoid any future arguments about whether the rights of the Indian nations superseded the authority of the Grand Council. The four groups were in a "firm league and friendship with each other for their common defense, the security of their liberties and their mutual and general welfare," and pledged to support each other "against all force offered to or attacks that might be made upon any or all of them."[60] Hence this alliance obligated member nations to defend each other in case of attack. This provision was a sharp departure from the tense relations that had existed between the Choctaw and the Chickasaw for some time and had led to their legal separation just six years before. The threat of an outside enemy outweighed internal squabbles between Native nations. The treaty provided a mechanism for new Indian nations to join and withdraw from the compact with the consent of the Grand Council. In fact, rather than using a process of secession and war, as in the case of the United States, withdrawing nations merely had to "give their reasons in writing, and be required to give notice of their intention to the Grand Council," which then had the power to "absolve them from all obligations of the Compact."[61]

Beyond the usual minutiae regarding the composition and terms of service of members of the Grand Council, the treaty also included provisions to support the Confederate war effort. In article 9, the signatories agreed to grant "right of way to all forces of the Confederate States of America through our territory," because such access served the "mutual protection and safety" of the member nations. This access was especially important to secessionists in Texas and Arkansas, who worried about federal troops in Kansas or Missouri.[62] Article 10 granted the Grand Council the power to ask member nations "to furnish any number of troops to repel invasion by a foreign enemy, or to suppress insurrections." Thus, not only could Confederate forces move freely through parts of Indian Territory, but also some Indian nations would provide soldiers to fight in the war.

The confederation of Indian nations, therefore, resolved to extend "right of way and free passage" not just to "all forces of the Confederate States of America" but also to "the forces of any Nation or Tribe who may desire to march their forces through to any part of the Indian Territory to repel the invading forces of abolition hands under Abraham Lincoln, whose army is now approaching our position."[63] This statement illustrates that while Indian soldiers might fight with Confederate forces against abolitionists and move through Indian Territory to do so, the confederation saw Indian forces as different from and not necessarily under the same command as Confederate troops, a fact that will be reiterated in other treaty provisions that I will discuss. Granting access to Confederate troops to travel in Indian country did not cover access for Native troops, so a separate statement had to be made. The opinion of Choctaw Sampson Folsom, who had early called for the creation of a Choctaw military force and participated in the treaty negotiations, must have been shared by members of other Indian nations to then appear in the final treaty with the Confederate States of America.[64]

As these Native groups were meeting in the summer of 1861 to declare their sympathies with the South, some Choctaw legislators had already tipped their hand and started to look to southern states for their financial security rather than rely on the good faith of the federal government. In July J. P. Folsom proposed a bill to place some Choctaw funds in southern banks. Eleven states had seceded, and the fate of the Union was uncertain. In the debate that followed Folsom's proposal, Charles Stewart urged the Choctaw Nation to remain neutral in the conflict and opposed the idea of placing any Choctaw money in southern banks; there were still a few holdouts for maintaining neutrality even as the Choctaw government made official statements of support for the Confederacy. Alfred Wade spoke in favor of the bill because he thought Choctaws should prepare for the eventuality that the United States would dissolve and "that we are in the midst of the Southern States, and of course we are considered Southerners and own slaves, and should join the Southern States." The bill passed, further uniting the fate of the Choctaw to the fate of the Confederacy.[65] Wade's comments highlight the affinity that Choctaws felt for other southerners in terms of geography and the practice of slavery. Further, he underscored the precariousness of the continued existence of the United States. For contemporaries, a Union victory was not assured. Finally, this debate between Choctaws demonstrates the wide-ranging impact of the American Civil War outside of the United States.

It was quite natural for the Choctaw lawmakers such as Folsom and Wade to turn southward to protect the nation's financial interests because the federal government had already invested the vast majority of funds held in trust for the Choctaw in southern stocks. The federal government held over $550,000 in stocks for the Choctaw Nation and had invested $450,000 of it in stocks connected to the state of Virginia; another $21,000 worth of stocks was invested in Missouri securities.[66] In general, the secretary of the Interior invested funds held in trust for individual Indian tribes in southern stocks. In 1859 the Indian Trust Fund amounted to nearly $3.5 million invested in securities in fourteen states and the United States. The fourteen states included nine of the eleven states of the Confederacy (Mississippi and Alabama were excluded), as well as the slaveholding states of Missouri, Kentucky, and Maryland that ultimately did not secede. In terms of dollar amounts, the investments in these states accounted for over $2.8 million, or more than 80 percent of the entire Indian Trust Fund.[67] The Choctaw legislators, then, would have seen their financial interests as clearly connected to slaveholding states and, perhaps, to the continued existence of economies based on the institution of slavery even if the Choctaw themselves did not already practice slavery.

In July, the Choctaw and Chickasaw Nations entered a "Treaty of Friendship and Alliance" with the Confederate States of America. The negotiations for this treaty had been part of the larger discussions held at North Fork that resulted in the compact between the Choctaw, Chickasaw, Muscogee, and Seminole Nations. So, after declaring their unity as a group and granting Confederate forces permission to travel through Indian Territory, the Choctaw and Chickasaw proclaimed that they would have "perpetual peace" as well as "an alliance offensive and defensive" with the Confederate States of America.[68] The Choctaw and Chickasaw reached treaty terms with the Confederacy together, reflecting the fact that the two nations had severed their unique political relationship only recently, in 1855. The nations may have seen some advantage in working together to hammer out an alliance with the seceding states. The treaty preamble began with a reference to the Confederate Congress's May agreement discussed earlier in this chapter, suggesting that the promise to honor federal debt to the tribes was a factor in gaining the support of the Choctaw.[69]

The specific terms of this treaty deserve some detailed attention because they reveal the uppermost concerns of the Choctaw and Confederate officials and are vital to understanding why Choctaws endorsed the South in the Civil War. At a moment when federal authorities had withdrawn from Indian Territory and did not offer much incentive to remain loyal, the Confederates seemed to offer Choctaws every conceivable benefit. The very detailed alliance treaty outlined many protections for the Choctaw and Chickasaw Nations. For instance, articles 2 and 3 reiterated that the nations were "under the protection" of and wards of the Confederate States of America. The Confederate government promised "never to desert or abandon" the nations, and "under no circumstances" would it "permit the Northern States or any other enemy to overcome them and sever the Choctaws and Chickasaws from the Confederacy." Instead, the Confederate government promised "at any cost and all hazards to protect and defend" the Choctaw and Chickasaw and "maintain unbroken the ties created by identity of interests and institution, and strengthened and made perpetual by this treaty."[70] This language was no doubt heartening after the abrupt withdrawal of federal troops in Indian Territory. Moreover, the Confederate government's promise to prevent the northern states from overrunning the territory must have reassured Natives worried about the federal response to the Choctaws' decision to ally with the South.

The next three articles of the treaty carefully outlined the boundaries of the Choctaw and Chickasaw Nations, both within Indian Territory and in relation to each other. Article 4 specifically referenced the 1820 Treaty of Doak's Stand and the 1830 Treaty of Dancing Rabbit Creek when describing the limits of the two nations' territory west of the Mississippi River.[71] The Confederate government's adherence to previously held treaty agreements was strategically clever because it conveyed several ideas that Native groups appreciated. First, the move assured the Indian nations that they need not negotiate new treaties with the Confederate states; that is, allying with the Confederacy would preserve the status quo. Second, referring to these treaties implicitly showed the Confederates' trustworthiness in honoring treaty agreements. The federal government and, frankly, southern states such as Georgia, Mississippi, and Alabama had already demonstrated a disregard for the boundaries of Indian nations as established by treaty agreements. The Confederate Congress was signaling that it aimed to do better. Finally, acknowledging these treaty agreements also reaffirmed Native sovereignty; the Choctaw entered those treaties as a sovereign and independent nation. As an added benefit for the Confederates, the treaties also affirmed that the Natives relinquished land claims in southern states.

After stipulating the territorial boundaries of the Choctaw and Chickasaw, the treaty moved to matters of access to land. Article 7 again referenced "An act for the protection of certain Indian tribes" passed in May, reiterated that the Confederate states rather than the United States now had a relationship with Indian country, and authorized Confederate military action in the territory. The clause confirmed Confederate military officers' ability to move troops or supplies through Indian Territory. Article 8 promised the Choctaw and Chickasaw that they would hold their territories "so long as grass shall grow and water run." Native peoples could only have interpreted this poetic language as a guarantee of a permanent home. Finally, the territory could not be surveyed or subdivided unless a majority of voters in each nation agreed to do so, and Confederate officials "solemnly" promised not to solicit such action. Again, through these treaty provisions, the Confederate government pledged to respect and protect Native land rights.[72]

Article 9 of the treaty preserved Choctaw land claims but simultaneously limited Choctaw sovereignty. The clause prohibited the Choctaw and Chickasaw Nations from selling, ceding, or disposing of land "to any foreign nation or to any State or government whatever." If such sale or cession was "made without the consent of the Confederate States, all the said lands shall thereupon revert to the Confederate States." The language affirmed Choctaw ownership of their territory but then undercut that ownership by insisting that any decisions to sell or cede land go through the Confederate government. The Confederate authorities certainly did not offer a reciprocal statement that they would not sell or cede land without Indian approval. Confederates surely feared that the Indian nations might reach some kind of agreement with the federal government, other states, or even other powers such as France, England, or Spain in exchange for land cessions. To further protect Confederate interests, officials included a penalty: Should the Choctaw or Chickasaw enter into such a land agreement, they forfeited the land to the Confederate States.[73]

On the other hand, in article 10 the Confederate government also promised the Choctaw and Chickasaw that "no State or Territory shall ever pass laws for the government of the Choctaw and Chickasaw nations." This article recalled laws passed by the Georgia and Mississippi state legislatures to extend their jurisdiction over Indian nations three decades prior. Choctaws whose memory of removal was particularly sharp must have met with trepidation the idea of allying with whites who had so recently clamored for Native land dispossession and tribal dissolution. Similarly, Confederate treaty negotiators must have recognized white southerners' part in the forced relocation of southeastern tribes to Indian Territory. Article 10 offered some assurance that this history would not be repeated. The seceding states also pledged not to seize any territory from the Choctaw or Chickasaw Nations for another territory or province, nor to convert their lands "into a State, or any other Territorial or political organization, or to incorporate it into any State previously created," without the express consent of the Choctaw and Chickasaw people.[74] In some ways, the Confederate government was endeavoring to make an alliance as attractive as possible to Indian nations, and these explicit protections of land rights and self-government are important to understanding the choices made by Indian nations.

Another provision of the treaty addressed jurisdictional disputes that arose because of previous Trade and Intercourse Acts. The American government had passed these acts to set the terms of trade between Native peoples and Americans and to settle matters of criminal jurisdiction. The 1834 iteration of the act had stipulated that cases in which both parties were Natives were matters for Indian courts to adjudicate, but proceedings in which one party was a non-Native, even if the crime was committed in Indian country, fell under the purview of American courts.[75] References to the resulting jurisdictional disputes appear in many letters to the Office of Indian Affairs, such as when cases involved the commission of crimes in Indian Territory by enslaved people owned by white men, or in the case of an intermarried white man who was murdered by Choctaw citizens.[76] The treaty of alliance with the Confederates confirmed some parts of the 1834 act but also resolved what had been a source of tension: legal jurisdiction over those non-Natives who married Choctaw or Chickasaw individuals and other non-Natives who had permanently relocated to Indian Territory.[77] The alliance treaty with the Confederates gave Choctaw and Chickasaw courts authority to settle legal disputes including those individuals.

A series of treaty articles protected Choctaw and Chickasaw property. Article 21 of the treaty promised that the Confederate government would "protect the Choctaws and Chickasaws from domestic strife, from hostile invasion, and from aggression by other Indians and white persons, not subject to the jurisdiction of the Choctaw or Chickasaw Nation."[78] The treaty already included an article to protect the Choctaw and Chickasaw from attack by the federal government and northern states, but this article went further to include attacks by other Natives and whites in general. In the past, depredations committed by whites in Indian country had been so egregious that even American officials commented on them and proposed laws to ameliorate the problem. As early as 1795, President George Washington had told Congress that "the provisions heretofore made with a view to the protection of the Indians from the violences of the lawless part of our frontier inhabitants, are insufficient. It is demonstrated that these violences can now be perpetrated with impunity."[79] Article 21 addressed that persistent problem, as well as tensions between Native groups. The Confederate government then guaranteed restitution "for all injuries resulting from such invasion or aggression" in an amount equivalent to that received by whites for "injuries or aggressions" committed by Indians.

Article 22 addressed intruders on Choctaw and Chickasaw lands and made the Confederate government responsible for their removal. Confederate authorities were to prevent intruders from entering the territory and not only pay for their removal but even resort to the use of military power to do so. If any Confederate citizens should steal property from any Choctaws or Chickasaws, the Confederate agent to the Natives would be responsible for recovering the property or providing "just remuneration," according to article 23. If the offending party did not provide recompense, the Confederate states agreed to pay for the loss.[80] These concessions were important; the Confederate government would be liable for damage caused by "foreigners" who entered the Choctaw and Chickasaw Nations, whether or not they were citizens of the Confederate States of America. Given the history of claims poorly processed by the War Department and then the Indian Office, whether these claims were filed by Natives or whites, the willingness of the Confederate government to take responsibility for such debts was a departure from federal inaction and encouraging for Choctaws.[81]

Perhaps the most remarkable concession in the alliance treaty was representation for the Choctaw and Chickasaw Nations in the Confederate Congress. The two nations would share a delegate to the Confederate House of Representatives to serve for a term of two years. This delegate had to be a member "by birth or blood, on either the father's or mother's side, of one of said nations" and would be "entitled to the same rights and privileges as may be enjoyed by delegate from any Territory of the Confederate States." One must note that recognizing either matrilineal or patrilineal descent to determine membership in the Choctaw and Chickasaw Nations was a departure from traditional practice within these groups. This treaty provision, then, reinforced the move away from reliance solely on matrilineal descent to determine legitimate membership in the groups. The language also highlights how Euro-Americans could impose their understanding of familial relationships upon Native groups in sometimes subtle ways. The delegate position would alternate between the two nations, first being elected by the Choctaw and then by the Chickasaw, and the Confederate agent would be in charge of the logistics for the elections.[82] This last condition was another small usurpation of Native sovereignty: why should the Confederate agent be in charge of running the election and declaring the winner for a Choctaw and Chickasaw representative? Both nations regularly conducted the elections of their own officials and were certainly capable of managing this election as well.

While the representative of the Choctaw and Chickasaw would not have the voting rights of other representatives of Confederate states, this level of representation as a territory was still a marked departure from the terms outlined for Choctaws in the 1830 Treaty of Dancing Rabbit Creek concluded with the federal government. That treaty had included the possibility of representation for the Choctaw in the US House of Representatives, but the language was lukewarm at best. Choctaw chiefs had suggested "that their people are in a state of rapid advancement in education and refinement and have impressed a solicitude that they might have the privilege of a Delegate on the floor of the House of Representatives extended to them." The commissioners had responded that they did "not feel that they can, under a treaty stipulation, accede to the request; but at their desire, present it in the treaty, that Congress may consider of and decide the application."[83] The US Congress had approved the treaty, surely to get access to the land cessions Choctaws made, and must have allowed the application, because in 1842 Charles Fenderich had captioned his portrait of Peter P. Pitchlynn with the following: "Choctaw delegate to the government of the United States."[84] In 1849, Pitchlynn had authored a remonstrance to Congress opposing a bill to place the Native groups west of the Mississippi River under a single government.[85] Thus, there was a precedent for considering the election of a Native delegate to Congress, and the Choctaw saw value in including an emissary to the Confederate legislature for their interests as they approached negotiations for an alliance with the seceding states.[86] Hence, thirty years after the Treaty of Dancing Rabbit Creek, the alliance treaty guaranteed representation with more declarative language.[87]

The Confederate treaty went a step further than offering a limited form of representation to the Choctaw and Chickasaw in the Congress: it also outlined a process to permit the two nations to join the Confederacy as a state "on equal terms, in all respects, with the original States, without regard to population; and all members of the Choctaw and Chickasaw nations shall thereby become citizens of the Confederate States." The creation of this new state would be dependent on a positive vote by a convention of Choctaw and Chickasaw delegates. Ostensibly, the Confederate states extended this possibility to the Indian nations because the Natives had demonstrated "uniform loyalty and good faith, and the tried friendship for the people of the Confederate States," and "their fitness and capacity for self-government." The Choctaw and Chickasaw had adopted governmental institutions and structures "to which the people of the Confederate States are accustomed," so Confederates could see these Natives as potential citizens.[88] The treaty writers carefully excluded the bands of Indians in the leased districts of these nations who had not created similar institutional forms and documents. Of course, there was a benefit for the Confederate states in granting possible statehood to the Natives: the condition for admission to the Confederate nation was that the Choctaw and Chickasaw had to hold their land in severalty and sell any additional lands "to citizens of the Confederate

States alone."⁸⁹ Pursuing statehood would have led to a radical reduction in Choctaw and Chickasaw landholdings.

Of course, these two provisions for representation in the Confederate Congress and statehood would not stand. Upon receipt of Confederate commissioner of Indian affairs Albert Pike's treaty report, Confederate president Jefferson Davis singled out these provisions "giving to certain tribes the unqualified right of admission as a State into the compact of the Confederacy, and, in the meantime allowing each of these tribes to have a delegate in Congress" as "impolitic" and "unconstitutional." He recommended that the Confederate Congress reject the seemingly unimpeded ability of the Choctaw and Chickasaw to pursue statehood and modify the treaty's language to permit Congress to decide future action about representation.⁹⁰ Davis's language suggests some hesitancy about the addition of an Indian state. While Confederates might have eagerly sought out an alliance with Indian nations, they were not ready to view them as equals. Davis was also reinforcing the idea of the Confederacy as a compact among equal states who together would determine who could vote in the Congress and who would be admitted into statehood. The Confederate Congress agreed with Davis's recommendations and amended the treaties so that the Choctaw and Chickasaw had a seat in the hall of the House of Representatives and could introduce measures and participate in debate but had no voting rights unless granted by the House of Representatives. Choctaw Robert M. Jones, the vocal supporter of the Confederate cause, would serve in this capacity.⁹¹ Statehood for the Choctaw and Chickasaw Nations, likewise, was a matter to be decided upon by the Confederate Congress.⁹²

Related to questions about jurisdiction, citizenship, and statehood was legal competence. The alliance treaty recognized members of the Choctaw and Chickasaw Nations as competent witnesses in legal proceedings in the Confederate states. As far back as 1834, the Committee on Indian Affairs had reported that "complaints have been made by Indians that they are not admitted to testify as witnesses; and it is understood that they are in some of the States excluded by law."⁹³ The treaty sought to address this perennial complaint; however, Jefferson Davis recommended that the Confederate Congress reject the article, which would have permitted Native people to testify in state courts. He believed that each state should have the power to decide this question of Indian legal competence.⁹⁴ The Confederate Congress agreed and added language asking rather than mandating that Confederate states allow Choctaws and Chickasaws to testify in court.⁹⁵

The alliance treaty between the Choctaw and Chickasaw and the

Confederate government also protected the practice of slavery. First, article 45 extended Confederate laws regarding the rendition of fugitive enslaved people to the Choctaw and Chickasaw Nations. Moreover, rules regarding the return of fugitives to their enslavers also applied to people enslaved by Choctaws and Chickasaws who escaped to other Indian nations or to the Confederate states.[96] Disputes over the recovery of fugitive enslaved people in some sense relate back to the issue of legal jurisdiction and questions of who had the authority to recover human property across what borders. This provision addressed those questions. Second, article 47 affirmed that the institution of slavery had existed in the Choctaw and Chickasaw Nations "from time immemorial" and stated that enslaved people were "personal property." The article also declared that the Choctaw and Chickasaw Nations' laws would determine property title and distribution after the owner's death.[97] On the surface, this part of the treaty seems superfluous because it simply reiterated existing practice: the Choctaw practiced slavery, and enslaved people were human property that could be transferred and inherited like any other personal property. Article 47, however, actually reified the legality of the institution of slavery in three nations, and in a war over slavery's continued existence, the Choctaw, the Chickasaw, and Confederates took every opportunity to confirm the lawfulness of this practice. Moreover, the provision about property inheritance suggests that Choctaws and Chickasaws were not relying solely on matrilineal inheritance to distribute property. Instead, the nations were writing laws that transferred property in other ways that required codification.

Of the terms offered by the Confederate states to the Choctaw and Chickasaw, perhaps none was as important as the financial obligation the southern states assumed in place of the federal government. Within the treaty language, the Confederate states acknowledged the debt due to the Choctaw Nation by the United States of America and carefully referenced the appropriate treaties while enumerating the amounts due for perpetual annuities, for the support of the lighthorsemen, to fund a blacksmith and materials, and for annual interest on $500,000 held in trust. This amounted to $35,520 due on July 1, 1861. In order to sever all ties between the Choctaw Nation and the federal government, the Confederate states agreed to pay these debts in the future "regularly and punctually." In addition, the Confederate states agreed to pay other debts to the Choctaw due from bonds invested in southern states prior to secession and even the value of investments of Choctaw funds made in northern states. The Confederate States also offered a "final settlement and full payment" once the war ended and peace was restored.[98] In other words, breaking ties with the federal government would not cost the Choctaw financially because the Confederate states would honor the monetary terms of old Choctaw treaties with the United States. Albert Pike and Confederate negotiators aimed to make allying with the Confederacy irresistible to Indian nations.

The Choctaw commitment to the Confederacy extended beyond just the concessions Indian nations might wring from the Confederate states; the Choctaw promised troops as well. Together, the Choctaw and Chickasaw Nations agreed to "raise and furnish a regiment of ten companies of mounted men to serve in the armies of the Confederate States for twelve months." They also agreed to provide troops in the future if asked by the president of the Confederacy "for the defence of the Indian country and the frontier of the Confederate States." The soldiers would elect their own officers, with the colonel to be appointed by the president of the Confederate states. Native troops electing their own officers meant that they could choose Native rather than white officers, unlike Black troops after the issuance of the Emancipation Proclamation. The Confederate government would also arm these troops with the "same pay and allowances as other mounted troops in the service."[99] If the war continued, Choctaw and Chickasaw authorities could request an advance of $50,000 and $2,000 respectively for the purchase of arms and ammunition for the war effort.[100] This difference in amounts likely reflects the perceived manpower each group could contribute. Importantly, article 49 stipulated that the Choctaw and Chickasaw troops would "not be marched beyond the limits of the Indian country west of Arkansas against their consent."[101] Brigadier General Ben McCulloch, posted to Fort Smith, Arkansas, remarked to the Confederate secretary of war that "the Indians are much opposed to marching out of their country. They are willing to organize for its defense, but want to remain in it."[102] These terms would allow the Choctaw and Chickasaw to maintain some control over their participation in the war and sovereignty over Indian troops. They would be fighting to protect their people, property, and lands in Indian Territory. Confederate officers would not be able to order Indian troops outside of Indian Territory without the agreement of Native officials.

Article 50 of the treaty prevented the Confederate states from asking for land or payment from the Choctaw or Chickasaw for "any part of the expenses for the present war, or of any war waged by or against the Confederate States." This limit must have resonated with those sympathetic to American patriots who had resented paying taxes to subsidize British military activity. Having seen the American example, Choctaws and Chickasaws did not want to receive a bill for the war at some later date. They would also have seen the article as an important way to protect landholdings. The Confederate states promised that, once the war ended, they would defend the frontiers of Indian Territory and prioritize the use of Native troops at forts within Indian Territory.[103] Here again, the treaty's guidelines offered Choctaws and Chickasaws enormous incentives to side with the Confederacy. Their allegiance to the Confederacy would not cost the Choctaw financially because the Confederate states would honor federal debts to them and Choctaw military participation would also be paid for by the Confederate government. In fact, given the federal government's history of late payments to Indian nations, the terms of the alliance treaty represented a financial gain for the Choctaw.

Representatives of the Choctaw and Chickasaw Nations and Confederate States of America reached the terms of this alliance treaty in July 1861, with official ratification including amendments completed in December of the same year. Some Choctaws, however, were so eager to join the Confederate cause that they did not wait for the alliance to become official. For instance, by September prominent Choctaw Sampson Folsom was already gathering troops. He wrote to Albert Pike, now a brigadier general, that the Choctaw had organized seven or eight volunteer companies "to serve the Confederate states." Moreover, he promised that several more companies would be formed that same month and stated that he was authorized to make arrangements with Confederate authorities to enlist the Choctaw companies into service. Folsom indicated that the Choctaw troops could serve on "the frontier or elsewhere," though according to the treaty, the troops could serve elsewhere only with the approval of Choctaw authorities. Folsom ended with a note that he had intended to send this offer directly to Jefferson Davis but preferred a "Mr. Hunt" to handle the matter for them.[104] Again, Folsom's willingness to contact the Confederate president and General Pike are indicators of his enthusiasm for the war effort.

The Choctaw companies were no doubt peopled by soldiers such as Peter P. Pitchlynn's brother Thomas. In a letter to his nephew Peter P. Howell, Peter Pitchlynn described Thomas as hating the Yankees and talking of "killing and scalping them all the time. He will no doubt seek an opportunity to carry into execution his wishes." Thomas would have welcomed news of plans to muster troops to fight against the federal forces. Pitchlynn went on to relate that Choctaws were "keeping up the War Dance" and "will commence drilling very soon."[105] Likewise, Lycurgus Pitchlynn, Peter's son, wrote of his intent to join in the war effort, saying he was determined not to let others "out general me." In fact, he planned a "Big War Dance" at his home and invited "the whole county" before his departure for service.[106]

These remarks highlight the ways in which traditional Choctaw practice coexisted with Euro-American expectations about how Natives might participate in the war. Choctaws such as Thomas Pitchlynn saw scalping as a part of wartime activity, while American soldiers decidedly did not.[107] And the Choctaw engaged in war dances in preparation for fighting. At the same time, Choctaws recognized that Confederate officials would expect Native troops to drill in the Euro-American manner.

Other Choctaws were enthusiastic about the war effort and the formation of companies, even if other circumstances prevented their service. Nat Grayham was "full mad" because his folks would not let him go to the war. Peter Pitchlynn warned his nephew John not to be "surprised to hear of me being on the warpath before a great while. . . . If it were possible for me to go I would be in your midst before another week." Instead, Pitchlynn was home nursing sick family members. He was also in his fifties at this time, so perhaps age was a factor in his decision to remain on the home front. And note, again, the use of traditional language to describe his would-be participation in the war: "being on the warpath." Pitchlynn then expressed pride at how well organized and united the troops were. Once more Pitchlynn demonstrated the ways in which Choctaw thinking melded traditional and American ideas. Finally, Pitchlynn mentioned the soldiers' hopes: "You only want a chance to make glory for yourselves and country."[108] This sentiment was similar for soldiers all over the Choctaw country as they prepared for war.

The decision by the Choctaw, Chickasaw, Muscogee, and Seminole Nations to open negotiations to discuss the terms of an alliance with the Confederacy must have increased the pressure on John Ross and the Cherokee to also commit to the South. By October, the Cherokee had issued a "Declaration of Causes" to explain the "circumstances beyond their control" that impelled them to break ties with the United States. In the document, the Cherokee described their conundrum: their "institutions are similar to those of the Southern States, and their interests identical with theirs," but the nation had also accepted the protection of the United States and had formed treaty agreements with the federal government. When sectional tensions culminated in secession, the Cherokee had attempted to remain faithful to their agreements with the United States despite their many institutional and geographical ties with the southern states and the actions of other Indian nations.[109]

The signatories of the Cherokee declaration—National Committee president Thomas Pegg, National Committee clerk Joshua Ross, Speaker of the Council Lacy Mouse, Council Clerk Thomas B. Wolfe, and Chief John

Ross—offered several indirect critiques of the federal government. The Confederate states had not invaded the northern states; rather, "they sought only to repel invaders from their own soil and to secure the right of governing themselves," which was a "privilege asserted by the Declaration of American Independence." Thus, the northern states were aggressors who denied the seceding states the right to self-governance; the southern position was all too familiar to Indian nations. The Confederate states also did not resort to violence, the suspension of laws, or the closing of courts. Its military had not usurped power from civilian authorities, and people in the Confederate States of America were not imprisoned because of their beliefs. The United States, on the other hand, was guilty of this litany of crimes and worse, including enlisting "the scum of cities" and prison inmates who then "committed the basest of outrages on women" and imprisoning women by arbitrary order.[110] What made these last crimes so egregious was that women were the victims. While some traditional conceptions of gender among Native peoples might have confounded Euro-Americans at the time, this idea that targeting women was especially shameful was apparently shared by Natives and whites alike.[111]

Given the description of federal actions in the Cherokee declaration, officials felt the nation could not remain neutral in the conflict. Cherokee leaders wrote that while they may have had cause to complain about the southern states in the past, "their interests and their destiny are inseparably connected with those of the South." As in other correspondence between Confederate officials and Indian nations, slavery was seen as a prime cause of the conflict: "The war now raging is a war of Northern cupidity and fanaticism against the institution of African servitude; against the commercial freedom of the South, and against the political freedom of the states, and its objects are to annihilate the sovereignty of those States." Moreover, the declaration stated that the Cherokee had been warned that the first goal of the federal government would be to "annul the institution of slavery in the whole Indian country, and make it what they term free territory and after a time a free State."[112] This statement was a direct reference to the warnings that had been issued by Confederate commissioner of Indian affairs David Hubbard to Chief John Ross in correspondence months earlier about abolitionists' true goals regarding Indian Territory. In sum, it had become impossible for the Cherokee Nation to maintain its neutrality in the face of the threats to its sovereignty and, more importantly, to its institutions.

Just as with slaveholders in the South, the war exacerbated fears about uprisings of enslaved people in the Choctaw Nation. Lycurgus P. Pitchlynn wrote to his father, Peter P. Pitchlynn, about events with Robert Jones's enslaved laborers who had to be disarmed by the Choctaw authorities after an insurrection. With his use of quotation marks, Lycurgus's description of events is almost sarcastic: "They (negroes) thought the 'feds' were in the Choctaw Nation and thought it was good time to 'rise' and strike for 'freedom.' Bad white men were at the head of it. Negroes all had long knives."[113] Once the Civil War had commenced in earnest, enslaved people all over the South did think the presence of federal officials could mean freedom and seized the opportunity to free themselves. Lycurgus blamed white men for the insurrection, as though he could not conceive of Jones's enslaved people seeking freedom on their own. Or perhaps, as a member of a slaveholding family himself, Lycurgus needed to blame white men for rebellious, armed enslaved people rather than imagine that he lived in the midst of people who were quietly plotting violence against him. This fear of insurrection by enslaved people likely led to the introduction of a measure in October 1861 "prohibiting negro slaves or free colored persons from carrying deadly weapons, in this Nation," which extended the 1836 prohibition on arms for enslaved people to free people of African descent.[114] Though the act was laid over, its introduction reflects real fears about what people of African descent might do and an understanding of the potential for the Civil War to change the racial status quo.

Around the same time that the Choctaw considered prohibiting people of African descent from carrying weapons in the nation, J. P. Folsom introduced a bill requiring all white persons aged twenty-one and older living in the Choctaw Nation to swear an oath to support the constitution of the Confederate States of America. Such whites were considered foreigners at that time. After some wrangling between the Choctaw House and Senate, the oath bill was enacted on November 5, 1861, and forwarded to county judges three months later.[115] This act was the legal manifestation of Lycurgus Pitchlynn's assumptions about who was dangerous in the Choctaw Nation: white people who could incite enslaved people to violence. In fact, such white people with abolitionist leanings were more dangerous than actual armed enslaved people—hence, this bill's passage while the bill to prohibit people of African descent from carrying deadly arms languished. The implicit assumption in Folsom's bill was that there was little Choctaw dissent from the Confederate position. Rather, white people were the potential malcontents who required an oath to stay in line.

By 1863, there were fears that some of this disagreement with the Confederate position had spread beyond "bad white men" to a few Choctaws as well. The Confederate commissioner of Indian affairs wrote in December that the Choctaw had held a meeting in the fall in Doaksville with the federal general Blount and that "one or two members of the nation were represented to have given utterance to sentiments that favored a wish to have the Choctaws ignore their treaty engagements with the Confederate States, and assume a position of neutrality during the remainder of the existing war." Confederate commissioner of Indian affairs S. S. Scott rushed to meet with Choctaw leaders to investigate the rumors and instead found that the Choctaw legislature had reaffirmed its commitment to the southern cause.[116] Choctaw leaders had also heard the swirling rumors about weakening Choctaw resolve toward the Confederate cause. In response, they passed an act declaring that any person making statements "to destroy the confidence of the Choctaw people in the ability of the Confederate States to sustain themselves in the present struggle" or who took steps to advocate neutrality or withdrawing their support from the Confederacy "shall be deemed and considered an enemy to this Nation of people and a traitor to the liberties of his common country and interest, and deserving the death of a traitor."[117] Thus, in the middle of the war, Choctaw lawmakers doubled down on their resolve to side with the Confederacy, so much so that even criticizing the Confederacy became punishable by death. And there must have been some truth to the idea that some Choctaws had grown disenchanted with the war and the South: officials did not target only white people with this law, as they had with the oath law.

While the Choctaw had entertained neutrality and debated the best course of action at the outset of hostilities, once they joined with the South, their commitment remained firm. Commissioner Scott even remarked in his annual report in 1863, "The Choctaws alone, of all the Indian nations, have remained perfectly united in their loyalty to this government. It was said to me by more than one influential and reliable Choctaw, during my sojourn in their country, that not only had no member of that nation ever gone over to the enemy, but that no Indian had ever done so, in whose vein coursed Choctaw blood."[118] Scott's informant surely employed some hyperbole in this comment; however, the remark still reflects a high level of unified sentiment among the Choctaw. In another report from the US Southern Superintendency later that same year, W. G. Coffin remarked, "The Choctaw nation almost *en masse* joined the rebels at the beginning of the rebellion, where they still remain. But very few in number have returned to their allegiance, and are now being subsisted, with other refugees, at the Sac and Fox agency."[119] Officials from both the Union and the Confederacy, then, acknowledged that Choctaws' support of the South was particularly fervent.

Scholars have attributed Native support for the Confederacy to a variety of largely external factors. Annie Heloise Abel placed particular emphasis on the ability of agents in Indian Territory to ensure that non-Natives who resided there had clear southern sympathies and that funds held in trust for the Native tribes were invested in southern companies. Abel also asserted that pressure from Arkansas and Texas was crucial to pushing Natives to side with the South.[120] Angie Debo ascribed Choctaw support for the Confederacy to slavery, the Confederate leanings of longtime agent to the Choctaws Douglas H. Cooper, fear of future land seizures by the Republican government, federal neglect, and pressure from southern sympathizers in Texas and Arkansas.[121] More recently, scholars have also added the Natives' cultural affinity with white southerners, both in terms of actual familial ties and in connections to a shared geography, to the list of factors contributing to their Confederate leanings.[122] Another line of argument is that the departure of Union forces from Indian Territory early in the war in particular left Natives little choice but to side with the secessionists.[123] Other than adoption of the institution of slavery, these explanations for Native support for the Confederacy tend to stress the actions of those outside of Indian nations to influence Indian behavior instead of motivations from within Native communities.

The idea that an alliance with the Confederacy was the only choice for Native nations has some basis in documents created by Choctaw Indians themselves. In June 1865, Peter P. Pitchlynn convened an extra session of the Choctaw legislature to communicate "that the Government of the Confederate States, to which we had under peculiar and unavoidable circumstances become allied, has ceased to exist." Note Pitchlynn's language: the Choctaw had become allies of the South because of "peculiar and unavoidable circumstances." He continued that the Choctaw's situation had not changed from four years prior "when the United States withdrew their troops from our country, and left us without any protecting power whatever." One of the "unavoidable circumstances" was the federal withdrawal of troops from Indian Territory and the concomitant loss of federal protection. Pitchlynn then clarified the terrible choice faced by the Choctaw: "The alternative of two evils was presented, that of immediate extermination as a people, or to aid and abet that party who had engaged in a crusade against their own Government." Joining the Confederacy, in Pitchlynn's recounting, was the only way to preserve the existence of the Choctaw Nation.[124] The alternative was "immediate extermination as a people"; in other words, death. In September of the same year, Pitchlynn again asserted that for Choctaws "the hostile hand would not have been raised in the late war, had not imperious circumstances over which they had no control impelled them." The Choctaw had "no wish to interfere" in a "fuss among the pale faced family to be settled in their own way," and "impartial history will show that they acted from motives of self-preservation and National protection." He again pointed out that the "Government of the United States at that time was powerless to protect us" and had "abandoned the Military Forts established in our country for our protection."[125] Pitchlynn's statements forcefully argued that the Choctaw's choice to side with the Confederacy was not a real choice at all; rather, circumstances, especially the withdrawal of federal troops, forced the Choctaw to join with rebelling southern states.

These statements about the coerced nature of Choctaws' support for the Confederacy came conveniently after the South lost the war. Choctaws' revision of their reasons for supporting the Confederacy mark them as quintessentially southern: white southerners also wrote slavery out of the war's causes on the heels of defeat.[126] Rather than an entirely accurate account of the decision to side with the Confederacy, these statements should be seen in light of the need to defend a disastrous choice and the desire to negotiate a new relationship with the federal government. Pitchlynn's explanation about the Choctaw Nation's lack of options elides the assignment of blame for the decision to side with the South and attempts to smooth over internal divisions. Indeed, by his account, no one was to blame for the decision. Instead, it had been the only choice, and reluctantly taken. He called for fellow Choctaws to "unite in restoring our country to law and order" and warned that "divisions among us now would soon end in certain destruction."[127] By September, Pitchlynn's words were self-consciously outward facing: "Now I appeal to every candid and unprejudiced man in the United States, was it not better for the Choctaw nation to join hands with the Southern States and thereby avert the demon of war from their country, to a considerable extent, than to have attempted neutrality, and thereby had the Country seized and taken possession of by the South, and the battle field with all its withering desolation brought to our doors."[128] He beseeched an American audience to understand the untenable position in which federal inaction had placed Choctaws. Pitchlynn also preempted any accusations that the Choctaw could have remained neutral, claiming the South would have "seized" Choctaw territory and brought the destruction of battle to their doorstep. Neutrality was at best a false option in this formulation. Again, this language avoids blaming the Choctaw for their stance and implicitly asks for some leniency from federal officials in the negotiations to come.

In a stunning turn, an 1870 feature on Peter Pitchlynn that appeared in the *Atlantic Monthly* erased the Choctaw alliance with the Confederacy by describing the Choctaw Nation as having "never, as a whole, been in hostile collision with, nor been subdued by, the United States." In this rendering, the fighting in Indian Territory did not count as a "hostile collision" between the Choctaw and the federal government. Moreover, "what certain individuals may have done during the late war ought not certainly to be charged against the nation at large."[129] The statement is full of obfuscating language: "certain individuals may have" taken action during the war. What individuals? What kind of action? Did action, in fact, take place? The answers to these questions did not matter because, in any case, those actions should not be held against the entirety of the Choctaw Nation.

In part, the sketch stakes this claim of Choctaw neutrality and even loyalty to the Union on Pitchlynn, whom the author describes as pursuing a neutral position but with a "heart" that "was for the Union." In an 1861 meeting between Pitchlynn and President Abraham Lincoln, Pitchlynn had "assured" Lincoln "of his desire to have the Choctaws pursue a neutral course" but also had declared "that, if the general government would protect them, his people would certainly espouse its cause." Pitchlynn then had returned to the Choctaw Nation to continue working his 600 acres of land with over 100 enslaved people. The war and Pitchlynn's neighbors thwarted his plans to resume the quiet life of a planter: "But the white men of Arkansas and Texas had already worked upon the passions of the Choctaws, and on reaching home he found a large part of the nation already infected with the spirit of rebellion. He pleaded for the national government, and, at the hazard of his life, denounced the conduct of the Southern authorities." In this version of events, some Choctaws such as Pitchlynn had not merely sought neutrality but had supported the Union, even when doing so was dangerous. And it had been southern white men who ginned up support among the Choctaw for the rebelling states, not Choctaws themselves. Confederate sympathizers then had spread stories that Pitchlynn had married Lincoln's sister and that he had accepted $400,000 to become an abolitionist.[130] In the *Atlantic Monthly* piece, Pitchlynn is the stand-in for the entire Choctaw Nation, fervently working to maintain loyalty to the Union and attacked and threatened by Confederates. At the time of publication in 1870, Reconstruction was in full swing, and the Choctaw, like the former Confederates, were chafing at its strictures. Rewriting history could help the Choctaw claim better treatment from the federal government.

Rather than consider the Choctaw alliance with the Confederacy as an outcome of southern states' desires or as a foregone conclusion, I take seriously Choctaw interests and the nation's decision-making process in choosing to side with the seceding states during the war. With conflict on the horizon, the Choctaw pursued a course of neutrality, along with other so-called Civilized Tribes. After all, both the federal government and southeastern states had been complicit in the devastation of removal. But Native peoples also understood that a potential civil war in the United States would have consequences for Native sovereignty and began to assess which combatant might respect it. The Choctaw quickly calculated that their interests lay with the seceding states. Thus, their initial statement of neutrality also included language about the strong affinity, the "indissoluble bonds," between the Choctaw people and their fellow southerners and signaled their intention to side with the southern states should war ensue. In spite of this resolution, late in the spring of 1861, after fighting commenced, some Choctaw leaders still hoped to maintain a position of neutrality in the conflict, but Robert M. Jones and others pushed the Choctaw legislature to follow their own economic, cultural, and social proclivities and side with the South.

Southern white civilians also worked to encourage an alliance between the new Confederacy and Native nations. Vigilance committees consisting of white Texans visited Choctaw leaders and attended a council meeting to press Choctaws to side more forcefully with the seceding states.[131] Because the federal government had abandoned all posts in Indian Territory in the spring of 1861, Native groups felt open to invasion from southern sympathizers in Texas or Arkansas.[132] The fear of what Confederate Texans might do was tangible.

Confederate officials offered substantial incentives to the Choctaw to side with the South. They promised to respect Native territorial claims in perpetuity. The treaty included provisions to handle long-standing questions about jurisdictional authority in cases involving Choctaw individuals or committed on Choctaw lands. Financially, the Confederate government would assume all of the debts owed to the Choctaw by the federal government. The Confederate government would pay for salaries and supplies for Choctaw soldiers who joined the war effort. And Choctaw soldiers would not be used outside of Indian Territory without the permission of Choctaw authorities. Though the Confederate Congress ended up pulling back from Albert Pike's initial offer of a representative with full voting rights in the Confederate House of Representatives, the Congress did offer the Choctaw a long sought-after delegate. As Choctaws Henry I. and Ida L. Falconer noted, "The confederates had promised more liberal agreements to take the place of these treaties in the event of the success of the secessionists."[133]

A host of factors converged, then, to lead to Choctaw support of the Confederate war effort. The combination of Choctaws' own practice of and economic interest in the institution of slavery, ties of geography and kin, pressure from white neighbors, and the concrete benefits offered by the Confederate government was compelling. But there were other options. The

Cherokee held the course on neutrality longer; in other cases, such as that of Creek leader Opothle Yahola, whom I will discuss more in depth in chapter 4, prominent Natives openly pushed against the official stance of the nation. Once the Choctaw committed to the Confederacy, on the other hand, they remained remarkably united, so much so that Confederate officials commented on Choctaw loyalty. And Choctaws themselves passed a measure making it illegal to say anything negative about the Confederacy. Such action cannot be attributed to outside pressures from southern white neighbors or Confederate officials; rather, it signals authentic internal Choctaw fervor for the Confederate cause, a fervor that was demonstrated in the enlistment records of the First Choctaw and Chickasaw Mounted Rifles, which I will discuss in the next chapter.

Chapter 4

We Know Dey Is Indians

RED SOLDIERS IN GRAY

Den jest as we starting to leave here come something across dat little prairie sho' nuff! We know dey is Indians de way dey is riding, and de way dey is all strung out. Dey had a flag, and it was all red and had a big criss-cross on it dat look lak a saw horse. De man carry it and rear back on it when de wind whip it, but it flap all 'roun de horse's head and de horse pitch and rear lak he know something going to happen, sho!

Bout dat time it turn kind of dark and begin to rain a little, and we git out to de big road and de rain come down hard. It rain so hard for a little while dat we jest have to stop de wagon and set dar, and den long come more soldiers dan I ever see befo'. Dey all white men, I think, and dey have on dat brown clothes dyed wid walnut and butternut, and old Master say dey de Confederate Soldiers.[1]

Lucinda Davis, owned by Creek Native Tuskaya-hiniha, offers one of the few existing accounts of the Battle of Honey Springs in July 1863.[2] She describes seeing Native troops approach carrying the Confederate battle flag, the changing weather conditions, and the arrival of white Confederate troops. Her account goes on to detail the roar of gunfire that sounded "lak hosses loping 'cross a plank bridge way off somewhar."[3] Davis offers compelling testimony about the far-reaching and destructive power of battle on the civilian population and on the landscape, but what I am most interested in for this chapter is the experience of those soldiers on horseback, whose riding style was so distinctive that Davis and her fellow spectators identified them as Indians from a distance. What can we say about their experiences with the Confederate army?

To answer this question, this chapter relies largely on service records—particularly the Compiled Service Records of Confederate Soldiers Who

Served in Organizations Raised Directly by the Confederate Government—from the National Archives.[4] The records offer a rich picture of the lives of Choctaw soldiers both on and off the battlefield, exposing some of the influences on Choctaw society, illuminating who enlisted and under what terms, and giving shape to the fighting that took place in Indian Territory, as well as its consequences. This Native military force operated in a manner entirely recognizable to white Americans in spite of ideas about Native savagery and disorganization. Finally, a politics of allegiances also emerges through the military records. While Confederate leadership may have wanted to control Native soldiers, the fact remained that Native soldiers were citizens of their respective nations, not of the Confederate States of America.

Before I discuss what these records reveal about Choctaw soldiers' experiences, I describe these records in detail for several reasons. First, scholars often assume written records about Native people are sparse; however, these records represent thousands of pages of documents. Second, some might question the reliability of documents that appear to be an artifact of the twentieth century. I contend that these records do accurately represent the often difficult-to-trace quotidian activities of common soldiers during the Civil War. Third, the transfer of this information onto government forms reinforces how numerous the records are: federal officials spent money to design and print these forms to organize a large body of information. Finally, this deep dive into the minutiae of the evidence reveals something of my methodology; in short, I want to give readers a sense of how I attempted to wring meaning from what may appear to be brief and generic forms. In particular, the records reveal patterns of enlistment that I contend represent Choctaws' enthusiasm for the war, an enthusiasm that seemed to decline after the Battle of Honey Springs.

The majority of the enlistment records consist of preprinted forms compiled by the War Department to facilitate determining individual eligibility for pensions and other veterans' benefits efficiently and rapidly. As head of the Record and Pension Office of the War Department, Brigadier General Fred C. Ainsworth directed the compilation of these service records of Confederate soldiers in 1903.[5] The preprinted forms were likely created at this time. Some of them included handwritten muster rolls that hint at the form of the original muster documents. Rather than an individual form or set of forms for each soldier, the original records were likely lists. In the available examples, a scribe neatly listed each officer by surname, then first name, then rank on a single line. Sometimes his script was quite small in order to include all of the important information on the single blank page. Often the scribe recorded a single statement that applied to everyone on the list, such as "muster in of Regt. Completed July 31/61 for 12 mos." Thus, all of the men on the list mustered in on July 31, 1861, and agreed to a twelve-month term of service. Sometimes the scribe added a note, such as "Col. Apptd May 30/61."[6] In this case, the colonel was appointed on May 30, 1861. The scribe also abbreviated ranks so that "C" meant captain or "1" indicated that the soldier held the rank of first lieutenant.[7] Copyists such as G. C. West, S. B. Woodward, and R. B. Duncan transferred this information onto the preprinted forms.[8]

Each record included a jacket with the soldier's name, company, and rank and listed the other cards associated with his record. This jacket also indicated whether the soldier's records appear elsewhere under a different spelling of his name. There were sufficient numbers of Choctaw troops that many of the preprinted jackets or envelopes noted "1 Choctaw Mounted Rifles. Also known as Cavalry. (Confederate.)." Other preprinted jackets included the names of both nations: "1 Choctaw and Chickasaw Mounted Rifles." The jacket often contained a fill-in-the-blank-style company muster roll. The company name and the information—"(Confederate.) 1 Choctaw and Chickasaw Mounted Rifles"—appeared preprinted on this form as well. The form lists the date, location, and term of enlistment. One version of the form asked for the enlistee's age, while a later version did not. Especially useful is the "Remarks" section. In most cases, this section merely indicated if an enlistee was still present at the end of his term of service, but sometimes it noted rich tidbits about promotions, work duties, or soldiers being absent without leave. A frequently included payroll form states whether the soldier received a commutation for clothing—a fee authorities paid soldiers to provide their own clothing—for six months, generally in the amount of twenty-five dollars. Sometimes a bounty pay and receipt roll for fifty dollars was in the file as well, along with petitions or official correspondence regarding the soldier. Less frequently, the soldier's jacket contained other miscellaneous documents, often handwritten.

The title of these records is something of a misnomer. It suggests that authorities from the Confederate States of America enlisted these troops into service; however, the Choctaw were quite motivated and had early allied with the Confederacy, agreeing to place a regiment of Choctaw troops numbering 1,000 men under Confederate officers, with the Confederacy committing to pay $500,000 to arm and equip them.[9] Consequently, despite the records' title, it is unclear whether Choctaw authorities or the Confederate government enlisted these troops. This uncertainty is also found in the

Enlistment record of Private Fullumini.
(NARA 258, roll 82: PDF 4007–4009; courtesy of National Archives)

actual enlistment documents examined below. In addition, I supplement the service records with firsthand accounts from Civil War soldiers more broadly to create a fuller picture of Choctaw soldiers' experiences.

The contemporary Choctaw Nation estimates that approximately 1,200 Choctaw troops served on the side of the Confederacy by the middle of the Civil War.[10] I have collected the service records of over 3,100 individuals in the 1 Choctaw Mounted Rifles for the totality of the Civil War. If one counts only the records for those persons who enlisted in 1861 and 1862, there are over 1,800 individuals, which is closer to Edward Elmer Prag's finding that 1,885 men made up the Choctaw and Chickasaw Confederate forces in June 1861.[11] Therefore, the Choctaw's own estimate of 1,200 for the number of Choctaws serving by the middle of the Civil War is likely quite low. Prag's number includes Chickasaw Confederates, whom I do not discuss here. To be sure, there is likely some duplication in my records: if two records shared the same name but differed in any other detail, I retained both entries. There are separate records for Chickasaw soldiers; thus, the individuals I included appear to be from the Choctaw Nation.

Some of these soldiers, however, were also white; for instance, Colonel Douglas Cooper, a federal agent to the Choctaw and Chickasaw Nations from Mississippi who became the commander of Indian troops at the outbreak of the Civil War, appears in these records. Moreover, Choctaw legislators' agreement to allow troops to serve under Confederate officers is unclear: was "Confederate officers" merely a euphemism for "white officers"? Some of the officers in the regiment were definitely Choctaw, such as Captain Iskitini Homa and Lieutenant Colonel Tandy Walker, so one cannot assume that all of the officers were white.[12]

The Chickasaw, on the other hand, appear to have agreed for at least one regiment to be commanded by white officers by the middle of the war. When Captain William L. Hunter received authority from the War Department in May 1863 to raise and command a regiment, the order stipulated that "all the officers [were] to be white and to be appointed by the Pres. of the C[onfederate] S[tates]."[13] No similar directive from the president of the Confederacy to appoint white officers to command Choctaw soldiers appears in the records. In light of the name of the regiment and the locations of enlistment, one can safely assume that the majority of the men who were enlisted in the First Choctaw and Chickasaw Mounted Rifles were Natives. And if one believes Principal Chief Peter P. Pitchlynn, the entire regiment comprised mostly Choctaws, so much so that he wanted to remove "Chickasaw" from the regiment's name.[14] Additionally, the disbursal of funds from the Confederate government to the Choctaw and Chickasaw Nations to support Native troops at a ratio of 25:1 affirms Pitchlynn's assertion.

In addition to white officers, some white soldiers did join the Indian regiments. White men and Indians of other tribes aged eighteen to forty-five residing in the Choctaw Nation were subject to militia duty by June 1861, according to Choctaw law.[15] The majority of white soldiers in Indian Territory, however, usually did not have ties to the Indian nations; that is, they were neither citizens nor residents of Indian Territory and also had not intermarried into the nations. Rather, as Captain B. W. Marston commented in 1864, white soldiers sought entry into Indian regiments to avoid service elsewhere that entailed stricter discipline. Marston thought these white men were a bad influence on the Indian soldiers because of their lack of skill and discipline.[16] Confederate negotiators had assured Native officials that Native troops would remain in Indian Territory; perhaps these white soldiers wanted to remain in the region as well.[17] Or perhaps these white soldiers, like many observers at the time, perceived Native troops as more relaxed about drilling and absenteeism. Marston estimated that as many as 1,000 white men might be serving in the Indian division (out of an estimated Confederate troop strength in Indian Territory of about 5,500 soldiers) and wished the men would be transferred to some white unit elsewhere.[18] According to Marston, these 1,000 troops were concentrated among the Cherokee forces rather than in the First Choctaw and Chickasaw Mounted Rifles: "The Chief white element in the Indian Division is in Watie's Brigade brought there under an authority which I am advised he has from the Sec of War to recruit within the enemy's line."[19] Marston's numbers seem high when one considers the real prejudices white soldiers had about serving under and with troops of color and how poorly provisioned the Native companies were.[20] In any case, by early 1865, Marston got his wish and was in command of "a separate battalion of white men in the Indian Division."[21]

In October 1861, not long after Choctaw authorities affirmed the ability of white men and Natives from other tribes to serve in the militia, officials introduced an act "prohibiting Negro slaves or free colored persons from carrying deadly weapons in this nation."[22] Ultimately, officials opted to table the measure, but the discussion came just four months after a unanimous vote on an act declaring "that the Constitution and laws of the Nation are Supreme and in full force within the limits of the Nation, and all persons, both white men as well as residents, and all sojourners are required to yield implicit obedience to the same."[23] These acts, in combination with the act clarifying who was subject to service in the militia, bespeak a polity reckoning with the question of who could be a legitimate soldier in the war. The answer for many Choctaws, not surprisingly, did not include people of African descent, whether enslaved or free. The Choctaw Nation, after all, was a society with a sizable enslaved population who performed important agricultural work. Moreover, while some Confederate officials and several southern legislatures had flirted with the idea of arming enslaved men, more serious calls to enlist enslaved men grew after 1863, as the manpower shortage became more dire. Still, the Confederate Congress did not authorize their use until March 1865 and with so many strictures that few enslaved men enlisted.[24] It would have been difficult to deploy soldiers of African descent in the Choctaw Nation alongside white Confederate troops early in the war, given white southerners' antagonism to the idea, so this Choctaw act, though tabled, is in keeping with the sentiments of the larger Confederate South.

The approximately 3,100 troops represented in the records translate into roughly 17.2 percent of the total Choctaw population, or 20 percent if one excludes the enslaved population. In the United States, soldiers accounted for approximately 14.6 percent of the northern population (2.7 million served out of a population of 18.5 million) and 8.3 percent of people in the Confederacy and border states, or 12.5 percent excluding their enslaved population.[25] Thus, while some 3,100 troops may seem like a small number in the aggregate, as a proportion of the Choctaw population, it is large. Of course, 3,100 troops is much lower than the 10,000 troops that Colonel Douglas H. Cooper had predicted in a letter to the president of the Confederacy, Jefferson Davis, that the Choctaw and Chickasaw would provide, a number all the more astonishing given that the combined total of the Choctaw and Chickasaw populations at this time was less than 23,000 people, including their enslaved populations.[26] Cooper had written, "The Choctaws and Chickasaw can furnish 10,000 warriors if needed. The Choctaws and Chickasaws are extremely anxious to form another regiment."[27] Cooper may have believed these numbers given the long-standing Choctaw reputation for military strength: eighteenth-century French observer Antoine du Pratz claimed that Choctaw warriors numbered 25,000, and fellow Frenchman Andre Penicaut thought the Choctaw and Chickasaw could summon 16,000 warriors in 1723.[28]

The data included in the Compiled Service Records not only tell us about individual soldiers but also reveal aspects of the changing nature of Choctaw society. For instance, the names on these records simultaneously demonstrate the influence of Euro-Americans and the resilience of traditional naming practices. Names include John Simpson, several Thomas Jeffersons, and a Jefferson Davis (a private, aged twenty-five) but also Cubbee, Eahantubbee, Haiokonubi, and Shumpalubbee. Some soldiers' names were a blend of traditional Choctaw names and European names: William Eyashahopaye, Shiaheka Thompson, Lewis Himakambi. The names suggest a society with a variety of cultural influences. Choctaw converts to Christianity, for instance, often took on new English names or the names of benefactors of the missionaries.[29] Other names resulted from marriages between Choctaws and Europeans or Euro-Americans. Many Choctaws, on the other hand, preserved their traditional names. Choctaw naming practices were important, especially to men, as I will discuss in the next chapter. The names suggest that service in the First Choctaw and Chickasaw Mounted Rifles was not the sole province of those who were most acculturated to American society. The surnames of prominent families within the Choctaw political arena also appear: the Folsoms, LeFlores, and McCurtains are three examples, each family having produced district or principal chiefs of the Choctaw Nation during the nineteenth century.

The age data on soldiers from the First Choctaw and Chickasaw Mounted Rifles provide some opportunity for comparison with similar data on American soldiers in the Civil War. Native soldiers were slightly older than their American counterparts. The average age for the Choctaw enlistees was 27.91, with a median age of 25. The average age of Union soldiers was 25.8, and the median age was 23.5. Similar data for Confederate soldiers does not exist; however, Civil War historian James McPherson offers some numbers based on a small sample size of 429 men: 26.5 years of age on average at enlistment, with a median age of 24.2.[30] The age data and name data also suggest relationships between soldiers. For example, the cluster of five Greenwood enlistees, aged 20 to 28, may have been related to each other in some way. Allen, Gibson, Harris, Hogan, and Sesson Greenwood all mustered into Company 1-E as privates on July 3, 1861, at Black Jack Court Ground. Similarly, Joseph Hunter, aged 43, and Stilon Hunter, aged 18, both joined Peter Maytubby's company at Goodland Station on September 2, 1864. Possibly they were a father and son joining together in hopes of watching out for one another. The sources are maddeningly silent about such connections.

As one would expect for military records, rank is an important piece of data that is consistently documented: more than 98 percent of the enlistment records include this information.[31] Of course, soldiers holding the rank of private predominate: over 85 percent of the soldiers were identified as privates.[32] The next most common rank was corporal, followed closely by sergeant. The number of lieutenants more than doubled the number of captains. Beyond the usual military ranks, Choctaw soldiers served in other capacities, including as buglers, blacksmiths, musicians, wagoners, quartermasters, and surgeons. Soldiers' changes in rank also appear. Thus, one can see Ben W. Lewis's promotion from first sergeant to second lieutenant and Tandy Folsom's rise from private to first sergeant.[33]

Company assignment was relatively straightforward: individuals mustered into Company A or 2-K or 2-D, among many others. As was common among other Confederate troops, some Choctaw companies were also known by names connected to their commanding officers. Captain Sinta Nowa's Company, for example, was also known as Walking Snake Company and Company I. Other companies were known as Captain Coleman E. Nelson's Company or Captain Edmond Gardner's Company or Captain Shemontah's (John Gibson) Company. Sometimes these unofficial names of companies were printed on the standardized forms, reinforcing the idea that these companies were well known by these less standard names.[34] The use of both Choctaw language and English names is also noteworthy. *Sinti* is "snake" in Choctaw, and *nowa* means "a walk" or "to walk."[35] Walking

Snake was a translation of Captain Sinta Nowa's name. Shemontah may come from the Choctaw word *shema*, meaning "to dress up or embellish."[36] A John Gibson aged 65 in 1899 appears on the Dawes Rolls as a Choctaw.[37] Shemontah/Gibson was certainly the right age to have served as a captain during the war. The Civil War was a defining moment for the United States, yet the presence of these Native names on Civil War military records exemplifies how much this American event included other peoples who did not identify as Americans.

The data on the date and place of muster reveal patterns in where and when soldiers enlisted into the First Choctaw and Chickasaw Mounted Rifles. Almost 70 percent of the records include this information.[38] Careful preservation of the enlistment date was crucial to determine when a soldier's term of service was complete. As one would expect, there was a surge of young men signing up to fight at the start of the Civil War in 1861. Of the records that include date and muster location data, half indicate enlistments that took place in 1861. June and July 1861 were especially popular months to enlist: the records include 950 enlistments for these two months alone. This Choctaw enthusiasm for the Confederacy is even more remarkable given that the Choctaw did not sign a treaty with the Confederacy until July 1861.[39] Thus, Choctaw citizens were committing to fight in the war even before the Choctaw legislature had officially sided with the Confederacy.

The Choctaw legislature had already passed a resolution in support of the southern states in February 1861, though the formal treaty alliance would not come for five more months, so gathering Choctaw support for enlistment may not have been so difficult.[40] Surely the Choctaw resolution was a response to the February 4 meeting of six southern states in Montgomery to form a provisional government and establish the Confederate States of America.[41] The Choctaw may have been waiting for the seceding states to create a more formal body before expressing Choctaw support. US Indian agent Douglas H. Cooper enrolled Indians for service as early as April 1861, again before an official treaty of alliance had been signed.[42] Muster rolls show over 100 Choctaw troops enlisted in May 1861, specifically on May 13, in Skullyville. Perhaps this enlistment fervor was prompted by the neighboring southern state of Arkansas's decision to join the Confederacy less than one week prior, on May 7, 1861.[43] Skullyville was located near the far eastern border of Choctaw Nation, very close to the shared border with Arkansas and Fort Smith, and was described by some Choctaws as a particular center for the settlement of enslavers due to agricultural conditions favorable to plantations.[44]

Doaksville, Fort Washita, Fort Arbuckle, Sulphur Springs, Goodland Station, Sugar Loaf, Boggy Depot, Black Jack Grove, and Perryville were all locations for clusters of enlistments in 1861. Doaksville and Boggy Depot each served as capitals of the Choctaw Nation, so these locations were logical sites for forming companies. Fort Washita and Fort Arbuckle were located within the Chickasaw Nation yet produced many Choctaw recruits. Because military encampments attracted military activity, individuals hoping to join the fight might have turned to forts to volunteer. That these locations in the Chickasaw Nation would attract Choctaw troops points to several other facts. First, Fort Washita is close to the shared border between the Choctaw and Chickasaw Nations. Brigadier General Albert Pike did not establish Fort McCulloch nearby within the Choctaw Nation until 1862, so soldiers could not enlist there in 1861.[45] Second, the two nations had shared a territory just six years prior; citizens of each nation were accustomed to moving about freely within that larger territory. Finally, the official designation of the unit was the First Choctaw and Chickasaw Mounted Rifles. Given the combined nature of the unit and the history of the relationship between these two nations, it is not surprising to see Choctaws enlist in this joint regiment inside the Chickasaw Nation. In all, the records indicate that over 1,000 Choctaw soldiers joined the mounted rifles in 1861 alone.[46]

In 1862, enthusiasm for the war among Choctaw Indians was still strong, as it was in the broader Confederacy: nearly 800 men enlisted in the regiment during the second year of the war. I will discuss some of the change in excitement to enlist among Choctaws and white Confederates below, but January, March, and July of 1862 in particular yielded a high number of Choctaw recruits. The almost 200 men who joined the regiment in January may have been spurred to action by the November and December battles that had taken place in Indian Territory: Round Mountain, Chusto-Talasah, and Chustenahlah.

All three engagements were efforts to subdue the wealthy Creek Indian Opothle Yahola and his followers. Initially hoping to remain neutral, the Creek leader had disagreed with the Creek Council's decision to ally with the Confederacy. While other Indian nations were negotiating treaties of alliance with Confederate officials, Indians loyal to the American federal government were coalescing around Opothle Yahola. Though his wife was a slaveholder, he promised freedom for enslaved people, and many in nearby Indian nations ran away to join him.[47] Phoebe Banks, whose parents had been owned by the Creek Perryman and McIntosh families, recalled her family joining "Old Gouge," as Opothle Yahola was known: "All our family join up with him, and there was lots of Creek Indians and slaves in the outfit when they made a break for the North. The runaways was riding ponies

Choctaw and Chickasaw Nations, 1860.
(Map by Rice University GIS/Data Center)

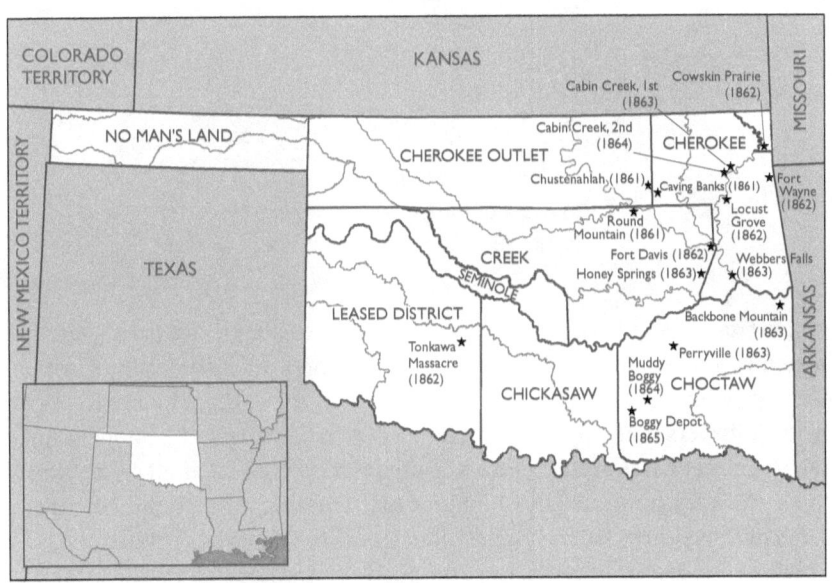

Civil War battle sites in Indian Territory.
(Map by Rice University GIS/Data Center)

Opothle Yahola.
(Courtesy of the Library of Congress
Prints and Photographs Division)

stolen from their masters."[48] Moreover, many free people of African descent also favored his Unionist stance and joined the loyal Creek camps, which were growing in size. Some estimated that Opothle Yahola had as many as 9,000 followers, but only 2,000 would have been fighting men. Colonel Douglas H. Cooper led over 1,400 Native Confederates supplemented by the Ninth Texas Cavalry to attack and pursue Chief Opothle Yahola and his band. Each of these three battles punctuated Opothle Yahola's flight to Kansas.[49]

Of the 105 deaths noted in the Compiled Service Records for the Choctaw Mounted Rifles for the entirety of the war (4 of which were horses), 7 were the result of this campaign against Opothle Yahola.[50] Cherokee Presbyterian minister Stephen Foreman wrote in his diary in January 1862 that he had heard "about 14" men were lost in the fighting.[51] Perhaps the additional deaths noted by Foreman came from the Ninth (Fourth) Texas Cavalry that Colonel Cooper had called in as reinforcements.[52] Despite these losses, the Confederate forces could claim a victory because they had forced so many loyal Indians into Kansas and neutralized the threat represented by Opothle Yahola. But would this threat remain outside of Indian Territory? Missionary Joseph Murrow worried that once weather conditions improved, "there will be squally times in this territory again, unless there is a considerable force of Confederate troops on the Kansas border to oppose 'Old Posey' [a nickname for Opothle Yahola] and his wild Indians and wilder Jayhawkers."[53] If this feeling was widespread within Indian Territory more broadly, and among Choctaws in particular, it may explain the burst of enlistments in January 1862. The men joined the regiment at Eagletown, Lukfahtah, and Doaksville, all located in Apukshunnubbee District in the southeastern corner of the nation, close to Texas and Arkansas. Nearly 230 more men enlisted in March, again from this same area: Lukfahtah and Nowood in Red River County in the southeast corner of the district. The companies raised in Red River County formed on March 10, most likely in response to the Battle at Pea Ridge (also known as Elkhorn Tavern, in nearby Arkansas) on March 7–8. The First Choctaw and Chickasaw Mounted Rifles failed to arrive on time at Pea Ridge, and the federal forces defeated the Confederate troops. The Confederate general Albert Pike pulled back his forces, leaving Indian Territory very isolated. The proximity of the fighting and the threat of southern failure may have spurred additional Confederate Choctaw companies to form. June and July brought still another 200 troops into service.

Fighting in the Cherokee Nation at Fort Wayne in October 1862 did not push a surge of recruits to the First Choctaw and Chickasaw Mounted Rifles. The Battle of Old Fort Wayne was actually a continuation of fighting that began at Newtonia, Missouri, in September. Union troops had fortified their presence in Newtonia because of its strategic value: described as the "granary of the Ozarks," the region produced cereal crops and was home to the mills that processed them. The nearby town of Granby produced lead for munitions. Finally, its location near free Kansas, Indian Territory, and Confederate Arkansas meant Newtonia could be a launching point for incursions into Confederate territory.[54] Colonel Cooper and the Texas Cavalry engaged Union troops from Wisconsin and Kansas near the small Missouri town, and Native soldiers fought on both sides of the battle. The tide seemed to be moving in the Union forces' favor until Lieutenant Colonel Tandy Walker led a charge of the regiment through town "singing their war-songs and giving the war whoop."[55] The victory came at a steep cost, however; the regiment lost eight men, including three officers: Lieutenant William Belvin, First Lieutenant Henry Van Osdol, and Captain Martin Folsom. Another seventeen men were wounded or taken prisoner.[56]

Cooper's forces would clash with federal troops again just a few weeks later at Old Fort Wayne, but with far different results. Some of Cooper's Indian troops failed to arrive in the Delaware District of the Cherokee Nation, and federal forces routed the Confederates, who then abandoned their supplies and fled to the Arkansas River. As Captain Sylvanus Howell from the Eleventh Texas Battery reported, "Nearly all the Batteries horses were shot in consequence of which we were unable to remove the battery from the field and the 4 guns, 3 six pounders and one 12 pound howitzer and 2 caissons were captured by the enemy."[57] Three more Choctaw soldiers fell at Fort Wayne: Chafatunobbee, Kelob Hoyupa, and Pisaryohtubbee. Soldiers from the federal Second Kansas Cavalry described the skirmish as a victory: "We engaged them and completely routed them, killing about 10 and wounding from 100 to 200."[58] Disgraced, Cooper was even accused of drunkenness, which allegedly had contributed to the defeat.[59] Such a result would hardly attract Choctaw recruits to the Confederate war effort.

At the same time of the Battle of Old Fort Wayne, the Tonkawa Massacre took place in the Leased District west of the Chickasaw Nation and highlighted the internecine conflict that the Civil War represented within Indian Territory. The Confederate-held Wichita Agency in the Leased District, the headquarters for the governmental official authorized to manage relations with the Wichita Indians and several other Native groups in the area, was at the center of the action.[60] The Wichita Indians claimed that their treaty with the Confederacy had been signed under duress, but other groups such as the Comanche and Tonkawa had signed willingly. The Confederate government was not able to meet its obligations for supplies and medicine included in the treaty. As Texans continued to make incursions at the agency despite their shared loyalty to the Confederacy, tensions rose to the point that Confederate Indian agent Matthew Leeper moved his family to the safety of Sherman, Texas. When pro-Union Natives, who reportedly included members of the Shawnee, Delaware, Kickapoo, Seminole, Cherokee, and Osage tribes, infiltrated the agency, some Confederate Indians joined the raiders because of their frustrations with Leeper and the Confederate government's unkept promises. Reports of the death of a Caddo boy and the suspected cannibalism of the Tonkawa suddenly focused the various groups' ire sharply on the Tonkawa. The Tonkawa reported to Superintendent S. S. Scott that they lost "twenty-three of their warriors, and about a hundred of their women and children," in the massacre.[61] The American

Civil War, then, could exacerbate tensions within Native groups and between Native groups, in some ways echoing the notion of the war as a fight that pitted brother against brother and friends against each other. Rather than stoke enthusiasm for the Confederacy, the Tonkawa Massacre revealed how convoluted the alliances between groups could be and how old grievances could persist.

By 1863, enlistment numbers had declined sharply: only 189 soldiers enlisted that year. Remember, officials had charted more than 1,000 enlistments in 1861 and nearly 800 in 1862. As in the larger Confederacy, by 1863 the Civil War had gone on much longer than anyone in Indian Territory expected. The realities of fighting, family separation, and being poorly provisioned dampened Choctaw enthusiasm for the war. As Confederate officer Edward W. Cade wrote to his wife in 1863, "I am sick of war" and "the separation from the dearest objects of life."[62] Surely many Choctaw soldiers would have agreed with this sentiment. For instance, Captain David Perkins resigned his command of Company E in the First Choctaw and Chickasaw Regiment in 1863 because of physical infirmity but also stated, "And last but not the least reason is, I have so many little children, unless I stay at home and provide for them they must necessarily suffer—as they have been during my first campaign."[63] These men felt the tug of family and home and knew the suffering of civilians as the war continued.

The few Choctaw enlistments that did occur clustered in the first half of 1863, in February, March, and April, with no enlistments occurring after July. Of course, on January 1, 1863, the Emancipation Proclamation issued by Abraham Lincoln took effect, ending slavery in rebelling states and parts of states. While it was unclear whether the proclamation applied to Indian Territory, news of emancipation did spread to Indian Territory.[64] If nothing else, Union troops often informed enslaved people in Indian Territory that the proclamation had changed their status; for example, Charlotte Johnson White learned of emancipation when soldiers arrived at her Cherokee enslaver's plantation.[65] Perhaps more relevant to Choctaw military enlistments was the activity in the Cherokee Nation in the first part of 1863. A pro-Union faction of Cherokees claimed rightful authority to govern and established a new legislature in February 1863. One of their first acts was to abolish slavery in the Cherokee Nation.[66] While many Cherokee slaveholders did not recognize the legitimacy of this new government and likely ignored this act, the fact remains that these actions brought abolition and the prospect of emancipation to the heart of Indian Territory. For some Choctaws, events in the Cherokee Nation may have hardened their resolve and led to the small clusters of enlistments in Skullyville and San Bois, locations in Mushulatubbee District close to the Cherokee Nation.[67] On the other hand, perhaps Cherokee emancipation and Lincoln's proclamation led many other Choctaws to see the Confederate chances for success declining, which softened overall enlistments.

In July, battles that included Union troops of African ancestry took place at Cabin Creek and Honey Springs, which also may have affected Choctaw enlistment numbers. Cabin Creek was located along the Texas Road, an important supply route for moving military matériel from Fort Scott, Kansas, to Indian Territory. The battle consisted of a series of skirmishes as Stand Watie's forces attempted to capture federal supplies. The Confederates eventually failed, and Watie blamed the defeat on his lack of cannon.[68] More remarkable is the diversity of forces present: troops from Colorado, Wisconsin, and Kansas; the Indian Home Guard; Confederate Indian troops; Texas Partisans; and the First Kansas Colored Volunteers all clashed on the battlefield.[69] Private Christopher Kimball of the Ninth Kansas Cavalry described the federal forces attempting the crossing: "Maj. Foreman assumed command, which consisted of the Indians, five companies of the colored regiment, the mounted men of the 2nd Colorado, and Capt. [Charles J.] Stewart's company, the 9th Kansas. Maj. Foreman, followed by Capt. [Bud Gritts], of the 3rd Indian, advanced into the stream."[70] Private Kimball's words paint a portrait of men of different races fighting together to preserve the country. In fact, historian Mark A. Lause suggests that the Union's tri-racial army in the west could have been a model for future race relations in the United States.[71]

Like Cabin Creek, Honey Springs was also located along the important supply route of the Texas Road. In July 1863, Confederate forces used the location as a staging ground to prepare an attack on Fort Gibson and push federal forces out of Indian Territory. Soldiers massed at Honey Springs and brought in supplies in preparation for the march to Fort Gibson.[72] Again, the fighting would include men of Native ancestry, men of African descent, and Euro-Americans, a fact not lost on those involved. As they waited for the command to advance, Colonel James M. Williams told the men of the First Kansas Colored Volunteers, "This is the day we have been patiently waiting for; the enemy at Cabin Creek [gave] you [the] opportunity of showing them what men can do fighting for their natural rights and for their recently acquired freedom and the freedom of their children and their children's children."[73] Colonel Williams also assessed his men's performance after the fighting: "They [the rebels] received a lesson which in my opinion, taught them not to despise on the battlefield, a race they had long tyrannized over as having no rights which a white man was bound to respect.

Choctaw battle flag. Choctaw troops flew this flag based on the seal of the Choctaw Nation in battle. Note the bow and two arrows and tomahawk at the center. (Wikimedia)

I had long been of the opinion that this race had a right to kill traitors and this day proved their capacity for the work."[74] Colonel Williams certainly understood the meaning of troops of African descent on this battlefield, for themselves and for the men they faced. Private Edward Folsom of the First Choctaw and Chickasaw Mounted Rifles was on the other side of the battle lines, and the troops of African descent made an impression on him as well. He remarked, "It was not long before the Federal cavalry found us and came over with Negro troops and give us fight. We had one side of Elk Creek and they the other. It was a stand up fight I never did see so many wounded Negro troops in a small fight."[75] Soldiers everywhere, not just in the South, were impressed and sometimes unsettled by the combat action of troops of African descent during the war, a force made possible by the Emancipation Proclamation.

The Confederates failed at Honey Springs because of inferior munitions supplies and, in part, the combined actions of the First Kansas Colored Regiment and the Indian Home Guard. The Confederates outnumbered the federals two to one but were outgunned three to one. And the inferior quality of the Confederate gunpowder meant that the downpour during the battle on July 17 rendered troops' arms useless, according to General Douglas Cooper.[76] As the fighting raged on, the federal regiment of Indian Home Guard inadvertently misled the Twentieth and Twenty-Ninth Texas Cavalry into thinking the federals were retreating. The Texans pursued, only to be met with a volley of bullets from the First Kansas Colored and forced to pull back. Then federal troops picked up the Texans' colors.[77] Tandy Walker arrived with Choctaw and Chickasaw troops late in the fight and was able to hold the federal forces as the Confederate forces continued to retreat. Dallas Bowman, a private from the First Choctaw and Chickasaw Mounted Rifles, remembered, "The Feds followed us about a half mile out on the prairie at which time our battalion charged on them and held them in check until the train could get out of the way."[78] Native troops, then, were important to both Confederate and federal forces in the battle. As the troops fled, General Cooper ordered the destruction of supplies and munitions located in Honey Springs. Corporal W. K. Makemson of the Confederate Indian Brigade led the squad that set fire to the commissary and quartermaster stores.[79] Henry Clay, who had been enslaved in the Creek Nation, remembered the smoke and fire as "the Yankees burn up Honey Springs," but in reality, he likely saw the results of Confederate efforts to keep supplies out of enemy hands rather than federal action.[80]

Some enslaved people also witnessed the battle and described the fighting and retreat years later. Creek freedwoman Lucinda Davis heard "de guns going all day, and along in de evening here come de South side making for a getaway. Dey come riding and running by whar we is, and it don't make no difference how much de head men hollers at 'em dey can't make dat bunch slow up and stop."[81] Davis's description matches Private Bowman's comments that Confederate troops scattered, "which caused confusion and we had a general stampede." Likewise, Private Edward Folsom reported that his company's picket "stampeded and broke for the mountains and most got away."[82] Phoebe Banks's uncle Jacob told her the fighting at Honey Creek "was the most terrible fighting he seen, but the Union soldiers whipped and went back into Fort Gibson. The Rebels was chased all over the country and couldn't find each other for a long time the way he tell it."[83] Banks's family had been owned by a Creek family and followed Opothle Yahola to Kansas. Uncle Jacob had returned to Indian Territory with federal troops to "fight the Indians who stayed with the South."[84] A disheartened Private R. McDermott from the Twentieth Texas Cavalry seems to confirm Uncle Jacob's account: "I belive [sic] they will whip us and whip us all the time until we are reinforced from Texas or some other point. I know it for I have tried them and they are as good as we are, better drilled and better armed. We got so much scatteredness in the stampede that we was 3 days getting together and not all have come in yet."[85] It seems that the Confederate soldiers truly had scattered across the country and did not immediately regroup for a counterattack or another engagement.

Battle of Honey Springs. ("The War in Arkansas—The Battle of Honey Springs, July 17. Defeat of the Rebels under General Cooper by the U.S. troops under Major-General James G. Blunt," from a sketch by James R. O'Neill, *Frank Leslie's Illustrated Newspaper*, August 29, 1863)

Some view Honey Springs as a turning point for Confederate forces in Indian Territory, after which white troops no longer defended the area in an organized manner; furthermore, the battle also marked a sharp decline in enlistments among Choctaw soldiers. The clash at Honey Springs proved to be the largest battle fought in Indian Territory based on numbers: approximately 9,000 men met in battle there, over 5,000 Confederates and some 4,000 Union soldiers. The Confederate loss left the Texas Road open for Union control and allowed federal troops to take Fort Gibson.[86] Moreover, the victory gave federal troops an avenue into the Choctaw Nation, "the fiercest and most steadfast of the Indian Nations in the Confederacy."[87] Given the scale of the fighting and the defeat, it comes as no surprise that the First Choctaw and Chickasaw Mounted Rifles did not see any new enlistments for the remainder of the year. The federals sent troops to Fort Gibson to strengthen its position in the territory, and July 1863 handed Confederate forces major losses.[88] Confederates were set back on their heels, and Choctaw soldiers may have viewed the southern effort as a losing one overall and declined mustering into service.

Whit Edwards states that the "desertion rate in the Confederate army in the Indian Territory was alarming" and attributes many desertions to the increased federal presence at Fort Gibson after the Battle of Honey Springs. However, the military records of the First Choctaw and Chickasaw Mounted Rifles indicate that in this unit, the vast majority of incidents of soldiers being absent without leave came before the actions at Cabin Creek or Honey Springs.[89] Rather, Choctaw soldiers were leaving their stations without permission most frequently in May 1863. May was a busy time for Choctaw agriculturalists. Soldiers may have returned home in order to plant crops with their families for the fall harvest.[90] And many soldiers returned to their companies in June before official rolls were taken on June 30, 1863. Perhaps soldiers had to appear on the June 30 roll to receive payment for their duty, or, again, had gone home to complete specific tasks and then returned to the fighting. War fatigue instead of the events of July may have been the explanation for permanently absent Choctaw soldiers. Nearly one-quarter of the deserters had enlisted in 1861 for a twelve-month term but remained on active duty in the summer of 1863. Another nearly 30 percent were in the middle of two-year enlistments, while 41 percent more were in the middle of three-year service terms. Such soldiers may have left their posts because they had tired of the war in general, not because of the specific battle losses.

The records for the Confederate Choctaw companies also reveal that desertion rates were higher in two companies in particular: Second Company C and Third Company H. Captain Willis Jones led Second Company C, in which thirty-five soldiers appeared as absent without leave. The soldiers had enlisted in July 1861 for twelve months and then reenlisted in July 1862 for two more years.[91] Thus, by May 1863, these soldiers had been serving for nearly two years. Perhaps some frustration with the length of the war was setting in. One officer, Second Lieutenant Abel McAfee, had been absent without leave since July 1862, when the company had reorganized and members reenlisted.[92] In Third Company H, the numbers are more startling: sixty-nine soldiers were listed as absent without leave. The company had formed in March 1862 with men enlisting for three-year terms. Clearly, something was driving the mass absenteeism in this unit in May 1863. Captain Lycurgus Pitchlynn led the unit, supported by Lieutenant Belvin Wilson. By November 1862, Lieutenant Wilson was dead, which likely decreased group morale. Moreover, Captain Pitchlynn himself was listed as a deserter and was dropped from the rolls by order of General Cooper in June 1863. Did the May absenteeism lead Pitchlynn to desert, or rather was his desertion symptomatic of a larger problem in the company?[93] Perhaps Pitchlynn's leadership was lacking and the soldiers voted with their feet. Or Pitchlynn may have tacitly approved of the men's actions because he himself planned to return home. Given Pitchlynn's own troubled past, which included a conviction for assault and battery with intent to kill and an admitted alcohol problem, the company's de facto dissolution under his command should come as no surprise.[94]

In 1864, the already sharply declining enlistment rates among the Choctaw dropped even further: there were only fifty-seven recorded enlistments. All of these fifty-seven soldiers enlisted in September at Goodland Station under the banner of Maytubby's Company. Goodland Station was located on the grounds of Goodland Academy, near the Choctaw Nation and Texas border in the southeast corner of Pushmataha District. Presbyterian and Congregational missionaries had founded the academy in 1848, and during the war Choctaw regiments camped on the school's grounds.[95] The company's namesake, Peter Maytubby, initially enlisted in June 1861 as a first lieutenant in Second Company D, formerly known as First Company H.[96] As a captain, he formed Maytubby's Company in 1864. The entire company enlisted for terms of "3 years or the war," phrasing I will discuss below. This slight boost in recruitment in 1864, which seems late in the war, may have been a response to some success achieved by General Cooper. Cooper consolidated his command and ambushed the Sixth Kansas Cavalry at Massard Prairie, located very close to Fort Smith on the border of Arkansas and Indian Territory, near Skullyville, on July 27, 1864. Earlier in July 1864, just prior to the events of Massard Prairie and the September bump in enlistments, the General Council of the Choctaw Nation also had passed an act directing the principal chief to form a brigade in conjunction with the Chickasaw for Confederate service for three years or "during the war." This may be the source of the language "or the war" for term lengths above.[97] So there may have been a broader push for recruits in the Choctaw Nation that led to the September enlistments. In the final year of the war, the records show just one enlistment, and that was to the US service rather than the Confederate regiment, in March.

Changes in the length of the term of service for Choctaw soldiers over the course of the Civil War reveal expectations about the length of the war and likely had something to do with waning enthusiasm for fighting. Over 1,000 enlistments record a twelve-month term of service. Almost without exception, these enlistments took place in 1861. That is, when Choctaw men joined the First Choctaw and Chickasaw Mounted Rifles early in the war, they agreed to serve twelve months. This term was in accordance with treaty agreements made between the Choctaw Nation and the Confederate States of America.[98] Moreover, many Choctaws probably could not have envisioned fighting that would last longer than one year. One young student at the University of Virginia predicted that the war would be brief because "the scum of the North cannot face the chivalric spirit of the South."[99] His northern counterpart in the Union army expressed a similar sentiment to his wife in early 1862: "You need not fret yourself about our staying in 3 years for we are whipping them too fast for that."[100] Other soldiers worried that the war would end before they could take part: a soldier in the Second Michigan wrote in 1861 that there was "a general fear that it will all be over before we have a chance to do anything."[101] Even Abraham Lincoln's first call for volunteers in April 1861 asked soldiers to enlist for only ninety days.[102] So confident was the northern public of the brevity of the war and of Union victory that civilians and senators arrived at the Battle of Bull Run in July 1861 with picnic baskets to observe the fighting, only to flee when the battle turned for the Confederacy.[103]

The Battle of Bull Run (known in the South as the Battle of Manassas) demonstrated to soldiers and civilians alike that the war might not merely be a brief spectacle but would be bloody and hard-fought. Recruits swelled the armies of both the Union and the Confederacy.[104] This phenomenon echoed in Indian Territory as well, with troops enthusiastically enlisting in the first year of the fighting. By 1862, Choctaw soldiers were no longer enlisting for twelve months but for longer terms. Over 400 soldiers enlisted for two years, and over 150 enlisted for three years. Many of the two-year enlistments came on the heels of twelve months of service. William Peter, for instance, enlisted in July 1861 at Perryville for twelve months and signed up for two more years of service at Camp Granite in July 1862. John Morrison started his military career at Skullyville in May 1861 and reenlisted in August 1862 at Camp Davis.[105] The majority of the three-year terms occurred in March 1862 in Nowood Red River County, long before the July 1864 act. Pissahonubbee initially enlisted for twelve months in May 1861 at Skullyville and then reenlisted ten months later at Nowood Red River County for three additional years. Another cluster of three-year enlistments were the Goodland enlistments for Maytubby's company in September 1864 discussed above. As mentioned, Maytubby's soldiers enlisted for "3 years or the war."[106] After three long, bloody years of fighting, perhaps officials recognized and hoped that the war might end before the soldiers' three-year term was over.

The military records show that by 1862, officials were offering Choctaw recruits a $50 bounty as a term of enlistment. Almost 400 Choctaw soldiers received the bounty, and the enlistments were concentrated in Doaksville, Eagletown, and Lukfahtah, locales all in the southern half of Apukshunnubbee District near the Red River and the states of Texas and Arkansas.

Almost all of the bounty recipients were members of Deneale's Company. The $50 bounty may have accounted for the high enlistment rates for 1862 and for the creation of Deneale's Company in particular. Remember, nearly 800 Choctaws enlisted in that year. According to a letter from Peter P. Pitchlynn to William Cass written in January 1862, Confederate president Jefferson Davis sent Colonel George E. Deneale to the Choctaw Nation "to raise a Regiment of Choctaw Warriors to go to Virginia." Further, Pitchlynn stated that that guns, horses, and clothing would be provided and asked for "healthy men" between the ages of eighteen and forty-five. The men were to meet at the Eagle County Court House and Doaksville. The monthly pay varied by rank: captains would receive $120, first lieutenants $94, and warriors (enlisted men) $24. In addition, warriors would also receive $25 for an initial purchase of clothes and a monthly clothing allowance of $2.50. By the end of the war, the warriors would receive a $40 bounty, which is less than the $50 listed on the enlistment records.[107] Pitchlynn did serve as a first lieutenant and received a $50 bounty but not the clothing commutation. While his letter suggests that officers in Deneale's Company would not receive the clothing allowance, the enlistment records indicate that officers such as Captain Ho Tubbee and Second Lieutenant Wilson Webster did.[108] And not every warrior received the clothing stipend, according to these records.[109]

Choctaw officials likely expected the Confederate government to pay the bounties. The Confederate States of America had agreed to "furnish now the above sum of five hundred thousand dollars to arm and equip said Regiment and maintain [it] in the field for that length of time [twelve months], and after the war and peace is established to reimburse the Choctaw, in said amount by the said Government of the Confederate States."[110] Likewise, soldiers in the various state militias and armies were offered bounties as an inducement to serve. By December 1861, it became clear that the war would not be short, and Confederate officials worried that the experienced soldiers would not continue to serve when their terms soon expired. Hence, the Confederate Congress passed an act to provide a $50 bounty and furlough of sixty days to those men who reenlisted.[111] Perhaps the $50 Confederate bounty in the rebelling states replaced the $40 mentioned by Pitchlynn.

Over 1,000 members of the First Choctaw and Chickasaw Mounted Rifles also received a $25 clothing commutation. For over 60 percent of these entries in the Compiled Service Record for the Choctaw Mounted Rifles, no date and place of muster was included, but the remaining records overwhelmingly represent enlistments that took place from May 1861 to June 1862, with a few outliers. The offer of bounties and clothing commutations mirrors recruitment efforts in the larger Confederacy. In February 1862, Joe Thompson's artillery company advertised a $50 bounty and $25 of commutation for "able-bodied men who wish to take part in driving the foe from Georgia's soil" near Savannah. In Dalton, a regiment raised by Colonel Jesse A. Glenn announced a bounty of $50, plus $50 annually for clothing, in addition to the monthly wage of $11 for enlistees. Colonel Glenn hoped to attract 1,000 volunteers with these inducements.[112]

By April, Confederate president Jefferson Davis had pushed a conscription act through the Confederate Congress to reinforce troop strength with soldiers who served longer enlistments and to centralize control over the Confederate forces.[113] However, one must also consider the fear that the bounties and furloughs would not attract enough soldiers as an impetus for the 1862 act and the Confederate conscription laws to follow. Each successive act enlarged the age pool of the men eligible for the draft, from males aged eighteen to thirty-five, then forty-five, to males aged seventeen to fifty, with men up to age sixty serving as home guards.[114] The Choctaw, on the other hand, did not resort to a draft to augment their troop strength. Rather, when Principal Chief George Hudson issued a proclamation in June 1861 stating "all citizens and residents of said nation between the ages of 18 and 45 years, subject to military duty, are required to enroll either in the volunteer or the reserve militia, according to law," with the aim of achieving a troop strength of 700 men, more than 950 men responded in June and July alone.[115] Historian Annie Heloise Abel describes Chief Hudson's proclamation as, "in effect, a conscription act."[116] The lack of coercive measures such as penalties for noncompliance and the flood of men who enlisted suggest that the proclamation was not quite a draft, despite Hudson's forceful language.

Instead, the Choctaw appear to have relied on volunteerism and inducements such as bounties and clothing commutations to fill the ranks of the First Choctaw and Chickasaw Mounted Rifles. As late as January 1865, Principal Chief Peter Pitchlynn recommended that the Choctaw General Council pass a "general Military law, which recognizes the volunteer system as just and efficient."[117] Again, Pitchlynn's language reinforces the idea that Hudson's proclamation was not regarded as a draft among Choctaws. Pitchlynn seemed to chafe at Confederate requests for the Choctaw Nation to contribute more troops to the war effort, because the nation needed men to remain to produce food and supplies for the families still living in the nation. Unlike the Confederate South, Pitchlynn continued, the Choctaw Nation lacked a large population of enslavers and therefore enslaved people to perform this important agricultural work. The Choctaw Nation was already doing its fair share for the Confederate cause. Moreover, within these volunteer units, Pitchlynn recommended that members of companies continue to select their own brigade and general officers by vote.[118] The commitment of Pitchlynn and the larger Choctaw population to a volunteer force came at a time when the Confederacy had already passed multiple iterations of conscription acts and was even debating the arming of enslaved people for the war effort.[119] There is no evidence of a discussion of the enlistment of enslaved people in the Choctaw legislative records.

As the war progressed, the lack of currency in the region west of the Mississippi River may have limited the Choctaw's ability to continue to offer funds for bounties and clothing commutations. When Confederate major general Theophilus Holmes took command of the Trans-Mississippi Department in August 1862, Holmes discovered that the western theater was basically bankrupt. Many of the troops had not received payment in as many as ten months, and civilian merchants were reluctant to sell supplies to the military because the Confederate War Department was already $13 million in debt.[120] General Holmes wrote, "The people refuse to sell any more to the Government on credit."[121] And if funds and supplies were limited for white soldiers, the situation was even more dire in Indian Territory. As historian Arrell M. Gibson noted, "Uniforms, weapons, and subsistence stores consigned to regiments in the District of Indian Territory were intercepted at Fort Smith and distributed among the Confederate troops massed about Belle Point."[122] That is, white Confederate troops confiscated supplies intended for Native soldiers.

Albert Pike was more direct about white troops seizing supplies intended for Native soldiers in a scathing letter to General Holmes in December 1862. Pike complained that General Thomas C. Hindman, commander of the Trans-Mississippi Department, had "stripped" Native soldiers of weapons and supplies that Holmes should have restored to Pike and his troops. Pike further accused Holmes:

> *You* will have *forced* the Indian to go to the North for protection. *You* will have *given away* their country to the enemy. *You* will have turned their arms against us. You will have done this by disobeying the orders of your Government, continuing the course it condemned, and to put an end to which it sent you out here; by falsifying its pledges and promises, taking for other uses the money which it sent out to pay the Indians, robbing them of the clothing sent by it to cover their

nakedness, and thus thrusting aside all considerations of common honesty, of justice, of humanity, and even of policy, expediency and common sense.[123]

In part, Pike was pushing back against allegations that he had mishandled funds himself; however, the common thread in the charges against Pike, Holmes, and Hindman is that Native troops were not being properly outfitted for the war. Instead, Native soldiers had to equip themselves.[124] When Pike resigned in July 1862, he wrote to the chiefs of the Cherokee, Creek, Seminole, Chickasaw, and Choctaw that troops had not been paid or supplied because those items had been intercepted.[125] Thus, cash and supplies were scarce, and the bounties and clothing commutations may have dried up.

The Choctaw, of course, already knew about shortages in supplies and currency despite the promises made by Confederate authorities in the alliance treaties. In February 1862, less than a year into the conflict, Choctaw major Mitchell LeFlore approached the Choctaw General Council to describe the condition of the Choctaw army. LeFlore said the troops were "suffering sickness & deaths" and presented a verbal petition for the appropriation of money for the army. He averred that if the council members saw the headquarters of the Choctaw troops, they would be convinced of the army's serious need. By October, presumably in response to a different request, the council discussed, amended, and passed an act allocating $2,500 to purchase munitions for the home guards and militia.[126] Despite the Confederate inability or unwillingness to meet its treaty obligations to supply the Choctaw war effort, Choctaw soldiers continued to enlist in large numbers, as discussed earlier. The numbers reflect the strong Choctaw commitment to the Confederate war effort, on which I will elaborate in chapter 5, before the turning point of the Battle of Honey Springs.

The other category of data on the muster records is the "Remarks" portion, and this section offers perhaps the most tantalizing information. By definition, information that showed up in the "Remarks" section was worthy of notation, that is, the record keeper thought it important enough to document and preserve. Most of the remarks concern whether or not soldiers were present or on the roll on particular dates, dates in August 1861, July and August 1862, and June 1863 being the most common; sometimes the remarks include information about soldiers who were wounded or killed in action or absent without leave, discussed earlier in this chapter. But other, sometimes revealing, information was also filed under "Remarks." These comments range from notations about horses to work details to promotions to petitions for action.

In view of the lack of supplies and the fact that the regiment was a mounted unit, perhaps the appearance of information regarding horses among the remarks was predictable. Moreover, horses had come to assume an important part in the economic and ceremonial lives of Choctaws since their introduction in the seventeenth century. For instance, horses were valuable tools in the deerskin trade and became a part of some Choctaw funerary rights. Choctaws even created a new Indigenous term to describe the animal, *isuba*, rather than adopt the Spanish term *caballo*, as some other Native groups did.[127] Thus, we find the report that Privates Robert Ballard, John W. Darnell, Edward Graves, and William B. Conner all lost horses at the Battle of Round Mountain in November 1862. Private Edwin Crawford's horse died at the Battle of Elkhorn Tavern (or Pea Ridge) on March 7, 1862. All five of these soldiers were affiliated with Company K. Surgeon Thomas Bond's records contain the note that three horses were mustered. While the note is brief, one might posit that additional horses may have helped Bond transport patients and supplies as he performed his medical duties. Horses ran away from Privates Cartilly, Alexander Durant, Kampillachubbee, and Thomas Charleston. While Private George McGee was present on June 30, 1863, his horse was gone for two weeks. Private Nicholas McGilberry left his horse at home. Even Private John Elias's and Second Lieutenant Jefferson Sexton's sick horses were noted in the official records. Sometimes soldiers were detailed to "hunt horses," as in the case of Private Lewis Hiarka and Sergeant Jimpson Jones. The horses were vital to the troops because the regiment was mounted, but horses also had other significance for Choctaws, an idea that I will return to in the next chapter.

In addition to assignments to hunt horses, the records include other details about the kind of work Choctaw soldiers performed. As discussed, the ranks of the soldiers included roles such as surgeon, bugler, musician, blacksmith, wagoner, and quartermaster. Additionally, the remarks reveal that several soldiers served as teamsters and hospital stewards. Private Thomas B. Stone served as farrier, taking care of the hooves of all of those important horses. Two soldiers from Company A, Ewing Moore and Jackson Perry, were tasked with transporting prisoners to Fort Smith. A number of soldiers, including Sowell Tamalacha, Ahhobantubbee, Alexander Gains, Sam John, John Lewis, Thompson Loring, Wall McCan, and Wilson Cage, all of whom were from Second Company K, spent time on duty searching for deserters. Several deserters, namely Privates Robert Joseph, John Paul, and Aaron Mishoontaba, were also from Second Company K, so it is likely that the soldiers assigned to find the deserters were looking for men they knew and may even have called friends. Moreover, all of these men, both the searchers and the deserters, had also enlisted at Sulphur Springs on June 12, 1861. Again, this hints at the potential for more than a casual acquaintance among the men. This example also demonstrates the benefits of looking at these records in the aggregate; possible connections among soldiers are revealed.

Military officials also recorded promotions and transfers under "Remarks." For instance, combining the information about rank and remarks shows Charles Strickland's movement through the ranks from corporal to sergeant major to second lieutenant and Albert Carney's move from private to second lieutenant to first lieutenant. William Loring was elected second lieutenant from the position of bugler. Simon Edward was elected to first lieutenant from private when John Levi was promoted to captain. And John Levi's records indicate that his election to captain came because S. R. Jones became a major. Likewise, John Martin moved from private to captain when Sampson Loring became a major. Soldiers would later elect Loring lieutenant colonel. The death of Nathan Talbert precipitated Cyrus Hamilton's promotion to fourth sergeant. June 1863 was a popular month for transfers, likely because it coincided with many men's reenlistment date: a few soldiers transferred to Captain Loring's company, and a larger number of soldiers transferred from the command of Captain Wilkins to Captain Krebbs. A few soldiers transferred to companies outside of Indian Territory. After serving for nine months in First Company K, William L. Wade transferred to Colonel Green's Texas regiment in March 1862. First Lieutenant Matt Daugherty chose Company E of the Twenty-Ninth Texas Cavalry when he reenlisted in 1862. Daugherty, who was from Denton, was likely white, given his ability to serve as an officer in the Twenty-Ninth Texas Cavalry, a non-Native unit.[128] Contrary to the negative perceptions of some white Americans, these details demonstrate that Native soldiers moved through the ranks and transferred between units in organized fashion, just like their white counterparts.

Sometimes the records of individual soldiers create a fuller narrative beyond muster dates and clothing commutations. When J. Mobbly joined the regiment in May 1861 as a lieutenant, he surely did not know what adventures would befall him. The documents in Mobbly's file present his story. Captured at Ponchatoula, Louisiana, in May 1863, Mobbly was placed on the steamer *Maple Leaf* by Union officials, along with ninety-six other captured Confederate officers. The ship was transporting the prisoners of war from Fort Monroe, Virginia, to Fort Delaware. The prisoners were bound for Johnson's Island in Ohio; however, on June 10, 1863, the prisoners overpowered the dozen guards on the *Maple Leaf*.[129] While some of the officers remained aboard and returned to Fort Monroe, the other seventy escaped to the banks of North Carolina on smaller boats. Local troops led by Captain Willis B. Sanderlin concealed the men, and civilians in the area fed them. Eventually, the escapees made their way to Richmond. There were enough men involved in this incident that record-keeping officials produced a preprinted form on which to record the particulars; Mobbly appeared on a "Roll of commissioned officers at New Orleans, La., captured in the Department of the Gulf," along with the date of his capture and a preprinted summary of the details. Read from bottom to top, Mobbly was among fifty commissioned officers received by Captain C. W. Killborn, provost marshal of the Parish of Orleans. Killborn had transferred the men to Major J. W. Burgess of the Sixth New York Regiment of Volunteers, who then delivered the prisoners to Major General John A. Dix at Fort Monroe. During the next stage of movement from Virginia to Delaware, the prisoners revolted.

The records do not report when Karrew Brown joined the Second Choctaw Regiment, but he does appear on a roll of prisoners of war captured at Gaines Spring in the Creek Nation in August 1863. Federal troops captured Durant Hicks and Erastus Hogue at the same time.[130] After Brown's capture, federal forces held him under guard at Fort Smith, Arkansas, until he was transferred to Fort Gibson. Officials then moved him from Fort Blunt in Indian Territory to Fort Scott in Kansas. A "Descriptive List" indicates that he was forty years of age, five feet eight inches tall, with dark hair and eyes. Under "Remarks," an official noted that he was "Indian." By October, he had become a "political prisoner" at Gratiot Street Military Prison in St. Louis, Missouri. Soon thereafter, officials listed Brown on a report of sick and wounded soldiers at the Gratiot Street Prison hospital. And by November 25, 1863, Brown had died from inflammation of the lungs. The brief notes about transporting prisoners and lists of sick and wounded present a narrative of the last few months of Brown's life, a story of confinement and illness.[131]

Had Brown lived, perhaps he would have followed the path of his fellow soldiers Hicks and Hogue. Like Brown, after being captured at Gaines Spring, these soldiers moved through various federal camps in the region until they arrived at Gratiot Street Military Prison in St. Louis.[132] A recuperated Brown then might have accompanied Hicks and Hogue from St. Louis to Camp Morton, Indiana, in November 1863. The men remained at Camp Morton until they were transferred to City Point, Virginia, by way of Baltimore, Maryland, for exchange in March 1865. Hicks and Hogue were among

3,499 Confederate soldiers, including 143 officers, exchanged at Boulware and Cox's Wharves on the James River. The next month Hicks, described as a twenty-year-old with a "very dark" complexion and black hair and eyes, took the oath of amnesty in Charleston, West Virginia. He swore before Provost Marshal William Gramm that he would

> henceforth faithfully, protect and defend the Constitution of the United States, and the union of the States thereunder, and that I will, in like manner, abide by and faithfully support all Acts of Congress, passed during the existing rebellion, with reference to slaves, so long and so far as not repealed, modified, or held void by Congress, or by decision of the Supreme Court; and that I will in like manner, abide by and faithfully support all proclamations of the President, made during the existing rebellion, having reference to slaves, so long and so far as not modified or declared void by decisions of the Supreme Court. And I furthermore swear, that I take and subscribe to this oath for no other purpose than that of *"restoring peace and establishing the national authority."* So help me God.[133]

Private Jameson Colbert also ended up at Camp Morton, Indiana, after being captured at Fort Smith in August 1863. Colbert had served in Cooper's Regiment only for "4 moons" and wanted to take the oath of allegiance and "remain loyal." In December 1863, First Lieutenant Mark Hoyt noted that Colbert was a Choctaw Indian and ended his account of Colbert's intentions to remain loyal with the comment "Doubtful." Perhaps Hoyt's feeling is the reason Colbert did not enlist in the US service until over a year later, in March 1865.[134]

The language of the oath of allegiance made plain the centrality of slavery to the cause of the war. Slavery appeared in the oath not once but twice. Oath takers pledged to abide by congressional acts and presidential proclamations made about the institution of slavery. Lincoln's Emancipation Proclamation, of course, loomed in the background. At the same time, the oath recognized the potential impermanence of such acts and proclamations. The acts could be "repealed, modified, or held void by Congress, or by decision of the Supreme Court," and presidential proclamations were effective "so long and so far as not modified or declared void by decisions of the Supreme Court." The oath read as an enticement to those Confederates who wanted to preserve the institution of slavery because the acts and proclamations that threatened it could be overturned or rescinded and slavery permitted to continue. If the Confederate government surrendered, the continuance of slavery would be up for negotiation, the oath suggested.

Finally, the oath asserted that the oath taker was motivated by "no other purpose than that of 'restoring peace and establishing the national authority.'" Committing to end slavery was not the purpose of swearing allegiance to the federal government, nor was fear of physical harm; instead, peace and national authority were the goals of oath takers. Confederates, whether from Indian Territory or southern states, sought to preserve slavery; hence, federal officials performed this verbal dance with the oath. The oath avoided the sting of emancipation by referring to it only obliquely and then implied emancipation could be undone. In this way, federal officials hoped to elicit the support of Confederate sympathizers for the Union.

The subsequent use of the loyalty oath outside of military service also highlights the puzzling legal status of Native peoples in relation to the federal and state governments. For instance, the federal government used the administration of loyalty oaths to citizens in Confederate states to determine which southern landowners could hire out the labor of "contraband" enslaved people who had sought refuge with the Union army.[135] In state elections in Maryland in 1863, voters decided to limit the suffrage to those who swore the strict loyalty oath, which included a statement "that one had never expressed a 'desire' for Confederate victory."[136] Later, white southerners who took the oath of loyalty could regain access to land and civil and political rights.[137] It is unlikely that federal officials considered Native landowners in Indian Territory potential employers of "contraband" enslaved people during the war. And Choctaw soldier Jameson Colbert was not a citizen of a southern state, nor did he have the right to vote in state or federal elections; thus, swearing this oath would not grant him later access to such rights. Choctaw and other Native soldiers could swear the oath of loyalty, but as citizens of other sovereign nations, the action did not come with other rights. Likewise, the federal government did not attempt to apply the acceptance of the oath as an index for readiness for self-governance among Native peoples as it did for southern states through action such as the 10 percent plan, which required 10 percent of the 1860 voting population to swear the oath of allegiance before a state could establish a new government and rejoin the Union.[138] Native nations were not seeking to join the federal government. Native soldiers, then, could swear this oath of allegiance, but with very different consequences.

The presence of prisoners of war and the oaths they took to achieve their freedom not only highlighted the importance of the issue of slavery and the ambiguous legal status of Native people, but Albert Pike claimed that the exchange of prisoners such as Hogue and Hicks also had another unintended consequence. He complained to Major General Holmes that federals used the exchanges to send messages to the Native populations in Indian Territory: "While *you* were thus stopping their clothing, and robbing the half-naked Indians to clothe other troops, the Federals were sending home the Choctaws whom they had taken prisoners, after clothing them comfortably and putting money in their pockets." Embedded in this statement was an explicit critique of Holmes for prioritizing white troops at the expense of Native troops. Moreover, Pike suggested that federal officials were filling that material void by providing supplies and currency to the Choctaw prisoners of war and then returning them to Indian Territory. How could Choctaw troops and civilians fail to see that the enemy was better provisioning Choctaw soldiers than their Confederate allies? Thus, Pike concluded, "no one need be astonished, when *all* the Indian[s] shall have turned their arms against us."[139] Hicks and Hogue may have returned to the Choctaw Nation and spread precisely this message, either intentionally or by their mere well-fed and well-clothed presence. Still other prisoners of war such as Private John Billy were not exchanged but were paroled instead. Private Billy reenlisted in July 1862 for two more years after completing his twelve-month term only to desert his company two months later. Two months after that, in November 1862, he was paroled in Fayetteville, Arkansas, by order of Union brigadier general John McAllister Schofield.[140]

The miscellaneous accompanying records reveal that the companies of the First Choctaw and Chickasaw Regiment also sometimes took prisoners while in battle. The Record of Events for Third Company H describes nine companies on scout from Camp Prairie Springs in June 1863. On the morning of June 16, they encountered federal forces and "Pins" about twelve miles away from Fort Gibson.[141] "Pins" or "Pin Indians" have variously been characterized as abolitionists or Unionists, though those terms are not the same thing, and are most often linked to the Cherokee and the Keetowah Society. Historians often describe members of Pin societies as "full-bloods" or less assimilated or less acculturated into American culture. The name seems to come from the practice of holding meetings in conjunction with bowling games using pins in the woods, in order to hide the true nature of their activities, as well as the pins they wore to identify themselves to other members.[142] In action against the Pins and federal soldiers, Third Company H suffered no casualties or deaths except for a horse. After five days of scouting "with 2 pins & three negroes," the company took five prisoners and would subsequently lose two more horses. The company record remains silent on the fate of the five prisoners.

A specific petition for the promotion of Colonel Sampson Folsom to brigadier general frequently appeared within the individual files of soldiers.

In fact, the request appeared regularly enough that when the military records for the First Choctaw and Chickasaw Mounted Rifles were consolidated in the early twentieth century, records officials created a preprinted form for such petitions. The signatories were all officers. The request from June 1862 read, "Petition to the Secretary of War from Officers of the Indian Regiments in the service of the Confederate States, requesting that Col. Sampson Folsom of the 1st Choctaw Regiment be appointed Brig. Gen. in the P. A. C. S."[143] PACS was the abbreviation for the Provisional Army of the Confederate States. The Confederate government had passed an "Act to raise Provisional Forces for the Confederates States of America, and for other purposes," which gave the president authority to control military operations, receive troops from the states, and form the Provisional Army of the Confederate States in February 1861.[144] The specific agreement between the Choctaw and Chickasaw and the Confederate government had permitted the Natives to elect their own officers below the rank of colonel and promised that the troops would "not be marched beyond the limits of the Indian country west of Arkansas against their consent."[145]

These petitions for Folsom's promotion reflect the tradition of electing officers below the rank of colonel but also recognize that the Confederate president had the power to choose the men who served at higher ranks. For their part, Native troops may have preferred being led by Native officers because of disputes about whether Indian troops could be ordered beyond Indian Territory against their consent by white leadership, in violation of the 1861 treaty between the Confederate government and the Choctaw and Chickasaw. For instance, despite General Albert Pike's attempts to honor treaty stipulations and not force Confederate Indian troops to fight outside of Indian Territory, Confederate command staff pushed for Pike to take his Indian soldiers into Arkansas to fight back the federal advance at Pea Ridge, also known as Elkhorn Tavern.[146] Early in the war when he was still a colonel, Douglas Cooper thought Indian troops should be sent wherever they might be needed in western military campaigns, especially as scouts.[147] The petitioners may have hoped that Folsom's promotion to brigadier general would give Natives more input in choices made about troop deployment and the disbursement of supplies.

Colonel Folsom was not the only Choctaw soldier supported by colleagues for a position. Officers urged the appointment of Dr. Thomas J. Bond as surgeon for the regiment in a handwritten petition in July 1862: "The undersigned commissioned officers in the 1st Regiment of the C&C M. Riflemen C. S. A. having confidence in the professional skill & ability of Dr. Thomas J. Bond, take pleasure in recommending him for the position of principle [sic]

Surgeon of the Regiment & Respectfully solicit his appoint for the same."[148] The petition also reveals that Major Mitchell LeFlore was likely illiterate, as he signed with "his x mark." The same officers made a similar recommendation for Dr. E. P. Kearby to serve as the assistant surgeon of the regiment.[149] And several soldiers signed testimonials on behalf of Lieutenant J. S. Tooly, though the preprinted forms do not reveal the nature or purpose of the testimonial.[150] Thus, petitioning for the promotion of fellow officers or affirming the character of colleagues was not unusual.

Other records that appear in individual files include typical statements about disability, resignations, and petitions for discharge from service. Often these statements were related. For instance, First Lieutenant Mitchell McCurtain's file included a certificate of disability from Surgeon George Lebantp, who found McCurtain to be "afflicted with paralysis of the left arm." McCurtain tendered his resignation "owing to disability to discharge" his duties.[151] Lieutenant John Mollattubbee resigned from his position in Company A on account of disability. His file includes a statement certifying his disability ("chronic ophthalmia and chronic otorrhea") from an examining board of surgeons.[152] Ophthalmia is eye inflammation, and otorrhea is a discharge of liquid from the ear. Captain Asa King's individual letter of resignation from July 1864 appears, along with an official special order that included King and the names of several other officers from outside of Indian Territory who were all resigning at this time; the list included two captains from the Texas cavalry and three officers from units in Louisiana.[153] As the war entered its fourth year, more soldiers lost the physical ability, and perhaps the enthusiasm, to continue fighting.

Unsurprisingly, the service records contain few references to women and offer little information about the experiences of women in Indian Territory during the war. The records reflect a broader omission; that is, material from the Indian Pioneer History Collection and WPA slave narratives offer only glimpses of women during the war. For instance, accounts of Opothle Yahola's flight to Kansas, such as Phoebe Banks's above, describe women and children as part of the Loyal Creek camps.[154] Mary Grayson, owned by the Creek Perryman family, remembered her mother crying when Grayson's father and uncle contemplated joining the Union war effort and bearing the brunt of Perryman's anger when the men did in fact leave.[155] And Lucinda Davis, from this chapter's opening, provides a firsthand account of the Battle of Honey Springs. These women represent the roles we might expect: refugee, civilian, and witness. But then there is Christine Bates's passing reference to Choctaw women who served as messengers during the war and risked torture if captured by northern soldiers.[156] Bates reminds us that

Choctaw Confederates included women who were willing to risk life and limb to support the Confederate cause. Given the demonstrated strength of Choctaw support for the Confederacy, the presence of such women should be expected, given our knowledge of women such as Rose Greenhow, Sarah Slater, or Olivia Floyd who served as Confederate spies during the war.[157]

The possibility of women being captured as prisoners of war, though slim, existed. Prominent Choctaw Peter P. Pitchlynn wrote to his nephew John early in the war about the treatment of female prisoners: "Should you take any female prisoners take good care of them and bring them home, but we don't want any abolitionists—let such go back to the north, way up beyond Kansas." He urged John to pass this admonishment respecting the treatment of female prisoners on to John's cousins William and Ebenezer Pitchlynn, who were both officers serving in the Choctaw regiment.[158] This brief statement came in the midst of news about sick relatives and assertions of enthusiasm for the war effort. Clearly Peter Pitchlynn thought it was possible that women would participate in fighting for the enemy or supporting the enemy, which perhaps reflected his own understanding that Choctaw women would do the same. And he encouraged good treatment for any female prisoners, perhaps demonstrating the hope that any Choctaw women taken prisoner would also be well treated. Pitchlynn's comments may refer to the idea circulating in Indian Territory that federal officials were imprisoning women. If official statements from the Cherokee government were to be believed, female prisoners were not just a possibility; they were a reality.[159]

The Compiled Service Records for the soldiers of the First Choctaw and Chickasaw Mounted Rifles provide a window into the experiences of Civil War soldiers in Indian Territory. These troops seldom left other kinds of records such as journals or diaries, and letters home were rare indeed. Service records include important information about when and where soldiers mustered for battle, the length of their enlistments, and why some of them left. Like their fellow Confederate soldiers, Choctaws rushed to serve early in the war, but their commitment waned as the war dragged on longer than anyone had anticipated and especially after the Battle of Honey Springs. Half of the men in the regiment enlisted in 1861. In particular, Opothle Yahola's opposition to allying with the Confederacy and fighting at Pea Ridge may have sparked some Choctaw enlistments. Age data from the records indicate that Choctaw soldiers were a little older than their American counterparts. And a wave of desertions in May and June 1863 may have had more to do with seasonal agricultural patterns than with specific battles or events.

The accompanying records in the service jackets, while uneven and unpredictable, offer further glimpses of daily life for Choctaw troops. The importance of horses, for instance, becomes apparent. For a mounted regiment, horses obviously would have been essential, and notes about lost or killed horses confirm that idea. The records track the movement of federal prisoners of war from camp to camp and show that some would choose to swear the oath of loyalty and even join federal units; other prisoners of war were exchanged. The records also include more mundane, though consequential, information such as petitions for promotion, letters of resignation, and certificates of disability. The records offer the opportunity to add meat to bare-bones data about troop movements and battle losses. They reveal a picture of enthusiastic enlistees at the beginning of the war whose support for it waned as they were plagued by poor provisions and increasing desertion as the war progressed. Choctaw Confederates were not so different from southern Confederates in many respects. What the Civil War meant for Choctaw notions of masculinity, on the other hand, did differ from ideas held by Euro-Americans, the topic of the next chapter.

Chapter 5

Earning One's Name

WARFARE AND
CHOCTAW MASCULINITY

Many texts discuss the transformative power of the Civil War experience on the lives of soldiers. Scholars explore how soldiers coped with the carnage and tremendous loss of life they witnessed and made meaning of the fighting.[1] Little of this literature considers Native soldiers. The records available in the Compiled Service Records of Confederate Soldiers Who Served in Organizations Raised Directly by the Confederate Government, discussed in the previous chapter, offer some insight into the military experience of Choctaw soldiers and glimpses of their interior lives, but this chapter examines the impact of military service on Choctaw notions of masculinity more broadly. The Civil War gave Choctaw men the opportunity to tap into some traditional masculine roles that had been limited by a changing political and economic landscape. Here I will first summarize the traditional ways that Choctaws conceptualized masculinity around warfare in the eighteenth century. Then I will trace the shift in Choctaw definitions of manhood as opportunities for warfare declined, with particular attention to the role of lighthorsemen in the nation. Finally, I will turn to the Civil War experience and the ideas about manliness that reemerged because of it. Some of the activity revealed in the personal correspondence and military records examined in chapter 4 take on different meaning when viewed through the lens of Choctaw ideas about masculinity.

Recall the discussion of traditional gender roles in Choctaw society from chapter 1. Choctaw women were agriculturalists who provided corn to their families, and Choctaw men provided meat through the hunt. Men also served as warriors. One index of the importance and value of warriors among the Choctaw was the ratio of warriors to non-warriors in their society. Gary Coleman Cheek Jr. found that the ratio varied among the Choctaw between 1:4 and 1:2, when the more populous Cherokees had ratios that ranged between 1:5 and 1:6.[2] That is, on the low end of the ratio, there was one Choctaw warrior for every four non-warriors, or as many as one Choctaw warrior for every two non-warriors. Such numbers reveal that a larger portion of the Choctaw population relative to other Indian populations in the southeastern United States, such as the Creek, Chickasaw, and Cherokee, served as warriors. Choctaw men were ranked in part based on their status as warriors: *mingoes* were peace and war chiefs, "beloved men" were leading warriors, common warriors had not distinguished themselves in some way, and then there were "those who have not struck a blow or who have killed only a woman or a child." Seating arrangements at ritual and political assemblies reflected this ranking, with venerated and older warriors occupying an inner circle surrounded by younger and less accomplished warriors.[3] In part, this emphasis on warriors may have stemmed from the coalescent origins of the Choctaw in which emerging groups competed with each other for resources and warriors protected communities.[4]

Early visitors to North America also commented on the importance of martial activity to ideas about masculinity among Indigenous groups that shared ideas about gender roles with the Choctaw.[5] For instance, French traveler Louis Armand Lahontan noted that among Natives, "the true Qualifications of a Man are ... to understand War."[6] Lahontan himself had been a soldier, so he had direct contact with Native warriors. He also spent several years journeying throughout the Great Lakes region, particularly among the Iroquois, in the late seventeenth century, and he learned to speak Algonquin.[7] Thus, Lahontan's observation that, within Natives' understanding, war was of vital importance in becoming a man holds some weight. Historian Gilles Havard summarized the observations of Jesuit missionary Joseph-François Lafitau, who worked among the Iroquois: "'The men ... are properly born only for great things, especially for warfare,' which they see as 'a necessary exercise.'"[8] Similarly, Lafitau also asserted that "war has, for all the Indians, such singular attractions that they seem to be born and live for it."[9] Lafitau's comments highlight the importance of warfare in Iroquois society: it was a "necessary exercise" that they seemed to "be born and live for." Moreover, among Natives warfare was the domain of men, in Lafitau's observation. These early French eyewitnesses in the Great Lakes region, then, offer some sense of the long history of the importance of warfare to masculine identity among the Iroquois in particular, which we can apply also to the Choctaw.

While this discussion focuses largely on the connection between masculinity and warfare for Choctaw men in the context of a male-female binary, I must note that there was also space for two-spirit individuals to participate in warfare because Native ideas about gender were more fluid. Historian Roger Carpenter comments on the involvement of both biologically male and biologically female two-spirit individuals in warfare. In many Native societies biologically male two spirits "doffed their feminine attire in wartime, picked up their weapons, and accompanied the other men into battle." Other warriors often found the presence of these two spirits beneficial because of the belief that two spirits had greater access to spiritual power.[10] Though less common, Carpenter also presents cases of biologically female two spirits among peoples of the Northern Plains and Plateau regions who served as warriors.[11]

Because warfare performed a different function in Native society than in Euro-American society, what constituted a victory also differed. Prior to the nineteenth century, Choctaws "intimately associated masculinity with spiritual power."[12] And because activity as a warrior was how a Choctaw youth became a man, Choctaws drew a connection between warfare and spiritual power as well. Success in warfare did not mean just the capture of specific territory or the slaying of one's foes: "Success in war satisfied the spirits of the deceased, weakened enemies, elevated one's standing in the community, and brought all the resulting benefits to a warrior's family, clan and village."[13] There was spiritual value to battlefield success, according to the Choctaw, and that value extended far beyond individual warriors. It is not surprising, then, that Choctaws and Euro-Americans might understand the same military event quite differently. Take the colonists' burning of unoccupied Cherokee villages in the mid-eighteenth century, for instance. Natives did not interpret this action as a victory because the colonists did not permanently occupy the settlement, nor did they defeat any warriors there. And burning crops was certainly not a manly activity, particularly given that agricultural work was performed by Cherokee women, not men. The colonists, however, could return to their white settlement and claim victory after such an event because they had destroyed Native homes and fields. Further, Native leaders did not consider retreat inglorious or a defeat, even when it included warriors. Rather, retreat was a prudent strategy to minimize risk to one's people.[14]

Nineteenth-century observer of the Choctaw H. B. Cushman described young Choctaw men's training as consisting of "war, hunting, and ball playing." These three activities, then, were central to notions of Choctaw masculinity. In preparation for warfare, young Choctaw men "were required to pass through many hard exercises of the body in order to inure them to hardships and suffering. They were required to receive inflictions of tortures on their naked bodies, once a year, and also to plunge into deep water and dive four times in about one minute, during one of the most cold and frosty mornings."[15] Training for battle was a serious matter and quite physically demanding. "Ancient Choctaws" viewed war as "the most patriotic avocation in which a man could engage."[16] Further, it was the province of men: Choctaw women's "maxim was—men for war and hunting; while home is the place for women." Hunting was an important activity that contributed meat to the diets of Choctaw families, meat that complemented the corn produced by Choctaw women. But hunting also incorporated a skill important for battle: marksmanship. Young men diligently honed their aim with the bow and "hardly ever miss a deer or turkey at the distance of fifty yards."[17] The last element of Choctaw young men's training was ball play. Sometimes called "the little brother of war," ball play provided an opportunity to break up the tedium of daily life outside of times of warfare and demonstrate the kind of strength, agility, and fearlessness a Choctaw man should possess as a warrior.[18] Ball play could also be used to settle disputes in avoidance of war, as when the Choctaw and Creek used a game to settle a dispute over ownership of a beaver pond in 1790.[19] Each of these defining activities of Choctaw masculinity was related to warfare: to its actual practice, to the skill involved, or as its substitute.

Among the Choctaw the connection between masculine identity and warfare was best demonstrated by naming practices. Choctaws often had several names over the span of their lifetimes. Choctaw parents usually named their children based on animal attributes or some event that occurred near the time of the child's birth.[20] In later life, Choctaws assumed a new name based on military exploits or some other event. For instance, prominent Choctaw chief Pushmataha was also known as Koi Hosh, which means "panther," as well as Ossi Hosh. *Ossi* means "eagle" in the Choctaw language.[21] These two names referred to his quick movements and "daring exploits in war." But Pushmataha was also known as Oka Chilohonfah, which means "falling water," because of the "sonorous and musical intonations of his voice."[22] And the name Pushmataha itself was a corruption of *A-num-pa-ish-ta-ya-u-bi*, which means "a messenger who kills."[23] Another Choctaw warrior who had been known by the name Ahaikahno, "the Careless," earned a new name after a skirmish with Muscogee Indians. Ahaikahno pursued the Muscogee ahead of his fellow warriors and was in the process of scalping one of the enemy when two Muscogee warriors rushed him. Ahaikahno could not see the men approaching, but his Choctaw comrades could and shouted a warning: *Chikke bulilih chia*, which translates to "Quickly run you!" Ahaikahno made his escape and thus carried the additional name Chikke Bulilih Chia.[24] The various names of these warriors demonstrate the transformative power of warfare for Choctaw men's identities. Names could also tell a story about the kind of warrior one was and thereby reveal important characteristics.

French captain Joseph Christophe De Lusser, stationed in Mobile in 1730, described a post-battle naming ceremony. De Lusser was in the Choctaw town of Chacachae and observed warriors returning from a battle one morning. The men arrived "bedaubed with paint like those of the Yellow Canes and passed howling" in front of De Lusser's cabin. Clearly, they were calling the attention of the community. The warriors who had participated in the fighting sat on the ground in a semicircle with the "captains and honored men" sitting on a bed of canes, in an example of ranked seating arrangements as described earlier. De Lusser and Reverend Father Beaudouin joined the place of honor on the bed of canes. He continued, "After this they made several warriors. . . . This ceremony consisted only of changing the names."[25] De Lusser's account suggests that the change wrought by war on men could be immediate: the men had scarcely returned from battle, and one of the first orders of business was to acknowledge their conversion to warriors and their new identities as men with a name-changing ceremony. As scholar Greg O'Brien asserts, "Names were the fundamental signifiers of masculinity, and they meant everything to a Choctaw male."[26]

The martial activity that earned Choctaw youth new names could also secure them positions of authority within their communities. Again, because of the connection between warfare, masculinity, and spiritual power, many Choctaws saw successful warriors as possessors or manipulators of spiritual power. Hence, those men were obvious candidates to serve in leadership positions, not only in matters of war but also in negotiations with outsiders.[27] In fact, by the nineteenth century, warriors had gained so much prominence in Choctaw society that they sometimes usurped the traditional social order by publicly challenging civil chiefs or altering the chiefly line of succession. Pushmataha and Mushulatubbee rose to power in the early nineteenth century because of their military success fighting Osage and Caddo Indians in the west. Mushulatubbee succeeded his father Chief Homastubbee instead of Homastubbee's nephew (his sister's child), as should have been the case because of the practice of matrilineal descent, on the basis of his military prowess. And Pushmataha was not connected to the chieftainship through maternal descent at all but managed to gain the position nonetheless due to his martial exploits.[28]

A lack of participation in martial activity could likewise erase one's name. H. B. Cushman related the story of the only son of a great Choctaw war chief, a story repeated by former principal chief of the Choctaws Peter P.

Pitchlynn in 1870.²⁹ As the subject of the story grew into a handsome young man, he discarded the name of his youth with the expectation that he would earn a new name as a warrior. Once he "distinguished himself in war either by slaying an enemy, taking a prisoner, or striking the dead," he would participate in the tribal councils of his people. While his fellow Choctaws knew him to be brave and of good character, he must earn this new name to become a full member of his community nonetheless. The new name, then, would be more than a name; rather, it would signify his ability to contribute to decision-making for his community. Moreover, until he earned this new name, he would also be unable to marry, despite the fact that he had a willing partner, a beautiful young Choctaw woman. She is notably unnamed in the legend, a point to which I will return. Somehow, the opportunity to show his bravery in battle never materialized, and so he never earned his new name. Instead, he became known as Chatah Osh Hochifoh Keyu, "the Nameless Chahtah."

Soon, circumstance offered Osh Hochifoh Keyu another opportunity to earn his name and a wife. Along with 400 Choctaw warriors, he prepared to go on an expedition against the Osages. Finally, he would earn his name and marry. But a strange turn of events again denied him the opportunity to fight. His compatriots were discovered and killed while he was away as a scout. Another Choctaw scout returned to the village and mistakenly reported Osh Hochifoh Keyu's death. In her grief, Osh Hochifoh Keyu's betrothed "at once began to droop and soon withered away." Meanwhile, Osage warriors pursued Osh Hochifoh Keyu for several days, and he lost his way so that "he found himself to be a bewildered man, wretched and forlorn." Osh Hochifoh Keyu did not return to his village for a year, and only then after an appeal and sacrifice to the Great Spirit and the intervention of a "snow white wolf of immense size." Upon Osh Hochifoh Keyu's arrival, no one in the village recognized him, and he did not reveal his identity. He found that the villagers were mourning the death of his betrothed, and he joined them by chanting "his wild songs ... to the memory of his loved one" and visiting her grave nightly until he died there. When community members found his body, they finally recognized him as Osh Hochifoh Keyu.³⁰

The legend of Osh Hochifoh Keyu is both a tragic love story and a cautionary tale. The tragedy lies in Osh Hochifoh Keyu's bad luck as a warrior and the false report of his death. Love stories center on the strength of the emotions between the lovers, and the feelings between Osh Hochifoh Keyu and his unnamed paramour were so powerful that neither could live while the other did not. The cautionary element of the story focuses on the importance for Choctaw men of earning their names through martial activity. Osh Hochifoh Keyu's inability to earn this new name became the most salient feature of his identity and placed him in a liminal space. This liminal position had real consequences. Osh Hochifoh Keyu could not marry; in other words, he could not claim an important right of manhood. For southeastern Natives more broadly, martial prowess qualified men for marriage. French traveler Louis LeClerk de Milford remarked in the late eighteenth century that Creek youth who did not manage to bring "back at least one scalp always bore his mother's name and was unable to find a wife." Milford's comment again emphasizes the importance of the name change to signify the transformation from youth to mature man. On the other hand, men who demonstrated an abundance of skill as warriors were able to marry more than one wife. Trader Thomas Nairne observed earlier in the same century that Chickasaw men who proved themselves to be great warriors often had multiple wives.[31] In one sense, Osh Hochifoh Keyu's inability to be successful as a warrior prevented him from being a fully adult male: he could not participate in the decision-making of the tribal council and could not marry. A new name would have signaled both his civic and his sexual maturity.

Also worth discussing is the lack of a name for the object of Osh Hochifoh Keyu's affections. She is beautiful, of course, and devoted, but her name (or lack of name) is not essential to the story. In fact, her name is irrelevant in a way that Osh Hochifoh Keyu's name most certainly is not. In one version of this tale, it is upon Osh Hochifoh Keyu's return to his village and discovery of his dead lover that we have a name for her: Osh Hochifoh Keyu refers to her as Imma, or the idol of warriors.[32] It is unclear, however, if this was a name she bore in life. If we combine both versions of the legend, it would appear that her community did not know her as Imma, because Osh Hochifoh Keyu's use of her name at her graveside did not reveal his own identity. We also do not know if she referred to herself by the name Imma privately or if Osh Hochifoh Keyu bestowed this name on her in his grief. More broadly, the legend suggests no need for a name change for Osh Hochifoh Keyu's lover to become eligible for marriage. Choctaw girls did not have to demonstrate their entrance into womanhood through external activity; rather, biology in the form of the onset of menstruation offered an obvious marker for this transition, demonstrating fertility and involving the potent substance of blood.[33] Traditional Choctaw practice required menstruating women to completely separate themselves from their families, with wives even avoiding the gazes of their husbands during their cycles.[34]

Thus, a Choctaw girl's entrance into reproductive maturity was a fairly public development that did not require a marker such as the assumption of a new name.

In general, names held power in Choctaw society. For instance, Choctaw women did not speak the names of their husbands, and observers insisted that Choctaws were reluctant to reveal their own names.[35] Like Choctaw men, Choctaw women might gain other names over the span of their lifetimes, as in the case of women who incorporated cattle into their names as they became more involved in the care and preparation of the animals. Some Choctaw women took on the name Wakaihoner, which means "cow cooker."[36] But Choctaw women's lack of new names did not preclude marriage or limit their social roles, as it did for Osh Hochifoh Keyu. This discussion of the meaning and power of names for Choctaws also adds weight to my contention in chapter 4 that the names recorded on the military enlistment records for the First Choctaw and Chickasaw Mounted Rifles, be they traditional, of European origin, or a blending of the two, reveal the cultural influences at play in the Choctaw Nation.

After the time of Osh Hochifoh Keyu and before the tensions that gave rise to the Civil War, Choctaw ideas about masculinity changed. Historian Greg O'Brien places the critical moment of change in the second half of the eighteenth century.[37] For O'Brien, contact with Europeans altered notions about what kinds of activities denoted "real" Choctaw men. Choctaws shifted from performing deeds to focusing on material goods to define masculinity.

Native groups traded with Europeans for goods such as guns, ammunition, and clothing, some of which also became signifiers of elite male status among the Choctaw. European-style clothing gained particular importance: Choctaw chief Appapaye asked British officials in 1771 to "make us look like men by Clothing us. . . . Let the great King be told that his Children and the Chactaws look like men."[38] This notion that one merely had to "look like men" is a remarkable departure from a sense of manhood derived from action. In traditional Choctaw thinking about manhood, outward appearance factored not at all; rather, a demonstration of bravery or skill in battle was paramount. After all, Osh Hochifoh Keyu was the son of a chief, well regarded by everyone in his community, and described as quite handsome, but none of this mattered in the absence of some accomplishment in battle. He could not earn a new name based on appearance or reputation. By contrast, Chief Appapaye's request placed appearance above action.

Specific trade goods were especially important in marking Choctaw masculinity. O'Brien observes, "Because red was the color of war, the red coats supplied by the British to elite Choctaw men during British rule in the Gulf South reinforced their positions as great warriors and war leaders." The red coats were so linked to British soldiers that the clothing became a kind of shorthand to refer to British troops. Thus, for Choctaws the red coat had a double connection to martial activity because of its color and its function, which meant red coats were that much more meaningful to masculine identity. Elite Choctaw men also favored medals stamped with images of European monarchs. The medals were a physical connection to other elite males in Europe and had the added benefit of entitling the bearer to "extra gifts while visiting European posts." Possession of one trade good yielded access to yet more trade goods. Trade goods such as manufactured clothing gained such esteem among Choctaws that a contemporary observed that Choctaws who could afford to do so preferred to be buried in European-made clothing and blankets, while poorer Choctaws wore animal skins in death.[39]

Trade goods had been an important marker of elite status, though not necessarily masculinity, long before the arrival of Europeans. Archaeological evidence indicates that as early as the period from 1100 to 1500, chiefs in the southeast region distributed luxury trade goods among community members to make claims to authority. Their ability to access items such as conch shells and copper from far-flung locales such as the Gulf Coast and the Great Lakes also cemented their status as elites. A loss in the ability to obtain and transmit such goods could lead to a chiefdom's collapse.[40] In some ways, then, European manufactured goods replaced these older valued items. The Europeans did not introduce a new system; rather, they introduced new items into an existing system that conferred status largely on men for distributing trade goods. Nonetheless, there was still space in these societies for individuals to earn merit. Patricia Galloway examined the arrangement of burial spaces and the goods associated with them to determine that, in a place such as Moundville, individuals' relative importance "was based on their achievements."[41] Given the descriptions of how Choctaw youth entered manhood through feats of warfare, access to such goods was not what made a man in this era, though it could improve a man's status.

So even though Choctaws had traditionally valued trade goods and used them as markers of elite status, it was not until the late eighteenth century, O'Brien argues, that access to and possession of European trade goods became implicated in notions of Choctaw masculinity.[42] The expanding market for Choctaw goods and products led the Choctaw to implement new systems of livestock management and cotton cultivation and fostered in turn a demand for liquor and manufactured goods on the part of the Choctaw, which led to indebtedness and land sales to pay off that debt, with devastating consequences, according to Richard White.[43] Choctaws became increasingly dependent on Europeans for goods vital to survival, such as food and clothing. The market also permitted the accumulation of goods and wealth that led to the increased stratification of Choctaw society, which could give rise to tensions between individuals. The reliance on outsiders to provide essential manufactured goods had important consequences for masculinity. That is, growing dependence on outsiders for the basics of survival, or being unable as a Choctaw man to provide some of these essentials, could be a blow to masculinity. As one Choctaw man said as early as 1772, "We are . . . incapable of making necessaries for ourselves, our sole dependence is upon you."[44] Choctaw men could no longer claim to be independent. And in the Choctaw context, independence meant both this ability to provide "necessaries" and also the ability to contribute to the well-being of their families and communities in partnership with Choctaw women.

Unlike Richard White, James Taylor Carson does not argue that the introduction of European trade goods led strictly to Native dependency. In his more nuanced consideration, Carson finds that the effect of European practices and products was uneven and could vary by gender. For instance, the presence of potshards at archaeological sites in multiple locations occupied in the eighteenth century suggests that Native women continued to make pottery and trade their wares alongside a growing number of European trade goods. On the other hand, as Native men increasingly relied on European firearms, they made fewer traditional items such as bows and arrows. Though Native men may have been able to repair the guns in their possession with some difficulty, they could not produce ammunition or make new guns, so they required trade to acquire more guns and more bullets.[45] Native men, then, were more dependent on the market and trade than were Native women.[46]

Carson also describes the cultivation of livestock, another activity introduced by Europeans, as a valuable part of the Choctaw economy. The Choctaw gained familiarity with raising pigs and horses in the eighteenth century and had begun raising cattle by the nineteenth century. By virtue of communal landownership, individual Choctaws had access to plenty of land on which their animals could forage. When they were ready, they rounded up animals to be penned and then transported the livestock to market. Before the mid-nineteenth century, Choctaw cattle holdings were substantial: Carson found that "in 1828 the cattle herd numbered over 43,000 head, a ratio of 2.07 cows per person," which exceeded the 1840 ratio for Mississippi of 1.8 cows per person.⁴⁷ Livestock became such an important part of the Choctaw economy that it entered into naming practices. Choctaw men and women sometimes incorporated *waka*, which meant "cow," into their names. In addition to Wakaihoner mentioned above, Choctaw men sometimes adopted the name Wakatubbee, or cow killer. Choctaw men and women owned this livestock individually, which raises interesting questions about how the care and control of livestock comported with Choctaw gender norms.⁴⁸ One might presume that animal husbandry would fall to Choctaw men because of their traditional role as hunters and providers of meat. For instance, the slaughter of the cows for meat would be performed by Choctaw men, hence the name Wakatubbee.⁴⁹ On the other hand, *alhpoa*, a Choctaw term for cattle, means "fruit trees such as are cultivated." This language permitted cattle to fall under the purview of Choctaw women as agriculturalists. Further, Carson posits that Choctaws were linking cattle to fruit trees because of their similarities: both produced valuable foodstuffs, milk or fruit, that were harvested by women.⁵⁰ I would suggest women's relationship to lactation as another reason that the care of cattle might fall to them. Choctaws were able to successfully incorporate livestock into their economy and address the care and slaughter of animals through existing ideas about gendered labor.

Choctaws' growing reliance on the care and raising of animals as part of their economy may have produced another consequence for ideas about masculinity. The experience of the Creek provides a parallel example. In their lands, cattle owned by European colonists often crowded out other animals, such as deer and bears, by damaging the flora that attracted such animals. Historian Claudio Saunt notes that many Creeks complained about the arrival of cattle in two separate treaties with Britain in 1763 and 1765. One Creek figure grumbled "that the west side of the Savannah River was 'settled all over the Woods with People Cattle and Horses, which has prevented them for some Time from being able to supply their Women and Children with Provisions as they could do formerly, their Buffalo, Deer and Bear being drove off the Land and killed.'" Creek hunters, then, could not reliably provide enough meat for their communities and turned to the raising of livestock themselves.⁵¹ In one sense, Creek men who became ranchers could still perform their traditional male role of meat providers for their families. On the other hand, they did so in a more sedentary fashion instead of through the chase or hunt. Would providing meat in this way carry the same social weight for masculinity as hunting? Choctaw men faced similar pressures on their ability to hunt and may also have embraced raising livestock to fill the need for meat. Moreover, as Choctaw women shouldered some of the work of livestock cultivation, the role of meat provider did not remain exclusive to men.

The Choctaw turn toward ranching also reflects the reality that deer populations had declined precipitously due to overhunting. European settlers' cattle and pigs may have trampled important grasses for deer subsistence or encroached on the territory of bears, but hunting for the market also put these animals in jeopardy. Even before the dawn of the nineteenth century, white-tailed deer in the Choctaw borderlands were so scarce that one observer reported in the 1770s "that during my circuit through the nation we never saw any."[52] The French had been cultivating a relationship with the Choctaw throughout the eighteenth century and offered advantageous terms to purchase all of the deerskins that Choctaw hunters could provide. By 1725, the French had traded for more than 4,000 deerskins from the Choctaw. In an astonishing uptick, during just two months in 1732, the French purchased 2,200 deerskins.[53] The French demand for deerskins must have seemed insatiable to Natives such as the Choctaw. French traders offered hunting items and military goods rather than domestic objects in exchange for deerskins, which led many Choctaw men to hunt for deerskins for trade with the French rather than for meat to provide for their families. And the deerskin trade may have seemed less restrictive to Native households because individuals could trade directly with Europeans for goods without elite Natives' oversight.[54] As nearby forests were depleted of deer, Choctaw men had to travel farther abroad to hunt.[55] So, again, incorporating livestock into their economy made a great deal of sense to many Choctaws, as it supplied meat reliably and close at hand and produced a surplus that could be sold outside of the nation for funds to purchase other goods.

The shift from the deerskin trade to animal husbandry had profound consequences for Natives of the broader southeastern region and reveals that Native peoples engaged in complex strategies to meet their own economic interests. Rather than view this shift as cause and effect—that overhunting of deer led to a turn to animal husbandry—zooarchaeologist Barnet Pavao-Zuckerman argues that the process was more of a push and pull. Her examination of faunal remains concludes that "deer were not extirpated from the inland Southeast." She posits that engaging in the deerskin trade suppressed the turn to animal husbandry because of the demands each made on time and labor, and it was when Creeks lost access to "hunting lands to grazing and white encroachment" that they embraced livestock cultivation, which required less land. But both strategies, hunting deerskin or raising livestock, gave Creeks access to manufactured goods, and Creeks adjusted their economic activity to the circumstances on the ground.[56]

Native peoples across the Southeast were engaged in a similar calculus as they determined which economic activities to adopt and how to incorporate those activities and attendant demands on labor into their existing gendered labor systems.

The expansion of stock raising among the Choctaw also reinforced the role of lighthorsemen in the Choctaw Nation, a position limited to men. H. B. Cushman describes the creation of the lighthorsemen as coinciding with the arrival of Christian missionaries to the Choctaw in the early nineteenth century, which is not to say that missionaries caused the formation of lighthorse companies.[57] Other southeastern Natives also adopted the use of lighthorsemen around this time. For instance, Cherokees created a mounted police force in 1797 that would be known as lighthorsemen in the 1820s.[58] And the Creek established a lighthorse force in an 1840 legal code.[59] While all of these groups were similarly targets of proselytization, Native people had their own reasons to formalize law enforcement bodies connected to changing economies, shifting ideas regarding property, and encounters with outsiders that required resolution. In the Choctaw Nation, each district had a company of armed police who traveled the countryside on horseback and settled disputes or arrested lawbreakers. Tradition had dictated that murderers be punished by relatives of the deceased, but lighthorsemen took over this function to serve as "sheriff, judge and jury."[60] The earliest mention of lighthorsemen in official documents appeared in the 1820 Treaty of Doak's Stand. Article 13 provided that chiefs "raise and organize a corps of Light-Horse, consisting of ten in each District, so that good order may be maintained, and that all men, both white and red, may be compelled to pay their just debts." This force had a social and economic function: to regulate behavior and enforce economic transactions. The lighthorsemen also removed "bad men," those without legal permission to be in the Choctaw Nation, from the territory.[61]

By 1827, Choctaw authorities extended the duties of lighthorsemen to include whipping thieves and outlined punishments when the stolen goods were livestock. The punishment varied depending on the item stolen: 100 lashes on the bare back for a stolen horse, 50 lashes for a cow, and 30 lashes for a pig. For other stolen items, a judge determined the number of lashes.[62] This statute is revealing in a number of ways, as discussed in chapter 1. First, it demonstrates the importance of livestock to the lawmakers: they attached specific punishments to the theft of these three items in particular, but judges made decisions about how many lashes should be administered for other stolen items. Second, the statute makes plain the value placed on each kind of livestock: clearly the horses were most valuable and the pigs the least so. Finally, the statute shows the growing importance of personal property. Choctaws were accumulating enough property that others would resort to theft to obtain it. Property accumulation was a marked departure for a society that held land communally and shared food. The office of the lighthorsemen developed, in part, to protect private property, and being mounted "enabled Choctaw males to maintain a martial function in their society" when they were participating in a less-than-warlike activity: protecting pigs, horses, and cattle.[63]

Christina Snyder, on the other hand, does not focus on changing economic forces as the impetus for changing concepts of Choctaw masculinity; rather, she turns to the declining practice of warfare. Snyder notes that Peter P. Pitchlynn had learned of the story of Osh Hochifoh Keyu as a boy and frequently told it as an elder. Perhaps the story resonated with Pitchlynn because he was born at a moment in Choctaw history when there were no longer wars to fight. By the end of the Seven Years' War, many European powers had already ceased to deploy Native groups against each other, a development that Choctaw men detested.[64] One Creek chief urged a federal agent to permit "the customary small-scale warfare between the Cherokees, Creeks, Choctaws, and Chickasaws" that had long been used by young men to practice their skills as warriors and enter manhood: "There is among us four Nations old customs, one of which is war. If the young, having grown to manhood, wish to practice the ways of the old people, let them try themselves at war."[65] War had held a meaning for southeastern Indians that went beyond struggles for territory or control over people; rather, it had shaped the fundamental transition from boy to man.

Without warfare, how would the young men of Pitchlynn's generation earn their new names and become eligible to marry and participate in the political life of their communities? How could they avoid the fate of Osh Hochifoh Keyu? Such young men "had to imagine a different future, another path to manhood."[66] Snyder posits that, for this generation of Choctaw youth, pursuing education at institutions such as the Choctaw Academy offered another way to defend their communities. English literacy was a valuable tool for Choctaws in economic transactions and political negotiations. Thus, while figures such as Pitchlynn might have had fewer opportunities to demonstrate their manliness during raids or in warfare, they could educate themselves to craft the most beneficial business deals and treaty agreements possible for the Choctaw Nation.[67] To that end, Pitchlynn attended Nashville University. He returned to the Choctaw Nation, assumed leadership of the lighthorsemen force in 1824, and then negotiated a treaty with the United States shortly thereafter to provide a permanent annuity to pay for this force.⁶⁸ Pitchlynn took full advantage of the ways to access masculinity available to him in the absence of regular warfare: obtaining an education, serving as a lighthorseman, and participating in political negotiations.

The growth of the responsibilities of lighthorsemen provided Choctaw men another way to express their identity as warriors when wars between Native peoples appeared to be declining. Legislation authorized lighthorsemen to kill armed, drunken men who committed crimes.⁶⁹ This legislation highlights the endemic growth of alcohol consumption and the problems associated with alcohol's overconsumption. Choctaw women who levied false rape allegations were subject to twenty-five lashes on the bare back to be administered by lighthorsemen.⁷⁰ Actual rape was punishable by thirty-five lashes.⁷¹ The combination of the passage of these two laws necessarily provokes difficult questions about whether the crime of rape and false allegations about rape were on the rise in the Choctaw Nation. Another statute gave lighthorsemen the latitude to determine sentences and execute people in the most serious criminal cases.⁷² If we cast lawbreakers as enemies of the Choctaw people, the lighthorsemen served to protect the people, sometimes with lethal authority, much as a warrior would have done in the past against other Native groups. Finally, the Choctaw General Council held in contempt anyone who "verbally abuses and threatens" members of the lighthorse company, which publicly demonstrated the esteem in which the lighthorsemen were held, again, much as warriors were held in high regard in the past.⁷³

A few years later, the Choctaw General Council passed other laws that targeted alcohol and included the lighthorsemen as law enforcement officers. For instance, the destruction of "any whiskey or other ardent spirits" brought into Choctaw Nation now fell to the lighthorsemen. Moreover, if a death resulted because someone took up arms and refused to hand over their whiskey for destruction, the lighthorsemen would not be held liable.⁷⁴ Another 1834 statute reiterated the power of members of the lighthorse company to execute criminals, in this case murderers.⁷⁵ The problem of alcohol consumption had grown enough that drunken criminals were no longer the only problem; now authorities wanted any whiskey to be destroyed, and those who fought to retain possession of their alcohol could be killed. In an attempt to discourage the importation of alcohol, the General Council fined anyone who brought whiskey into the nation in order to sell it. To encourage informants to report such activity, they would receive a reward paid from the fine. If the offender could not pay the fine, the lighthorsemen were empowered to impound the offender's property and sell it in order to pay the fine.[76] In another preemptive move to decrease alcohol consumption, the General Council stipulated that lighthorsemen "visit all of the neighborhoods in their respective districts at least twice in every year, and to advise the people to abstain from spirituous liquors."[77] Again, the council referenced alcohol as a problem. Moreover, implicit in this directive that lighthorsemen urge people to abstain from alcohol was the idea that lighthorsemen were seen as respectable figures of authority in the larger Choctaw populace.

The lighthorsemen also had important duties that increased over time regarding livestock. Unclaimed stray cattle (those having roamed for at least six months and with no identifying marks) were to be sold after six months, with the proceeds to be divided between the person who found the animals and the national public fund. The lighthorsemen were in charge of this process.[78] A year later, the General Council passed similar legislation with regard to stray horses; however, the time scale was longer. Stray horses would be held for twelve months before being sold, again with the proceeds divided between the finder and the Choctaw Nation. District clerks would receive one dollar for each stray animal sold within their district. Lighthorsemen would manage the sales.[79] Peter Pitchlynn eventually proposed that the lighthorsemen also provide full descriptions of all stray horses and cattle to the district courts.[80] Other statutes regarding livestock did not mention the lighthorsemen directly, but enforcement likely fell under their purview. For instance, abusing a horse "by ill usage and by disfiguring him by shaving his tail and mane" was punishable by a fine of up to ten dollars.[81] Individuals surely reported accusations of abuse to lighthorsemen, who then had to collect the fines. Another legal provision prohibited "Indian" doctors from confiscating the personal possessions of a patient who died under their care, specifically "horses, cattle, hogs, or guns." If a doctor's treatments were effective, he could accept whatever payment was offered to him "but such as goods he shall have a right to take."[82] It would have been lighthorsemen who intervened when doctors demanded payment despite bad outcomes or who returned the property to the patient's family. All of this legal activity concerning livestock also underscores the value Choctaws placed on the animals and the growing importance of raising livestock to the Choctaw economy.

Choctaw authorities reaffirmed and expanded upon the duties of lighthorse companies in their constitution after the nation's removal to Indian Territory. First, the 1838 Choctaw Constitution gave lighthorsemen the very important job of managing elections.[83] The lighthorsemen directed the candidates for office to form their lines of electors and appointed the judges who counted the votes. Within the judicial system, the lighthorsemen performed many valuable functions. Under the direction of judges, the lighthorsemen summoned persons accused of crimes and witnesses to court.[84] A year later, the Choctaw General Council would strengthen this power when it declared that "any person or persons refusing to obey the summons of the Officers aforesaid, by taking up arms or weapons against said Officers shall be liable to be killed or taken by force of arms."[85] Legal proceedings, especially criminal trials, would have difficulty moving forward without the work of the lighthorsemen. And the council empowered the lighthorse companies to carry out these functions important to the operation of the judiciary. Lighthorsemen also were responsible for removing people who settled in the wrong location, too close to saltworks, or within 450 yards of other citizens' improvements.[86] Salt was valuable in food preparation and preservation as well as in the raising of livestock. While Choctaws held land communally, disputes could arise over improvements, so more widely dispersing settlement mitigated conflict. All of these expanded powers and duties of lighthorse companies led Robert M. Jones to propose that four additional men be appointed to each district in 1839, though his proposal does not appear to have been approved.[87]

The management of noncitizens, that is, individuals whom Choctaws understood as outsiders, also fell to the lighthorse companies. Lighthorsemen figured prominently in a capacious law intended to manage the issue of free people of African descent in the nation. The 1840 act included a provision for the expulsion of all free people of African descent "unconnected with the Choctaw and Chickasaw blood" within six months. Clearly, individuals had ignored the prohibition on settlement for "free negroes" already contained in the 1838 Choctaw Constitution.[88] Now the lighthorsemen would round up, hold in custody, and then sell to the highest bidder those free people of African descent who remained in Choctaw country. The captain of the lighthorsemen would provide the legal bill of sale. With virtual impunity, lighthorsemen could kill or maim free people of African descent who engaged in "hostile resistance" to being placed in custody. Choctaw citizens who attempted to evade the law's intent by harboring or hiring free people of African descent without Choctaw or Chickasaw blood were subject to fines between $250 and $500 or the physical punishment of fifty lashes on the bare back. Previous legislation made the lighthorsemen responsible for collecting fines and administering corporal punishment; thus, while not named explicitly, the lighthorsemen would have punished Choctaws who aided free people of African descent illegally in the Choctaw Nation. The statute ordered white men who aided or concealed "free negroes" to leave the nation. Interestingly, the chief or the agent would be the responsible party in cases involving white men, presumably because lighthorsemen did not have jurisdiction over American citizens, under the Trade and Intercourse Acts discussed in chapter 3.[89]

Another category of noncitizens was enslaved people emancipated by their Choctaw enslavers. While Choctaw legislators had intended the 1838 constitutional provision to prevent the settlement of free people of African descent in the nation and the 1840 statute to expel any free people of African descent without Choctaw or Chickasaw ancestry from the nation, neither legal maneuver addressed the possibility of emancipation as a source for a growing population of noncitizens of African descent. Thus, in 1846 Choctaw lawmakers required enslavers to petition the General Council to free enslaved people of African descent. Enslavers had to demonstrate that they had no outstanding debts because enslaved property could, of course, satisfy claimants. Then the General Council could pass an act emancipating the enslaved person. Last, emancipated people had to leave the Choctaw Nation within thirty days of the passage of the General Council's act to free them. Failure to comply would lead to dire consequences: any person of African descent freed in this manner who returned to the Choctaw Nation would be "subject to be taken by the light-horse-men and exposed to public sale for the term of five years."[90] In other words, emancipated people who returned to the Choctaw Nation to be near family and friends, the familiarity of their old neighborhoods, or Choctaw culture faced five years of what amounted to indentured servitude. Again, lighthorsemen enforced this act to limit the number of noncitizens of African descent in the Choctaw Nation.

Lighthorsemen played an important role in the regulation of enslaved human property as well. While an 1840 Choctaw statute called on everyone to apprehend suspected fugitive enslaved people, it was the lighthorsemen who managed their sale after six months.[91] This law calling on civilian assistance in capturing runaway enslaved people resonates with provisions of the Fugitive Slave Act of 1850. The language of the Choctaw statute is forceful: "it shall be the duty of any one in this Nation to take up a negro whom he may suspect as a runaway." Just ten years later, section 5 of the American law stated that "all good citizens are hereby commanded to aid and assist in the prompt and efficient execution of this law, whenever their services may be required."[92] That is, enslavers seeking runaway enslaved people in the United States could call on the aid of any citizen to recapture his or her human property. The laws obligated bystanders in both the Choctaw Nation and the United States, no matter their feelings about the practice of slavery nor their relation to the institution, to participate in the capture of suspected fugitive enslaved people. In some ways, the lighthorsemen's responsibilities regarding both enslaved and free people of African descent were remarkably similar to their responsibilities regarding livestock: rounding up people, holding them until sale, providing official documentation of the purchase. The status of enslaved people as chattel, as property, in this scenario cannot be clearer.

Because the lighthorsemen functioned as a national police force in the Choctaw Nation, the General Council also passed a series of laws outlining more mundane responsibilities for the company and its management. For instance, lighthorsemen presented those who disturbed religious meetings to judges in order to be assessed fines.[93] The General Council also provided for lighthorsemen to be assigned to each of the various public schools in the nation with duties to include returning runaway children to the schools.[94] To punctuate the national nature of the lighthorsemen's duties, the General Council designated the pistols issued to the force by the United States government as public rather than personal property. Hence, upon the death or resignation of a lighthorse company member, his pistol became the property of his successor rather than a family member or some other heir.[95] The General Council also passed various laws over time regarding the pay and size of the lighthorse force and expanded their duties as a part of legislative activity. For instance, one lighthorseman from each district was to be present at General Council meetings to serve as sergeants at arms.[96] The lighthorse force in different districts could vary: recall that the Treaty of Doak's Stand had called for ten lighthorsemen for each district, and Robert Jones's had requested four more lighthorsemen for each district in 1839, but in 1842 the General Council gave chiefs in Pushmataha and Mushulatubbee districts the authority to reduce their forces to six.[97] Later, these districts would again add more members.[98] Pay for lighthorsemen increased over time with the possibility of earning extra money for performing additional duties, such as serving as the above-mentioned sergeants at arms.[99]

The position of the lighthorsemen offered Choctaw men an opportunity to enact their masculinity at a moment when the traditional method of facing an outside enemy in battle and returning triumphantly was less possible. Rather than threats to security or from people from other Indigenous groups, Choctaws faced attacks on sovereignty, on land possession, and on the practice of traditional activities. The lighthorsemen were an adaptation to new realities. The raising and sale of livestock became important parts of the Choctaw economy, and lighthorsemen protected and regulated stray animals. Choctaw people increasingly valued property in general and guns in particular, and lighthorsemen also worked to preserve this property. Elections became a central part of Choctaw governance to determine the chief and the composition of the General Council; lighthorsemen organized the election process. As Choctaws moved away from clan law to adjudicate disputes and relied on a judicial system with judges and witnesses, lighthorsemen ensured that the witnesses and criminals would appear in courts. Lighthorsemen also meted out punishment by collecting fines and confiscating property, whipping guilty parties, and carrying out executions in the most serious cases. Thus, in the absence of warfare, some Choctaw men might turn to negotiation to protect their nation's political and economic interests, while others could turn to the protection of the public welfare through the work of the lighthorsemen. Lighthorsemen defended innocent people from criminals and brought justice to the guilty. Moreover, the lighthorsemen performed their duties atop horses, another connection to Choctaw men's former roles as warriors and hunters.

Many of the duties of lighthorsemen centered around the control of livestock and alcohol, a development with interesting connotations if we consider historian James Taylor Carson's assertion that "to fulfill their traditional roles and responsibilities, men had to find new ways to demonstrate their social and economic worth. Drinking and raiding offered two viable and popular alternatives to hunting and warring."[100] Because by the nineteenth century raiding typically involved stealing horses from the farms of white settlers and trading them for alcohol, it combined two important responsibilities of the lighthorse company. To reiterate, Choctaw men were not engaging in warfare as frequently because European powers and then Americans frowned upon and discouraged this activity. Choctaw men were also hunting less frequently because overhunting had caused a dramatic decline in the populations of animals such as deer and bears. Traditional notions of manhood based on prowess as a warrior or hunter were under assault. Lighthorsemen, then, were asserting a new form of Choctaw masculinity by limiting other Choctaw men's ability to tap into different kinds of masculinity in the form of horse raiding and drinking alcohol.

In the American context, horse raiding and theft have a complicated history, because these activities connect to traditional Native practices but could also have specific meaning in relation to white settlers. Historian William McLoughlin describes horse raiding as "an understandable and acceptable source of plunder" in wartime and "a source of revenge, of excitement, of courageous achievement for those denied other means of self-esteem and success" during peacetime. Horses were acceptable spoils of war that victors could claim and transport to home villages. Their acquisition could tangibly mark a warrior's skill. As traditional game animals declined, hunters who did not want to return empty-handed might steal horses to sell or trade for valuable foodstuffs or manufactured goods. In this case, the stolen horses were something of a consolation prize. The theft of horses could also serve another function: McLoughlin describes horse theft as a way to enact revenge on white interlopers and demonstrate one's wit or bravery, something more akin to the function of warfare. That is, warfare gave men the opportunity to exact revenge on enemies and show their daring and cleverness, and so did horse theft. Horse raids were also far more profitable while being less time-consuming than planting and harvesting crops for market.[101] Thus, for Choctaw men who did not want to engage in farming and wanted a more familiar way to articulate notions of masculinity, horse theft may have held some appeal. Raiding the settlers for horses and cattle was often one way Choctaw men could both punish these squatters and express Choctaw masculinity.[102]

Choctaws referred to alcohol, which they frequently obtained through the trade of raided horses, as *oka homi*, or "bitter water," and *oka humma*, or "red water." Bitter water referred to alcohol's taste, but using the color red to describe alcohol, Carson argues, connected alcohol to warfare. Choctaws were not the only Native population to link alcohol and warfare. For instance, Izumi Ishii finds that Cherokees viewed alcohol "as a war medicine" to be consumed in preparation for going to battle, as well as an "accoutrement of war," among gifts such as guns and ammunition frequently presented to warriors by Europeans.[103] Carson posits that the overindulgence in alcohol was generational among the Choctaw; that is, while men and women of all ages imbibed rum, "chiefs and colonial officials identified young men as the most conspicuous and troublesome consumers of alcohol." Young "warriors" without the traditional outlet of warfare were the most likely to engage in drunken and violent behavior, both among themselves and against white settlers.[104] Because article 4 of the 1786 Treaty of Hopewell empowered Choctaws to punish American citizens who attempted to settle on Choctaw lands, young warriors likely felt justified about their drunken depredations against nearby white property owners, as well as about those committed while sober.[105] One can see, then, how alcohol consumption and horse raiding could become inextricably intertwined, because of the trade of horses for rum. Moreover, because both of these activities could be related to warfare, they also served as substitutes for the martial activity that so defined Choctaw masculinity. Thus, young Choctaw men who could not engage in traditional warfare could turn to horse raiding and alcohol consumption to demonstrate manliness.

The laws governing the responsibilities of lighthorsemen reveal the growing concern about the use and abuse of alcohol among the Choctaw. An act passed in 1848 gave lighthorsemen the power to call on civilians to aid them in capturing criminals "charged with high crime against this nation" and, especially important for this discussion, in destroying any whiskey. Those civilians who refused to assist the lighthorsemen were liable for a fine of up to five dollars.[106] One year later, Nicholas Cochnauer, who would later serve as chief of Pushmataha District, proposed that anyone who hindered a lighthorseman from performing his duty to destroy "spiritous liquors" be penalized by a fine between five and ten dollars, half of which would go to the lighthorseman.[107] The next day, October 11, 1849, the General Council went a step further: those who assisted the lighthorsemen in destroying alcohol would be paid one dollar for their service. These three acts taken together suggest a progression: the lighthorsemen were tasked with destroying alcohol but might not be able to do so on their own, so they could call on civilians for aid. Civilians, though, did not always aid the lighthorsemen in the destruction of alcohol, even upon pain of a fine; they sometimes actively obstructed the lighthorsemen's work. Therefore, rather than use punitive threats to encourage civilian support in the destruction of whiskey, the General Council offered a financial reward for those who helped the lighthorsemen. By 1850 Choctaw authorities had expanded the lighthorsemen's power to destroy alcohol to include the ability to search "any person's house or dwellings wagon boat pack horse or any persons bag or saddle bags where they may have good reason or evidence to suspect of having any intoxicating whiskey wines or other intoxicating liquors." The act directed lighthorsemen to destroy both the liquor and its vessel, once found.[108] In the span of a few years, the General Council passed several acts in an attempt to not just control but eliminate alcohol use among the Choctaws.

While opportunities to participate in warfare between Indigenous groups declined in the eighteenth and nineteenth centuries, conflicts between whites offered another chance for Choctaw men to reconnect with older notions of manhood and how to achieve it. Thus, in the eighteenth century some young Native males saw the American Revolution as an opportunity to prove themselves on battlefields once more and ignored older chiefs who urged neutrality on the advice of the Spanish and the Americans.[109] The younger generation may have been less concerned about what the war, which seemed like an internal dispute in any case, meant for Native people more broadly but, instead, focused on how the war could permit them to transition into manhood in the traditional way.

Similarly, some of the enthusiasm for Civil War–era enlistment discussed in the previous chapter may also have been the result of Choctaw youth imagining service in the Confederacy as a way to claim, or reclaim, their identities as warriors. Even the terminology used by some officials to describe Choctaw troops utilized this "warrior" language. Peter Pitchlynn referred to Colonel DeNeale's efforts "to raise a Regiment of Choctaw Warriors." Even Pitchlynn's enumeration of the differences in pay for the various ranks styled enlisted men as "warriors."[110] The then colonel Douglas H. Cooper thought the Choctaw and Chickasaw could provide "10,000 warriors."[111] Neither white soldiers nor soldiers of African descent were regularly described as "warriors." For some, this language likely contained a tinge of racism: they imagined Native soldiers as "savage" and used the term "warrior" to convey the meaning that such troops were somehow different from, perhaps fiercer than, white soldiers from Georgia or Ohio. But for others, the term "warrior" was precisely what they meant: Choctaw troops would engage in the time-honored practice of warfare and perform brave deeds so that they could become men.

When the American Civil War provided Choctaw men the opportunity to be warriors again, some lighthorsemen transitioned into soldiers. One prominent example is Iskitini Homa, who served as a captain in Second Company K during the war.[112] Homa is likely the same Ishkitini Homma who was paid by an act of appropriation in June 1858 for his two months of service as a lighthorseman.[113] A lighthorse company would be a natural place to turn for military leadership once the Choctaw legislature decided to participate in the war. District chiefs had certainly chosen men who were already well regarded in their communities to serve in lighthorse companies. The larger district population would have been familiar with the lighthorse company members because traveling through their districts was a part of the company's duties. And fellow Choctaws' esteem for the lighthorsemen probably grew as these men protected public welfare from criminals, regulated appropriate behavior, collected fines, and meted out punishments. Thus, lighthorsemen would be obvious choices for service as officers and noncommissioned officers in the First Choctaw and Chickasaw Mounted Rifles. And lighthorsemen, given their experience in law enforcement, may have readily sought out military service.

This examination of Choctaw masculinity and its traditional connection to warfare adds a different valence to Choctaw men's enthusiasm for enlistment during the American Civil War. The eager throngs of Choctaw men signing up for military service even before the Choctaw Nation had officially taken a side in the dispute reflected a desire to reinvigorate older notions of manhood. I have devoted a lot of space here to discussing the lighthorse companies and how their duties allowed members to claim masculine identities because, while the number of lighthorse positions never exceeded ten per district, the influence of lighthorsemen was enormous. Their duties encompassed activities vital to the functioning of Choctaw society such as overseeing elections, capturing and punishing thieves, protecting private property, and controlling noncitizens in the Nation. Thus, though not many Choctaw men could use these positions to make claims to manhood, the lighthorsemen were outsized representations of masculinity. Other activities, such as pursuing an education or engaging in diplomacy with foreign powers, provided alternative ways to express masculinity and protect Choctaw sovereignty, but the Civil War offered the chance to the masses to once again earn one's name. And Choctaw men embraced it, at least initially. This is not to suggest that the other reasons Choctaws entered into an alliance with the Confederacy that I discussed in chapter 3 are any less valid. Rather, my goal is to demonstrate that Choctaw soldiers attached profound meaning to their experience as soldiers.

Horse hunting, an important activity in the military as mentioned in chapter 4, gains new meaning in light of what we know about Choctaws' changing notions of masculinity in the nineteenth century. Official records noted sick horses, horses killed in battle, lost horses, and soldiers on duty hunting horses. Read one way, these notations reflect the importance of horses for soldiers to perform in battle in a cavalry unit. Read in light of William McLoughlin's discussion of horses as a prize in traditional Native warfare and of horse raiding as an activity that could substitute for warfare to demonstrate Native masculinity, the notations also reify the continued importance of horses to Choctaw notions of manhood. Moreover, Choctaw officers who sent soldiers away from battle to hunt horses were not relegating them to light duty. Soldiers such as Privates Lewis Hiarka and Jim Yellow or Sergeant Jimpson Jones may not have interpreted such orders to mean they were missing out on battle and an opportunity to be warriors; instead, those men were engaged in manly behavior, aiding their fellow soldiers by providing them with horses.[114] The role of soldiers out hunting horses for the cavalry also dovetailed nicely with the duties of lighthorse company members to manage the population of stray horses and livestock and with ideas that included horse raiding as a demonstration of manhood. Thus, the traditional practice of warfare and newer ways to access masculinity doubly confirmed the manliness of horse hunting among Choctaw troops in the Civil War.

The decision of some Choctaws to use war dances to send off young men who enlisted to fight in the Civil War also takes on importance as more than a throwback to traditional practice; rather, the dances invoked specific traditional ideas about manhood and its connection to war. Thus, when Peter Pitchlynn told his nephew, "We are keeping up the War Dance, but will commence drilling very soon," he was describing not just the juxtaposition of Native traditions and Euro-American ideas regarding warfare but also the reanimation of an important Choctaw practice that was a part of the transition from youth to manhood.[115] Lycurgus Pitchlynn arranged for a "Big War Dance" at his home on a Wednesday night and invited the "whole county." The next morning he planned to leave for service "without any doubt of failure."[116] According to H. B. Cushman, an evening war dance conformed to traditional practice: "The opening of hostilities was always preceded by the famous hoyopahihla, war-dance. Night was the chosen time for engaging in that time-honored ceremony." Lycurgus Pitchlynn's event likely also included the large bonfire, *hoyopataloah*, or war songs, and *hoyopa-tassuhah*, or war whoops, that Cushman recounted.[117] Again, the war dance was an important prelude to battle but also another part of the rite in which young Choctaws participated to become both warriors and men.

The meaning of manhood and war's importance in Choctaw society also imbue Choctaw men's complaints about their inability to participate in the war with more meaning. Nat Grayham was "full mad" because his family "would not let him go to the Wars." Grayham was likely so angry because the war represented his opportunity to earn his name and enter manhood, but his family stood in the way. Did they believe that Grayham was too young to make the decision for himself? Did he have obligations to his family that he could not ignore? Peter Pitchlynn's 1861 letter to his nephew John about the matter does not offer any answers.[118] The enlistment records for the First Choctaw and Chickasaw Mounted Rifles, however, do offer a suggestive possibility. A private named Nat Graham appeared on an undated payroll in 1862 for Company F.[119] If Nat Grayham and Nat Graham were one and the same, it suggests that Grayham overcame his family's resistance and seized the opportunity to claim his full identity as a man by enlisting. In the same letter Pitchlynn assures his nephew John, "If it were possible for me to go I would be in your midst before another week." Instead Pitchlynn was nursing sick relatives. Pitchlynn's generation had come of age when there were no longer wars to fight to access identity as Choctaw men; finally, when an opportunity to fight arose, Pitchlynn had too many familial obligations, and was perhaps too old, to participate. His inability to fight in the Civil War may have been especially bittersweet: while he could not serve as a warrior, his sons and nephews could.

This chapter considered Choctaw ideas about masculinity and how they can shape our understanding of Choctaw men's participation in the war. I began with an examination of how Choctaws traditionally defined male identity through warfare. Male Choctaw youths earned new names and new identities as sexually mature men through martial activity such as taking scalps or demonstrating daring bravery or skill in battle. These new names and identities entitled warriors to marry and take on leadership roles within their communities. As opportunities for warfare declined, Choctaw men turned to other activities to define their identities, such as pursuing education or protecting the interests of their communities through political and business negotiation. Service in lighthorse companies allowed Choctaw men to exercise some of the same functions of warriors in terms of community protection. In this case, the enemy was no longer members of other Native groups or other outsiders; rather, thieves, murderers, and lawbreakers in general became the focus of the lighthorsemen's attention. There were few lighthorsemen positions, however, and some men simply preferred other activities to express their manhood, such as horse raiding and drinking.

In view of these changes in Choctaw thinking about masculinity, Choctaw men's participation in the American Civil War takes on different meaning. Choctaw enthusiasm to enlist reflected an interest in the question of slavery and the issue of sovereignty but also the reclamation of a warrior identity. War dances represented a retention of traditional practice but also claimed a specific rite of manhood that had been closed off to Choctaw youth. Choctaw youth could once again earn their names as warriors and become real Choctaw men. Choctaw enlistment in the Confederacy and participation in war dances also preserved the spiritual meaning of certain traditional practices in the face of a changing landscape. Once in battle, ideas about duties such as hunting horses might have different meaning for Choctaw soldiers, as might evaluations of what constituted a military victory. By the end of the war, however, all Confederate soldiers, be they from the Choctaw Nation or southern states, had to contend with the reality of defeat. Choctaw Confederates, like their southern white counterparts, faced the task of reconciling with the federal government and negotiating the place of newly emancipated people of African descent in their society, the subject of the next chapter.

Chapter 6

Dis Land Which Jines Dat of Ole Master's

RECONSTRUCTION IN THE
CHOCTAW NATION

In January 1865, the Choctaw Nation was wavering on the precipice of chaos. Principal Chief Peter P. Pitchlynn, the same man who just a few short months earlier had described a Choctaw commitment to the Confederate cause that exceeded southern white soldiers', now sounded real alarm because of what the war had wrought for his people. Pitchlynn stated that the war had "suspend[ed] the civil law, destroy[ed] the moral force and organic structure of society, and subject[ed] the citizens rights to military rule, or physical force, and lawless violence." He watched as citizens became "selfish and unprincipled, the soldier licentious and profligate," and "anarchy, devastation, ruin and famine" threatened Choctaw society. The situation was particularly worrisome in the Northern District, where "citizens despoiled of their property by lawless violence, have been compelled to abandon their homes and seek south of the mountains refuge and subsistence." Unfortunately, a recent drought compounded the shortage of food, as did the presence of cavalry troops along the Red River who rapidly consumed the supplies that were "the only hope of preventing famine from visiting the land." Though Pitchlynn attempted to sound a hopeful note about the prospects of the Confederate cause, he ended his address by urging the Choctaw people to stay the course, even if the war might be prolonged to "an indefinite period."[1] Little did he know that the war would soon be over and the Choctaw people would have to negotiate not with the Confederate government but with the federal government about the fate of enslaved people of African descent in the Choctaw Nation.

As the preceding chapters make clear, the Choctaw Nation and Indian Territory more broadly offer a unique perspective on slavery. One can simultaneously see the similarities between slavery in the American South and among Indian nations, as well as how sovereign Native groups crafted their own practice of the institution to fit particular traditional customs or beliefs. Choctaw Indians and other Native groups did not blindly adopt state laws regarding the behavior and treatment of enslaved people, nor did they always engage in the same kind of commercial activity as their southern counterparts. Choctaws sided with the South because of their interest in preserving Native sovereignty and protecting the institution of slavery, and the Confederate government also offered Choctaws many other inducements to support the South. During the fighting, Choctaw soldiers shared some experiences with their Confederate allies, but the war also carried different meanings and repercussions for Choctaw masculinity. It should be expected, then, that while Reconstruction in Indian Territory bore some resemblance to Reconstruction in the former Confederate states, it had some distinguishing features as well.

At the conclusion of the war, the Choctaw Nation found itself subject to federal authority, like the rest of the Confederate South. The federal government attempted to reestablish friendly relations with the Choctaw Nation and to create a new position within Choctaw society for individuals formerly held as slaves by members of the Choctaw Nation. Thus, federal authorities negotiated a treaty with the Choctaw Nation, and other Indian nations, that included provisions for granting formerly enslaved people Choctaw citizenship, civil rights, and access to land, something that the federal government neglected to do for its own newly emancipated population. The Choctaw Nation, however, circumvented these measures.

This chapter examines the terms under which Reconstruction took place in the Choctaw Nation. Part of the Choctaw Reconstruction story is in the treaty requirements and legislative action taken to address the position of newly freed people in Choctaw society. The other part of the story, however, is more individual and considers the experiences of formerly enslaved people. How did the people formerly enslaved by Choctaw Indians, and in Indian Territory more generally, discuss and imagine freedom within this context? To answer this question I turn again to the WPA slave narratives. As discussed in the introduction, I often present the words of enslaved people as they appear in the narratives rather than replace their words with my own. Because the Oklahoma narratives include the accounts of individuals enslaved outside of Indian Territory as well as those with non-Native enslavers, I indicate when an interviewee had a Native enslaver in the text. Formerly enslaved people from Indian Territory often described enslavers and overseers and the announcement of emancipation in very similar language used by formerly enslaved people from the Confederate states. Where their accounts differ markedly, however, is in terms of their access to land once the Civil War ended and the more formal process of Reconstruction began. The formerly enslaved people of Native peoples in Indian Territory gained rights to land, while those from the southern states did not. Property ownership, however, did not necessarily improve the political or legal status of the freedpeople in Indian Territory. As it turns out, Choctaw officials opposed the extension of full citizenship rights to their formerly enslaved people almost as fiercely as many white southerners did.

My discussion of Reconstruction starts with the Emancipation Proclamation.[2] Choctaws and other Native groups adamantly insisted on their claims to sovereignty; thus, from their perspective, the Emancipation Proclamation did not have any direct impact on their policies. The Supreme Court case of *Worcester v. Georgia* had affirmed tribal sovereignty in 1832, and though southern states such as Georgia and Mississippi ignored it, the legal principle of tribal sovereignty stood.[3] Moreover, Abraham Lincoln did not make any reference within the proclamation to Indian Territory or Indian nations. Rather, Lincoln enumerated the states and parts of states in rebellion where the act applied: "Arkansas, Texas, Louisiana, (except the Parishes of St. Bernard, Plaquemines, Jefferson, St. John, St. Charles, St. James Ascension, Assumption, Terrebonne, Lafourche, St. Mary, St. Martin, and Orleans, including the City of New Orleans) Mississippi, Alabama, Florida, Georgia, South Carolina, North Carolina, and Virginia, (except the forty-eight counties designated as West Virginia, and also the counties of Berkley, Accomac, Northampton, Elizabeth City, York, Princess Ann, and Norfolk, including the cities of Norfolk and Portsmouth[)], and which excepted parts, are for the present, left precisely as if this proclamation were not issued."[4] Historian Louis Gerteis contends that exempt areas "were deemed sufficiently loyal by the president to be allowed to continue to debate the future of slavery."[5] Lincoln could not be confused about the loyalty of some Indian nations: the Choctaw, Chickasaw, Seminole, and Creek Nations had already officially sided with the Confederacy through treaty arrangements made in July 1861. These nations were clearly in rebellion, yet Lincoln made no mention of them.

One way to read the omission of the Indian nations from this list is as a tacit recognition of Native sovereignty. That is, if Lincoln thought that Indian nations fell under the authority of the federal government as Confederate states did, he would have included them in this proclamation. If Lincoln imagined the Indian nations to be similar to states in terms of the limits of their sovereign authority, he could have imposed federal authority over them. One might argue that Lincoln was wary of further antagonizing Indian nations by ignoring their claims to sovereignty, but as Indian nations were officially allied with the Confederacy and were contributing troops to the southern war effort, one wonders what further antagonism could occur. Moreover, recent events in Minnesota in 1862, in which American forces had quashed a conflict with the Lakota people, showed Lincoln's willingness to apply federal authority to Native populations. So, while both Indian nations and Confederate states asserted rights to self-government, the federal government recognized only Indian claims. The Native nations had more ground on which to stake their claim that the Emancipation Proclamation did not apply to them. Indian authorities thought of themselves as outside of US jurisdiction. And at least one legal decision after the war supported that claim: one federal court judge "asserted that both the Emancipation Proclamation and the Thirteenth Amendment applied to Indian Territory" only to have a higher court reject his opinion.[6]

While the applicability of the Emancipation Proclamation to the Indian nations of Indian Territory may have been in question among federal officials, enslaved people in the territory seized upon freedom whenever and wherever possible. Freedom came to those enslaved people of African descent owned by Choctaws, and to enslaved people in Indian Territory more broadly, in ways that matched the experiences of enslaved people in southern states. For instance, enslavers were not always forthcoming with news about emancipation. Mollie Barber's mother, an enslaved woman in the Creek Nation, did not learn about freedom until she had a serendipitous conversation with a passerby. She had been cooking dinner for her mistress, but upon learning of her freedom, "she run back in de house, grab up what little clothes she had, made a bundle and leave dat place wid de dinner 'most ready. Bless her old black heart! She was glad to be free!"[7] Red Richardson of Texas claimed that his father's enslaver did not free him until the "second threat from President Lincoln."[8] Perhaps Richardson was distinguishing between the preliminary executive order of September 1862 and the final one of January 1, 1863, or he may have been referring to the passage of the Thirteenth Amendment, or the late dissemination of news about the Emancipation Proclamation in the state of Texas. Joanna Draper was an enslaved person in Mississippi whose enslaver bound her out to the Deeson family during the war. She had been with the family for four years before deciding to run away because of her bad treatment. After her escape, she discovered she was free: "I never will forgive that white man for not telling me I was free, and not helping me git back to my mammy and pappy. Lots of white people done that."[9] Decades later, one can still feel Draper's deep resentment about the Deesons' dishonesty. One can only guess at how long the Deesons would have continued to exploit Draper's labor and permit her to call them "master" without cause. Perhaps Draper's experience was similar to that of Robert Williams, who had been enslaved in Mississippi. He recalled matter-of-factly, "Even after freedom he [Williams's enslaver] owned a darky or two; I was one."[10]

On the other hand, many enslavers did inform their enslaved people of emancipation and held true to their obligation to release these people from bondage. Mary Lindsay's Chickasaw enslaver informed Lindsay and another household enslaved person of their freedom: "She say, 'You and Vici jest as free as I am.'"[11] She then offered the women room, board, and several dresses if the freedwomen would continue to work for her. Formerly enslaved people both from Indian Territory and from southern states repeated similar stories of enslavers using this kind of phrasing, "as free as I am." For instance, Phyllis Petite, Sina Banks, L. B. Barner, and Doc Daniel Dowdy each recalled enslavers using similar language when they gathered enslaved people together to inform them of emancipation.[12] Unlike the story of the Deeson family and Joanna Draper, Sina Banks's young enslaver also told her, "It is my duty to take you back to your mother, but if you will stay with me and help me till I get my crop in I will take you home."[13] Banks agreed to stay.

Sarah Wilson's Cherokee enslaver Ben Johnson told his enslaved people of emancipation only reluctantly. After refugeeing those enslaved people to Texas, across the border from the Choctaw Nation, he received word of emancipation from Fort Smith. Unable to read, he asked his daughter to read the letter: "He went wild and jumped on her and beat the devil out of her. Said she was lying to him. It near about killed him to let us loose, but he cooled down after awhile and said he would help us all get back home if we wanted to come."[14] Wilson described her former enslaver as a "hellion"; however, despite his resentment for this change in status for his human property, he still honored it. Alice Rawlings's old enslaver Major Jackson was not violent when he informed his enslaved people of their freedom, but he did conveniently wait until after the crop had been harvested, "six months after all the rest was free."[15] Even this delayed admission may have been forced: Rawlings's father had talked with a friendly planter from a neighboring plantation who may have shared the news of emancipation. Perhaps Jackson would have kept this information from his bondpeople longer if it had been possible. In both cases, enslavers Johnson and Jackson did not want to relinquish their hold on their human property. Johnson found the idea of the end of slavery so inconceivable that he physically assaulted his daughter when she gave him the news of emancipation. And Jackson was so dependent on his workforce that he withheld information from them in order to keep them on the plantation.

Still other formerly enslaved people learned about freedom from the arrival of Yankee soldiers. Charlotte Johnson White, who had been owned in the Cherokee Nation, remembered nearly 100 soldiers arriving at the house: "Dey was a pretty sight settin' on dey horses, and de men had on blue uniforms wid little caps. 'All de slaves is free' one of de men said."[16] George Kye left Arkansas to serve in the army in his enslaver Abe Stover's stead and drove a team of mules for the "Sesesh soldiers from Van Buren to Texarkana and back" for two years. After some fighting, a federal soldier approached Kye and asked who owned the mules, to which Kye replied, Abe Stover. The soldier then said, "Let me tell you, black boy, you are as free now as old Abe Stover his own self!"[17] Some Union troops seemed to relish informing enslaved people about emancipation. Eliza Evans, formerly enslaved in Alabama, did not learn of her freedom from Union troops; rather, a soldier taught her to be sassy. The Union soldier asked Evans her name and she replied, "Liza." When prodded for her surname, Liza replied that she did not have one, so he asked who owned the "Big House" on the plantation. Eliza told him the owner was Mr. John Mixon. The soldier concluded that she should call herself "Miss Liza Mixon." At his direction, when called a "nigger" by her enslaver, she replied "real pert like, 'I ain't no nigger, I's a Negro and I'm Miss Liza Mixon.'" For this impertinence, Evans received a whipping from her grandmother.[18]

Some formerly enslaved people were quite specific about the date of their freedom. Sally Henderson Moss remembered that Choctaw freedpeople celebrated emancipation on August 4, the date that the Choctaw freed their enslaved people, according to Moss.[19] Similarly, Cherokee freedman R. C. Smith also linked emancipation to August 4, 1866.[20] Interestingly, Smith did not invoke February 1863, the date when the Cherokee General Council abolished slavery in the Cherokee Nation, as the moment of his emancipation. This likely reflects the division within the Cherokee Nation: the nation officially sided with the Confederacy in 1861, but many nation members then actually fought with the Union army, and Confederate Cherokees were not recognizing legislation passed by Union sympathizers in the Cherokee government.[21] Moss and Smith might have been referencing the August date, rather than the issuance of the Emancipation Proclamation or the ratification of the Thirteenth Amendment, because the summer of 1866 coincided with the ratification of the treaties between the federal government and the various Native groups in Indian Territory that sided with the Confederacy

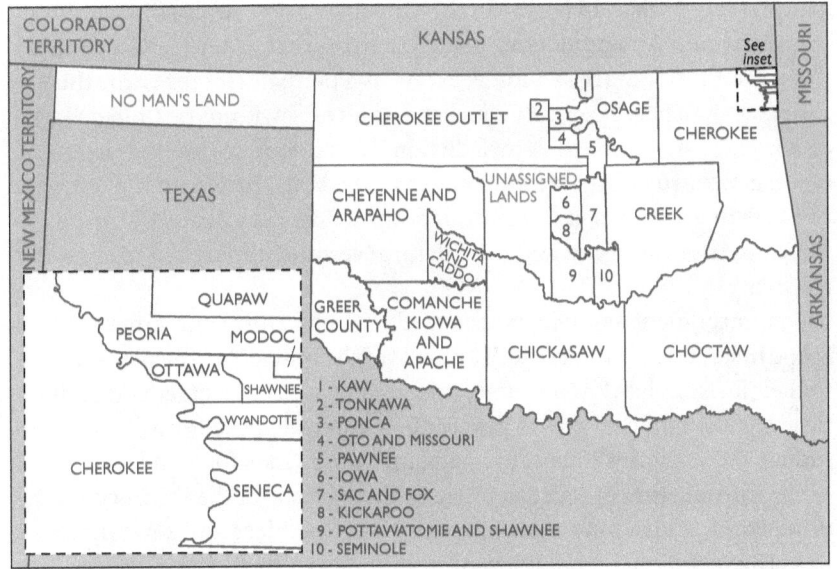

Indian Territory, 1866.
(Map by Rice University GIS/Data Center)

during the Civil War. The stipulations of the treaties included the abolition of slavery among Confederate Indians. Ida Henry, formerly enslaved in Texas, recalled the familiar Juneteenth date (June 19) for her emancipation.[22] Katie Rowe, also formerly enslaved in Texas, described her own emancipation with remarkable clarity and detail: being interrupted at work, gathering in the overseer's yard, and receiving the news from a stranger. She concluded, "It was de fourth day of June in 1865 I begins to live, and I gwine take de picture of dat old man in de big black hat and long whiskers, setting on de gallery and talking kind to us, clean into my grave wid me."[23]

Slavery officially ended in the Choctaw Nation with the April 1866 treaty reestablishing friendly relations between the federal government and the Choctaw and Chickasaw Nations. The second article of the treaty stated that "the Choctaws and Chickasaws hereby covenant and agree that henceforth neither slavery nor involuntary servitude, otherwise than in punishment of crime whereof the parties shall have been duly convicted, in accordance with laws applicable to all members of the particular nation, shall ever exist in said nations."[24] The article abolished slavery and involuntary servitude except in the case of people convicted of a crime and prohibited the future practice of slavery among the Choctaw and Chickasaw. The language of the article freeing enslaved people in the Choctaw Nation borrows heavily from the Thirteenth Amendment to the US Constitution, which reads, "Neither slavery nor involuntary servitude, except as a punishment for crime thereof the party shall have been duly convicted, shall exist within the United States, or any place subject to their jurisdiction."[25] The similarities between these two clauses is to be expected: the states ratified the Thirteenth Amendment in December 1865, just a few short months before representatives from the Choctaw, the Chickasaw, and the federal government convened to negotiate the treaty.

Some argument might have been made that the Thirteenth Amendment's scope included Indian Territory because of the phrase "or any place subject to their jurisdiction."[26] Of course, this perspective is that of federal authorities who thought the federal government controlled the Native nations of Indian Territory and thus could open up Native lands for white settlement or the introduction of railroads. The Indian nations of the territory, on the other hand, understood themselves to be independent and sovereign entities. The fact that the abolition of slavery had to be included in the individual treaties of 1866 between Confederate Indian nations and the federal government suggests that federal authorities also recognized Indian sovereignty and did not think that the Thirteenth Amendment had abolished slavery among the Choctaw or other Indians.

Formerly enslaved people differed in their descriptions of what emancipation meant to them individually, and this variation was similar among the formerly enslaved people of Indian Territory and also those from nearby southern states. Some formerly enslaved people, such as Paul Garnett Roebuck's father, who had been enslaved among the Choctaw and Chickasaw Indians, told their children that emancipation did not mean a change in their treatment: they had been treated well under slavery and continued to receive fair treatment from their former enslavers' families after the Civil War.[27] Matilda Poe experienced better material conditions as an enslaved person in the Chickasaw Nation than as a freedwoman: "I never did know I was a slave, 'cause I couldn't tell I wasn't free. I always had a good time, didn't have to work much, and allus had something to eat and wear and that was better than it is with me now."[28] Eliza Evans went so far as to assert that John Mixon's slaves did not want to be freed and that they hated Yankee soldiers.[29] These comments recall the discussion of kind enslavers from chapter 2. Roebuck, Poe, and Mixon may have accurately remembered the kinder treatment of their enslavers, but their recollections may also have been colored by their impoverished state on the heels of the Great Depression. Moreover, these informants likely had not experienced a great change in their legal or social status because of legalized segregation and legislative activity to prevent African Americans from exercising all of their political and civil rights.

Other formerly enslaved people described cruel enslavers and emancipation as a moment of jubilation. Annie Hawkins, formerly enslaved in Texas, recalled, "We was the happiest folks in the world when we knowed we was free. We couldn't realize it at first but how we did shout and cry for joy when we did realize it." Hawkins and her fellow enslaved people feared their "fetched mean" enslaver so much that, initially, they were afraid to leave the plantation because they feared their mistress would bring them back.[30] Similarly, Lou Smith, formerly enslaved in Texas, described her mistress, Miss Jo, as "low brow" with little experience in how to treat enslaved people. Accordingly, Miss Jo treated her human property like dogs, even denying them food.[31] Upon hearing news of her emancipation, eleven-year-old Lou Smith hid in the plum orchard and repeated to herself, "I'se free, I'se free; I ain't never going back to Miss Jo." Katie Rowe understood emancipation as the end of brutal punishment: "No, bless God, I ain't never seen no more black boys bleeding all up and down de back under a cat o'nine tails, and I never go by no cabin and hear no poor nigger groaning, all wrapped up in a lardy sheet no more." In fact, Rowe was sure she herself would have died had she remained under the authority of her cruel former overseer, Mr. Saunders.[32] These recollections do not suggest continuity between informants' lives as enslaved and as free people; rather, emancipation represented a sharp rupture from their lives in bondage.

For other formerly enslaved people, emancipation meant the possibility of reuniting families separated by sale or the war.[33] Acemy Wofford's second enslaver moved her from Mississippi to Texas, apparently leaving behind her husband. Once the war was over, her husband came to Texas to find her, and they then farmed near the town of Midway.[34] The Perrymans owned Mary Grayson's family in the Creek Nation. When some of the men in Grayson's family ran away to join the Union army, the enslavers tried to move their human property to prevent additional runaways. The family returned to the Creek Agency at the war's end, where Grayson's mother "met a Negro who had seen pappy and knew where he was, so we sent word to him and he came and found us."[35] Sale separated Johnson Thompson's grandmother and father; his grandmother remained in Indian Territory, while the rest of the family lived in Texas with their new enslaver, John Harnage. Thompson recalled that when the war ended, "Pappy wanted to go back to his mother" and made a deal to drive for a white man who was moving into Indian Territory.[36] William Curtis's enslaved parents married in Georgia but were also separated through sale: "It nigh broke our hearts when he [Curtis's father] had to leave and old Master sho' done everything he could to make it up to us."[37] After the war, however, Curtis's father returned to the family. Curtis stated plainly, "Dat was de best thing about de war setting us free, he could come back to us."[38] Clearly other formerly enslaved people agreed with Curtis and sometimes went to great lengths to reconnect with parents, spouses, children, and siblings.

Reunions were made possible by some freedpeople's newfound freedom of movement, but other formerly enslaved people remained on the plantations where they had long labored for enslavers. For instance, Anthony Dawson and Eliza Bell each described their families and fellow enslaved people remaining with their enslavers.[39] Similarly, Ebenezer Cutnezer Kemp's father continued to farm for his former enslaver, Jackson Kemp, long after emancipation.[40] Mary Ellen Phillips Wynn's mother married into the Choctaw Nation when Wynn was a girl, and her Choctaw stepfather claimed that the people his family had enslaved remained with the family after emancipation and continued to work the land.[41] Some freedpeople worked for shares and others for pay or food and shelter.[42] Formerly enslaved person Ed Butler thought some enslaved people favored freedom, but others feared starvation and did not know how to care for themselves.[43] Perhaps this anxiety led some enslaved people to remain on plantations. Eliza Elsey, formerly enslaved in Texas, explained that some enslaved people stayed on the plantation because "they didn't know how to sell cattle or hogs, or sugar cane, and the Master sell part of the crops and give the Negroes some of the money."[44] William Curtis's newly reunited family initially chose to stay with their former enslaver: "Yes, we was free but we didn't know what to do. We didn't want to leave our old Master and our old home."[45] The transformation from property to person occurred fairly quickly, and it was likely comforting for some to remain in communities with families and within established relationships in which both parties, former enslavers and formerly enslaved people, knew what to expect from the other. Further, it was unclear to newly emancipated people what their economic options were. Still other formerly enslaved people feared violent reprisal if they left their former enslavers.[46]

Enslavers who desperately needed a labor source to stay afloat financially likely met the decision of some formerly enslaved people to remain on their enslavers' land with relief. William Hutson's enslaver, Dr. Allison, informed his enslaved workforce of the end of slavery but also wanted the laborers to remain until the harvest was completed in the fall. According to Hutson, no one left, and no one celebrated the news of freedom. Dr. Allison must have appreciated having his crop harvested before the newly emancipated people from his plantation sought work in town, although the freedpeople on Dr. Allison's farm surely chafed at the inability to even mark the end of slavery.[47] William Curtis had been enslaved in Georgia, and his family remained on the plantation after the Civil War. When his old enslavers passed away, their son took over the running of the farm. Curtis's assessment of the son's abilities is brusque: "He couldn't a'done nothing without us niggers. He didn't know how to work."[48] This led to an arrangement in which the young man divided the crops with his parents' formerly enslaved people.

The overseer at the plantation where Daniel William Lucas was enslaved informed the laborers of their freedom but quickly reported, "But Old Master don't want you to leave. He just wants you to stay right on here where at is your home. That's what the Master say is best for you to do."[49] The overseer framed the choice to remain on the plantation as being in the best interest of the formerly enslaved, but of course it was also in the best interest of the enslaver. In return for Lucas's labor, "Master Doctor" paid Lucas ten dollars per month, plus gave him room and board and medical treatment. Millie Garnes's old enslaver Terry Harris paid her family for their labor in "meat, lard, corn and other food stuff" and leased some land on which he built the family a home. The old mistress gave Garnes's mother some chickens. Even so, the family eventually moved forty miles away.[50] The Harrises seemed to make every effort to keep Garnes's family from moving. These apparently generous terms make sense when one considers that landholders possessed an almost worthless commodity in land without labor to extract the land's wealth.

When enslavers could not use persuasion or offer enough inducements to convince formerly enslaved people to continue to till their fields, they strove to control access to their labor in other ways. Because emancipation had obliterated enslavers' authority over enslaved people, the master class used state legislatures to enact statutes in the form of the Black Codes, designed to force freedpeople to continue to labor.[51] While some of the provisions of the Mississippi Black Codes, for instance, addressed the new rights of freedpeople to legally marry, appear as witnesses in court, and enter into contracts, the bulk of the Black Codes' provisions concerned labor. Lawmakers permitted freedpeople to rent or lease land only in urban areas, preventing them from renting land to farm independently. Freedpeople had to provide evidence of employment and faced penalties if they "deserted" their job prior to the end of the contract and without good cause. Penalties for individuals who attempted to entice freedpeople away from their work included a fine of any amount between $25 and $200 or two months in jail and being liable to the employer for damages.[52] According to contemporary observer Sidney Andrews, "The whole struggle between the whites on the one hand and the blacks on the other hand is a struggle for and against compulsion. The negro insists, very blindly perhaps, that he shall be free to come and go when he pleases; the white insists that he shall only come and go at the pleasure of his *employer*. . . . Even the best men hold that each state must have a negro code."[53] These laws ensured that freedpeople had few economic opportunities save laboring for others.

While some enslavers in the Choctaw Nation may have wanted to retain the labor of the formerly enslaved, the official stance of the Choctaw government would eventually be to demand that formerly enslaved people be removed, despite apparent agreement to do otherwise. As part of the treaty agreement reached in April 1866 between the federal government and the Choctaw and Chickasaw Nations, the Choctaw and Chickasaw had ceded territory known as the Leased District to the United States for $300,000, which was to be invested and held in trust for the nations "until the legislatures of the Choctaw and Chickasaw Nations respectively shall have made such laws, rules, and regulations as may be necessary to give all persons of African descent, resident in the said nation at the date of the treaty of Fort Smith, and their descendants, heretofore held in slavery among said nations, all the rights, privileges, and immunities, including the right of suffrage, of citizens of said nations, except in the annuities, moneys, and public domain claimed by, or belonging to, said nations respectively." In other words, the Choctaw would not be able to access the funds from their land cession until they provided for legal citizenship for their formerly enslaved people and their descendants held in the nation. The citizenship rights of formerly enslaved people in the Choctaw Nation would not include rights to the public domain or funds received in exchange for land cessions; however, formerly enslaved individuals would receive forty acres of land "on the same terms as the Choctaws and Chickasaws." Choctaw freedpeople who did not wish to remain in the Choctaw Nation and become Choctaw citizens would receive $100.[54]

The Choctaw legislature had two years to comply with the treaty of 1866 and grant the formerly enslaved people of the nation citizenship rights or face the loss of funds. If the Choctaw refused to fulfill the treaty's terms, the freedpeople of the Choctaw and Chickasaw Nations would receive the proceeds of the Leased District, and the United States would handle the removal of "said persons of African descent . . . in such a manner as the United States shall deem proper."[55] Initially, there was some support for the inclusion in the two nations of the freedpeople. In a joint circular, Chickasaw governor

George Colbert and Choctaw chief Peter P. Pitchlynn argued that the labor of the freedpeople was valuable and that the small size of the population of freedpeople limited the potential threat their presence posed. These leaders also worried that the removal of the freedpeople of the Choctaw and Chickasaw Nations to the Leased District by the federal government would transform the district into a colony for people of African descent and attract other freedpeople from nearby states. Thus, the population in the district would swell, and the freedpeople would form a "large Negro nation upon the borders of the Choctaw-Chickasaw country."[56]

The larger populations of the Choctaw and Chickasaw Nations, however, wanted those formerly enslaved to be removed. Choctaw citizens made clear their desires by choosing representatives in the next election who then formally requested that the commissioner of Indian affairs expel the freedpeople, and the Chickasaw quickly followed suit. By 1868, Holmes Colbert and Sampson Folsom, as representatives of the Choctaw and Chickasaw Nations, were urging the federal government to enforce the terms of the treaty by removing the freedpeople from their nations.[57] In later years, Choctaw lawmakers claimed that they would have accepted their freedpeople as citizens but for the recalcitrance of the Chickasaw to grant their freedpeople citizenship.[58] In any case, it would seem that for many Choctaws and Chickasaws, the potential loss of $300,000 for the nations was not enough of an inducement to expand the polity to include formerly enslaved people.

The question of the loss of funds may have been muddied, however, by the actions of the federal government. In July 1866, Congress appropriated $200,000 as a partial payment to the nations for the Leased District, $150,000 of which was paid to the Choctaw treasurer. Perhaps Congress hoped to persuade Choctaw and Chickasaw citizens to grant the freedpeople citizenship rights and assumed the nations' acceptance of the funds reflected an implicit agreement to do so.[59] Congress also may not have conceived of the possibility that the Choctaw and Chickasaw would opt to refuse the funds and request that the freedpeople be ejected; thus, legislators saw no harm in appropriating and disbursing the funds quickly. In fact, Congress also appropriated $15,000 as interest, which was paid by August 1866, and even appropriated and disbursed another $15,000 in 1869, after both nations had already refused to extend citizenship to the freedpeople.[60] From the Choctaw perspective, it might appear that nothing was lost by denying formerly enslaved people citizenship. Because the nation had already received the funds promised without having complied with the stipulation about citizenship for freedpeople, there was no incentive to extend those rights if the Choctaw population was not so inclined.

This push to remove freedpeople also reflects traditional Choctaw understandings of kinship: formerly enslaved people did not have matrilineally figured clan memberships. Thus, Choctaw people had no obligations to fulfill regarding the freed population, and there was little space for them in Choctaw society. Moreover, emancipation also meant that Choctaw men no longer had the ability to control the labor of enslaved people. As discussed in chapter 2, the introduction of enslaved labor often led to Choctaw men making decisions about agricultural work and directing the labor of enslaved people in the fields in ways that Choctaw men had not traditionally. This was a way for Choctaw men to participate in agriculture without threatening traditional notions of gender; however, emancipation spelled the end of this practice. Choctaw freedpeople fell outside both traditional clan relations and gender systems, which may have added weight to the desire to force them out of the bounds of the Choctaw Nation.

In short, most Choctaws seem to have wanted freedpeople removed from the nation at precisely the moment that white southerners were going to great lengths to keep their former bondpeople tied to the land. Though both groups had exploited the labor of people of African descent, their responses to emancipation were quite different: expulsion versus a reification of old economic and social relationships. To be sure, without the institution of slavery to set the terms of most interactions between people of African descent and whites, many southern whites expressed a desire to remove people of African descent from the South. Mary Ann Lenoir of North Carolina, for instance, described the end of the institution of slavery as a "relief to my mind" and added, "If we could only get *rid* of the negroes, but, there is the *rub*! . . . I have served a pretty long apprenticeship to ours and would be glad to be free of them."[61] Mary Ann Lenoir, like her brother Walter, preferred a landscape without people of African descent if those people were no longer enslaved. Once formerly enslaved people began to depart from her family's plantation after learning of their emancipation, Ella Gertrude Clanton Thomas "renounced any further interest in their welfare."[62] In her view the end of slavery meant the end of Thomas's obligation to formerly enslaved people, a sentiment that echoes Mary Ann Lenoir's feeling of relief regarding emancipation and surely also reflects these women's resentment toward freedpeople. Thomas and Lenoir recognized that emancipation would alter their economic and social lives. In the end, however, many southern whites also recognized that their economy depended on the labor of African Americans, even as they grew uncomfortable with the notion that whites and formerly enslaved people might also be competitors in the economic marketplace.[63]

Besides the Black Codes, white southerners also adopted language in labor contracts that safeguarded the interests of landowners rather than formerly enslaved people. Initially, agents of the Bureau of Refugees, Freedmen, and Abandoned Lands (known as the Freedmen's Bureau) encouraged the use of these contracts to protect emancipated people and, of course, to ensure that freedpeople continued to labor. The vast majority of freedpeople lacked the resources to purchase land for themselves on which to labor, and the Freedmen's Bureau, despite its long official name, did not redistribute the land of former Confederate landholders. Moreover, many landowners would not sell or rent land to the formerly enslaved.[64] Many whites, from both the North and the South, feared the large population of potentially idle and landless individuals represented by the freedpeople. Federal officials intended such contracts to lay out reasonable terms for how freedpeople would work and under what conditions and to ensure that landowners would compensate freedpeople. Former enslavers used the contracts to enforce certain labor standards. William Grimes of North Carolina, for instance, insisted that "work of every description, particularly the work on fences and ditches, . . . be done to my satisfaction, and must be done over until I am satisfied that it is done as it should be."[65] Grimes wanted to be sure that he controlled the labor of freedpeople in the same manner he once had managed the labor of enslaved people. Other planters inserted language in these contracts requiring "perfect obedience" and insisting that a laborer "be 'prompt and faithful' in the performance of his duties, and to maintain a proper demeanor."[66] These stipulations were less about working conditions than about replicating the social system in place under slavery. Former enslavers were reluctant to cede control over the behavior of formerly enslaved people.

Planters' desire to control the behavior and the labor of freedpeople and freedpeople's lack of resources to purchase land led to the development of the sharecropping system in the American South. At its most basic level, sharecropping addressed a crucial post-emancipation problem: freedpeople had labor but no land, and planters had land in abundance but no labor. That is, the majority of freedpeople had few skills outside of agricultural work, but they did not have the means to purchase land on which to labor. Planters owned large tracts of land but did not have ready cash to pay others to perform the agricultural labor to make that land profitable. In sharecropping arrangements, planters divided their land into tracts to be worked by individual families. The planter generally provided seed, some of the implements to work the land, and work animals, and croppers paid for their use of the land with a portion of the crop they produced. If the croppers could supply their own seed, implements, and work animals, the croppers could retain a larger portion of the crop.[67] In sharecropping's most positive iteration, this system gave landless freedpeople access to land, permitted them some autonomy in allocating their own labor, and provided a stable labor force for cash-strapped landowners. Unfortunately, sharecropping often took a more malignant form that resembled slavery: landowners tightly controlled the behavior of laborers who were practically tied to the land through unfair labor contracts and impossible debt.

In the Choctaw Nation, however, sharecropping did not dominate agricultural production as it would in the American South. Recall that the 1866 treaty included a provision for formerly enslaved people to receive forty acres of land "on the same terms as the Choctaws and Chickasaws." This figure resonated with the idea of "forty acres and a mule" and General William Tecumseh Sherman's Special Field Order No. 15 of January 1865, which would later popularly be misunderstood to grant land and mules to all freedpeople, but it is unclear whether either the federal authorities or Choctaw officials had been referencing Sherman's order during treaty negotiations. While the Choctaw government demanded the removal of the freedpeople, the federal government did not comply, and for almost twenty years the freedpeople in the Choctaw Nation existed in a kind of legal limbo, until the passage of the Freedmen Bill in 1883. During this time, Choctaw authorities treated the freedpeople as American citizens, and as such the freedpeople generally fell under the legal jurisdiction of federal courts. Likewise, the Choctaw Nation did not provide any schools for the children of freedpeople, which induced federal authorities to do so. On the other hand, by common consent, Choctaws permitted the freedpeople to cultivate as much land as they desired in the nation, though they had no rights in the public domain.[68]

The Choctaw traditional practice of communal landownership attached access to land to citizenship; thus, one could interpret the Choctaw authorities' and average Choctaw Nation member's willingness to allow formerly enslaved people to cultivate land as an acknowledgment that the Choctaw freedpeople had some, if unequal, right to be in the nation. Moreover, despite the pressures of the federal government and surrounding Americans, among the Choctaw the concept of individual landownership had not displaced older understandings of peoples' relationship to the land. At the same time, a division between newly emancipated people and their former enslavers was emerging. The freedpeople often formed separate towns away from Choctaw Indians, perhaps to till their land in relative peace.[69]

Despite the Choctaw freedpeople's ability to access land and congregate in their own separate communities, they chafed at some of the limits placed on their rights by the Choctaw Nation. For instance, a delegation of freedmen traveled to Washington, DC, in 1869 to entreat the authorities to enforce the stipulations of the 1866 treaty, and still others met in a convention and penned a resolution that complained that the Indians "failed to fulfill their obligations."[70] Other freedpeople registered their grievances by sending petitions to the federal government, a fact that so irked Choctaw lawmakers that in 1872 the Choctaw General Council directed the principal chief to do everything in his power to aid the United States "in any measures it may adopt in the removal of the said Freedmen petitioners" because of their "pretended grievances."[71] This Choctaw act dismissed the complaints of the Choctaw freedpeople as false yet found the petitioners so troublesome that the lawmakers wanted those freedpeople ejected. Other Choctaw and Chickasaw freedpeople wrote to President Ulysses S. Grant in 1872 to state their desire to remain in the territory and to object to the efforts of an outsider to convince freedpeople to agree to be removed.[72] Even members of the Arkansas state legislature wrote the US Congress in 1869 to urge the body to use influence to convince the Choctaw and Chickasaw governments to allow freedpeople to remain in their nations, receive forty acres of land, and exercise rights including suffrage.[73] Undoubtedly, the legal status of freedpeople and even their ability to remain in the Choctaw Nation was uncertain at best, in spite of the 1866 treaty between the Choctaw and the federal government.

The Choctaw Freedmen Bill of 1883 finally clarified the status of the roughly 3,500 Choctaw freedpeople and enumerated their rights in the nation.[74] The freedpeople gained citizenship rights, including suffrage; the right to equal process in civil and criminal matters in the Choctaw courts; forty acres of land to be held in the manner of other Choctaws (though other Choctaws held land communally and could improve as much land as they wished); equal educational opportunities; and the right to hold political offices in the nation, other than principal or district chief.[75] The freedpeople were not entitled, however, to any annuity moneys from previous treaty agreements or access to the public domain of the nation, which would have meant they could receive payments for future land cessions.[76] Nor could freedpeople confer Choctaw citizenship on others through marriage.[77] Those freedpeople who chose to leave the nation were entitled to $100.[78] Before the end of 1883, the law was tightened: the General Council voted to revoke the freedmen's right to hold any political offices whatsoever.[79]

While Choctaw freedpeople lacked the full legal and political rights of Choctaw citizens by blood, their access to land was a concrete and significant benefit of citizenship, one that the freedpeople in southern states lacked and desperately wanted.[80] Choctaw freedwoman Frances Banks remarked, "After de War I was what you call a freedman. De Indians had to give all dey slaves forty acres of land. I'se allus lived on dis land which jines dat of Ole master's and I'se never stayed away from it long at a time."[81] Sally Henderson Moss recalled that her stepfather, Robert Wright, had a right to land in the Choctaw Nation as a freedman.[82] Squire Hall and his wife both received allotments as freedpeople "partly in the rich land of the Arkansas River bottom and the remainder on the high ground which skirts the valley land."[83] Robert Lewis stated, "I had a lot of relatives there who owned quite a bit of land that they had been allotted; they were freedmen."[84] While the Choctaw Freedmen Bill confirmed the forty acres specified in the 1866 treaty, once again the source of the amount of land stipulated is uncertain. Perhaps more pertinent is that Choctaw Indians did not have any restrictions placed on the amount of land they could improve in the nation at that time.

Ownership of this land by these freedpeople had consequences for their children as well; the children could inherit this property or this right to land. Lula Neighbors lived on land she obtained through her mother, a Choctaw freedwoman: "This forty acres where I live now was given to me after statehood; it is my claim. I have a 'right' from Mother's being a freedwoman."[85] Similarly, Thomas Franklin described his mother as "slave-Choctaw" and stated, "When I was born in 1873, I became a member of the tribe and years later I received an allotment of forty acres in Garvin County."[86] And there were greater consequences for this distribution of land to freedpeople in Indian Territory: some of these allotments would become the basis of the creation of all-Black towns such as Boley in Oklahoma in the early twentieth century.[87] However, the people of African descent did not always manage to maintain title to this land: Matthew Maytubbie, born in 1889 not long after the passage of the Freedmen Bill, noted with chagrin, "We all had land given us by the government but fiddled it away drinking and gambling. My pappy didn't drink and I wish I didn't."[88] This inability to retain possession of these allotments was part of a larger pattern of land loss because of federal policy; tribal groups had controlled 138 million acres of land in the nineteenth century, prior to allotment, but only 55 million acres by 1934, around when many of these Indian Pioneer History and Works Progress Administration interviews were recorded.[89]

White Americans had long recognized the possibility of improving one's economic standing by marrying Native women to gain access to land, and some commented on how people who had been enslaved by Indians also had a right to land.[90] For some African Americans from southern states, the ability for the freedpeople to access land suggested that there was more opportunity for people of African descent in general in Indian Territory.[91] Lula Neighbors's African American father was a "state man" who moved to the Choctaw Nation from Georgia: "When he saw that the Civil War was over he decided to come west where colored people were given a better chance to make a living. He came to the Choctaw Nation and married my mother, a freedwoman."[92] This marriage enabled Neighbors's father to access landownership more readily than would have been possible in Georgia. Lucy Cherry's mother moved to Indian Territory from Alabama after emancipation and married William Crush, a Choctaw Indian.[93] One cannot help but wonder if the attraction of this move for Cherry's mother, just as it was for Neighbors's father, was the perception that conditions for freedpeople might be better in Indian Territory.

The ability of freedpeople to own land in Indian Territory attracted other people of African descent to migrate to the area. For instance, in Topeka, Kansas, William Eagleson's company promoted the land and climate of Oklahoma Territory and claimed it as a space where black people "could enjoy freedom and could fearlessly exercise [their] rights as citizen[s]."[94] Eagleson also edited the newspaper the *Colored Citizen*. The pages of African American publications included promising tidbits about life in Indian Territory. J. A. Broadnax wrote in the *Christian Reporter* about missionary work taking place among the Seminole Indians: "I am presiding Elder of the Seminole nation and agent for the Chickasaw, to assist them in getting the rights of the colored people and have them adopted in that nation as full-blooded Indians. We have in view a nice location for building a high school in the nation for the freemen.... I want seven active ministers to come out at once; married men preferred.... This is my 12 year in the territory and I have not been hungry a day on account of hard times."[95] For Broadnax's readers, Indian Territory promised a religious community, educational opportunity, and economic security. Another article offered a description of an idyllic interracial religious service with a "negro" interpreter and meal in which "Creeks, negroes and whites sat down together at a long table under an arbor."[96] Guidon provided a detailed and more critical evaluation of conditions for people of African descent in the Indian nations, stating that some groups offered more legal rights and options for schooling to freedpeople than others. Yet Guidon still closed with "Dear readers, consider what an opportunity here is to do good."[97] The implication was that, even if the availability of schools, churches, or jobs for people of African descent was uneven in the territory, it was still an attractive place to go to "civilize" the population, both Native and Black, and pursue the establishment of churches and schools. Hence, Edward P. McCabe, one of the leaders of the Black town of Nicodemus, Kansas, promoted Oklahoma as a potential Black state or a place where African Americans could hold the balance of political power.[98] Likewise, George M. Jackson would write to the governor of Kansas claiming that many African Americans hoped Congress would open land ceded by Indian nations in 1866 for settlement.[99] By the early twentieth century, the pages of the *Chicago Defender* broadcasted the call for Black migration out of the South far and wide.[100]

Other freedpeople may have come to Indian Territory to flee the racialized violence spreading across the South in the wake of Reconstruction. According to statistics compiled by Monroe Work, the number of known lynchings peaked around 1892, and the vast majority of lynchings that took place from 1882 to 1968 occurred in southern states. Moreover, other scholars suggest that a great deal of violence that targeted African Americans in the South immediately after the Civil War has not yet been studied or quantified.[101] *Chicago Defender* editor Robert S. Abbott and his staff were often willing to recount the graphic details of the torture inflicted upon African American victims of white lynch mobs.[102] Such descriptions surely led some African Americans to try their luck outside of the South. Western states in general may have been attractive because significantly fewer lynchings took place there, and mobs there executed more white victims than African American or Native victims.[103] For instance, Work's figures for Oklahoma included eighty-two white victims and forty African American victims. Some westerners drew distinctions between acts of "'Southern lynching,' popularly understood as the torture, mutilation, and murder of African Americans through mob violence," and western vigilantism, a controlled response to a crime when legal mechanisms were inadequate to the task.[104] They claimed such vigilante activity took place without regard to race and often condemned the activities of white southerners.

Historian Murray R. Wickett points out that in 1896, the total number of lynchings reported in the *Chicago Tribune* for Indian Territory and Oklahoma Territory combined (ten) was surpassed only by Louisiana, Tennessee, Alabama, and Florida, arguing that Indian Territory was very southern in its racial thinking.[105] Civilian mobs in Indian Territory assuredly took the punishment of alleged criminals into their own hands; however, this figure does not capture the racial identities of the victims of the mobs. The presence of a large Native population complicated the racial picture in Indian Territory. James Elbert Cutler's compilation of figures from the *Chicago Tribune* also indicates that from 1882 to 1903, of ninety-five victims of lynch mobs in Indian Territory, seven were African American and fifteen were "Others" (a category that presumably included Native peoples), while the rest were white. The composition of the victims of mob violence in Indian Territory is a marked departure from that of a location such as Mississippi, where 294 of 334 victims were African American, or South Carolina, where 109 of 117 victims were African American.[106] Again, the African American population's awareness of these regional differences in mob violence, combined with stories about black landownership, could have made Indian Territory seem like an enticing destination with the possibility of economic independence and fairer treatment.

Alice Alexander had been enslaved in Louisiana and walked to Oklahoma with her husband and other freedpeople "in search of education.... We come to Oklahoma looking for de same thing then that darkies go North looking fer now. But we got disappointed."[107] Alexander and her fellow freedpeople were likely unaware of the resistance Native groups displayed toward incorporating their formerly enslaved population into Native societies and their unwillingness to provide schools for people of African descent immediately after the war, whether newly arrived or long established. Upon passage of the Freedmen Bill, Choctaw authorities created neighborhood schools and, later, a boarding school for the formerly enslaved; however, citizens of African descent would later complain to American officials about the inadequacy of such institutions.[108]

The concessions of the Freedmen Bill were an obvious improvement in the condition of the freedpeople of the Choctaw Nation, and more than the freedpeople of the American South were able to achieve, particularly with respect to land. Yet they also exposed the resistance of the Choctaw Nation to incorporating freedpeople into the country. Choctaw authorities declared that the freedpeople possessed "all the rights, priviliges [sic] and immunities" of Choctaw citizens but then carefully circumscribed those rights.[109] Thus, the freedpeople had access to land but not to the public domain or annuity funds that resulted from the sale of Choctaw land. Some freedpeople would later complain to American officials that Choctaws also prevented their possession of their promised forty acres.[110] The freedpeople could vote but not hold particular political offices. And citizenship rights did not extend to the spouses of freedpeople, who were obligated, in the case of men, to obtain permits to reside in the nation "and allowed to remain during good behavior only."[111] The language of this limit on freedpeople's ability to bestow Choctaw citizenship on their spouses assumed that such spouses would be other freedpeople from nearby states. This limit, then, also ensured that a larger population of people of African descent would not be incorporated into the Choctaw Nation. The entire process, with its constant renegotiation of terms, as well as the resulting limits on the rights of freedpeople, demonstrates the lack of enthusiasm with which the Choctaw approached including freedpeople in the nation as citizens.

In 1885, not long after the Choctaw freedpeople had received civil and some political rights in the nation, the Choctaw legislature passed a marriage act to clarify further the limits of the freedpeople's new rights. The legislation declared simply, "It shall not be lawful for a Choctaw and a negro to marry." Choctaw men or women who violated this statute faced felony charges in Choctaw circuit court and, if found guilty, would receive fifty lashes on the bare back.[112] While the freedpeople might have obtained Choctaw citizenship, participated in the Choctaw courts as legal actors, and voted in Choctaw elections, they could not legally marry Choctaw Indians. In the language of the day, civil and political equality might be permissible, but social equality was not. Thus, the law declared an entire class of Choctaw citizens unmarriageable, though these people were no longer enslaved and possessed some rights in the nation. The target of the earlier anti-amalgamation statute discussed in chapter 2 was the race—the African ancestry—of the enslaved, not their status. The race of enslaved people was what made relationships with them distasteful enough to be declared illegal.

While Choctaw lawmakers were prohibiting marriages between people of African descent and Choctaws, they provided a legal means for such unions between Euro-Americans and Choctaws. The most complicated iteration of marriage laws governing unions between white men and Choctaw women came in 1875.[113] The General Council continued to require that white men, who could be citizens of the United States or some other foreign government, obtain a marriage license from a Choctaw circuit clerk or judge in order to marry in the nation but also added the stipulation that a man swear an oath or provide some other evidence that he was not still legally married elsewhere. This part of the intermarriage law echoes the sentiments of the earlier 1849 prohibition of polygamous unions. Moreover, he had to present a "certificate of good moral character, signed by at least ten respectable Choctaw citizens by blood, who shall have been acquainted with him at least twelve months immediately preceding the signing of such certificate." The certificate requirement is illuminating in several respects. First, Choctaw legal authorities did not trust just any citizen to testify to the "good moral character" of a white male applicant for marriage; other intermarried white men, for instance, were not acceptable signatories. Thus, while these intermarried white men might have been Choctaw citizens legally, Choctaw authorities saw them as different in some way. Choctaw citizens by blood had to be willing to endorse an applicant for marriage. Second, the requirement that the signatories of the certificate know the applicant for at least twelve months reflects a desire to be certain about the applicant's character. Presumably, those signatories knew the applicant because he had resided in the nation for those twelve months prior to seeking a marriage license. Choctaws, then, were wary of white men who moved into Choctaw territory and immediately sought Choctaw wives and, thereby, access to Choctaw citizenship. Finally, these signatories were always Choctaw men; that is, Choctaw men had some control over the ability of Choctaw women to introduce outsiders to the nation, which also reaffirmed Choctaw men's protection of Choctaw sovereignty, as discussed in chapter 2.

The procedure for obtaining a marriage license did not end with demonstrating that one was not married elsewhere and presenting a certificate of good moral character; the applicant still had to pay a twenty-five-dollar fee and swear an oath of allegiance to the Choctaw government. The oath stated, "I do solemnly swear that I will honor, defend, and submit to the constitution and laws of the Choctaw nation, and will neither claim nor seek from the United States government or from the judicial tribunals thereof, any protection privilege, or redress incompatible with the same as guaranteed to the Choctaw nation by the treaty stipulations entered into between them, so help me God."[114] The oath was an attempt to navigate the complications created by marriages between citizens of different sovereign nations. For instance, in the case of the commission of a crime, what court had jurisdiction to punish an intermarried citizen? To what court would an intermarried citizen submit a complaint or attempt to seek restitution? If the Choctaw Nation and the United States engaged in a war, not so far-fetched a prospect given the Trail of Tears and the Civil War, for whom might intermarried citizens fight? Choctaw legal officials hoped, through the oath, to transform outsiders into citizens, to provide a clear answer to these kinds of questions. In marrying Choctaw women, white men made not only a financial commitment (for the license fee was not small) but a legal and civic commitment as well.

While much of the intermarriage legislation applied to marriages between Choctaw women and "foreign" men, lawmakers did recognize that some Choctaw men married "foreign" women. According to the language of the act, however, the General Council did not oblige white women to obtain a marriage license, prove that they were not already married elsewhere, find Choctaws by blood to attest to their good character, or swear an oath of allegiance to the Choctaw government. Clearly, Choctaw authorities found intermarried white women less threatening and saw less need to carefully monitor white women's access to Choctaw citizenship. Perhaps the long history of adopting non-Choctaw women into the nation explains the exemption of white women from the requirements of the intermarriage law. Choctaws also likely realized that white women exercised few property rights upon marriage in American society and were thus unlikely to expect these rights upon marrying their Choctaw husbands. In contrast, Choctaw authorities' careful circumscription of the property rights of white men who married Choctaw women indicates that white men did presume that they would have authority over their wives' property upon marriage.

Where white women do appear in this intermarriage act is as widows and absent partners.[115] A white woman preceded in death by her Choctaw husband continued to enjoy the privileges of Choctaw citizenship unless she remarried any white person "having no rights of Choctaw citizenship by blood." Marrying even another widowed intermarried white person, it seems, would lead to the loss of Choctaw citizenship for intermarried white women and men. Widowed intermarried whites presented a problem for Choctaw authorities: such individuals lacked clan affiliations and a connection to the nation but also had not done anything to provoke a loss of citizenship except experience the misfortune of losing a spouse. These individuals also might be responsible for raising Choctaw children who did have clan membership and whom the Choctaw would want to keep in the nation. Widowed intermarried whites who then married each other presented a larger problem: they could produce children who would be Choctaw citizens but lacked clan membership and kinship ties, a prospect that many Choctaw would have found anathema because of the importance of clan identity, even as it experienced a nineteenth-century decline.

Abandoning one's Choctaw spouse also led to the loss of Choctaw citizenship, as well as a declaration of intruder status and removal from the nation, for both white women and white men. This provision attempted to prevent whites from marrying solely to gain citizenship rights in the nation and then quickly deserting their Choctaw spouses. It is unclear from the statute whether any kind of legal separation or divorce between a Choctaw Indian and a white person might qualify as abandonment. Thus, the end of a long marriage might also result in the revocation of the white partner's legal citizenship and ejection from the nation.

Not long after the passage of this more detailed intermarriage act, a court decision in Indian Territory would demonstrate the force of intermarriage laws and the continuation of the trend in changing social organization suggested by the passage of earlier laws about marriage and property inheritance. While the 1878 murder case against James E. Reynolds, an intermarried white man in the Choctaw Nation accused of murdering another intermarried white man, focused on the issue of jurisdiction and who had authority in legal matters concerning intermarried white people in Indian Territory, the decision also established patrilineal descent as equal to matrilineal descent in determining Choctaw citizenship.[116] The court's decision regarding which judicial system, American or Indian, had the authority to hear the case depended on the citizenship of the wives: if the women were Choctaws by birth, their husbands obtained Choctaw citizenship through marriage, and the Choctaw courts would decide the case. The court found that the wives were in fact Choctaw based on their descent from a common male Choctaw ancestor; thus, Choctaw courts had jurisdiction over the prosecution of Reynolds. Many Choctaws had likely accepted the children of white women and Choctaw men, for instance, as citizens of the nation prior to this decision, but the decision validated the practice. The decision also confirmed that matrilineal descent and clan membership were no longer the central principle for social organization in the Choctaw Nation.

By 1886, just three years after finally making freedpeople in the nation citizens, the General Council passed an act to define "the quantity of blood necessary for citizenship." Quite tellingly, the act stipulated that "all applicants for rights in this Nation shall prove their mixture of blood to be white and Indian."[117] While the act did not apply to freedpeople and others who were already citizens in the Choctaw Nation, it did mean that in the future, people of mixed Choctaw and African ancestry could not claim Choctaw citizenship, a departure from older practice that would have permitted such individuals with blood ties to Choctaw Nation members to access citizenship. The act also closed an entry point to citizenship for freedpeople who might migrate to the nation in the future. In the Choctaw Nation, Reconstruction led to the inclusion of freedpeople as citizens, and this citizenship came with land; however, this land did not come with equality.

Conclusion

Focusing our attention on the Choctaw Nation, as well as on Indian Territory more broadly, during the Civil War exposes the many ruptures the war represented. These fissures transcend easy and familiar binaries: North versus South, blue versus gray, free states versus slave states, industrialization versus agrarianism, and a largely white North fighting a South where the Black population was concentrated. As scholars continue to widen and deepen our understanding of the Civil War by moving beyond its battlefields, they demonstrate the war's sweeping consequences for everyone within and beyond the borders of the United States. Including Indian Territory injects the question of Native sovereignty into the dispute over whether federal or state governments held more authority. Federal and state officials disagreed about who held ultimate power in questions about slavery, but they also did not see eye to eye about the nature of Indian sovereignty. Thus, as we saw in chapter 1, the Mississippi state legislature took steps to extend its jurisdiction over the Choctaw ahead of federal efforts to negotiate and enact a policy of removing Native groups from the southeastern United States. For their part, the Choctaw saw the potential relationship between state sovereignty and the sovereignty of Indigenous nations that, to an important degree, led them to side with the Confederacy during the war.

The Civil War is also irrevocably tied to the history of the West, as well as to the complex, promise-filled but sometimes ugly origin story of the United States. Because of disagreement about the place of slavery in society, the founders forged compromises about the slave trade and political representation that would not last as settlement moved west. By the antebellum period, Americans increasingly linked westward expansion to the question of slavery's expansion. As American colonizers marched across the North American continent, sometimes pushing Natives off their homelands, at other times decimating their numbers, the issue of whether settlers would take slavery with them grew in importance and precipitated the Missouri Compromise and the Compromise of 1850. Eventually, tensions between federal and state authorities regarding slavery's expansion and the control of enslaved populations erupted into war.

It behooves us, then, to take seriously what people in those western spaces thought of slavery, the balance between state and federal power, and definitions of citizenship. Even if one argues that the western theater of fighting had little effect on events in the East, one can at least concede Mary Jane Warde's assertion that the war had a profound impact on the inhabitants of Indian Territory and on Native sovereignty.[1] Further, ideas about sovereignty, expansion, and citizenship that were being worked out in Indian Territory had consequences for the United States. Obviously, Native people inhibited US expansion with their mere existence in the West, as well as their organization into sovereign nations. Moreover, land cessions by Native peoples were the basis for the creation of many western states. But the presence of self-governing Indigenous peoples also reordered the racial hierarchy in ways manifested in the Oklahoma state constitution.[2] Finally, congressmen simultaneously juggled beliefs about the readiness for American citizenship of people of African descent and Indigenous peoples, who often were not, in fact, interested in joining the American polity at all.[3]

Both the Choctaw Nation and southern states fought to maintain their access to the labor of enslaved people. Yet, the racial hierarchies these societies created to support the institution of slavery differed, because in the Choctaw Nation, Euro-Americans did not control political power. Choctaws used enslaved people to grow corn and, to a lesser degree, cotton and to manage livestock, agricultural priorities that differed from those of many white southerners. To preserve control over this labor force, Choctaw lawmakers passed laws regulating interracial marriage and prohibiting literacy for enslaved people without the permission of their enslavers. This legislative activity created a social hierarchy in which race played an essential part.

While some of this legislative activity would have been familiar to white southerners, there were also sharp differences. The Choctaw General Council did not just prohibit marriages between Choctaw citizens and people of African descent; it also carefully policed white men who married Choctaw women. Choctaws continued to honor matrilineal descent; thus, people of African descent who also claimed descent from Choctaw women could still access legal rights in the nation in ways that were not possible for people of mixed African and European ancestry in southern states. In general, Choctaws created a racial order that distinguished and privileged Choctaw identity over whiteness. In other words, a black-and-white racial binary did not fit the reality of the Choctaw Nation.

Choctaws traditionally held different ideas about gender, especially women's labor and access to and control of property, and those notions persisted in the nineteenth century. Clan membership continued to follow matrilineal descent, as did leadership positions. Choctaw women were also the primary agriculturalists and controlled land use. These practices imparted a great deal of power to women in Choctaw society.

The Confederate government promised to respect the Choctaw Nation's territorial boundaries and right to self-governance and to preserve the institution of slavery, but officials also offered numerous other incentives to encourage the Choctaw to join the southern cause. Jefferson Davis's agents offered money for Choctaw soldiers' pay, bounties, uniforms, and weapons. Confederate officials also promised to honor treaties made between the Choctaw and the federal government and secured all unpaid funds due the Choctaw treasury. Shortly after taking a secession vote, Texas immediately sent emissaries to Indian Territory to gain the support of Native nations. Individual white southerners from Texas and Arkansas also exerted pressure by attending Choctaw political meetings and sometimes even overtly threatened Natives in hopes of gaining support for the Confederacy. And while Choctaw leaders initially expressed a desire to remain neutral, they quickly joined the fight on behalf of the South.

Choctaw participation in the war was greater than previous estimates suggested, and the Confederate records illuminate the enthusiasm with which Choctaw men enlisted for the fight. Additional records that accompany the enlistment papers in conjunction with nineteenth-century narratives and personal papers offer valuable glimpses of the experiences of Choctaw soldiers in the war. The Civil War also presented an opportunity for Choctaw men to reclaim traditional notions of masculinity that had waned over the course of the first half of the nineteenth century. Choctaws had always connected warfare and masculinity, so that full male adulthood was impossible without participating in war. But interactions with Euro-Americans and concomitant declines in warfare between Native groups had led Choctaws to reconfigure notions of masculinity to include activities such as educational attainment, diplomatic negotiation, horse raiding, and alcohol consumption. The prospect of battle against federal troops permitted Choctaw soldiers to preserve sovereignty, slavery, and a particular racial hierarchy while demonstrating their right to be men, to once again claim their names in the traditional way.

Once the war ended, the Choctaw Nation faced the same dilemma as the Confederate South: how and under what terms to reestablish a relationship with the federal government. One of the terms of its 1866 treaty with the United States was the inclusion of people formerly enslaved in the Choctaw Nation as citizens. The General Council initially resisted this requirement and finally acquiesced nearly twenty years later. For Choctaw freedpeople, citizenship came not only with legal rights, though circumscribed, but also with access to land due to practices of communal landholding among the Choctaw. In some sense, that mythologized "forty acres and a mule" for freedpeople materialized in the Choctaw Nation in a way that it did not in southern states. Some of these landholdings became the basis for all-Black towns in the later state of Oklahoma. Again, expanding our view to include Indian Territory in our understanding of the American Civil War reveals a story that can feel familiar but with startlingly different consequences.

The Civil War and the Reconstruction that followed raised fundamental questions about the meaning of citizenship in both Native nations and the United States. The era's attempted legal resolutions continue to reverberate today, as descendants of Choctaw freedpeople currently cannot obtain citizenship in the Choctaw Nation unless they can demonstrate descent from an individual enrolled by the Dawes Commission as a "by blood" member of the Choctaw Nation.[4] Similar requirements have led some descendants of people enslaved by Indigenous enslavers in the larger Indian Territory—specifically in the Cherokee and Seminole Nations—to pursue legal action to gain full citizenship rights in their respective nations.[5] Just as in the nineteenth century, the question of who should determine the citizenship status of formerly enslaved people and their descendants in Native nations continues to raise uncomfortable questions about governmental authority, Native sovereignty, and race.

While the larger Choctaw story in the nineteenth century is about change to some of the Choctaw's basic social relationships of gender and race, it is also a story that presents an alternative way to imagine these relations. The Choctaw example gives us other ways to think about gender roles and how to define them and a different standard for organizing racial hierarchy. The experience of Choctaw freedpeople also invites us to consider the missed opportunities of landownership for formerly enslaved people outside of Indian Territory. That is, do the Choctaw Nation and Indian Territory more broadly offer some hint of what a fully realized plan for land redistribution for formerly enslaved people in the larger South might have meant? Tulsa, Oklahoma, was home to Greenwood, also known as the Black Wall Street because of its thriving African American community. Perhaps the prosperity of African Americans in Greenwood was possible because some freedpeople had access to landownership through citizenship in Indian nations. More darkly, perhaps the Tulsa Race Massacre that later targeted Greenwood reveals something about white Americans' inability to disentangle anxieties about race and economics. In another divergence from the Confederate South, the citizens of the Choctaw Nation did not subscribe to the "Lost Cause" narrative or embark on a campaign to create statues of and monuments to Confederate soldiers in the years after the Civil War ended.[6] That choice offers us another way to think about how Americans and many white southerners in particular commemorate the Civil War. In the end, telling the story of the Civil War from the perspective of the Choctaw Nation challenges ideas about who and what experiences are southern; reorients Civil War historiography to consider the importance of locations beyond the traditional Union and Confederacy; and complicates our thinking about the historical relationship between Native populations and people of African descent.

Acknowledgments

In many ways, this book took me far too long to write; however, I could not have written it until now. Along the way, I was guided and supported by many people and institutions. I was able to work through some of the ideas in this book through presentations at conferences and symposia hosted by institutions including the University of Florida; the Clements Center for Southwest Studies at Southern Methodist University; the University of New Mexico; Saint Louis University; the University of Alabama; and Rice University's collaboration with Universidade Estadual de Campinas and Instituto Mora. The questions asked and lively conversations that emerged improved this book immeasurably.

I received financial support from the University of Oklahoma and Rice University to conduct research for this project. I would like to give special thanks to Laurie Scrivener at the University of Oklahoma for all of her help accessing materials, even after I was no longer a faculty member there. A fellowship from the National Endowment for the Humanities and a teaching release provided by Rice University's Humanities Research Center gave me the time to complete this manuscript. Amy Ferguson with Rice University's GIS/Data Center created the beautiful maps.

Numerous colleagues and friends have encouraged me throughout the process. In Norman, the company of Jane Wickersham, Sandie Holguin, Kathleen Brosnan, Melissa Stockdale, and Jennifer Davis gave me something to look forward to after long days staring at microfilm. Jane also let me stay at her home during some of my summer visits to the University of Oklahoma's libraries. At Rice, Lora Wildenthal acted as a writing accountability buddy during one semester of leave, and Carl Caldwell gently reminded me to get work done. Lunches with Lora, Moramay Lopez-Alonso, Lisa Balabanlilar, Sayuri Guthrie Shimizu, and Kerry Ward fed my spirit and my mind. And Alex Byrd and Ed Cox have been my private brain trust, helping me to think about the other parts of my life as a faculty member and sharing their warm friendship.

Joanne Melish and Caleb McDaniel generously read this manuscript in full and offered helpful suggestions to clarify my language and reframe my interpretations. Meg Olsen's careful eye has saved me from many errors. Despite our disparate research interests, my colleague Michael Maas kindly read my work at a crucial moment. Our "hallway conversations" are always a revelation about how connected people and ideas are, even when separated by thousands of years and thousands of miles.

At the University of North Carolina Press, Debbie Gershenowitz has been an enthusiastic and patient advocate for my work, and her publication staff operates with enviable efficiency. Through Debbie, I was able to receive cogent criticisms to sharpen my analysis and push my thinking from Greg Smithers and an anonymous reader.

I would like to thank the University of South Carolina Press for granting permission to reprint portions of chapter 1, which appeared as "Women, Labor, and Power in the Nineteenth-Century Choctaw Nation" in *Gender and Sexuality in Indigenous North America*, edited by Sandra Slater and myself. I would also like to thank the University of California Press for allowing me to reprint material in chapter 6, which appeared as "'Dis Land Which Jines Dat of Ole Master's': The Meaning of Citizenship for the Choctaw Freedpeople" in *Civil War Wests: Testing the Limits of the United States*, edited by Adam Arenson and Andrew R. Graybill.

Last, I would like to thank my family. My parents, James and Okie Yarbrough, gave me time in the archives by providing valuable childcare, and my brother, Roy, and his wife, Erin, opened up their home to me numerous times for research trips. My in-laws, the Terry and Leveston families, are always supportive of my work, though I am sure they have been puzzled by my slow progress. And as always, I have to thank Arthur Terry for his patience and love. He is my biggest cheerleader and has faith in my abilities, even when I have doubts. My children, Wilson and Rivers, have lived with this book for their whole lives and without complaint. In fact, they think I am cool for writing books. I think they are cool for loving books. This one is for you both.

Notes

Abbreviations

CLCN 1839–1851	*The Constitution and Laws of the Cherokee Nation: Passed at Tahlequah, Cherokee Nation, 1839–1851* (Tahlequah, Cherokee Nation, 1852). Electronic copy accessed through the Library of Congress website, http://lccn.loc.gov/28014182.
CLCN 1840	*The Constitution and Laws of the Choctaw Nation*, vol. 13 of *Constitutions and Laws of the American Indian Tribes* (1840; repr., Wilmington, DE: Scholarly Resources, 1975)
CLCN 1847	*The Constitution and Laws of the Choctaw Nation*, vol. 14 of *Constitutions and Laws of the American Indian Tribes* (1847; repr., Wilmington, DE: Scholarly Resources, 1975)
CLCN 1852	*The Constitution and Laws of the Choctaw Nation*, vol. 15 of *Constitutions and Laws of the American Indian Tribes* (1852; repr., Wilmington, DE: Scholarly Resources, 1975)
CLCN 1869	*Constitution and Laws of the Choctaw Nation: Together with the Treaties of 1855, 1865 and 1866* (New York City: Wm. P. Lyon and Son, 1869)
CNR	Choctaw National Records Microfilm Series, Oklahoma Historical Society, Oklahoma City
CTLCN	*Constitution, Treaties and Laws of the Choctaw Nation: Made and Enacted by the Choctaw Legislature* (1887; repr., Wilmington, DE: Scholarly Resources, 1975)
FRB	*The Freedmen and Registration Bills*, vol. 18 of *Constitutions and Laws of the American Indian Tribes* (1883; repr., Wilmington, DE: Scholarly Resources, 1975)
IPH	Indian Pioneer History Collection, Western History Collection, University of Oklahoma, Norman
NARA 258	Compiled Service Records of Confederate Soldiers Who Served in Organizations Raised Directly by the Confederate Government, microcopy 258, National Archives, Washington, DC

Introduction

1. Typescript of speech "The Inaugural Address of Gov. Pitchlynn," pp. 1 and 3, box 6, folder 6, document ID 2196, Peter Perkins Pitchlynn Papers, Western History Collection, University of Oklahoma, Norman.

2. Grahame-Smith, *Abraham Lincoln*.

3. CNR, roll CTN 8, vol. 295: 32, 210, 229; roll CTN 8, vol. 297: 179, 184; and roll CTN 16, document 18302: 251–52, 301–2.

4. Pesantubbee, *Choctaw Women in a Chaotic World*, 97. McKee and Schlenker find that most Choctaws were aware of enslaved Africans by 1750; see *Choctaws*, 39.

5. Krauthamer, *Black Slaves, Indian Masters*, 21–23.

6. DeRosier, *Removal of the Choctaw Indians*, 137.

7. Katz, *Black Indians*, 135.

8. Mary Cole claimed to have learned the Choctaw language before she learned to speak English. IPH, roll 33, vol. 100: 56–59. Paul Garnett Roebuck's enslaved grandfather acted as an interpreter for Choctaw and Chickasaw Indians in federal court at Paris, Texas, roll 27, vol. 81: 438–41.

9. *CLCN* 1840, 19, 20–21.

10. See article 1, section 9.4, of the *Constitution of the Confederate States of America*.

11. Galloway, *Choctaw Genesis*, 27–29, 115–16, and 120–27. See also Etheridge, *From Chicaza to Chickasaw*, 2 (citations refer to 2013 edition); and Cheek's summary of Choctaw origins in "'We Are Clay People,'" 13–24.

12. For more discussion of settler colonialism, see Wolfe, "Settler Colonialism"; and Wolfe, *Settler Colonialism*. See also Lorenzo Veracini's *Settler Colonialism*. Bowes offers a nice summary of settler colonialism in the context of Indian removal in the United States in *Land Too Good for Indians*, 12–13.

13. Perdue and Green, *Cherokee Removal*, 119–20. This language comes from an excerpt of President Andrew Jackson's State of the Union address, December 6, 1830.

14. To see the distribution of the enslaved population in the South via map and raw numbers, see Hergesheimer, *Map Showing the Distribution of the Slave Population*. See Melish's *Disowning Slavery* for more on the connection between ideas about race and the institution of slavery in New England in spite of the region's smaller population of enslaved people and the fact of gradual emancipation after the Revolutionary War.

15. Nelson and Sheriff, *People at War*, chap. 7.

16. McPherson, *Battle Cry of Freedom*.

17. A. Bailey, *Invisible Southerners*.

18. Ural, *Civil War Citizens*, 7.

19. Lause, *Race and Radicalism*.

20. Hauptman, *Between Two Fires*, xii.

21. See Confer's *Cherokee Nation in the Civil War*; Gaines's *Confederate Cherokees*; and Knight's *Red Fox*. There is also an autobiography of G. W. Grayson of the Creek Nation edited by Baird titled *A Creek Warrior for the Confederacy*.

22. Warde, *When the Wolf Came*; Clampitt, *Civil War and Reconstruction*.

23. See Abel's *American Indian as Slaveholder and Secessionist* and *American Indian as Participant in the Civil War*, which are part of her three-volume series, *The Slaveholding Indians*.

24. Baird, *Peter Pitchlynn*, x.
25. Smithers, "Cherokee 'Two Spirits,'" 637.
26. See Mellon, *Bullwhip Days*, xvi–xviii; Starling, *Slave Narrative*, esp. chap. 4; D. Bailey, "Divided Prism"; Spindel, "Assessing Memory"; Escott, *Slavery Remembered*, 7–13; Foster, *Witnessing Slavery*, esp. chaps. 4 and 7; and Sekora and Turner's edited volume of essays, *Art of Slave Narrative*.
27. Woodward, "History from Slave Sources," 472.
28. Baker and Baker, *Oklahoma Slave Narratives*, 5.
29. Woodward, "History from Slave Sources," esp. 475.
30. Shaw, "Using the WPA Ex-slave Narratives," 624–26.
31. Fox-Genovese, *Within the Plantation Household*, 32–34.

Chapter 1

1. Lowery, "Original Southerners," 20.
2. There is some disagreement about whether "moiety," "ethnic group," or "phratry" is the correct terminology for these groups. For the use of "moiety," see McKee and Schlenker, *Choctaws*, 16. See also Swanton, *Social and Ceremonial Life of the Choctaw Indians*, 76–79. O'Brien refers to the two groups as "ethnic groups" in *Choctaws in a Revolutionary Age*, 15. Lambert prefers the term "phratry," *Choctaw Nation*, 23–24.
3. Swanton, *Social and Ceremonial Life of the Choctaw Indians*, 77; Pesantubbee, *Choctaw Women in a Chaotic World*, 10; Cushman, *History of the Choctaw, Chickasaw and Natchez Indians*, 59n14 and 87; McKee and Schlenker, *Choctaws*, 29; Galloway, *Choctaw Genesis*, 2. For examples of clan names among the Choctaw, see Smithers, *Native Southerners*, 22.
4. Galloway, *Choctaw Genesis*, 2.
5. IPH, roll 3, vol. 7: 170.
6. See Cushman, *History of the Choctaw, Chickasaw and Natchez Indians*, 194–95; and McKee and Schlenker, *Choctaws*, 29, for more on Choctaw naming practices.
7. Swanton, *Social and Ceremonial Life of the Choctaw Indians*, 134. *Ogla* refers to family or clan. Swanton is quoting David I. Bushnell Jr.
8. Both quotes from White, *Roots of Dependency*, 38. See also Cushman, *History of the Choctaw, Chickasaw and Natchez Indians*, 157; Swanton, *Social and Ceremonial Life of the Choctaw Indians*, 104–7; and Debo, *Rise and Fall of the Choctaw Republic*, 21–22.
9. Cushman, *History of the Choctaw, Chickasaw and Natchez Indians*, 203–6.
10. Pesantubbee, *Choctaw Women in a Chaotic World*, 46.
11. Cushman, *History of the Choctaw, Chickasaw and Natchez Indians*, 157; White, *Roots of Dependency*, 42.
12. Pesantubbee, *Choctaw Women in a Chaotic World*, 46.
13. Swanton offers the accounts of several observers who remarked on the reluctance of Choctaws to wage offensive wars but who noted that they fought valiantly when attacked. See *Social and Ceremonial Life of the Choctaw Indians*, 164–70, esp. 164. Choctaws' reluctance also stemmed from a desire for strategic advantage, and to be sure they took the scalps of men, "which is a greater mark of valour" than "content[ing]" themselves with the scalps of women and children.

14. White, *Roots of Dependency*, 108.
15. Cushman, *History of the Choctaw, Chickasaw and Natchez Indians*, 88.
16. Galloway, *Choctaw Genesis*, 2; Searcy, "Choctaw Subsistence," 35.
17. See Debo, *Rise and Fall of the Choctaw Republic*, 16.
18. Cushman, *History of the Choctaw, Chickasaw and Natchez Indians*, 88.
19. Swanton, *Social and Ceremonial Life of the Choctaw Indians*, 131; Debo, *Rise and Fall of the Choctaw Republic*, 16.
20. Galloway, *Choctaw Genesis*, 2. See Yarbrough, *Race and the Cherokee Nation*, 27-28, for more on the benefits of polygamous marriage for women in matrilocal households in the case of Cherokee Indians.
21. *CTLCN*, 155-56. It is unclear whether the husband, the wives, or all were liable for prosecution for the crime of polygamy.
22. McKee and Schlenker, *Choctaws*, 29.
23. Galloway, *Choctaw Genesis*, 2.
24. McKee and Schlenker, *Choctaws*, 29. See also White, *Roots of Dependency*, 20.
25. IPH, roll 33, vol. 99: 394. Sofkey, also spelled "sofke," is a sour corn drink or soup.
26. IPH, roll 22, vol. 65: 238.
27. Pesantubbee, *Choctaw Women in a Chaotic World*, 102.
28. Estrada, "Two-Spirit Histories," 166. Estrada offers a historiographical overview of the literature on two-spirit peoples in the Southwest, 166-74. Carpenter offers a brief review of the broader literature in "Womanish Men and Manlike Women," 147-48.
29. Smithers, "Cherokee 'Two Spirits,'" 631-32.
30. Carpenter, "Womanish Men and Manlike Women," 148 and 149.
31. Cushman, *History of the Choctaw, Chickasaw and Natchez Indians*, 174.
32. IPH, roll 17, vol. 51: 223.
33. Pesantubbee, *Choctaw Women in a Chaotic World*, 124.
34. IPH, roll 34, vol. 101: 488.
35. IPH, roll 15, vol. 46: 286-87.
36. See Debo, *Rise and Fall of the Choctaw Republic*, 18; and Pesantubbee, *Choctaw Women in a Chaotic World*, 164.
37. IPH, roll vol. 63: 136.
38. Cushman, *History of the Choctaw, Chickasaw and Natchez Indians*, 173-74; Swanton, *Social and Ceremonial Life of the Choctaw Indians*, 37-38.
39. Pesantubbee discusses these various uses of corn in *Choctaw Women in a Chaotic World*, 124-25.
40. White, *Roots of Dependency*, 26; Cushman, *History of the Choctaw, Chickasaw and Natchez Indians*, 309-11; Swanton, *Social and Ceremonial Life of the Choctaw Indians*, 127-38.
41. See Swanton, *Social and Ceremonial Life of the Choctaw Indians*, 161; and Cushman, *History of the Choctaw, Chickasaw and Natchez Indians*, 122.
42. Pesantubbee, *Choctaw Women in a Chaotic World*, 125.
43. Cushman, *History of the Choctaw, Chickasaw and Natchez Indians*, 174.
44. White, *Roots of Dependency*, 21-22.
45. Swanton, *Social and Ceremonial Life of the Choctaw Indians*, 38.
46. Pesantubbee, *Choctaw Women in a Chaotic World*, 125.

47. Champagne, *Social Order and Political Change*, 106–9.
48. White, *Roots of Dependency*, 120. See also Champagne, *Social Order and Political Change*, 149.
49. Champagne, *Social Order and Political Change*, 152; and Lambert, *Choctaw Nation*, 38.
50. Pitchlynn, *Gathering of Statesmen*, 19–20, 47, 51, 53, and 57.
51. For more on the backgrounds of figures who served in the Choctaw government, see Kidwell, *Choctaws and Missionaries*, 18–20; and Faiman-Silva, *Choctaw at the Crossroads*, 30.
52. Champagne, *Social Order and Political Change*, 152.
53. Pitchlynn, *Gathering of Statesmen*, 51.
54. Pitchlynn, 78, clauses 106–7, 127, and 219.
55. Pitchlynn, 85–89.
56. See Carson, "Greenwood LeFlore," 229; Pitchlynn, *Gathering of Statesmen*, 27; and Champagne, *Social Order and Political Change*, 152, for more on the spread of Christian religion among the Choctaws at this time.
57. Kidwell, *Choctaws and Missionaries*, 25.
58. Krauthamer, *Black Slaves, Indian Masters*, 48.
59. Kidwell, *Choctaws and Missionaries*, 76 and 120.
60. Krauthamer notes that some missionaries described their work among the Indians as "more than a 'duty enjoined by the Gospel'; it was also an 'act of justice' toward Indians," *Black Slaves, Indian Masters*, 48.
61. Pitchlynn, *Gathering of Statesmen*, 92–93, clauses 137–40.
62. Pitchlynn, 93–94, clauses 141–44.
63. Pitchlynn, 95–96, clauses 146–49.
64. Pitchlynn, 100, clauses 157–59.
65. Pitchlynn, 101–3, clauses 161 and 166.
66. Snyder, *Great Crossings*, 32 and 72; McGrath, *Illicit Love*, chap. 1.
67. Gabriel, *Elias Boudinot*, 61.
68. McGrath, *Illicit Love*, esp. 35–41.
69. Pitchlynn, *Gathering of Statesmen*, 114–16, clauses 192–98.
70. White, *Roots of Dependency*, 103. See also Carson, "Native Americans."
71. White, *Roots of Dependency*, 20.
72. Saunt, *New Order of Things*, 171. See chap. 7 for more discussion of the change in Creek thinking about property.
73. See O'Brien, *Choctaws in a Revolutionary Age*, 111, for more on this transition prior to the nineteenth century.
74. Pitchlynn, *Gathering of Statesmen*, 118, clause 201.
75. Pitchlynn, 72–73, clauses 91–94.
76. Pitchlynn, 122–25, clauses 209–16.
77. Pitchlynn, 73, clauses 95–96.
78. Pitchlynn, 130–31, clauses 226–28.
79. See Saunt's book *New Order of Things* for the most thorough discussion of changing ideas about property among southeastern native groups, specifically the Creeks. Other works on other groups also discuss changes in Native legal practices to protect property: Gibson, *Chickasaws*, chap. 6; and Strickland, *Fire and the Spirits*, chap. 5.

80. White, *Roots of Dependency*, 124–27.
81. For more on the religious revivals in the Choctaw Nation at this time, see Carson, "Greenwood LeFlore," 228–29; and Champagne, *Social Order and Political Change*, 152–53.
82. Kidwell, *Choctaws and Missionaries*, 134.
83. Krauthamer, *Black Slaves, Indian Masters*, 48.
84. Champagne, *Social Order and Political Change*, 150–55; Kidwell, *Choctaws and Missionaries*, 134–38. See also DeRosier, *Removal of the Choctaw Indians*, chap. 7; and Foreman, *Indian Removal*, chap. 1. DeRosier's depiction of the events suggests that LeFlore was even more dastardly in his intentions, carrying on secret negotiations with the federal government after being deposed from his position of authority.
85. See Perdue and Green, *Cherokee Removal*, 116–17, for a copy of the Indian Removal Act. For a discussion of the part that state courts played in removal, see Garrison, *Legal Ideology of Removal*; and for more on the landmark cases involving the Cherokee Nation, see Norgren, *Cherokee Cases*. For a discussion of the removal of Native groups north of the Ohio River, see Bowes, *Land Too Good for Indians*.
86. Champagne, *Social Order and Political Change*, 126.
87. S. Wells, "Federal Indian Policy," 182–85.
88. Kidwell, *Choctaws and Missionaries*, 133.
89. *Laws of the State of Mississippi*, 207–8.
90. DeRosier, *Removal of the Choctaw Indians*, 104–6. See also Kidwell, *Choctaws and Missionaries*, 133–34.
91. Wolfe, "Settler Colonialism," 388.
92. DeRosier, *Removal of the Choctaw Indians*, 106.
93. DeRosier, 107. DeRosier lays out these arguments quite succinctly.
94. Kidwell, *Choctaws and Missionaries*, 134–35; DeRosier, *Removal of the Choctaw Indians*, 113.
95. DeRosier, *Removal of the Choctaw Indians*, 116. DeRosier quotes the magazine *Niles Register* from September 1830.
96. Kidwell, *Choctaws and Missionaries*, 135.
97. Kidwell, 134.
98. DeRosier, *Removal of the Choctaw Indians*, 116–17. See also Prucha, *American Indian Treaties*, 168.
99. Pitchlynn, *Gathering of Statesmen*, 19. Similarly, the Cherokee were deeply divided over removal; see Davis, "Chaos in the Indian Country."
100. McKee and Schlenker, *Choctaws*, 17; DeRosier, *Removal of the Choctaw Indians*, 120–21; Champagne, *Social Order and Political Change*, 155; the quotation is from Swanton, *Social and Ceremonial Life of the Choctaw Indians*, 96.
101. Kidwell, *Choctaws and Missionaries*, 140; Champagne, *Social Order and Political Change*, 154.
102. Kidwell, *Choctaws and Missionaries*, 139–40.
103. Perhaps the most famous example of missionaries defending the sovereignty of southeastern Native groups is the Supreme Court case *Worcester v. Georgia* from 1832. The state of Georgia, in a move similar to Mississippi's, extended its jurisdiction over the Cherokee Nation and required whites living there to take an oath of allegiance to the state. Several missionaries, including Samuel Worcester, refused

to take this oath, insisting that the state had no authority over the Cherokee Nation because it was a sovereign nation. The case eventually reached the Supreme Court, and the majority found in favor of Worcester: Georgia did not have the authority to enforce its laws within the Cherokee Nation.

104. DeRosier, *Removal of the Choctaw Indians*, 120–21.
105. DeRosier, 122–23.
106. Champagne, *Social Order and Political Change*, 155; Kidwell, *Choctaws and Missionaries*, 140.
107. DeRosier, *Removal of the Choctaw Indians*, 123–24; Kidwell, *Choctaws and Missionaries*, 140.
108. The text of the 1830 Treaty of Dancing Rabbit Creek is widely available online. The Choctaw Nation provides a copy on its website, choctawnation.com. DeRosier offers the text of the treaty in the appendix of *Removal of the Choctaw Indians*.
109. 1830 Treaty of Dancing Rabbit Creek, article 4.
110. 1830 Treaty of Dancing Rabbit Creek, articles 6 and 7.
111. 1830 Treaty of Dancing Rabbit Creek, article 3.
112. 1830 Treaty of Dancing Rabbit Creek, article 16.
113. 1830 Treaty of Dancing Rabbit Creek, article 17.
114. 1830 Treaty of Dancing Rabbit Creek, article 20.
115. 1830 Treaty of Dancing Rabbit Creek, article 14.
116. 1830 Treaty of Dancing Rabbit Creek, article 22.
117. 1830 Treaty of Dancing Rabbit Creek, article 15.
118. 1830 Treaty of Dancing Rabbit Creek, article 19.
119. Champagne, *Social Order and Political Change*, 156; DeRosier, *Removal of the Choctaw Indians*, 132–33; Foreman, *Indian Removal*, 29–30.
120. DeRosier, *Removal of the Choctaw Indians*, 126–27.
121. McKee and Schlenker, *Choctaws*, 76; DeRosier, *Removal of the Choctaw Indians*, 129–32.
122. DeRosier, *Removal of the Choctaw Indians*, 132.
123. Wright, "Removal of the Choctaws," 113–15.
124. IPH, roll 15, vol. 46: 146–64.
125. Wright, "Removal of the Choctaws," 115–19.
126. Wright, 120–23; DeRosier, *Removal of the Choctaw Indians*, 153.
127. Wright, "Removal of the Choctaws," 123.
128. McKee and Schlenker, *Choctaws*, 87.
129. Lambert, *Choctaw Nation*, 41.
130. *CLCN* 1840, 6–7, article 3.
131. 1837 Treaty with the Choctaw and Chickasa, article 1.
132. 1837 Treaty with the Choctaw and Chickasa, article 3.
133. Champagne, *Social Order and Political Change*, 160–64; Paige, Bumpers, and Littlefield, *Chickasaw Removal*, chap. 3; Gibson, *Chickasaws*, chap. 7. For more on the land lost through sale, see Paige, Bumpers, and Littlefield, *Chickasaw Removal*, 60.
134. Paige, Bumpers, and Littlefield, *Chickasaw Removal*, 28.
135. Cushman, *History of the Choctaw, Chickasaw and Natchez Indians*, 18–21.
136. McKee and Schlenker, *Choctaws*, 7–8. McKee and Schlenker offer several other versions of the Choctaw origin story as well, 5–12.

137. Swanton, *Social and Ceremonial Life of the Choctaw Indians*, 5–37, esp. 12–27.

138. Galloway, *Choctaw Genesis*, 324. See 324–37 for a longer discussion of various origin stories and what can be gleaned from them.

139. Galloway, 316–20.

140. Gibson, *Chickasaws*, 4.

141. Gibson, 18–21; Swanton, *Social and Ceremonial Life of the Choctaw Indians*, 76–79.

142. *CLCN* 1840, 3.

143. *CLCN* 1840, 5–10, articles 2–6. These articles stipulate the distribution of powers, as well as the duties of each branch of the government.

144. *CLCN* 1840, 4–5, article 1.

145. *CLCN* 1840, 6, sections 7 and 5.

146. *CLCN* 1840, 8, section 4. Emphasis mine.

147. *CLCN* 1840, 9, section 5.

148. *CLCN* 1840, 10, article 6, section 3.

149. *CLCN* 1840, 12, section 14. For just several early examples of laws passed by the General Council that carefully use "person or persons" in describing punishment, see *CLCN* 1840, 13–15, sections 2, 3, 4, 5, 7, 8, 11, and 12.

150. Cushman, *History of the Choctaw, Chickasaw and Natchez Indians*, 88.

151. Cushman, 89.

152. *CLCN* 1840, 15, section 8.

153. *CLCN* 1840, 14–15, section 7.

154. *CLCN* 1840, 18, section 2.

155. *CLCN* 1847, 63, section 14.

156. *CLCN* 1847, 20.

157. White, *Roots of Dependency*, 127.

158. *CLCN* 1869, 100.

159. *CLCN* 1869, 100.

160. *CLCN* 1869, 100.

161. While I do not discuss it here, anthropologist Sandra Faiman-Silva also points to "technological innovations such as commoditized livestock ranching" as well as to the use of enslaved laborers in agriculture as contributors to Choctaw women's declining status, *Choctaw at the Crossroads*, 29.

162. Gibson, *Chickasaws*, 137–38; Yarbrough, *Race and the Cherokee Nation*, chap. 1; Zellar, *African Creeks*, 21–22; Saunt, *Black, White, and Indian*, 23; Smithers, *Native Southerners*, 138–39.

Chapter 2

1. Fite, "Development of the Cotton Industry," 343.

2. Pesantubbee, *Choctaw Women in a Chaotic World*, 97. McKee and Schlenker find that most Choctaws were aware of enslaved Africans by 1750. See *Choctaws*, 39.

3. DeRosier, *Removal of the Choctaw Indians*, 137.

4. McKee and Schlenker, *Choctaws*, 120–21.

5. Katz, *Black Indians*, 135.

6. See Krauthamer, *Black Slaves, Indian Masters*; and Fortney, "Robert M. Jones."

7. McKee and Schlenker, *Choctaws*, 115, 120.

8. Krauthamer, *Black Slaves, Indian Masters*, 80.
9. Fite, "Development of the Cotton Industry," 346.
10. Fortney, "Robert M. Jones," 1.
11. Fortney, 146; Fite, "Development of the Cotton Industry," 347.
12. Doran, "Negro Slaves," 341.
13. Quoted in Foreman, *Five Civilized Tribes*, 53.
14. Fite, "Development of the Cotton Industry," 346-47. Littlefield also discusses the practice of using enslaved labor for cash crop production among the Chickasaw in *Chickasaw Freedmen*, 11-12. See also St. Jean, *Remaining Chickasaw*, 35-36.
15. Baker and Baker, *Oklahoma Slave Narratives*, 325.
16. Yetman, *Voices from Slavery*, 56. See also Blassingame, *Slave Community*, 250.
17. Baker and Baker, *Oklahoma Slave Narratives*, 28.
18. Yetman, *Voices from Slavery*, 316.
19. See Blassingame, *Slave Community*, 114-23, for more on enslaved people, music, and labor.
20. Baker and Baker, *Oklahoma Slave Narratives*, 86-89.
21. Fox-Genovese, *Within the Plantation Household*, 120.
22. Baker and Baker, *Oklahoma Slave Narratives*, 259-62, 325.
23. Baker and Baker, 87-88, 258-59.
24. Baker and Baker, 324.
25. Krauthamer, *Black Slaves, Indian Masters*, 33.
26. For more on enslaved people's familiarity with horses, see Ainsworth's article on fugitive enslaved people in Texas, "Field Hands, Cowboys, and Runaways."
27. Baker and Baker, *Oklahoma Slave Narratives*, 88.
28. Baker and Baker, 326n1. Footnote 1 describes Poe as eighty years old at the time of the interview in 1937.
29. Baker and Baker, 258, 260.
30. Baker and Baker, 248-50.
31. Krauthamer, *Black Slaves, Indian Masters*, 33-34. See also Yarbrough, "Women, Labor, and Power," 135-36, for some discussion of Choctaw gender roles and labor.
32. Baker and Baker, *Oklahoma Slave Narratives*, 89, 260.
33. Mellon, *Bullwhip Days*, 185-87. See the MSGenWeb Slave Narrative Project, http://msgw.org/slaves/, for Dixon's full narrative and details about Dixon.
34. Raboteau, *Slave Religion*, esp. chaps. 2 and 5.
35. Lankford, *Bearing Witness*, 48.
36. For some discussion of how planters allocated their resources, see Genovese, *Political Economy of Slavery*, 46 and 131-36.
37. Fite, "Development of the Cotton Industry," 347-48.
38. Graebner, "Pioneer Indian Agriculture," 235.
39. Baker and Baker, *Oklahoma Slave Narratives*, 303.
40. Baker and Baker, 195.
41. Baker and Baker, 315.
42. Baker and Baker, 257-64.
43. IPH, roll 28, vol. 85: 468.
44. White, *Roots of Dependency*, 99-106. See Pitchlynn, *Gathering of Statesmen*, ix, for some background details about the Pitchlynns.

45. Doran, "Negro Slaves," 341.
46. Fortney, "Robert M. Jones," chap. 3; Lambert, *Choctaw Nation*, 42–43.
47. Baker and Baker, *Oklahoma Slave Narratives*, 196.
48. Baker and Baker, 376–77.
49. White, *Roots of Dependency*, 105.
50. Doran, "Negro Slaves," 341.
51. See Yetman, *Voices from Slavery*, 267, as well as 124 and 190. The aforementioned Amanda Oliver described corn shuckings in which men shucked corn and sang all night long while women sewed quilts. A big dance followed. See Baker and Baker, *Oklahoma Slave Narratives*, 303.
52. Genovese, *Political Economy of Slavery*, 135.
53. Baker and Baker, *Oklahoma Slave Narratives*, 128.
54. Baker and Baker, 201.
55. Lankford, *Bearing Witness*, 59–60.
56. Lankford, 69.
57. Blassingame, *Slave Community*, 250.
58. Genovese, *Political Economy of Slavery*, chap. 5.
59. See Hitchcock, *Traveler in Indian Territory*, 187.
60. For a brief primer on the topic of "squaw drudges" and the persistence of the image, see Smits, "'Squaw Drudge.'" See also Stidolph, "Medicine Worse Than the Malady," chaps. 1 and 5.
61. Naylor, *African Cherokees in Indian Territory*, 77.
62. Baker and Baker, *Oklahoma Slave Narratives*, 325.
63. Baker and Baker, 86.
64. Baker and Baker, 83.
65. See Berlin, *Generations of Captivity*, 77–78, especially his discussion of the task system.
66. Baker and Baker, *Oklahoma Slave Narratives*, 109.
67. Baker and Baker, 257–64.
68. Baker and Baker, 259–60.
69. McLoughlin, Conser, and McLoughlin, *Cherokee Ghost Dance*, 343–47.
70. See Saunt, "Paradox of Freedom"; Halliburton, *Red over Black*; Naylor, *African Cherokees in Indian Territory*; and Krauthamer, *Black Slaves, Indian Masters*.
71. IPH, roll 33, vol. 100: 56–59. Paul Garnett Roebuck's enslaved grandfather acted as an interpreter for Choctaw and Chickasaw Indians in federal court at Paris, Texas. See IPH, roll 27, vol. 81: 438–41.
72. Baker and Baker, *Oklahoma Slave Narratives*, 108.
73. McKee and Schlenker, *Choctaws*, 39.
74. See Naylor, *African Cherokees in Indian Territory*, 98–99; and Krauthamer, *Black Slaves, Indian Masters*, 57.
75. Krauthamer also discusses how enslaved proselytizers among the Indians might have thought of their position and its potential access to authority. See *Black Slaves, Indian Masters*, 58.
76. Shaw, "Using the WPA Ex-slave Narratives," 626.
77. Woodward, "History from Slave Sources," 474. The entire essay addresses the potential hazards of the WPA slave narratives but also notes that all sources have peculiarities that require careful handling.

78. Baker and Baker, *Oklahoma Slave Narratives*, 444.
79. Baker and Baker, 262.
80. Bibb, *Narrative of the Life and Adventures of Henry Bibb*, 152–55.
81. Baker and Baker, *Oklahoma Slave Narratives*, 219.
82. Pitchlynn, *Gathering of Statesmen*, 139, clauses 240–44.
83. Pitchlynn, 142–43, clauses 245–48.
84. *CLCN* 1840, 19.
85. *CLCN 1839–1851*, 55–56.
86. Yarbrough, *Race and the Cherokee Nation*, 47–48.
87. Baker and Baker, *Oklahoma Slave Narratives*, 356.
88. Baker and Baker, 380, 497.
89. Baker and Baker, 351.
90. See Philadelphia Female Anti-slavery Society, *Extracts from the American Slave Code*, for a pamphlet enumerating various laws regarding slavery; and Genovese, *Roll, Jordan, Roll*, 561–62.
91. Baker and Baker, *Oklahoma Slave Narratives*, 233–34.
92. Baker and Baker, 384. Mollie Watson remembered a slave who was missing part of his forefinger as punishment for learning to read and write. See Baker and Baker, 352–53.
93. Krauthamer, *Black Slaves, Indian Masters*, 56–57.
94. Lankford, *Bearing Witness*, 22–23.
95. Lankford, 38.
96. Lankford, 35; Douglass, *Narrative of the Life of Frederick Douglass*, 66–67.
97. Douglass, *Narrative of the Life of Frederick Douglass*, 63.
98. Krauthamer, *Black Slaves, Indian Masters*, 57.
99. *CLCN* 1840, 20–21.
100. See Dusinberre, *Them Dark Days*. For some discussion of the flexibility the task system could offer, see 180 and 317. For examples of enslaved people accumulating some property on rice plantations, see 182, 273, 317, 324, 335, and 342–43. Dusinberre is quick to point out that plantation owners did not adopt the task system because they were benevolent; rather, they could forgo providing some items for enslaved people, such as meat or clothing, by giving enslaved people the time to hunt or sew themselves. See 181, 183, and 187.
101. *CLCN* 1840, 20–21.
102. *CLCN* 1840, 12, section 14.
103. *CLCN* 1840, 11, section 6. The Choctaw and Chickasaw Indians were united through treaty agreement, as discussed in chapter 1, which accounts for this exception for those of Chickasaw blood.
104. *CLCN* 1840, 12, section 15.
105. *CLCN* 1847, 32–33, emphasis in the original.
106. Berlin, *Slaves without Masters*, chap. 11; Atkins, "Party Politics." Virginia did pass a law in 1806 that permitted manumission but required freed blacks to leave the state within six months in response to Gabriel's rebellion. Virginia eventually rescinded this law. See Wolf, *Race and Liberty*, esp. chaps. 2–4. Tennessee and North Carolina passed similar statutes regarding manumission and expulsion in the aftermath of Nat Turner's revolt. Klebaner, "American Manumission Laws," see the table on 448.

107. See Berlin, *Slaves without Masters*, esp. 372–74, for more on Arkansas; and for more on the terms of the law, see Higgins, "Act 151 of 1859."
108. *CLCN* 1847, 61.
109. *CLCN* 1847, 23.
110. *CLCN* 1847, 45.
111. *CLCN* 1847, 61.
112. *CLCN* 1847, 61.
113. *CLCN* 1840, 27–28.
114. K. Fischer, *Suspect Relations*, 102–3. See also Wallenstein, *Tell the Court I Love My Wife*, 116.
115. *CLCN* 1840, 12, section 14; *CLCN* 1840, 11, section 6. Recall the shared history of the Choctaw and Chickasaw Nations and their unusual shared territorial agreement discussed in chapter 1, which explain the exception made for those of Chickasaw descent in this statute.
116. IPH, roll 34, vol. 102: 81–88. Future laws will be discussed in chapter 6.
117. IPH, roll 23, vol. 70: 286–89.
118. IPH, roll 13, vol. 39: 24–26.
119. For more on sexual interactions between Natives and people of African descent, see Yarbrough, "Power, Perception, and Interracial Sex." See also Pascoe, *What Comes Naturally*; Hodes, *Sex, Love, Race*; Hodes, *White Women, Black Men*; K. Fischer, *Suspect Relations*; Rothman, *Notorious in the Neighborhood*; and Fox-Genovese, *Within the Plantation Household*.
120. IPH, roll 35, vol. 104: 366–67. Cole had detailed knowledge of Choctaw marriage laws and offered a summary on 363–66. Quoted material comes from Cushman's account, *History of the Choctaw, Chickasaw and Natchez Indians*, 314–15.
121. Cushman, *History of the Choctaw, Chickasaw and Natchez Indians*, 315.
122. *CLCN* 1840, 22.
123. *CLCN* 1840, 22.
124. *CLCN* 1847, 33–34.
125. *CLCN* 1869, 106.
126. *CLCN* 1869, 106.
127. O'Meara, *Daughters of the Country*, 45–47. See also Riley, *Women and Indians on the Frontier*, 133; and White, *Roots of Dependency*, 161.
128. IPH, roll 2, vol. 4: 8–10.
129. Axtell, *European and the Indian*, 154–56.
130. *CLCN* 1840, 20–21.
131. *CLCN* 1840, 19.
132. See Robinson, *Union Indivisible*, for more on the border states' decision to remain in the Union. See also Gerteis, "Slaves, Servants, and Soldiers," 170.

Chapter 3

1. *War of the Rebellion*, ser. 1, vol. 1: 682.
2. T. Smith, "Nations Colliding," 299.
3. *War of the Rebellion*, ser. 4, vol. 2: 353.
4. Warde, *When the Wolf Came*, 42–43.

5. Abel, *American Indian as Slaveholder and Secessionist*, 127.
6. L. P. Walker to Douglas H. Cooper, May 13, 1861, box 48, folder 16, Choctaw Nation Papers, Western History Collection, University of Oklahoma, Norman.
7. Harkins (Doaksville, Choctaw Nation) to Peter P. Pitchlynn, April 27, 1856, box 2, folder 78, Peter Perkins Pitchlynn Papers, Western History Collection, University of Oklahoma, Norman.
8. Agnew, "Our Doom as a Nation Is Sealed," 66–67.
9. Walker, "Inaugural Address of R. J. Walker," 329–30 and 336.
10. Jordan, "Politician of Expansion."
11. Debo, *History of the Indians of the United States*, 147.
12. Abel, *American Indian as Slaveholder and Secessionist*, 75–76.
13. CNR, roll CTN 8, vol. 295: 210.
14. See the Choctaw Nation website, choctawnation.com, for a useful timeline and summary about the various principal chiefs and district chiefs of the Choctaw Nation over time.
15. Peter Folsom to Peter P. Pitchlynn, January 19, 1861, Pitchlynn Papers.
16. 1830 Treaty of Dancing Rabbit Creek. The full text of the treaty is available in a variety of sources, including Barnett, *Mississippi's American Indians*, appendix 1, 214–24.
17. Debo, *The Rise and Fall of the Choctaw Republic*, 132–34.
18. United States Office of Indian Affairs, *Annual Report*, 446.
19. *Acts and Resolutions of the General Council of the Choctaw Nation*, 68–69.
20. United States Office of Indian Affairs, *Annual Report*, 446.
21. Debo describes how important annuity funds were for the maintenance of Choctaw schools. See *Rise and Fall of the Choctaw Republic*, 42 and 60.
22. T. Smith, "Nations Colliding," 285.
23. *War of the Rebellion*, ser. 4, vol. 1: 322–23.
24. *War of the Rebellion*, ser. 1, vol. 1: 682.
25. *War of the Rebellion*, ser. 1, vol. 1: 682.
26. Jacob Folsom to Peter P. Pitchlynn, January 9, 1861, Pitchlynn Papers. See Baird, *Peter Pitchlynn*, 65, for a reference to the familial relationship between Folsom and Pitchlynn.
27. Fitz, "'Suspected on Both Sides,'" 299. For a broader discussion of Native response to the American Revolution, see also Calloway, *American Revolution in Indian Country*. See O'Brien, *Choctaws in a Revolutionary Age*, for more on Choctaw efforts to navigate relations with Europeans and Euro-Americans during the American Revolution.
28. Jacob Folsom to Peter P. Pitchlynn, January 9, 1861, Pitchlynn Papers.
29. Peter Folsom to Peter P. Pitchlynn, January 19, 1861, Pitchlynn Papers.
30. Baird, *Peter Pitchlynn*, 126.
31. Fitz discusses this idea of military neutrality in her work on Mohawk chief Little Abraham during the Revolutionary War. See "'Suspected on Both Sides,'" 300.
32. For more on Spencer Academy, see Baird, *Peter Pitchlynn*, 64–66; and Kidwell, *Choctaws and Missionaries*, 161.
33. Abel, *American Indian as Slaveholder and Secessionist*, 77–78. For the full account from S. Orlando Lee, see 75–79.

34. Abel, 77–78.

35. Sampson Folsom to Peter P. Pitchlynn, May 14, 1861, Pitchlynn Papers. Emphasized words in the original.

36. *War of the Rebellion*, ser. 1, vol. 1: 683–84.

37. *War of the Rebellion*, ser. 1, vol. 1: 683–84.

38. John Ross to Arkansas governor Henry M. Rector, February 22, 1861, Confederate Imprints, microfilm 615, reel 72, item 2385: Cherokee correspondence.

39. David Hubbard to John Ross, June 12, 1861, Confederate Imprints, microfilm 615, reel 72, item 2385: Cherokee correspondence.

40. David Hubbard to John Ross, June 12, 1861.

41. Mark Bean, W. B. Welch, E. W. MacClure, John Spencer, J. A. McColoch, J. M. Lacy, and J. P. Carnahan to John Ross, May 9, 1861, Confederate Imprints, microfilm 615, reel 72, item 2385: Cherokee correspondence. Ross enclosed the letter with his letter to Lieutenant Colonel Kannady of Fort Smith dated May 18, 1861. The gentlemen wanted to know whom the Cherokee would support in the war.

42. John Ross to Brigadier General Ben McCulloch, June 17, 1861, Confederate Imprints, microfilm 615, reel 72, item 2385: Cherokee correspondence.

43. John Ross to CSA commissioner of Indian affairs David Hubbard, June 17, 1861, Confederate Imprints, microfilm 615, reel 72, item 2385: Cherokee correspondence.

44. May 17, 1861, Proclamation to the Cherokee People, Confederate Imprints, microfilm 615, reel 72, item 2385: Cherokee correspondence.

45. See, for instance, T. Smith, "Nations Colliding," 290; and Agnew, "Our Doom as a Nation Is Sealed," 72–74. See also *Confederate States Almanac and Repository of Useful Knowledge*, 34–36.

46. R. Miller, *Confederate States Chronology*, 57.

47. Fortney, "Robert M. Jones and the Choctaw Nation: Indigenous Nationalism in the American South, 1820–1877," 196.

48. Fortney, "Robert M. Jones," 187–88.

49. Abel, *American Indian as Slaveholder and Secessionist*, 77. For more on Robert Jones's ardent secessionist sentiment, see chap. 4 of Fortney, "Robert M. Jones."

50. Baird, *Peter Pitchlynn*, 127.

51. "Acts and Resolutions passed at the called Session of the General Council of the Choctaw Nation, in June 1861," June 11, 1861, folder Choctaw Manuscript Materials 3, Pitchlynn Papers (hereafter "Acts and Resolutions"). Choctaw Manuscript Materials 3 is one folder that contains numerous legislative documents.

52. For discussion of southerners' vacillating position on states' rights and federal power, see Potter, *Impending Crisis*, 294–96; and Yanuck, "Garner Fugitive Slave Case," 59–65. Some legal scholars argue that southerners seceded because the federal government did not do more to force northern states' compliance with federal laws, not because of a desire to respect states' rights. See Neff, "Secession and Breach of Compact," 411–12; and Finkelman, "States' Rights."

53. "Acts and Resolutions."

54. "Acts and Resolutions."

55. "Acts and Resolutions."

56. "Acts and Resolutions." Page 3 includes a notation of the compact being approved on October 23, 1861, but does not include the text.

57. "Declaration by the People of the Cherokee Nation."

58. "Articles of Confederation Entered Into between Muscogees, Seminoles, Choctaws, and Chickasaws and the Confederate States of America" (hereafter "Article of Confederation"). The text of the treaty comes from the Choctaw Nation website, choctawnation.com. This version uses the term "Muscogee" rather than "Creek." The manuscript reference to the treaty in the Pitchlynn Papers does not include the Confederate States of America as a party to the treaty.

59. "Articles of Confederation," article 1.

60. "Articles of Confederation," article 2.

61. "Articles of Confederation," articles 8 and 13.

62. Lieut. Col. J. R. Kannady of Fort Smith to John Ross, May 15, 1861, Confederate Imprints, microfilm 615, reel 72, item 2387: Cherokee correspondence.

63. "Articles of Confederation," articles 9, 10, and part of 13.

64. Acts, Bills, and Resolutions of the Choctaw Nation, box 49, folder 7, Choctaw Nation Papers. The document is a warrant for payment to Sampson Folsom for his service at the treaty negotiations in July.

65. CNR, roll CTN 8, vol. 295: 220–28.

66. United States Office of Indian Affairs, *Annual Report*, 448.

67. Abel, *American Indian as Slaveholder and Secessionist*, 61; United States Office of Indian Affairs, *Annual Report*, 452.

68. Confederate States of America, *Statutes at Large of the Provisional Government*, 311, article 1.

69. Confederate States of America, 311, preamble.

70. Confederate States of America, 312, articles 2 and 3.

71. Confederate States of America, 312, article 4. Articles 5 and 6 do not reference previous treaty agreements but do outline territorial boundaries and provide for Choctaws to have free passage through the Chickasaw district.

72. Confederate States of America, 313, articles 7 and 8.

73. Confederate States of America, 313–14, article 9.

74. Confederate States of America, 314, article 10.

75. For an early version of the law, see US Laws, Statutes, Etc., *Act to Regulate Trade and Intercourse with the Indian Tribes*. For the 1834 version of the Trade and Intercourse Act, see *United States Statutes at Large*, 23rd Cong., chap. 161. See also Prucha, *American Indian Policy*.

76. See, for instance, Letters Received by the Office of Indian Affairs, 1824–1881, Choctaw Agency West, 1825–1838, microfilm 890, roll 184, frames 243–48; and Letters Received by the Office of Indian Affairs, 1824–1881, Choctaw Agency, 1824–1876, 1860–1866, microfilm 890, roll 176, frames 140–46.

77. Confederate States of America, *Statutes at Large of the Provisional Government*, 315.

78. Confederate States of America, 317, article 21.

79. Prucha, *American Indian Policy*, 191.

80. Confederate States of America, *Statutes at Large of the Provisional Government*, 317, articles 22 and 23.

81. Prucha, *American Indian Policy*, 209–10.

82. Confederate States of America, *Statutes at Large of the Provisional Government*, 318.

83. 1830 Treaty of Dancing Rabbit Creek, article 22.

84. Fenderich, *P. P. Pitchlynn*.
85. Pitchlynn, "Remonstrance of Col. Peter Pitchlynn."
86. It remains unclear, however, whether Pitchlynn was specifically a delegate to the House of Representatives under treaty terms or a more general representative of the Choctaw Nation to the federal government and what rights he exercised. The perception of whether such Native representation existed in Congress in the past is muddled. See Debo, *Rise and Fall of the Choctaw Republic*, 83; and Ahtone, "Cherokee Nation Is Entitled to a Delegate." For a discussion on congressional representation for the Cherokee Nation, see also Rosser, "Nature of Representation."
87. Debo, *Rise and Fall of the Choctaw Republic*, 83n13.
88. Confederate States of America, *Statutes at Large of the Provisional Government*, 318.
89. Confederate States of America, 318–19.
90. *Message of the President, and Report of Albert Pike*, 4.
91. CNR, roll CTN 16, file 1, document 18302: 295; see also Warde, *When the Wolf Came*, 127.
92. Confederate States of America, *Statutes at Large of the Provisional Government*, 330–31.
93. United States Department of the Interior, *Federal Indian Law*, 542.
94. *Message of the President, and Report of Albert Pike*, 4.
95. Confederate States of America, *Statutes at Large of the Provisional Government*, 331.
96. Confederate States of America, 321–22, article 45.
97. Confederate States of America, 322, article 47.
98. Confederate States of America, 323–24.
99. Confederate States of America, 322.
100. Confederate States of America, 329.
101. Confederate States of America, 322, article 49.
102. *War of the Rebellion*, ser. 1, vol. 3: 594–95.
103. Confederate States of America, *Statutes at Large of the Provisional Government*, 322–23, article 50.
104. Sampson Folsom to General A. Pike, September 5, 1861, Pitchlynn Papers. This may have been Confederate colonel William Hunt, who practiced law in New Orleans as a civilian, or Captain William L. Hunter, whom I discuss in chapter 4.
105. Peter P. Pitchlynn to Peter P. Howell, October 20, 1861, Pitchlynn Papers.
106. Lycurgus P. Pitchlynn to Peter P. Pitchlynn, 1861, Pitchlynn Papers.
107. Warde, *When the Wolf Came*, 101–2.
108. Peter P. Pitchlynn to John, 1861, Pitchlynn Papers.
109. "Declaration by the People of the Cherokee Nation."
110. "Declaration by the People of the Cherokee Nation."
111. See Shoemaker, *Strange Likeness*, esp. chap. 5, for more on some of the ideas about gender shared between Native peoples and Europeans in their early encounters.
112. "Declaration by the People of the Cherokee Nation."
113. Lycurgus P. Pitchlynn to Peter P. Pitchlynn, 1861, Pitchlynn Papers.
114. CNR, roll CTN 8, vol. 297: 214.
115. CNR, roll CTN 8, vol. 295: 32, 38, 42–43, 55, and 12–13.

116. Confederate States of America, *Report of the Commissioner of Indian Affairs 1863*, 34–41.
117. CNR, roll CTN 16, document 18302: 301–2.
118. Confederate States of America, *Report of the Commissioner of Indian Affairs*, January 1863, 3.
119. United States Office of Indian Affairs, *Annual Report of the Commissioner of Indian Affairs—Yr. 1862–63*, 177.
120. Abel, *American Indian as Slaveholder and Secessionist*, 59–64.
121. Debo, *Rise and Fall of the Choctaw Republic*, 80.
122. Warde, *When the Wolf Came*, 44; Clampitt, *Civil War and Reconstruction*, 5.
123. See F. T. Smith, "'Most Destitute' People in Indian Territory"; Bean, "Who Defines a Nation?"; and Cobb-Greetham, "Hearth and Home," all in Clampitt, *Civil War and Reconstruction in Indian Territory*, 95, 111, and 162.
124. P. P. Pitchlynn to "Fellow Citizens of the Senate and of the House of Representatives," June 15, 1865, folder Choctaw Manuscript Materials 3, Pitchlynn Papers, 26–28.
125. P. P. Pitchlynn to "Fellow Citizens of the Senate and of the House of Representatives," September 1, 1865, folder Choctaw Manuscript Materials 3, Pitchlynn Papers, 41–56.
126. Nolan, "Anatomy of the Myth," 15 and 19–20.
127. P. P. Pitchlynn to "Fellow Citizens of the Senate and of the House of Representatives," June 15, 1865.
128. P. P. Pitchlynn to "Fellow Citizens of the Senate and of the House of Representatives," September 1, 1865.
129. "Peter Pitchlynn, Chief of the Choctaws," *Atlantic Monthly*, April 1870, 486–97, in box 6, folder 5, Pitchlynn Papers.
130. "Peter Pitchlynn, Chief of the Choctaws," 490.
131. Abel, *American Indian as Slaveholder and Secessionist*, 77; Baird, *Peter Pitchlynn*, 126–27.
132. Gibson, "Native Americans and the Civil War," 387.
133. IPH, roll 21, vol. 64: 103–12, esp. 108.

Chapter 4

1. Baker and Baker, *Oklahoma Slave Narratives*, 113.
2. Baker and Baker, 108.
3. Baker and Baker, 113.
4. See NARA 258, rolls 81, 82, 83, 84, 85, and 91.
5. Pamphlet accompanying NARA 258, 1.
6. NARA 258, roll 83: PDF 1727.
7. See NARA 258, roll 83: PDF 1728, PDF 1729, and PDF 1730 for some examples.
8. See the bottom of the records of NARA 258, roll 83: PDF 15, PDF 488, and PDF 1905 for the copyists' signatures.
9. CNR, roll CTN 16, document 18302: 254–56.
10. Iti Fabʋssa, "Choctaw Nation and the American Civil War."
11. Prag, *Confederate Diplomacy*, 65.
12. *Iskitini* means "small," and *homa* or *homma* means "red" in the Choctaw

language. See Byington, *Dictionary of the Choctaw Language*. For more on Tandy Walker, see Kidwell, *Choctaws in Oklahoma*, 48.

13. NARA 258, roll 81: PDF 5.

14. "Message of P. P. Pitchlynn, Principal Chief of the Choctaw Nation, Delivered before the Choctaw Council, in Extra Session," January 9, 1865, Confederate Imprints, microfilm 615, reel 72, item 2391.

15. CNR, roll CTN 16, file 1, document 18304: 356.

16. Ashcraft, "Confederate Indian Troop Conditions," 448; Warde, *When the Wolf Came*, 119.

17. Wright, "General Douglas H. Cooper," 178; Warde, *When the Wolf Came*, 54.

18. For troop numbers, see Albert Pike to Major General Holmes, December 30, 1862, Confederate Imprints, microfilm 615, reel 92, items 2814R–2860: 2814R; Prag, *Confederate Diplomacy*, 65; and Ashcraft, "Confederate Indian Troop Conditions," 445.

19. Ashcraft, "Confederate Indian Troop Conditions," 448.

20. Warde, *When the Wolf Came*, 116.

21. Ashcraft, "Confederate Indian Troop Conditions," 448.

22. CNR, roll CTN 8, vol. 297: 214.

23. CNR, roll CTN 8, vol. 297: 185.

24. Moore, *Conscription and Conflict*, 342–50; Gallagher and Waugh, *American War*, 94; Levine, *Confederate Emancipation*, 16–18, 39, 95–97, and chap. 6; and Beringer et al., *Why the South Lost the Civil War*, 368–76.

25. Population estimates from the National Parks Service website, accessed October 2, 2018, https://www.nps.gov/civilwar/facts.htm. The caveat is, of course, that the numbers for Confederate enlistments are less accurate.

26. For Choctaw Nation and Chickasaw Nation population estimates in 1860, see Abel, *American Indian as Slaveholder and Secessionist*, 211. Katz, *Black Indians*, 135, describes the Choctaw population of 1860 as 14 percent enslaved. Another population estimate for Native nations in the Indian Territory may be found in Warde, *When the Wolf Came*, 264; and *Confederate States Almanac and Repository of Useful Knowledge*, 35.

27. Abel, *American Indian as Slaveholder and Secessionist*, 211; Colonel Douglas H. Cooper to Jefferson Davis, July 25, 1861, *War of the Rebellion*, ser. 1, vol. 3: 614.

28. Cheek, "'We Are Clay People,'" 31–34.

29. Vickers, "Mississippi Choctaw Names," esp. 121.

30. McPherson, *For Cause and Comrades*, viii.

31. In my database, 3,083 of 3,126 records for individuals include the soldier's rank. Some individual records include more than one rank for an individual.

32. Some of these privates were promoted and will also be counted among other rank totals.

33. See database in author's possession.

34. See NARA 258, roll 82, records for Abelauli, Abitishteya, Ahtuklowtubbi, and Alfred for examples. See the pamphlet describing National Archives Record Group 109, microcopy 861, Compiled Records Showing Service of Military Units in Confederate Organizations, for examples of unit names from southern states.

35. Byington, *Dictionary of the Choctaw Language*, 561, 281.

36. Byington, 328.

37. Dawes Enrollment Number 4938, Census Card Number 1745, Oklahoma and Indian Territory, Dawes Census Cards for Five Civilized Tribes, 1898–1914, online database, Ancestry.com; and Enrollment Cards for the Five Civilized Tribes, 1898–1914, NAI Number 251747, Records of the Bureau of Indian Affairs, Record Group Number 75, National Archives, Washington, DC.

38. Over 2,000 of the 3,126 records include date and location of muster.

39. "Articles of Confederation Entered Into between Muscogees, Seminoles, Choctaws, and Chickasaws and the Confederate States of America."

40. Prag, *Confederate Diplomacy*, 47. See also "Resolutions Expressing the Feelings and Sentiments of the General Council of the Choctaw Nation," 682.

41. Freehling, *Road to Disunion*, 503.

42. Abel, *American Indian as Slaveholder and Secessionist*, 207.

43. Kidwell, *Choctaws in Oklahoma*, 57.

44. Interview with Henry I. and Ida L. Falconer, IPH, roll 21, vol. 64: 107.

45. Wright, "General Douglas H. Cooper," 167.

46. See database in author's possession.

47. Hitchcock, *Traveler in Indian Territory*, 148. Hitchcock mentions Opothle Yahola's wife sending Hitchcock a gift and message through her "negress."

48. Baker and Baker, *Oklahoma Slave Narratives*, 31.

49. See Warde, *When the Wolf Came*, 64–87, for a detailed account of the pursuit of Opothle Yahola to Kansas.

50. See database in author's possession.

51. Warde, *When the Wolf Came*, 90–91.

52. Warde, 70.

53. Warde, 90.

54. See Warde, 128; and "Battle of Newtonia (1862)."

55. Kidwell, *Choctaws in Oklahoma*, 65; Knight, *Red Fox*, 124–28.

56. See database in author's possession.

57. Edwards, *"Prairie Was on Fire,"* 31.

58. Edwards, 32; see esp. Captain Daniel S. Whittenhall. Lieutenant David R. Coleman also used this language of a complete rout.

59. Warde, *When the Wolf Came*, 129; Knight, *Red Fox*, 135; Kidwell, *Choctaws in Oklahoma*, 65; "Fort Wayne, Battle of."

60. For more on Indian agencies, see Prucha, *American Indian Policy*, chap. 4. While this describes the responsibilities of agents in the federal system, the Confederate government followed similar practices; see Prucha, *American Indian Treaties*, 263–64.

61. Warde, *When the Wolf Came*, 123–25; L. Fischer, *Civil War Era*, 79–80.

62. McPherson, *For Cause and Comrades*, 13.

63. Capt. David Perkins to Genl. D. H. Cooper, December 17, 1863, NARA 258, roll 85: PDF 0198–0199.

64. Historian Claudio Saunt points out in "Paradox of Freedom," 77–78, that federal officials were unsure if the Thirteenth Amendment actually applied to Indian Territory.

65. Baker and Baker, *Oklahoma Slave Narratives*, 466.

66. Warde, *When the Wolf Came*, 137.

67. In the larger Confederacy, the threat of the emancipation of enslaved people

in the form of Abraham Lincoln's proclamation firmed the resolve of many. See Gallagher and Waugh, *American War*, 125.

68. Edwards, *"Prairie Was on Fire,"* 60

69. Warde, *When the Wolf Came*, 156–59; see also "Cabin Creek Battlefield Historic Site."

70. Edwards, *"Prairie Was on Fire,"* 59–60.

71. Lause, *Race and Radicalism*, 2.

72. "Battle of Honey Springs."

73. Warde, *When the Wolf Came*, 166.

74. Edward, *"Prairie Was on Fire,"* 63.

75. Edwards, 67.

76. Knight, *Red Fox*, 170; Edwards, *"Prairie Was on Fire,"* 66; Hood, "Twilight of the Confederacy," 425–26.

77. See also "Battle of Honey Springs"; and Warde, *When the Wolf Came*, 169.

78. Edwards, *"Prairie Was on Fire,"* 67.

79. Edwards, 68.

80. Baker and Baker, *Oklahoma Slave Narratives*, 83.

81. Baker and Baker, 113.

82. Edward, *"Prairie Was on Fire,"* 67–68.

83. Baker and Baker, *Oklahoma Slave Narratives*, 32.

84. Baker and Baker, 30–32.

85. Edwards, *"Prairie Was on Fire,"* 69.

86. Knight, *Red Fox*, 166.

87. Knight, 173.

88. Edwards, *"Prairie Was on Fire,"* 71.

89. See database in author's possession. Of 173 cases, 170 occurred in 1863.

90. For more on the importance of May as a planting time among the Choctaw Indians, see Iti Fabussa, "Traditional Choctaw Agriculture."

91. NARA 258, roll 84: PDF 1729.

92. See database in author's possession.

93. NARA 258, roll 84: PDF 1735.

94. William McKean (Van Buren Ark) to Peter P. Pitchlynn, May 21, 1857, and Lycurgus Pitchlynn to Peter P. Pitchlynn, April 28, 1857, both in box 2, folder 92, Peter Perkins Pitchlynn Papers, Western History Collection, University of Oklahoma, Norman.

95. For more information about the academy, see "Our History"; see also "Short History of Goodland Presbyterian Children's Home."

96. NARA 258, roll 84: PDF 1730.

97. CNR, roll CTN 16, file 1, document 18302: 322.

98. See "An act entitled an Act ratifying the compact entered into between the Creeks, Seminoles, Choctaws and Chickasaws at North Fork Village, Creek Nation, on the first day of July 1861," and "Acts and Resolutions passed by the General Council of the Choctaw Nation in October 1861," box 7, folder 7, Pitchlynn Papers.

99. McPherson, *For Cause and Comrades*, 17.

100. McPherson, 156.

101. McPherson, 30.

102. J. Wells, *House Divided*, 79. This call for soldiers came in two parts: Lincoln's

"Proclamation Calling Militia and Convening Congress" in April 1861, available in *Collected Works of Abraham Lincoln*, 4:332; and the requests made by Secretary of War Simon Cameron to the various state governors. For an example, see the request made to the governor of New York, New York State Military Museum and Veterans Research Center website, Front Matter, vol. 1, p. 6, accessed October 26, 2018, https://dmna.ny.gov/historic/reghist/civil/MusterRolls/.

103. For the description of the battle from the point of view of the US Senate, see "Senators Witness the First Battle of Bull Run."

104. Gallagher and Waugh, *American War*, 38–39; Manning, *What This Cruel War Was Over*, 44–45.

105. See database in author's possession.

106. See Benjamin Roebuck's entry in the database in author's possession.

107. Peter P. Pitchlynn to William Cass, January 16, 1862, box 3, folder 98, Pitchlynn Papers.

108. See database in author's possession.

109. See, for example, Private Henry Gibson, Joseph Harkin, or Cyrus Holly, to name a few. See database in author's possession.

110. See "An act entitled an Act ratifying the compact entered into between the Creeks, Seminoles, Choctaws and Chickasaws at North Fork Village, Creek Nation, on the first day of July 1861," and "Acts and Resolutions passed by the General Council of the Choctaw Nation in October 1861," box 7, folder 7, Pitchlynn Papers.

111. Moore, *Conscription and Conflict*, 7–8.

112. *Southern Confederacy*, February 13, 1862, Digital Library of Georgia, https://gahistoricnewspapers.galileo.usg.edu/regions/atlanta/?docId=bookreader/asc/asc1862/asc1862-0086.mets.xml.

113. Moore, *Conscription and Conflict*, 12–14.

114. Lonn, *Desertion during the Civil War*, 6.

115. *War of the Rebellion*, ser. 1, vol. 3: 593–94.

116. Abel, *American Indian as Slaveholder and Secessionist*, 156.

117. "Message of P. P. Pitchlynn, Principal Chief of the Choctaw Nation, Delivered before the Choctaw Council, in Extra Session," January 9, 1865, Confederate Imprints, microfilm 615, reel 72, items 2368–2391: 2391, p. 4.

118. "Message of P. P. Pitchlynn, Principal Chief of the Choctaw Nation," 4.

119. Moore, *Conscription and Conflict*, 334.

120. Scheiber, "Pay of Troops," 352.

121. Quoted in Scheiber, 354.

122. Gibson, *Chickasaws*, 233.

123. Albert Pike to Major General Holmes, December 30, 1862, Confederate Imprints, microfilm 615, reel 92, items 2814R–2860: 2814R. Italics in the original.

124. Gibson, *Chickasaws*, 233.

125. Albert Pike to the Chiefs and people of the Cherokees, Creeks, Seminoles, Chickasaws, and Choctaws, July 31, 1862, Confederate Imprints, microfilm 615, reel 92, items 2814R–2860: 2819.

126. CNR, roll CTN 8, vol. 295: 17.

127. Carson, "Horses and the Economy," 497. See also Weik, "Engendering Labor," for more on the importance of horses among the Chickasaw and southeastern Natives more broadly.

128. Grear and Salyer, "Twenty-Ninth Texas Cavalry."

129. NARA 258, roll 84: PDF 2194 and PDF 2195. The State Library of North Carolina has some information about the escape on the *Maple Leaf*; see "*Maple Leaf*: A Great Escape."

130. NARA 258, roll 91: PDF 2329, PDF 2330, PDF 2331, PDF 2332, and PDF 2333. Brown variously appears as Karren, Kerrin, Canon, Karrew, and Kairn. The documents are not in chronological order. See database in author's possession for Hicks and Hogue.

131. For more on illness during the Civil War, see Downs, *Sick from Freedom*.

132. NARA 258, roll 91: PDF 2359, PDF 2364, PDF 2368, PDF 2369, and PDF 2370.

133. NARA 258, roll 91: PDF 2360, PDF 2361, PDF 2362, PDF 2363, PDF 2365, PDF 2371, PDF 2372, and PDF 2373.

134. One document says Colbert was captured at Fort Scott in Kansas. Given the pattern in other records, Colbert was likely transferred to Fort Scott and not captured there. NARA 258, roll 83: PDF 2805, PDF 2806, PDF 2807, and PDF 2808.

135. Hahn, *Nation without Borders*, 276.

136. Foner, *Short History of Reconstruction*, 18–19.

137. Hahn, *Nation without Borders*, 297, 300, and 326.

138. Hahn, 274.

139. Confederate Imprints, microfilm 615, reel 92, items 2814R–2860: 2814R, p. 6.

140. NARA 258, roll 82: PDF 2481–2485.

141. NARA 258, roll 82: PDF 1783–1784.

142. See Cowsert, "Confederate Borderland," 75–76; T. Smith, "Nations Colliding," 291–92; King, "Forgotten Warriors," esp. 109–10, 139–43, 206, 244–45, and 317–20; Abel, "Indians in the Civil War," 289; and Abel, *American Indian as Slaveholder and Secessionist*, 216n86.

143. Record of First Lieutenant Henry Clay, NARA 258, roll 82: PDF 302.

144. Confederate States of America, *Statutes at Large of the Provisional Government*, 43–44.

145. Confederate States of America, 322–24.

146. Edwards, *"Prairie Was on Fire,"* 15.

147. Wright, "General Douglas H. Cooper," 142–84, esp. 163.

148. NARA 258, roll 82: PDF 2582–2584.

149. NARA 258, roll 84: PDF 1229–1231.

150. NARA 258, roll 82: see PDF 316, 353, 417, 487, and 640 for examples.

151. NARA 258, roll 84: PDF 1918–1921. Lebantp is the spelling of the name in the original.

152. NARA 258, roll 91: PDF 2394–2399.

153. NARA 258, roll 91: PDF 2384–2387.

154. Baker and Baker, *Oklahoma Slave Narratives*, 31–32.

155. Baker and Baker, 173–74.

156. IPH, roll 5, vol. 14: 10–21.

157. For a popular account of female spies for the Union and Confederacy, see Winkler, *Stealing Secrets*. Hall's *Women on the Civil War Battlefront* considers women's role in the war a bit more broadly.

158. Peter P. Pitchlynn to John, 1861, Pitchlynn Papers. See database in author's

possession for information about the service of William B. Pitchlynn and Ebenezer Pitchlynn.

159. "Declaration by the People of the Cherokee Nation."

Chapter 5

1. McPherson, *For Cause and Comrades*; Faust, *This Republic of Suffering*; and J. Smith, *Black Soldiers in Blue*, are just three examples of the available scholarship. Essays by Stephen Kantrowitz ("Fighting Like Men") and John Stauffer ("Embattled Manhood and New England Writers") in Clinton and Silber's *Battle Scars* consider ideas about manhood among Black and white abolitionists and northern white writers, respectively, to demonstrate that the war could change gendered ideas, even for those men who did not fight in battles.
2. Cheek, "'We Are Clay People,'" 31–32.
3. Faiman-Silva, *Choctaws at the Crossroads*, 10.
4. Cheek, "'We Are Clay People,'" 30.
5. Carson remarks that the Iroquois and Choctaw "shared similar gender conventions regarding work" but also reminds us that the history of gender and work in these societies was not the same. See *Searching for the Bright Path*, 12–13. Noel offers a clear summary of scholarship on gender among the Iroquois in "Revisiting Gender in Iroquoia." See also Leacock's "Women's Status in Egalitarian Society" for more discussion of Iroquois gender roles. Shoemaker discusses some of the shared concepts, including gender, that allowed Native peoples and Europeans to communicate in eighteenth-century North America in *Strange Likeness*, chap. 5. Implicit in this formulation is that Native peoples also shared similar understandings of concepts such as gender.
6. Quoted by Boulware in "'We Are Men,'" 53–54.
7. Virtual Museum of New France, "The Explorers."
8. Havard, *Great Peace of Montreal*, 46.
9. Boulware, "'We Are Men,'" 53.
10. Carpenter, "Womanish Men and Manlike Women," 148–49. Note that Carpenter uses the term "berdache," which many find offensive because of its etymology in Arabic meaning "male prostitute." For more on the term "berdache," see Estrada, "Two-Spirit Histories," 165–66; Smithers, "Cherokee 'Two Spirits,'" 630–31; and Lang, *Men as Women*, 6. Lang's work offers a broad overview of two-spirit people across a wide range of Native populations.
11. Carpenter, "Womanish Men and Manlike Women," 158–61.
12. O'Brien, "Trying to Look Like Men," 50–51.
13. Boulware, "'We Are Men,'" 53–54.
14. Boulware, 63–64.
15. Cushman, *History of the Choctaw, Chickasaw and Natchez Indians*, 308.
16. Cushman, 197.
17. Both quotes from Cushman, 309.
18. Carson, *Searching for the Bright Path*, 18. For a description of the modern game of stickball among the Choctaws, see D'Urso, "World Series of Choctaw Stickball." For Cushman's contemporary description of ball play, see *History of the Choctaw,*

Chickasaw and Natchez Indians, 123–30. Hitchcock also offered a description of a ball game that included women in *Traveler in Indian Territory*, 157–58.

19. Cushman, *History of the Choctaw, Chickasaw and Natchez Indians*, 132–33.

20. Cushman, 46–47.

21. See the guide to Choctaw animal words on the Native Languages of the Americas website, http://www.native-languages.org/choctaw_animals.htm.

22. Cushman, *History of the Choctaw, Chickasaw and Natchez Indians*, 264–65.

23. Cushman, 479. O'Brien suggests Pushmataha's name is a shortened version of *A-push-a-ma-ta-hah-ub-i*, which had a similar meaning: "a messenger of death; literally one whose rifle, tomahawk, or bow is alike fatal in war or hunting." See O'Brien, "Pushmataha"; and Swanton, *Social and Ceremonial Life of the Choctaw Indians*, 121.

24. Cushman, *History of the Choctaw, Chickasaw and Natchez Indians*, 180.

25. Swanton, *Social and Ceremonial Life of the Choctaw Indians*, 167. Pesantubbee describes De Lusser and his location in *Choctaw Women in a Chaotic World*, 29.

26. O'Brien, "Trying to Look Like Men," 51.

27. O'Brien, 53.

28. White, *Roots of Dependency*, 111.

29. Mould, *Choctaw Tales*, 88–92. Cheek offers a summary of the implications of lacking a name for Choctaw males in "'We Are Clay People,'" 40–42, as does Snyder in *Great Crossings*, 18–19.

30. See Cushman, *History of the Choctaw, Chickasaw and Natchez Indians*, 218–22, for the full story.

31. Both comments from O'Brien, "Trying to Look Like Men," 54.

32. Mould, *Choctaw Tales*, 88–92.

33. Pesantubbee, *Choctaw Women in a Chaotic World*, 24; Carson, *Searching for the Bright Path*, 20.

34. Swanton, *Social and Ceremonial Life of the Choctaw Indians*, 115–16.

35. Swanton, 120; Cushman, *History of the Choctaw, Chickasaw and Natchez Indians*, 144.

36. Carson, *Searching for the Bright Path*, 77.

37. O'Brien, "Trying to Look Like Men," 49–50.

38. O'Brien, 57.

39. O'Brien, 58.

40. Galloway, *Choctaw Genesis*, 40–41.

41. Galloway, 61.

42. O'Brien, "Trying to Look Like Men," 58–59.

43. White, *Roots of Dependency*, 146.

44. Quoted in Carson, *Searching for the Bright Path*, 51.

45. Braund, *Deerskins and Duffels*, 66. Braund quotes James Adair's description of Native men as clever craftsmen who figured out how to make some repairs on their guns, but such repairs could take time. For Adair's original, see Adair, *History of the American Indians*, 413.

46. Carson, *Searching for the Bright Path*, 51–52.

47. Carson, 73–74.

48. Carson, 77.

49. Carson, 76.

50. Carson, 77.

51. Saunt, *New Order of Things*, 47–48.
52. Carson, *Searching for the Bright Path*, 64. Carson quotes Bernard Romans.
53. Pesantubbee, *Choctaw Women in a Chaotic World*, 134.
54. Meyers finds that in the prehistoric period in the Southeast, elites controlled the production of craft goods and trade. See "Political Economy and Craft Production," 397.
55. Pesantubbee, *Choctaw Women in a Chaotic World*, 135–36. McLoughlin discusses a similar process of overhunting among the Cherokee that he also extends to the larger southeastern United States in *Cherokee Ghost Dance*, 7.
56. Pavao-Zuckerman, "Deerskins and Domesticates," 28–31, first quote from 29 and second quote from 30.
57. Cushman, *History of the Choctaw, Chickasaw and Natchez Indians*, 157. For more on missionaries among the Choctaw Indians, see Kidwell, *Choctaws and Missionaries*.
58. Luna-Firebaugh, *Tribal Policing*, 18.
59. Blackburn, "From Blood Revenge to the Lighthorsemen," 63.
60. Cushman, *History of the Choctaw, Chickasaw and Natchez Indians*, 157.
61. 1820 Treaty of Doak's Stand.
62. Pitchlynn, *Gathering of Statesmen*, 72–73.
63. Carson, *Searching for the Bright Path*, 76. O'Brien makes a similar case for the lighthorse companies representing elite Choctaws' "commitment to the new economy and its altered notion of masculinity" in "Trying to Look Like Men," 65.
64. Carson, *Searching for the Bright Path*, 52.
65. McLoughlin, "Cherokee Anomie," 9.
66. Snyder, *Great Crossings*, 19; Mould, *Choctaw Tales*, 88–92. Pitchlynn's version of the tale is included and dated 1870.
67. Snyder, *Great Crossings*, 40.
68. Debo, *Rise and Fall of the Choctaw Republic*, 45–46.
69. Pitchlynn, *Gathering of Statesmen*, 74.
70. Pitchlynn, 127–28.
71. Pitchlynn, 80.
72. Pitchlynn, 90.
73. Pitchlynn, 75–76.
74. *CLCN* 1840, 2, session 1, section 2. Page 13 is misnumbered as page 2 under the laws section.
75. *CLCN* 1840, 14–15, session 1, section 7.
76. *CLCN* 1840, 27, session 4, section 10.
77. *CLCN* 1840, 15, session 1, section 13.
78. *CLCN* 1840, 16, session 2, section 1.
79. *CLCN* 1840, 18, session 3, section 3 covers the sale of stray horses. *CLCN* 1840, 26, session 4, section 6 requires the one-dollar payment to the district clerk.
80. *CLCN* 1840, 32, session 6, section 5.
81. *CLCN* 1840, 26, session 4, section 5.
82. *CLCN* 1840, 27, session 4, section 8.
83. *CLCN* 1840, 6–7, article 3, section 8.
84. *CLCN* 1840, 9, article 5, section 5.
85. *CLCN* 1840, 33–34, session 6, section 10.

86. *CLCN* 1840, 30, session 5, section 8; and 31, session 6, section 2.
87. *CLCN* 1840, 33, session 6, section 7.
88. I discuss the constitutional limit in chap. 2. See also *CLCN* 1840, 12, section 15.
89. *CLCN* 1847, 32–33.
90. *CLCN* 1847, 61.
91. *CLCN* 1847, 35.
92. The text for the 1850 and 1793 Fugitive Slave Acts can be found in Spooner's *Defence for Fugitive Slaves*. This quote is from p. 2.
93. *CLCN* 1847, 62.
94. *CLCN* 1852, 33; see two separate acts: "An Act attendance of light-horse-men at the Schools" and "An Act return of runaway children from the schools."
95. *CLCN* 1847, 33.
96. *CLCN* 1852, 59.
97. *CLCN* 1852, 35
98. *CLCN* 1852, 51 and 94.
99. *CLCN* 1852, 97; *Acts and Resolutions of the General Council of the Choctaw Nation*, 33, 34, 44, 67.
100. Carson, *Searching for the Bright Path*, 52–53.
101. McLoughlin, "Cherokee Anomie," 31–32. McLoughlin specifically discusses the Cherokee context, but I think many of his observations can be extended to discussion of the Choctaw.
102. Carson, *In Search of the Bright Path*, 63.
103. Ishii, *Bad Fruits of the Civilized Tree*, 32–33, 165.
104. Carson, *In Search of the Bright Path*, 63.
105. Treaty of Hopewell.
106. *CLCN* 1852, 59–60.
107. *CLCN* 1852, 67. For a history of Choctaw chiefs, see Hudson, "Story of Choctaw Chiefs."
108. *CLCN* 1852, 77–78. The lack of punctuation is from the original.
109. Carson, *Searching for the Bright Path*, 62.
110. Peter P. Pitchlynn to William Cass, January 16, 1862, Peter Perkins Pitchlynn Papers, Western History Collection, University of Oklahoma, Norman.
111. Abel, *American Indian as Slaveholder and Secessionist*, 211; Colonel Douglas H. Cooper to Jefferson Davis, July 25, 1861, *War of the Rebellion*, ser. 1, vol. 3: 614.
112. See database in author's possession.
113. *Acts and Resolutions of the General Council of the Choctaw Nation*, 35.
114. See database in author's possession.
115. Peter P. Pitchlynn to Peter Howell, October 20, 1861, Pitchlynn Papers.
116. Lycurgus P. Pitchlynn to Peter P. Pitchlynn, 1861, Pitchlynn Papers.
117. Cushman, *History of the Choctaw, Chickasaw and Natchez Indians*, 197.
118. Peter P. Pitchlynn to John, 1861, Pitchlynn Papers.
119. See database in author's possession.

Chapter 6

1. Message of P. P. Pitchlynn, Principal Chief of the Choctaw Nation, delivered before the Choctaw Council, in Extra Session, held at Goodwater Seminary, C.N., on

the Second Monday in January, 1865, Confederate Imprints, microfilm 615, reel 72, item 2391. Quotes from 1 and 8.

2. See Foner, *Reconstruction*.

3. For more of the legal details, see Garrison, *Legal Ideology of Removal*, chap. 7; and Norgren, *Cherokee Cases*, 114–22.

4. Emancipation Proclamation.

5. Gerteis, "Slaves, Servants, and Soldiers," 172.

6. Saunt, *Black, White, and Indian*, 114.

7. Baker and Baker, *Oklahoma Slave Narratives*, 44.

8. Baker and Baker, 352.

9. Baker and Baker, 132–37.

10. Baker and Baker, 487.

11. Baker and Baker, 251.

12. Baker and Baker, 319, 40, 61, and 130.

13. Baker and Baker, 40.

14. Baker and Baker, 497–98.

15. Baker and Baker, 341.

16. Baker and Baker, 466.

17. Baker and Baker, 242–43.

18. Baker and Baker, 145–46. "Liza" was clearly short for "Eliza." She did not indicate the origin of her surname of Evans in her interview. Perhaps she gained it through marriage.

19. IPH, roll 36, vol. 108: 465–73.

20. Baker and Baker, *Oklahoma Slave Narratives*, 401.

21. Abel, *American Indian as Slaveholder and Secessionist*. See especially chap. 4 for an extensive discussion of the alliances made between the Confederacy and various tribes in Indian Territory.

22. Baker and Baker, *Oklahoma Slave Narratives*, 199.

23. Baker and Baker, 370–71. In her narrative, Rowe mentions several times living near Bois d'Arc Creek, and that waterway is located in Texas.

24. Treaty with the Choctaw and Chickasaw, 1866, article 2.

25. Rachel Purvis and Melinda Miller discussed this language in work presented at the Gilder Lehrman Center's 2013 conference, "Indigenous Enslavement and Incarceration in North American History," at Yale University and in "Reconstructing the Cherokee Nation: Emancipation and Citizenship in a Native Nation," presented at the symposium "Race and Nation in the Age of Emancipations" at Rice University in 2014.

26. Saunt, *Black, White, and Indian*, 258n19.

27. IPH, roll 27, vol. 81: 438–48, esp. 442–43.

28. Baker and Baker, *Oklahoma Slave Narratives*, 325–26.

29. Baker and Baker, 146.

30. Baker and Baker, 191.

31. Baker and Baker, 391.

32. Baker and Baker, 370–71.

33. See Litwack, *Been in the Storm So Long*, 229–47; and Williams, *Help Me to Find My People*, for a fuller discussion of the phenomenal efforts freedpeople all over the South made to reunite with loved ones.

34. Baker and Baker, *Oklahoma Slave Narratives*, 500.
35. Baker and Baker, 177.
36. Baker and Baker, 421.
37. Baker and Baker, 96.
38. Baker and Baker, 98.
39. Baker and Baker, 122, 54.
40. IPH, roll 2, vol. 6: 75–78, esp. 75.
41. IPH, roll 31, vol. 94: 459–68, esp. 461.
42. For examples of freedpeople receiving wages, see Baker and Baker, *Oklahoma Slave Narratives*, 207, 360–61. Hal Hutson, who was born in Tennessee, mentioned earning five dollars per month. Harriett Robinson, who was enslaved in Texas, described monthly pay varying from four dollars to ten dollars, depending on the age of the worker.
43. IPH, roll 6, vol. 17: 473–76, esp. 475. Butler and his family were most likely owned by Choctaw Indians. He named Samson Folsom as his enslaver.
44. Baker and Baker, *Oklahoma Slave Narratives*, 142.
45. Baker and Baker, 98.
46. For examples of enslavers' coercive efforts to keep formerly enslaved people on plantations, see Litwack, *Been in the Storm So Long*, 193–94.
47. Baker and Baker, *Oklahoma Slave Narratives*, 210.
48. Baker and Baker, 98–99.
49. Baker and Baker, 266.
50. Baker and Baker, 166.
51. Foner offers a discussion of southern legislative attempts to maintain control of the labor of formerly enslaved people in *Short History of Reconstruction*, 92–95.
52. Teed and Teed, *Reconstruction*, 202–5. See also Litwack, *Been in the Storm So Long*, 408; and Masur, *Civil War*, 82.
53. Andrews, *South since the War*, 398. Emphasis mine.
54. Treaty with the Choctaw and Chickasaw, 1866, article 3.
55. Treaty with the Choctaw and Chickasaw, 1866, article 3.
56. Debo, *Rise and Fall of the Choctaw Republic*, 101.
57. "Choctaw and Chickasaw freedmen. Letter from the Secretary of the Interior, transmitting, in response to the resolution of the Senate of December 18, 1897, copy of a communication from the Commissioner of Indian Affairs containing a full statement in regard to the Choctaw and Chickasaw freedmen," American Indian and Alaskan Native Documents in the Congressional Serial Set, 4.
58. "Choctaw and Chickasaw freedmen," 5 and 23.
59. Debo, *Rise and Fall of the Choctaw Republic*, 101.
60. Debo, 101–2.
61. Quoted in Barney, *Making of a Confederate*, 148.
62. Painter, *Southern History across the Color Line*, 76.
63. Painter, 77–79.
64. Litwack, *Been in the Storm So Long*, 402–3. Litwack also discusses the deeply felt expectation many Black people had that they should and would receive land, especially that of their former enslavers, 399–402. See also Foner, *Short History of Reconstruction*, 46. See Litwack, 407, for the reluctance of white landowners to sell land to formerly enslaved people.

65. "A Sharecropper's Contract." This contract is also a part of the Grimes Family Papers (#3357), 1882, in the Southern Historical Collection, University of North Carolina at Chapel Hill.

66. Litwack, *Been in the Storm So Long*, 409.

67. Litwack, 446–48; Foner, *Short History of Reconstruction*, 79–80.

68. Debo, *Rise and Fall of the Choctaw Republic*, 102–4.

69. Kidwell, *Choctaws in Oklahoma*, 81. This separation occurred in other Indian nations as well. See Chang, *Color of the Land*, 152–53.

70. "Choctaw and Chickasaw freedmen," 4, 6. See also Schreier, "Different Shades of Freedom," 84–85.

71. Principal Chief William Bryant included the text of the March 4, 1872, act in correspondence to the president of the United States dated March 18, 1872, Letters Received by the Office of Indian Affairs, 1824–1881, microcopy 234, roll 180, Choctaw Agency, 1824–1876, 1872–1873, National Archives, Washington, DC. Records courtesy of Sarah Rois.

72. March 28, 1872, petition, Charles Anderson to Ulysses Grant, Letters Received by the Office of Indian Affairs, 1824–1881, microcopy 234, roll 180, Choctaw Agency, 1824–1876, 1872–1873, National Archives.

73. See the Arkansas state legislature's petition at "Arkansas Petition for Freedmen's Rights 1869."

74. CNR, roll CTN 5, 1872–1908 Documents, document 13631. The citizenship commission reported 14,476 Choctaws in the Choctaw Nation, with an additional 1,777 Choctaws residing in the Chickasaw Nation. The total number of Choctaw freedmen was 3,985, which included 468 Choctaw freedmen residing in the Chickasaw Nation.

75. *FRB*, 1–4. Vol. 18 contains three separate sections with separate titles: "The Freedmen and Registration Bills," "Laws of the Choctaw Nation," and "Chahta Okla Nan Uhlpesa."

76. *FRB*, 2 (section 1).

77. *FRB*, 3 (section 7).

78. *FRB*, 3 (section 6).

79. *Laws of the Choctaw Nation* 1883, 23.

80. See Wickett, *Contested Territory*, 53; and Litwack, *Been in the Storm So Long*, 399–408.

81. Baker and Baker, *Oklahoma Slave Narratives*, 28.

82. IPH, roll 36, vol. 108: 465–73, esp. 466.

83. IPH, roll 31, vol. 92: 77–84, esp. 84. Given the surrounding records, Hall was likely a Choctaw freedman.

84. IPH, roll 35, vol. 106: 342–49, esp. 345.

85. IPH, roll 13, vol. 37: 473–81, esp. 479.

86. IPH, roll 30, vol. 91: 455–56.

87. Deutsch, "Being American," 102–3. Creek freedmen land claims were at the center of the founding of Boley. See also Chang, *Color of the Land*, 158–59, 163. For a more popular perspective, see Previch, "Diversity," 25.

88. IPH, roll 12, vol. 34: 326–35, esp. 335. Maytubbie is listed as a Choctaw freedman, though he should have been able to claim Choctaw Nation membership on the "By Blood" rolls. He described his grandmother as a native of Africa who was purchased by a member of the Choctaw Nation and then freed so that she could marry

her enslaver's son. See also *Final Rolls of Citizens and Freedmen of the Five Civilized Tribes in Indian Territory*.

89. Stremlau, *Sustaining the Cherokee Family*, 5.

90. See Wickett, *Contested Territory*, 36–37; and Yarbrough, *Race and the Cherokee Nation*, 30–31, 58–59.

91. See IPH, roll 3, vol. 7: 296–305, esp. 302; and IPH, roll 31, vol. 92: 264–68, esp. 265. The descendants of John Guest, who had been enslaved by Zadoc John Harrison's grandfather, continued to live in the vicinity of the family farm: "Those of the descendants of that old darkey who survived at the time of the allotment of land were each given their lawful share, as freemen."

92. IPH, roll 13, vol. 37: 473–81, esp. 473. Chang discusses the tensions that sometimes arose in the Creek Nation between Creek freedpeople who received allotments and "State Negroes," as Black Creeks referred to African American migrants to Indian Territory. *Color of the Land*, 159.

93. IPH, roll 26, vol. 79: 155–73, esp. 155–56.

94. Franklin, *Journey toward Hope*, 12.

95. J. A. Broadnax, "Oklahoma. EL RENO.–Our Church Here Is Ahead of All Other Churches," *Christian Recorder*, April 26, 1894.

96. "The Indian Territory," *Christian Recorder*, June 21, 1888.

97. Guidon, "Schools in the Indian Territory."

98. Franklin, *Journey toward Hope*, 13.

99. Athearn, *In Search of Canaan*, 164–65. Of course, many in Kansas were hoping to stem the tide of Black migration to the state and looking for other possible destinations for this population, which may have colored their enthusiasm for Indian Territory.

100. Grossman, "Blowing the Trumpet."

101. Dana Chandler, "Lynchings Stats Year Dates Causes," Lynching Information, Tuskegee University Archives Repository, January 14, 2021, http://archive.tuskegee.edu/repository/wp-content/uploads/2020/11/Lynchings-Stats-Year-Dates-Causes.pdf. See also Northwestern University School of Law, "Lynching Statistics." Of course, as Pfeifer points out, these numbers can be problematic because they include errors and begin in the 1880s, rather than when lynching began. See "State of the Field of Lynching Scholarship," 844. See also Waldrep's work on defining lynching, such as "War of Words"; and Trotti, "What Counts."

102. Grossman, "Blowing the Trumpet," 85.

103. See the tables in Cutler, *Lynch-Law*, 179–85.

104. Labode, "'Stern, Fearless Settlers of the West,'" 390–92.

105. Wickett, *Contested Territory*, 155–56.

106. Cutler, *Lynch-Law*, 179–80.

107. Baker and Baker, *Oklahoma Slave Narratives*, 24.

108. Debo, *Rise and Fall of the Choctaw Republic*, 109, 249.

109. FRB, 1.

110. Kidwell, *Choctaws in Oklahoma*, 143.

111. FRB, 3 (section 7).

112. CTLCN, 156–57.

113. CTLCN, 171–72.

114. The oath duplicates the language of a similar oath required of white men

seeking to marry Cherokee women in 1855. The Choctaw oath adds "so help me God." See Yarbrough, *Race and the Cherokee Nation*, chap. 3, esp. 56–58.

115. *CTLCN*, 172, sections 5 and 6.

116. Cherokee National Records Microfilm Series, roll CHN 73, vol. Cherokee (Tahlequah) Courts 1878: 12–28. Page numbering restarts in each year, though there are no actual volume titles. This case appeared in Cherokee court at the request of Choctaw authorities. Indian courts assumed that because both the victim and alleged perpetrator were Choctaw citizens, Indian courts had the authority to prosecute the case and mete out justice; however, American courts might have interpreted the legal status of intermarried whites differently. Federal courts might have attempted to exercise authority over this case because neither the accused nor the victim was a native Choctaw. See Yarbrough, *Race and the Cherokee Nation*, 56–57, for more on this case in the Cherokee context.

117. *Laws of the Choctaw Nation 1891*, 8–9.

Conclusion

1. Warde, *When the Wolf Came*, 299.

2. For more in the racial hierarchy that developed in Oklahoma, see Wallenstein, "Native Americans are White"; and Yarbrough, *Race and the Cherokee Nation*, 125–26.

3. Joshua Paddison discusses the impact of the racial diversity of the larger West on discussions of citizenship during the Reconstruction era. See Paddison, "Race, Religion, and Naturalization."

4. Emphasis from the original Certificate of Degree of Indian Blood application, available on the Choctaw Nation of Oklahoma website, choctawnation.com.

5. For more on the controversy over freedpeople, see Krauthamer, *Black Slaves, Indian Masters*, 154; Yarbrough, *Race and the Cherokee Nation*, chap. 7; Naylor, *African Cherokees in Indian Territory*, 206–19; Miles, *Ties That Bind*, preface; and S. Miller, *Coacoochee's Bones*, 183–88. Saunt's work *Black, White, and Indian* focuses on a Creek family and also addresses contemporary discussions about race, particularly people of African descent.

6. Jeff Fortney, "Lest We Remember," 526; Lowery, "Original Southerners," 22.

Bibliography

Primary Sources

ARCHIVAL COLLECTIONS

National Archives, Washington, DC
  Compiled Records Showing Service of Military Units in Confederate Organizations, Record Group 109, microcopy 861.
  Compiled Service Records of Confederate Soldiers Who Served in Organizations Raised Directly by the Confederate Government, microcopy 258, rolls 81, 82, 83, 84, 85, and 91, also available at Bizzell Memorial Library, University of Oklahoma, Norman. I have compiled information from these service records into a database that includes soldiers' names, ranks, companies, ages, dates of enlistment, remarks, receipts of clothing, commutations, terms of service, and information about reenlistment.
  Dawes Enrollment Number 4938, Census Card Number 1745, Oklahoma and Indian Territory, Dawes Census Cards for Five Civilized Tribes, 1898–1914, online database, Ancestry.com.
  Enrollment Cards for the Five Civilized Tribes, 1898–1914, NAI Number 251747, Records of the Bureau of Indian Affairs, Record Group Number 75.
  Final Rolls of Citizens and Freedmen of the Five Civilized Tribes in Indian Territory. Microfilm publication T529, 3 rolls, ARC ID 608958, Records of the Office of the Secretary of the Interior, Record Group 48.
  Letters Received by the Office of Indian Affairs, 1824–1881.
Oklahoma Historical Society, Oklahoma City
  Cherokee National Records Microfilm Series
  Choctaw National Records Microfilm Series
Western History Collection, University of Oklahoma, Norman
  Choctaw National Records Microfilm Series
  Choctaw Nation Papers
  Indian Pioneer History Collection
  Native American Manuscripts
  Peter Perkins Pitchlynn Papers

CONFEDERATE RECORDS

Confederate Imprints, microfilm 615, University of Oklahoma Libraries, Norman.
The Confederate States Almanac and Repository of Useful Knowledge: For the Year 1863: Being the Third Year of the Independence of the Confederate States of America. Augusta, GA: H. C. Clarke, 1863. Available on Sabin Americana, Gale, Cengage Learning, http://galenet.galegroup.com.ezproxy.rice.edu/servlet/Sabin?af=RN&ae=CY102947109&srchtp=a&ste=14.

Confederate States of America. *Report of the Commissioner of Indian Affairs.* Richmond: War Department, Office of Indian Affairs, January 12, 1863. Hathi Trust Digital Library, hathitrust.org.

———. *Report of the Commissioner of Indian Affairs.* Richmond: War Department, Office of Indian Affairs, December 7, 1863.

———. *The Statutes at Large of the Provisional Government of the Confederate States of America, from the Institution of the Government, February 8, 1861, to Its Termination, February 18, 1862, Inclusive. Arranged in Chronological Order. Together with the Constitution for the Provisional Government and the Permanent Constitution of the Confederate States, and the Treaties Concluded by the Confederates States with Indian Tribes.* Edited by James M. Matthews. Richmond: R. M. Smith, Printer to Congress, 1864. Electronic edition available through University of North Carolina at Chapel Hill Libraries.

Constitution of the Confederate States of America. Confederate Imprints, microfilm 615, Rice University Libraries, Houston, TX. https://avalon.law.yale.edu/19th_century/csa_csa.asp.

Message of the President, and Report of Albert Pike, Commissioner of the Confederate States to the Indian Nations West of Arkansas, of the Results of His Mission. Richmond: Enquirer Book and Job Press, Tyler, Wise, Allegre and Smith, 1861.

GOVERNMENT DOCUMENTS

1820 Treaty of Doak's Stand. Available on the Choctaw Nation website, https://www.choctawnation.com/history-culture/history/government-treaties.

1830 Treaty of Dancing Rabbit Creek. Available on the Choctaw Nation website, https://www.choctawnation.com/history-culture/history/government-treaties.

1834 Trade and Intercourse Act, *United States Statutes at Large*, 23rd Cong., chapter 161. Available on the Library of Congress website, http://www.loc.gov/law/help/statutes-at-large/23rd-congress.php.

1837 Treaty with the Choctaw and Chickasa. In *Indian Affairs: Laws and Treaties*, vol. 2, compiled and edited by Charles J. Kappler. Washington, DC: Government Printing Office, 1904.

American Indian and Alaskan Native Documents in the Congressional Serial Set: 1817–1899, University of Oklahoma College of Law, S. Doc. No. 84, 55th Congress, 2nd Session (1898).

"Articles of Confederation Entered Into between Muscogees, Seminoles, Choctaws, and Chickasaws and the Confederate States of America, July 1, 1861." Available on the Choctaw Nation website, choctawnation.com.

"Declaration by the People of the Cherokee Nation of the Causes Which Have Impelled Them to Unite Their Fortunes with Those of the Confederate States of America." Available on the Cherokee Nation website, http://www.cherokee.org/About-The-Nation/History/Events/Cherokee-Declaration-of-Causes-October-28-1861.

"Resolutions Expressing the Feelings and Sentiments of the General Council of the Choctaw Nation in Reference to the Political Disagreement Existing between the Northern and Southern States of the American Union." *The Miscellaneous Documents of the House of Representative for the Second Session of the Fifty-Second Congress, 1892–93; in Thirty Volumes.* Washington, DC: Government Printing Office, 1893.

Treaty of Hopewell. Yale Law School's Avalon Project, accessed May 30, 2019, http://avalon.law.yale.edu/18th_century/choc1786.asp.

Treaty with the Choctaw and Chickasaw, 1866. Available on the Choctaw Nation website: https://www.choctawnation.com/history-culture/history/government-treaties.

United States Department of the Interior. *Federal Indian Law.* Clark, NJ: The Lawbook Exchange, 2008.

United States, Office of Indian Affairs. *Annual Report of the Commissioner of Indian Affairs, for the Year 1859.* University of Wisconsin–Madison Libraries, Digital Collections, http://digicoll.library.wisc.edu.

———. *Annual Report of the Commissioner of Indian Affairs—Yr. 1862–63.* Washington, DC: Government Printing Office, A. O. P. Nicolson, 1863. Hathi Trust Digital Library, hathiturst.org.

US Laws, Statutes, Etc. *An Act to Regulate Trade and Intercourse with the Indian Tribes, and to Preserve Peace on the Frontiers.* Philadelphia: Francis Childs, 1796. Available on the Library of Congress website, https://www.loc.gov/item/rbpe.2230070a/.

The War of the Rebellion: A Compilation of the Official Records of the Union and Confederate Armies, 128 vols. Washington, DC: Government Printing Office, 1881.

LEGAL CODES

Acts and Resolutions of the General Council of the Choctaw Nation. Vol. 16 of *Constitutions and Laws of the American Indian Tribes.* 1859. Reprint, Wilmington, DE: Scholarly Resources, Inc., 1975.

The Constitution and Laws of the Cherokee Nation: Passed at Tahlequah, Cherokee Nation, 1839–1851. Tahlequah, Cherokee Nation, 1852. Electronic copy accessed through the Library of Congress website, http://lccn.loc.gov/28014182.

The Constitution and Laws of the Choctaw Nation. Vol. 13 of *Constitutions and Laws of the American Indian Tribes.* 1840. Reprint, Wilmington, DE: Scholarly Resources, Inc., 1975.

The Constitution and Laws of the Choctaw Nation. Vol. 14 of *Constitutions and Laws of the American Indian Tribes.* 1847. Reprint, Wilmington, DE: Scholarly Resources, Inc., 1975.

The Constitution and Laws of the Choctaw Nation. Vol. 15 of *Constitutions and Laws of the American Indian Tribes.* 1852. Reprint, Wilmington, DE: Scholarly Resources, Inc., 1975.

Constitution and Laws of the Choctaw Nation: Together with the Treaties of 1855, 1865 and 1866. New York City: Wm. P. Lyon and Son, 1869.

Constitution, Treaties and Laws of the Choctaw Nation: Made and Enacted by the Choctaw Legislature. 1887. Reprint, Wilmington, DE: Scholarly Resources, Inc., 1975.

The Freedmen and Registration Bills. Vol. 18 of *Constitutions and Laws of the American Indian Tribes.* 1883. Reprint, Wilmington, DE: Scholarly Resources, Inc., 1975.

Laws of the Choctaw Nation. Vol. 18 of *Constitutions and Laws of the American Indian Tribes.* 1883. Reprint, Wilmington, DE: Scholarly Resources, Inc., 1975.

Laws of the Choctaw Nation Made and Enacted by the General Council, from 1886–

1890 Inclusive. Vol. 21 of *Constitutions and Laws of the American Indian Tribes.* 1891. Reprint, Wilmington, DE: Scholarly Resources, Inc., 1975.

Laws of the State of Mississippi: Embracing All Acts of a Public Nature from January Session, 1824, to January Session, 1838, Inclusive. Baltimore: John D. Toy, 1838, Google eBook.

OTHER RECORDS

Andrews, Sidney. *The South since the War: As Shown by Fourteen Weeks of Travel and Observation in Georgia and the Carolinas.* Boston: Ticknor and Fields, 1866.

"Arkansas Petition for Freedmen's Rights 1869." National Archives Records of Rights website, http://recordsofrights.org/records/271/arkansas-petition-for-freedmens-rights/0.

Baker, T. Lindsay, and Julie Baker, eds. *The WPA Oklahoma Slave Narratives.* Norman: University of Oklahoma Press, 1996.

Bibb, Henry. *Narrative of the Life and Adventures of Henry Bibb, an American Slave, Written by Himself.* New York, 1850. Available on Uncle Tom's Cabin & American Culture: A Multi-media Archive, http:utc.iath.virginia.edu.

Byington, Cyrus. *A Dictionary of the Choctaw Language.* Edited by John R. Swanton and Henry S. Halbert. Washington, DC: Government Printing Office, 1915. See https://archive.org/stream/choctawlanguagoobyinrich/choctawlanguagoobyinrich_djvu.txt; and Choctaw-English Dictionary, Glosbe Multilingual Online Dictionary, https://en.glosbe.com/cho/en/homa.

Certificate of Degree of Indian Blood application. Available on the Choctaw Nation of Oklahoma website, choctawnation.com.

Collected Works of Abraham Lincoln, vol. 4. University of Michigan Digital Collections, https://quod.lib.umich.edu/l/lincoln/lincoln4/1:527?rgn=div1;view=fulltext.

Emancipation Proclamation. Transcript available on the National Archives website, https://www.archives.gov/exhibits/featured-documents/emancipation-proclamation.

Fenderich, Chas. *P. P. Pitchlynn, Speaker of the National Council of the Choctaw Nation and Choctaw Delegate to the Government of the United States.* Lithograph. Washington, [DC]: Chas. Fenderich, 1842. Available on the Library of Congress website, https://www.loc.gov/resource/pga.06453/.

Guidon. "Schools in the Indian Territory." *Christian Recorder,* September 12, 1878.

Havard, Gilles. *The Great Peace of Montreal of 1702: French Native Diplomacy in the Seventeenth Century.* Translated by Phyllis Aronoff and Howard Scott. Montreal: McGill-Queen's University Press, 2001.

Hergesheimer, E. *Map Showing the Distribution of the Slave Population of the Southern States of the United States. Compiled from the Census of 1860.* Washington: Henry S. Graham, 1861. Available on the Library of Congress website, https://www.loc.gov/item/99447026/.

Hitchcock, Ethan Allen. *A Traveler in Indian Territory: The Journal of Ethan Allen Hitchcock.* Edited by Grant Foreman. 1930. Reprint, Norman: University of Oklahoma Press, 1996.

Hudson, Peter J. "A Story of Choctaw Chiefs." University of Oklahoma Libraries Digital Collection, accessed May 31, 2019, https://digital.libraries.ou.edu/utils/getfile/collection/choctawnat/id/7510/.../7511.pdf.

Philadelphia Female Anti-slavery Society. *Extracts from the American Slave Code.* Philadelphia, 1820.

Pitchlynn, Peter Perkins. *A Gathering of Statesmen: Records of the Choctaw Council Meetings 1826–1828.* Edited and translated by Marcia Haag and Henry J. Willis. Norman: University of Oklahoma Press, 2013.

———. "Remonstrance of Col. Peter Pitchlynn, Choctaw Delegate, against the Passage of the Bill to Unite under One Government the Several Indian Tribes West of the Mississippi River, February 3, 1849." H.R. Misc. Doc. No. 35, 30th Cong., 2nd Sess. (1849).

"A Sharecropper's Contract." Grimes Family Papers (#3357), 1882, in the Southern Historical Collection, University of North Carolina at Chapel Hill. Accessed October 22, 2019, http://web.archive.org/web/20180204155312/http://www.learnnc.org/lp/editions/nchist-newsouth/4765.

Spooner, Lysander. *A Defence for Fugitive Slaves, against the Acts of Congress of February 12, 1793, and September 18, 1850.* Boston: B. Marsh, 1850.

Walker, Robert J. "Inaugural Address of R. J. Walker, Governor of Kansas Territory. Delivered in Lecompton, K. T., May 27, 1857." In *Transactions of the Kansas State Historical Society, 1888–'96; Together with Addresses at Annual Meetings; Copies of Official Papers and Executive Minutes*, vol. 5, edited by F. G. Adams, 328–41. Topeka: Press of the Kansas State Printing Company, J. K. Hudson, State Printer, 1896.

Secondary Sources

Abel, Annie Heloise. *The American Indian as Participant in the Civil War, 1862–1865.* Cleveland: Arthur H. Clark Company, 1919.

———. *The American Indian as Slaveholder and Secessionist.* Lincoln: University of Nebraska Press, 1991. Originally published as *An Omitted Chapter in the Diplomatic History of the Southern Confederacy.* Cleveland: Arthur H. Clark Company, 1915.

———. "The Indians in the Civil War." *American Historical Review* 15, no. 2 (January 1910): 281–96.

Adair, James. *The History of the American Indians.* Edited by Kathryn E. Holland Braund. Tuscaloosa: University of Alabama Press, 2005.

Agnew, Brad. "Our Doom as a Nation Is Sealed: The Five Nations in the Civil War." In Clampitt, *Civil War and Reconstruction in Indian Territory*, 64–87.

Ahtone, Tristan. "The Cherokee Nation Is Entitled to a Delegate in Congress. But Will They Finally Send One?" *Yes! Magazine*, January 4, 2017. https://www.yesmagazine.org/people-power/the-cherokee-nation-is-entitled-to-a-delegate-in-congress-but-will-they-finally-send-one-20170104.

Ainsworth, Kyle. "Field Hands, Cowboys, and Runaways: Enslaved People on Horseback in Texas's Planter-Herder Economy, 1835–1865." *Journal of Southern History* 86, no. 3 (August 2020): 557–600.

Ashcraft, Allan C. "Confederate Indian Troop Conditions in 1864." *Chronicles of Oklahoma* 41, no. 4 (Winter 1963–64): 442–49.

Athearn, Robert G. *In Search of Canaan: Black Migration to Kansas, 1879–1880.* Lawrence: Regents Press of Kansas, 1978.

Atkins, Jonathan M. "Party Politics and the Debate over the Tennessee Free Negro Bill, 1859–1860." *Journal of Southern History* 71, no. 2 (May 2005): 245–78.

Axtell, James. *The European and the Indian: Essays in the Ethnohistory of Colonial North America*. Oxford: Oxford University Press, 1981.

Bailey, Anne J. *Invisible Southerners: Ethnicity in the Civil War*. Athens: University of Georgia Press, 2006.

Bailey, David Thomas. "A Divided Prism: Two Sources of Black Testimony on Slavery." *Journal of Southern History* 46 (August 1980): 381–404.

Baird, W. David. *A Creek Warrior for the Confederacy: The Autobiography of Chief G. W. Grayson*. Norman: University of Oklahoma Press, 1988.

———. *Peter Pitchlynn: Chief of the Choctaws*. Norman: University of Oklahoma Press, 1972.

Baker, Jean. "The Civilian Experience of the Civil War." National Park Service website, accessed October 29, 2018, https://www.nps.gov/resources/story.htm%3Fid%3D249.

Barnett, James F., Jr. *Mississippi's American Indians*. Jackson: University of Mississippi Press, 2012.

Barney, William L. *The Making of a Confederate: Walter Lenoir's Civil War*. Oxford: Oxford University Press, 2008.

"The Battle of Honey Springs." Oklahoma Historical Society website, accessed October 18, 2018, http://www.okhistory.org/sites/hsbattle.

"Battle of Newtonia (1862)." Community Conflict: The Impact of the Civil War in the Ozarks website, accessed October 17, 2018, http://www.ozarkscivilwar.org/archives/336.

Bean, Christopher B. "Who Defines a Nation? Reconstruction in Indian Territory." In Clampitt, *Civil War and Reconstruction in Indian Territory*, 110–31.

Beringer, Richard E., Herman Hattaway, Archer Jones, and William N. Still Jr. *Why the South Lost the Civil War*. Athens: University of Georgia Press, 1986.

Berlin, Ira. *Generations of Captivity: A History of African-American Slaves*. Cambridge, MA: Harvard University Press, 2003.

———. *Slaves without Masters: The Free Negro in the Antebellum South*. New York: New Press, 1974.

Blackburn, Bob L. "From Blood Revenge to the Lighthorsemen: Evolution of Law Enforcement Institutions among the Five Civilized Tribes to 1861." *American Indian Law Review* 8, no. 1 (1980): 49–63.

Blassingame, John W. *The Slave Community: Plantation Life in the Antebellum South*. 1972. Reprint, New York: Oxford University Press, 1979.

Boulware, Tyler. "'We Are Men': Native American and Euroamerican Projections of Masculinity during the Seven Years' War." In *New Men: Manliness in Early America*, edited by Thomas A. Foster, 51–70. New York: New York University Press, 2011.

Bowes, John P. *Land Too Good for Indians: Northern Indian Removal*. Norman: University of Oklahoma Press, 2016.

Braund, Kathryn E. *Deerskins and Duffels: The Creek Indian Trade with Anglo-America, 1685–1815*. Lincoln: University of Nebraska Press, 1993.

"Cabin Creek Battlefield Historic Site." Oklahoma Historical Society website, accessed October 18, 2018, http://www.okhistory.org/sites/cabincreek.

Calloway, Colin G. *The American Revolution in Indian Country: Crisis and Diversity in Native American Communities*. Cambridge: Cambridge University Press, 1995.

Carpenter, Roger. "Womanish Men and Manlike Women." In Slater and Yarbrough, *Gender and Sexuality in Indigenous North America*, 146–64.

Carson, James Taylor. "Greenwood LeFlore: Southern Creole, Choctaw Chief." In *Pre-removal Choctaw History*, edited by Greg O'Brien, 221–36. Norman: University of Oklahoma Press, 2008.

———. "Horses and the Economy and Culture of the Choctaw Indians, 1790–1840." *Ethnohistory* 42, no. 3 (Summer 1995): 495–513.

———. "Native Americans, the Market Revolution, and Culture Change: The Choctaw Cattle Economy, 1690–1830." In *Pre-removal Choctaw History*, edited by Greg O'Brien, 183–99. Norman: University of Oklahoma Press, 2008.

———. *Searching for the Bright Path: The Mississippi Choctaws from Prehistory to Removal*. Lincoln: University of Nebraska Press, 1999.

Champagne, Duane. *Social Order and Political Change: Constitutional Governments among the Cherokee, the Choctaw, the Chickasaw, and the Creek*. Stanford: Stanford University Press, 1992.

Chang, David A. *The Color of the Land: Race, Nation, and the Politics of Landownership in Oklahoma, 1832–1929*. Chapel Hill: University of North Carolina Press, 2010.

Cheek, Gary Coleman, Jr. "'We Are Clay People': The Struggle against Choctaw Communal Dissolution, 1801–1861." PhD diss., Mississippi State University, 2020.

Clampitt, Bradley R., ed. *The Civil War and Reconstruction in Indian Territory*. Lincoln: University of Nebraska Press, 2015.

Clinton, Catherine, and Nina Silber, eds. *Battle Scars: Gender and Sexuality in the American Civil War*. Oxford: Oxford University Press, 2006.

Cobb-Greetham, Amanda. "Hearth and Home: Cherokee and Creek Women's Memories of the Civil War in Indian Territory." In Clampitt, *Civil War and Reconstruction in Indian Territory*, 153–71.

Confer, Clarissa W. *The Cherokee Nation in the Civil War*. Norman: University of Oklahoma Press, 2007.

Cowsert, Zachery Christian. "Confederate Borderland, Indian Homeland: Slavery, Sovereignty, and Suffering in Indian Territory." Master's thesis, West Virginia University, 2014.

Cushman, H. B. *History of the Choctaw, Chickasaw and Natchez Indians*. Edited by Angie Debo. Norman: University of Oklahoma Press, 1999.

Cutler, James Elbert. *Lynch-Law: An Investigation into the History of Lynching in the United States*. London: Longmans, Green, and Co., 1905.

Davis, Kenneth Penn. "Chaos in the Indian Country: The Cherokee Nation, 1828–1835." In *The Cherokee Indian Nation: A Troubled History*, edited by Duane H. King, 129–47. Knoxville: University of Tennessee Press, 1979.

Debo, Angie. *A History of the Indians of the United States*. Norman: University of Oklahoma Press, 1970.

———. *The Rise and Fall of the Choctaw Republic*. 1934. Reprint, Norman: University of Oklahoma Press, 1982.

DeRosier, Arthur H., Jr. *The Removal of the Choctaw Indians*. Knoxville: University of Tennessee Press, 1970.

Deutsch, Sarah. "Being American in Boley, Oklahoma." In *Beyond Black and White: Race, Ethnicity, and Gender in the U.S. South and Southwest*, edited by Stephanie Cole and Alison M. Parker, 97–122. College Station: Texas A&M University Press for University of Texas at Arlington, 2004.

Doran, Michael F. "Negro Slaves of the Five Civilized Tribes." *Annals of the Association of American Geographers* 68, no. 3 (September 1978): 335–50.

Douglass, Frederick. *Narrative of the Life of Frederick Douglass, an American Slave, Written by Himself, with Related Documents*. Edited by David W. Blight. Boston: Bedford/St. Martin's, 2003.

Downs, Jim. *Sick from Freedom: African-American Illness and Suffering during the Civil War and Reconstruction*. Oxford: Oxford University Press, 2012.

D'Urso, William. "The World Series of Choctaw Stickball: They Remember, the Little Brother of War." SBNation.com, accessed May 14, 2019, https://www.sbnation.com/2015/9/2/9224451/they-remember-the-little-brother-of-war.

Dusinberre, William. *Them Dark Days: Slavery in the American Rice Swamps*. New York: Oxford University Press, 1996.

Edwards, Whit. *"The Prairie Was on Fire": Eyewitness Accounts of the Civil War in the Indian Territory*. Oklahoma City: Oklahoma Historical Society, 2001.

Escott, Paul D. *Slavery Remembered: A Record of Twentieth-Century Slave Narratives*. Chapel Hill: University of North Carolina Press, 1979.

Estrada, Gabriel S. "Two-Spirit Histories in Southwestern and Mesoamerican Literatures." In Slater and Yarbrough, *Gender and Sexuality in Indigenous North America*, 165–84.

Etheridge, Robbie. *From Chicaza to Chickasaw: The European Invasion and the Transformation of the Mississippian World, 1540–1715*. 2010. Reprint, Chapel Hill: University of North Carolina Press, 2013.

Faiman-Silva, Sandra. *Choctaw at the Crossroads: The Political Economy of Class and Culture in the Oklahoma Timber Region*. Lincoln: University of Nebraska Press, 1997.

Faust, Drew Gilpin. *This Republic of Suffering: Death and the American Civil War*. New York: Alfred A. Knopf, 2008.

Finkelman, Paul. "States' Rights, Southern Hypocrisy, and the Crisis of the Union." *Akron Law Review* 45, no. 2 (2012): 449–78.

Fischer, Kirsten. *Suspect Relations: Sex, Race, and Resistance in Colonial North Carolina*. Ithaca: Cornell University Press, 2002.

Fischer, LeRoy H. *The Civil War Era in Indian Territory*. Los Angeles: Lorrin L. Morrison, 1974.

Fite, Gilbert C. "Development of the Cotton Industry by the Five Civilized Tribes in Indian Territory." *Journal of Southern History* 15, no. 3 (August 1949): 342–53.

Fitz, Caitlin A. "'Suspected on Both Sides': Little Abraham, Iroquois Neutrality, and the American Revolution." *Journal of the Early Republic* 27, no. 3 (Fall 2008): 299–335.

Foner, Eric. *Reconstruction: America's Unfinished Revolution, 1863–1877*. Updated ed. New York: Harper Perennial Modern Classics, 2014.

———. *A Short History of Reconstruction*. New York: Harper and Row, 1990.

Foreman, Grant. *The Five Civilized Tribes: Cherokee, Chickasaw, Choctaw, Creek, Seminole*. Norman: University of Oklahoma Press, 1934.

———. *Indian Removal.* 11th ed. Norman: University of Oklahoma Press, 1989.
Fortney, Jeff. "Lest We Remember: Civil War Memory and Commemoration among the Five Tribes." *American Indian Quarterly* 36, no. 4 (Fall 2012): 525–44.
———. "Robert M. Jones and the Choctaw Nation: Indigenous Nationalism in the American South, 1820–1877." PhD diss., University of Oklahoma, 2014.
"Fort Wayne, Battle of." Oklahoma Historical Society website, accessed October 16, 2018, http://www.okhistory.org/publications/enc/entry.php?entry=FO048.
Foster, Frances Smith. *Witnessing Slavery: The Development of Antebellum Slave Narratives.* 2nd ed. Madison: University of Wisconsin Press, 1994.
Fox-Genovese, Elizabeth. *Within the Plantation Household: Black and White Women of the Old South.* Chapel Hill: University of North Carolina Press, 1988.
Franklin, Jimmie Lewis. *Journey toward Hope: A History of Blacks in Oklahoma.* Norman: University of Oklahoma Press, 1982.
Freehling, William W. *The Road to Disunion: Secessionists Triumphant, 1854–1861.* Oxford: Oxford University Press, 2007.
Gabriel, Ralph Henry. *Elias Boudinot, Cherokee, and His America.* The Civilization of the American Indian Series, no. 20. Norman: University of Oklahoma Press, 1941.
Gaines, W. Craig. *The Confederate Cherokees.* Baton Rouge: Louisiana State University Press, 1989.
Gallagher, Gary W., and Joan Waugh. *The American War: A History of the Civil War Era.* State College, PA: Flip Learning, 2015.
Galloway, Patricia. *Choctaw Genesis, 1500–1700.* Lincoln: University of Nebraska Press, 1995.
Garrison, Tim Alan. *The Legal Ideology of Removal: The Southern Judiciary and the Sovereignty of Native American Nations.* Athens: University of Georgia Press, 2002.
Genovese, Eugene D. *The Political Economy of Slavery: Studies in the Economy and Society of the Slave South.* 4th ed. Middletown, CT: Wesleyan University Press, 1989.
———. *Roll, Jordan, Roll: The World the Slaves Made.* New York: First Vintage Books Edition, 1972.
Gerteis, Louis. "Slaves, Servants, and Soldiers: Uneven Paths to Freedom in the Border States, 1861–1865." In *Lincoln's Proclamation: Emancipation Reconsidered*, edited by William A. Blair and Karen Fisher Younger, 170–94. Chapel Hill: University of North Carolina Press, 2009.
Gibson, Arrell M. *The Chickasaws.* Norman: University of Oklahoma Press, 1971.
———. "Native Americans and the Civil War." *American Indian Quarterly* 9, no. 4 (Autumn 1985): 385–410.
Graebner, Norman Arthur. "Pioneer Indian Agriculture in Oklahoma." *Chronicles of Oklahoma* 23, no. 3 (1945): 232–48.
Grahame-Smith, Seth. *Abraham Lincoln: Vampire Hunter.* New York: Grand Central Publishing, 2010.
Grear, Charles D., and Steven P. Salyer. "Twenty-Ninth Texas Cavalry." *Handbook of Texas Online*, accessed November 5, 2018, http://www.tshaonline.org/handbook/online/articles/qkt07.
Grossman, James R. "Blowing the Trumpet: The 'Chicago Defender' and Black

Migration during World War I." *Illinois Historical Journal* 78, no. 2 (Summer 1985): 82–96.

Hahn, Steven. *A Nation without Borders: The United States and Its World in an Age of Civil Wars, 1830–1910*. New York: Viking, 2016.

Hall, Richard. *Women on the Civil War Battlefront*. Lawrence: University Press of Kansas, 2006.

Halliburton, R. *Red over Black: Black Slavery among the Cherokee Indians*. Westport, CT: Greenwood Press, 1977.

Hauptman, Laurence M. *Between Two Fires: American Indians in the Civil War*. New York: Free Press, 1996.

Higgins, Billy D. "Act 151 of 1859." Encyclopedia of Arkansas website, accessed March 14, 2021, https://encyclopediaofarkansas.net/entries/act-151-of-1859-4430/.

Hodes, Martha. *White Women, Black Men: Illicit Sex in the 19th-Century South*. New Haven: Yale University Press, 1997.

———, ed. *Sex, Love, Race: Crossing Boundaries in North American History*. New York: New York University Press, 1999.

Hood, Fred. "Twilight of the Confederacy in Indian Territory." *Chronicles of Oklahoma* 41, no. 4 (Winter 1963–64): 425–41.

Ishii, Izumi. *Bad Fruits of the Civilized Tree: Alcohol and the Sovereignty of the Cherokee Nation*. Lincoln: University of Nebraska Press, 2008.

Iti Fabvssa. "Choctaw Nation and the American Civil War." October 2011, Choctaw Nation website, https://www.choctawnation.com/sites/default/files/2015/10/14/2011.10_Choctaw_Nation_and_the_American_Civil_War.pdf.

———. "Traditional Choctaw Agriculture (Part I)." Chahta Anumpa Aiikhvna School of Choctaw Language website, accessed October 24, 2018, http://www.choctawschool.com/home-side-menu/iti-fabvssa/2011-articles/traditional-choctaw-agriculture-(part-i).aspx.

Jordan, H. Donaldson. "A Politician of Expansion: Robert J. Walker." *Mississippi Valley Historical Review* 19, no. 3 (1932): 362–81.

Kantrowitz, Stephen. "Fighting Like Men: Civil War Dilemmas of Abolitionist Manhood." In Clinton and Silber, *Battle Scars*, 19–40.

Katz, William Loren. *Black Indians: A Hidden Heritage*. New York: Atheneum, 1986.

Kidwell, Clara Sue. *Choctaws and Missionaries in Mississippi, 1818–1918*. Norman: University of Oklahoma Press, 1995.

———. *Choctaws in Oklahoma: From Tribe to Nation, 1855–1970*. Norman: University of Oklahoma Press, 2007.

King, Patricia Jo Lynn. "The Forgotten Warriors: Keetoowah Abolitionists, Revitalization, the Search for Modernity and the Struggle for Autonomy in the Cherokee Nation, 1800–1866." PhD diss., University of Oklahoma, 2013.

Klebaner, Benjamin Joseph. "American Manumission Laws and the Responsibility for Supporting Slaves." *Virginia Magazine of History and Biography* 63, no. 4 (October 1955): 443–53.

Knight, Wilfred. *Red Fox: Stand Watie and the Confederate Indian Nations during the Civil War Years in Indian Territory*. Glendale, CA: Arthur H. Clark, 1988.

Krauthamer, Barbara. *Black Slaves, Indian Masters: Slavery, Emancipation, and Citizenship in the Native American South*. Chapel Hill: University of North Carolina Press, 2013.

Labode, Modupe. "The 'Stern, Fearless Settlers of the West': Lynching, Region, and Capital Punishment in Early Twentieth-Century Colorado." *Western Historical Quarterly* 45, no. 4 (Winter 2014): 389–428.

Lambert, Valerie. *Choctaw Nation: A Story of American Indian Resurgence*. Lincoln: University of Nebraska Press, 2007.

Lang, Sabine. *Men as Women, Women as Men: Changing Gender in Native American Cultures*. Austin: University of Texas Press, 1998.

Lankford, George E., ed. *Bearing Witness: Memories of Arkansas Slavery; Narratives from the 1930s WPA Collections*. Fayetteville: University of Arkansas Press, 2003.

Lause, Mark A. *Race and Radicalism in the Union Army*. Urbana: University of Illinois Press, 2009.

Leacock, Eleanor Burke. "Women's Status in Egalitarian Society: Implications for Social Evolution." In *Native Women's History in Eastern North America before 1900: A Guide to Research and Writing*, edited by Rebecca Kugel and Lucy Eldersveld Murphy, 79–106. Lincoln: University of Nebraska Press, 2007.

Levine, Bruce. *Confederate Emancipation: Southern Plans to Free and Arm Slaves during the Civil War*. New York: Oxford University Press, 2006.

Littlefield, Daniel F., Jr. *The Chickasaw Freedmen: A People without a Country*. Westport, CT: Greenwood Press, 1980.

Litwack, Leon F. *Been in the Storm So Long: The Aftermath of Slavery*. New York: Vintage Books, 1979.

Lonn, Ella. *Desertion during the Civil War*. Lincoln: University of Nebraska Press, 1998. iBook.

Lowery, Malinda Maynor. "The Original Southerners: American Indians, the Civil War, and Confederate Memory." *Southern Cultures* 25, no. 4 (Winter 2019): 16–35.

Luna-Firebaugh, Eileen. *Tribal Policing: Asserting Sovereignty, Seeking Justice*. Tucson: University of Arizona Press, 2007.

Manning, Chandra. *What This Cruel War Was Over*. New York: Vintage Books, 2007.

Masur, Louis P. *The Civil War: A Concise History*. Oxford: Oxford University Press, 2011.

McGrath, Ann. *Illicit Love: Interracial Sex and Marriage in the United States and Australia*. Lincoln: University of Nebraska Press, 2015.

McKee, Jesse O., and Jon A. Schlenker. *The Choctaws: Cultural Evolution of a Native American Tribe*. Jackson: University Press of Mississippi, 1980.

McLoughlin, William G., Walter H. Conser Jr., and Virginia Duffy McLoughlin. *Cherokee Ghost Dance: Essays on the Southeastern Indians, 1789–1861*. Macon, GA: Mercer University Press, 1984.

McPherson, James M. *Battle Cry of Freedom: The Civil War Era*. New York: Oxford, 2003.

———. *For Cause and Comrades: Why Men Fought in the Civil War*. New York: Oxford University Press, 1997.

Melish, Joanne Pope. *Disowning Slavery: Gradual Emancipation and "Race" in New England, 1780–1860*. Ithaca: Cornell University Press, 1998.

Mellon, James. *Bullwhip Days: The Slaves Remember*. New York: Weidenfeld and Nicolson, 1988.

Meyers, Maureen. "Political Economy and Craft Production before and after the Collapse of Mississippian Chiefdoms." In *Beyond Collapse: Archaeological*

Perspectives on Resilience, Revitalization, and Transformation in Complex Societies, edited by Ronald K. Faulseit, 380–403. Carbondale: Southern Illinois University Press, 2016.

Miles, Tiya. *Ties That Bind: The Story of an Afro-Cherokee Family in Slavery and Freedom*. Berkeley: University of California Press.

Miller, Richard F., ed. *The Confederate States Chronology and a Reference Guide for South Carolina in the Civil War*. Vol. 6 of *States at War*. Lebanon, NH: University Press of New England, 2018. Google book.

Miller, Susan A. *Coacoochee's Bones: A Seminole Saga*. Lawrence: University of Kansas Press, 2003.

Moore, Albert Burton. *Conscription and Conflict in the Confederacy*. New York: Macmillan, 1924.

Mould, Tom. *Choctaw Tales*. Jackson: University of Mississippi Press, 2004.

National Park Service. "*Maple Leaf* (Shipwreck Site.)" National Park Service website, accessed November 5, 2018, https://www.nps.gov/articles/mapleleaf.htm.

Naylor, Celia E. *African Cherokees in Indian Territory: From Chattel to Citizens*. Chapel Hill: University of North Carolina Press, 2008.

Neff, Stephen C. "Secession and Breach of Compact: The Law of Nature Meets the United States Constitution." *Akron Law Review* 45, no. 2 (2012): 405–29.

Nelson, Scott, and Carol Sheriff. *A People at War: Civilians and Soldiers in America's Civil War, 1854–1877*. New York: Oxford University Press, 2008.

Noel, Jan V. "Revisiting Gender in Iroquoia." In Slater and Yarbrough, *Gender and Sexuality in Indigenous North America*, 54–74.

Nolan, Alan T. "The Anatomy of the Myth." In *The Myth of the Lost Cause and Civil War History*, edited by Gary W. Gallagher and Alan T. Nolan, 11–34. Bloomington: Indiana University Press, 2000.

Norgren, Jill. *The Cherokee Cases: The Confrontation of Law and Politics*. New York: McGraw-Hill, 1996.

Northwestern University School of Law. "Lynching Statistics." *Journal of the American Institute of Criminal Law and Criminology* 9, no. 1 (May 1918): 144–46.

O'Brien, Greg. *Choctaws in a Revolutionary Age, 1750–1830*. Lincoln: University of Nebraska Press, 2002.

———. "Pushmataha: Choctaw Warrior, Diplomat, and Chief." Mississippi HistoryNow website, accessed May 8, 2019, http://www.mshistorynow.mdah.ms.gov/articles/14/pushmataha-choctaw-warrior-diplomat-and-chief.

———. "Trying to Look Like Men: Changing Notions of Masculinity among Choctaw Elites in the Early Republic." In *Southern Manhood: Perspectives on Masculinity in the Old South*, edited by Craig Thompson Friend and Lorri Glover, 49–70. Athens: University of Georgia Press, 2004.

Olsen, Monty. *Indices of Choctaw and Chickasaw Confederate Soldiers*. Calera, OK: Bryan County Heritage Association, 1996.

O'Meara, Walter. *Daughters of the Country: The Women of the Fur Traders and Mountain Men*. New York: Harcourt, Brace, and World, 1968.

"Our History." Goodland Academy website, accessed October 25, 2018, http://www.goodland.org/about/our-history/.

Paddison, Joshua. "Race, Religion, and Naturalization: How the West Shaped Citizenship Debates in the Reconstruction Congress." In *Civil War Wests: Testing the Limits of the United States*, edited by Adam Arenson and Andrew R. Graybill, 181–201. Oakland: University of California Press, 2015.

Paige, Amanda L., Fuller L. Bumpers, and Daniel F. Littlefield Jr. *Chickasaw Removal*. Ada, OK: Chickasaw Press, 2010.

Painter, Nell Irvin. *Southern History across the Color Line*. Chapel Hill: University of North Carolina Press, 2002.

Pascoe, Peggy. *What Comes Naturally: Miscegenation Law and the Making of Race in America*. New York: Oxford University Press, 2009.

Pavao-Zuckerman, Barnet. "Deerskins and Domesticates: Creek Subsistence and Economic Strategies in the Historic Period." *American Antiquity* 72, no. 1 (January 2007): 5–33.

Perdue, Theda, and Michael D. Green, eds. *The Cherokee Removal: A Brief History with Documents*. Boston: Bedford/St. Martin's, 1995.

Pesantubbee, Michelene E. *Choctaw Women in a Chaotic World: The Clash of Cultures in the Colonial Southeast*. Albuquerque: University of New Mexico Press, 2005.

Pfeifer, Michael J. "The State of the Field of Lynching Scholarship." *Journal of American History* 101, no. 3 (December 2014): 832–46.

Potter, David M. *The Impending Crisis, 1848–1861*. Compiled and edited by Don E. Fehrenbacher. New York: Harper and Row, 1976.

Prag, Edward Elmer. "The Confederate Diplomacy with the Five Civilized Tribes." Master's thesis, University of Oklahoma, 1966.

Previch, Chad. "Diversity: Oklahoma Once Had 40 All-Black Towns, Formed Because Their Citizens Weren't Welcome Elsewhere—Longtime Resident Fears Worst for Boley—He Says Lure of Cities, Stagnant Economies Are Leading to Town's Death." *The Oklahoman*, April 22, 2007.

Prucha, Francis Paul. *American Indian Policy in the Formative Years: The Indian Trade and Intercourse Acts, 1790–1834*. Cambridge, Mass.: Harvard University Press, 1962.

———. *American Indian Treaties: The History of a Political Anomaly*. Berkeley: University of California Press, 1994.

Raboteau, Albert J. *Slave Religion: The "Invisible Institution in the Antebellum South."* Oxford: Oxford University Press, 1978.

Riley, Glenda. *Women and Indians on the Frontier, 1825–1915*. Albuquerque: University of New Mexico Press, 1984.

Robinson, Michael D. *A Union Indivisible: Secession and the Politics of Slavery in the Border South*. Chapel Hill: University of North Carolina Press, 2017.

Rosser, Ezra. "The Nature of Representation: The Cherokee Right to a Congressional Delegate." *Boston University Public Interest Law Journal* 15, no. 91 (Fall 2005): 91–152. https://ssrn.com/abstract=842647.

Rothman, Joshua D. *Notorious in the Neighborhood: Sex and Families across the Color Line in Virginia, 1787–1861*. Chapel Hill: University of North Carolina Press, 2003.

Saunt, Claudio. *Black, White, and Indian: Race and the Unmaking of an American Family*. New York: Oxford University Press, 2005.

———. *A New Order of Things: Property, Power, and the Transformation of the Creek Indians, 1733–1816*. Cambridge: Cambridge University Press, 1999.

———. "The Paradox of Freedom: Tribal Sovereignty and Emancipation during the Reconstruction of Indian Territory." *Journal of Southern History* 70 (February 2004): 63–94.

Scheiber, Harry N. "The Pay of Troops and Confederate Morale in the Trans-Mississippi West." *Arkansas Historical Quarterly* 18, no. 4 (Winter 1959): 350–65.

Schreier, Jessie Turner. "Different Shades of Freedom: Indians, African Americans, and Race in the Choctaw Nation, 1800–1907." PhD diss., University of California, Los Angeles, 2008.

Searcy, Margaret Zehmer. "Choctaw Subsistence, 1540–1830: Hunting, Fishing, Farming, and Gathering." In *The Choctaw before Removal*, edited by Carolyn Keller Reeves, 32–54. Jackson: University Press of Mississippi, 1985.

Sekora, John, and Darwin T. Turner, eds. *Art of Slave Narrative: Original Essays in Criticism and Theory*. Macomb: Western Illinois University Press, 1982.

"Senators Witness the First Battle of Bull Run." United States Senate website, accessed October 29, 2018, https://www.senate.gov/artandhistory/history/minute/Witness_Bull_Run.htm.

Shaw, Stephanie J. "Using the WPA Ex-slave Narratives to Study the Impact of the Great Depression." *Journal of Southern History* 69 (August 2003): 623–58.

Shoemaker, Nancy. *A Strange Likeness: Becoming Red and White in Eighteenth-Century North America*. Oxford: Oxford University Press, 2004.

"A Short History of Goodland Presbyterian Children's Home." Goodland Academy website, accessed October 25, 2018, goodland.org/01_aboutus/01-history/1-sketches/hsk_04.pdf.

Slater, Sandra, and Fay A. Yarbrough, eds. *Gender and Sexuality in Indigenous North America, 1400–1850*. Columbia: University of South Carolina Press, 2011.

Smith, F. Todd. "'The Most Destitute' People in Indian Territory: The Wichita Agency Tribes and the Civil War." In Clampitt, *Civil War and Reconstruction in Indian Territory*, 88–109.

Smith, John David, ed. *Black Soldiers in Blue: African American Troops in the Civil War Era*. Chapel Hill: University of North Carolina Press, 2002.

Smith, Troy. "Nations Colliding: The Civil War Comes to Indian Territory." *Civil War History* 59, no. 3 (September 2013): 279–319.

Smithers, Gregory D. "Cherokee 'Two Spirits': Gender, Ritual, and Spirituality in the Native South." *Early American Studies: An Interdisciplinary Journal* 12, no. 3 (Fall 2014): 626–51.

———. *Native Southerners: Indigenous History from Origins to Removal*. Norman: University of Oklahoma Press, 2019.

Smits, David D. "The 'Squaw Drudge': A Prime Index of Savagism." In *Native Women's History in Eastern North America before 1900: A Guide to Research and Writing*, edited by Rebecca Kugel and Lucy Eldersveld Murphy, 27–50. Lincoln: University of Nebraska Press, 2007.

Snyder, Christina. *Great Crossings: Indians, Settlers, and Slaves in the Age of Jackson*. New York: Oxford University Press, 2017.

Spindel, Donna J. "Assessing Memory: Twentieth-Century Slave Narratives Reconsidered." *Journal of Interdisciplinary History* 27 (Autumn 1996): 247–61.

Starling, Marion Wilson. *The Slave Narrative: Its Place in American History*. 2nd ed. Washington, DC: Howard University Press, 1988.

State Library of North Carolina. "*Maple Leaf*: A Great Escape." State Library of North Carolina website, accessed November 6, 2018, http://digital.ncdcr.gov/cdm/ref/collection/p15012coll8/id/11069.

Stauffer, John. "Embattled Manhood and New England Writers, 1860–1870." In Clinton and Silber, *Battle Scars*, 120–39.

Stidolph, Julie. "Medicine Worse Than the Malady: Indian Health, Colonization, and the Wind River Reservation, 1800–1928." PhD diss., University of Oklahoma, 2014.

St. Jean, Wendy. *Remaining Chickasaw in Indian Territory, 1830s–1907*. Tuscaloosa: University of Alabama Press, 2011.

Stremlau, Rose. *Sustaining the Cherokee Family: Kinship and the Allotment of an Indigenous Nation*. Chapel Hill: University of North Carolina Press, 2011.

Strickland, Rennard. *Fire and the Spirits: Cherokee Law from Clan to Court*. Norman: University of Oklahoma Press, 1975.

Swanton, John R. *Source Material for the Social and Ceremonial Life of the Choctaw Indians*. Tuscaloosa: University of Alabama Press, 2001. Swanton's work was originally published by the Smithsonian Institution in 1931 as *Bureau of American Ethnology Bulletin 103*.

Teed, Paul E., and Melissa Ladd Teed. *Reconstruction: A Reference Guide*. Santa Barbara: ABC-CLIO, 2015.

Trotti, Michael Ayers. "What Counts: Trends in Racial Violence in the Postbellum South." *Journal of American History* 100, no. 2 (September 2013): 375–400.

Ural, Susannah J., ed. *Civil War Citizens: Race, Ethnicity, and Identity in America's Bloodiest Conflict*. New York: New York University Press, 2010.

Veracini, Lorenzo. *Settler Colonialism: A Theoretical Overview*. New York: Palgrave Macmillan, 2010.

Vickers, Ovid. "Mississippi Choctaw Names and Naming: A Diachronic View." *Names: Journal of the American Name Society* 31 (June 1983): 117–22.

Virtual Museum of New France. "The Explorers." Canadian Museum of History, accessed May 6, 2019, https://www.historymuseum.ca/virtual-museum-of-new-france/the-explorers/louis-armand-de-lom-darce-baron-lahontan-1684-1689/.

Waldrep, Christopher. "War of Words: The Controversy over the Definition of Lynching, 1899–1940." *Journal of Southern History* 66, no. 1 (February 2000): 75–100.

Wallenstein, Peter. "Native Americans Are White, African Americans Are Not: Racial Identity, Marriage, Inheritance, and the Law in Oklahoma, 1907–1967." *Journal of the West* 39 (January 2000): 55–63.

———. *Tell the Court I Love My Wife: Race, Marriage, and Law—an American History*. New York: Palgrave Macmillan, 2002.

Warde, Mary Jane. *When the Wolf Came: The Civil War in Indian Territory*. Fayetteville: University of Arkansas Press, 2013.

Weik, Terrance M. "Engendering Labor, African Enslavement, and Human-Horse Relations in Chickasaw Territory." *Journal of African Diaspora Archaeology and Heritage* 8, nos. 1–2 (July 2019): 110–130. https://doi.org/10.1080/21619441.2019.1644830.

Wells, Jonathan Daniel. *A House Divided: The Civil War and Nineteenth-Century America*. New York: Routledge, 2012.

Wells, Samuel J. "Federal Indian Policy: From Accommodation to Removal." In *The Choctaw before Removal*, edited by Carolyn Keller Reeves, 181–213. Jackson: University of Mississippi Press, 1985.

White, Richard. *The Roots of Dependency: Subsistence, Environment, and Social Change among the Choctaws, Pawnees, and Navajos*. Lincoln: University of Nebraska Press, 1983.

Wickett, Murray R. *Contested Territory: Whites, Native Americans and African Americans in Oklahoma, 1865–1907*. Baton Rouge: Louisiana State University Press, 2000.

Williams, Heather Andrea. *Help Me to Find My People: The African American Search for Family Lost in Slavery*. Chapel Hill: University of North Carolina Press, 2012.

Winkler, H. Donald. *Stealing Secrets: How a Few Daring Women Deceived Generals, Impacted Battles, and Altered the Course of the Civil War*. Naperville, IL: Cumberland House, 2010.

Wolf, Eva Sheppard. *Race and Liberty in the New Nation: Emancipation in Virginia from the Revolution to Nat Turner's Rebellion*. Baton Rouge: Louisiana State University Press, 2006.

Wolfe, Patrick. "Settler Colonialism and the Elimination of the Native." *Journal of Genocide Research* 8, no. 4 (December 2006): 387–409.

———. *Settler Colonialism and the Transformation of Anthropology: The Politics and Poetics of an Ethnographic Event*. London: Cassell, 1999.

Woodward, C. Vann. "History from Slave Sources." *American Historical Review* 79 (April 1974): 470–81.

Wright, Muriel H. "General Douglas H. Cooper, C.S.A." *Chronicles of Oklahoma* 32, no. 2 (1954): 142–84.

———. "The Removal of the Choctaws to the Indian Territory, 1830–1833." *Chronicles of Oklahoma* 6, no. 2 (1928): 103–28.

Yanuck, Julius. "The Garner Fugitive Slave Case." *Mississippi Valley Historical Review* 40, no. 1 (June 1953): 47–66.

Yarbrough, Fay A. "Power, Perception, and Interracial Sex: Former Slaves Recall a Multiracial South." *Journal of Southern History* 71, no. 3 (August 2005): 559–88.

———. *Race and the Cherokee Nation: Sovereignty in the Nineteenth Century*. Philadelphia: University of Pennsylvania Press, 2008.

———. "Women, Labor, and Power in the Nineteenth-Century Choctaw Nation," In Slater and Yarbrough, *Gender and Sexuality in Indigenous North America*, 123–45.

Yetman, Norman R., ed. *Voices from Slavery: 100 Authentic Slave Narratives*. 1970. Reprint, Mineola, NY: Dover, 2000.

Zellar, Gary. *African Creeks: Estelvste and the Creek Nation*. Norman: University of Oklahoma Press, 2007.

Index

Note: Page numbers in italic refer to illustrative matter.

Abbott, Robert S., 196
Abel, Annie Heloise, 8, 108–9, 138
Aboha Kulla Humma (chief), 15, 16, 41–42
abolition, 129–30, 180–84, 229n67. *See also* Emancipation Proclamation; enslaved people of African descent; freedpeople of African descent; slavery
abuse, 57–58, 165, 166
African American soldiers, 2, 130, 173
Africans. *See* enslaved people of African descent; freedpeople of African descent
Agnew, Brad, 77
agricultural production and labor: gender roles in, 16–18, 23–24, 43, 50–51, 54–56, 160–62; important crops in, 53–54; in plantation farming, 47–51; recently freed people and, 188–91; sharecropping, 191–92; task system in, 63, 221n100. *See also* corn; cotton; livestock; slavery
Ahaikahno, 154
Ainsworth, Fred C., 116
Alabama, 3, 6, 11, 91, 95, 96. *See also* Confederate States of America
alcohol use, 165–66, 170, 171–72, 176
Alexander, Alice, 197
American Board of Commissioners for Foreign Missions, 20, 22, 31
Andrews, Sidney, 188
animal husbandry. *See* livestock
Appapaye (chief), 158–59
Arkansas, 9, 82, 109. *See also* Confederate States of America
Atlantic Monthly (publication), 110–11

Bailey, Anne J., 7
Baker, William Edward, 17
Ballard, Robert, 141
ball playing, 30, 153–54
Banks, Frances, 50
Banks, Phoebe, 124, 132, 148
Banks, Sina, 181
Barber, Mollie, 180
Barner, L. B., 181
Bates, Christine, 148
Battle Cry of Freedom (McPherson), 7
Battle of Bull Run (1861), 136
Battle of Cabin Creek (1863), 130
Battle of Elkhorn Tavern. *See* Battle of Pea Ridge (1862)
Battle of Honey Springs (1863), 2, 115, 130, 131, *133*, 148
Battle of Locust Grove (1862), 2, *125*
Battle of Manassas. *See* Battle of Bull Run (1861)
Battle of Old Fort Wayne (1862), 127–28
Battle of Pea Ridge (1862), 127, 141
Battle of Round Mountain (1862), 141
Bell, Eliza, 186
berdache, as term, 233n10. *See also* two spirits
Berlin, Ira, 57
Bibb, Henry, 59–60
Billy, John, 146
Black Codes, 187–88, 191
blood vengeance. *See* revenge tradition
boarding schools, 33. *See also* education
Boggy Depot, 123, 124, *125*
Bond, Thomas J., 147–48
Boudinot, Elias, 22
bounties, 136–37

Bowman, Dallas, 132
Bowman, Elam, 62
Broadnax, J. A., 195
Brown, John, 65–66, 73
Brown, Karrew, 143
Butler, Ed, 186, 238n43

Cade, Edward W., 129
Campbell Jones, R., 55
Camp Davis, 136
Camp Granite, 136
Carpenter, Roger, 17, 153
Carson, James Taylor, 160, 170
Case, Lucy, 17
Champagne, Duane, 18–19
Cheatham, Henry, 50
Cheek, Gary Coleman, Jr., 151–52
Cherokee Constitution, 19, 44
Cherokee language, 58
Cherokee Nation: abolition of slavery on, 129; "Declaration of Causes" by, 105–6; enslaved people on, 62, 181, 182; maps, *6, 77, 183*; Native alliances of, 80, 92, 95; sovereignty of, 179, 216n103; war neutrality of, 86–88, 92, 113. *See also* Indian Territory, overview
Cherokee people: on alcohol use, 171; citizenship rights of, 206; forced removal of, 26, *37*, 88–89; gender roles of, 153; as soldiers, 120, 140
Cherry, Lucy, 195
Chickasaw Constitution, 44
Chickasaw Nation: Confederate treaty with, 95–102; enslaved people on, 49, 181, 219n14; incorporation into Choctaw Nation, 38–39; maps, *5, 6, 77, 125, 183*; Native alliances of, 80, 92, 95, 105; sovereignty of, 27, 38–39. *See also* Choctaw Nation; Indian Territory, overview
Chickasaw people: historical relationship with Choctaw of, 39–40; matrilineality of, 102; removal of, 4–5, 13, 27–28, 37–39. *See also* Choctaw and Chickasaw Confederate soldiers
childcare, 50

Chilton, William P., 76
Choctaw and Chickasaw Confederate soldiers: ages and ranks of, 122–23; bounties for, 136–37, 138; desertions of, 133–34, 141–42, 149; disabilities of, 148; duties of, 141–42; enlistment of, 113, 117–18, 123–24, 129–30, 135, 137, 173; flag of, *131*; laws in support of, 2; lighthorsemen and, 173–76; names of, 121, 123; oath on slavery of, 144–45; offensive and defensive strategies of, 213n13; as prisoners of war, 142–46; promotions and transfers of, 142–44, 147–48; service records of, 8, 115–18; supply shortages of, 140–41; terms of, 135–36; troop establishment of, 93–94, 104–5, 119; warrior role and, 172–73; white soldiers and, 119–20, 139–40. *See also* Civil War battles; warriors
Choctaw Constitution, 8, 14, 24, 41, 44, 64, 120, 166–68, 199
Choctaw Freedman Bill (1883), 193–94, 197
Choctaw language, 40, 58, 212n8
Choctaw Nation: 1866 treaty of, 182–83, 184, 188, 192–94, 206; abolition of slavery on, 183–84; Chickasaw incorporation into, 38–39; Confederate allegiance of, 2–3, 75–76, 80–82, 107–10, 113; Confederate alliance treaty of, 76, 90–104, 112; Confederate payments to, 102–4; enslaved people on, 2–3, 5, 19, 24, 48–60, 181; federal payments to, 34, 79–80, 81, 83, 94–95, 104, 189; governance of, 18–20, 24–26, 40–41, 44–45; land cessions and acquisitions of, 3, *4*, 30–31, 44, 188; laws and treatment of freedpeople on, 65–67, 178–79, 188–98, 201, 204; livestock management of, 54–56; maps, *5, 6, 77, 79, 125, 183*; marriage laws and practices on, 44, 60, 67–69, 72–73, 198–201; Native alliances of, 80, 92, 95; ownership of slaves on, 2–3, 5, 19, 24; population statistics on, 3, 35, 239n74; proposal to federal government for voluntary removal, 28–30;

INDEX 261

racial ideology of, 41; racial laws of, 65–69; sovereignty of, 2–3, 10–11, 27, 39, 76; war neutrality of, 75, 76, 83–84, 89–90, 110–12; women's rights in, 41–42; written laws and criminality on, 18–20, 32. *See also* citizenship, Choctaw; Indian Territory, overview

Choctaw people: changes to concepts of gender, 20–21; clan organization of, 13–16; historical relationship with Chickasaw of, 39–40; livestock production of, 23–24, 54–56, 161–62; marriage of, 16, 21–23, 44, 60, 67–68; matrilineality of, 14, 16–18, 44, 45, 69–70, 71, 99, 201, 204–5; property rights of, 21–24, 42–44, 164; removal of, 25–37, *37*; traditional gender roles of, 16–18, 20–21, 41, 70, 205. *See also* Choctaw and Chickasaw Confederate soldiers; lighthorsemen

Christianity. *See* missionaries

citizenship, Choctaw: for enslaved people of African descent, 6, 68; for freedpeople of African descent, 73, 179, 188–89, 193–94, 197–98, 201, 206; land and, 192, 206; for white people, 70, 71, 199–200. *See also* Choctaw Nation; removal; sovereignty

citizenship, U.S., 33, 204

Civil War battles: (1861) Battle of Bull Run, 136; (1862) Battle of Pea Ridge, 127, 141; (1862) Battle of Locust Grove, 2, *125*; (1862) Battle of Old Fort Wayne, 127–28; (1862) Battle of Round Mountain, 141; (1863) Battle of Cabin Creek, 130; (1863) Battle of Honey Springs, 2, 115, 130, 131, *133*, 148; reenactment of, 1. *See also* Choctaw and Chickasaw Confederate soldiers

Clampitt, Bradley R., 8

clan organization, 13–16. *See also* matrilineality; patrilineality

Clay, Henry, 56

Cochnauer, Nicholas, 172

Coffee, John, 30, 31

Coffin, W. G., 108

Colbert, Buck, 57–58

Colbert, Frank, 53, 57, 58, 59
Colbert, George, 189
Colbert, Holmes, 54, 189
Colbert, Jameson, 144, 145, 232n134
Colbert, Levi, 49
Colbert, Polly, 50, 51, 52, 54, 56
Cole, Jefferson L., 17
Cole, Mary, 58, 212n8
Comanche, 128
communal landholding, 17, 22, 23, 29, 47, 54, 160, 164, 167, 192–93, 206. *See also* landownership

Compiled Service Records of Confederate Soldiers Who Served in Organizations Raised Directly by the Confederate Government (document), 115–18, 126, 137, 149–50, 151

Confederate Congress, 95, 96, 99, 101, 112, 120, 137–38

Confederate Constitution, 3, 101, 107

Confederate soldiers, overview, 121–22, 137. *See also* Choctaw and Chickasaw Confederate soldiers; Civil War battles; white soldiers

Confederate States of America: Choctaw allegiance to, 2–3, 75–76, 80–82, 107–10, 113; Choctaw alliance treaty with, 76, 90–102, 112. *See also* Choctaw and Chickasaw Confederate soldiers; *and names of specific states*

Conner, William B., 141

constitutions: of Cherokee, 19, 44; of Chickasaw, 44; of Choctaw, 8, 14, 24, 41, 44, 64, 120, 166–68, 199; of Confederate States of America, 3, 101, 107; of Creek, 44; of Kansas, 77, 78; of Oklahoma, 204; of U.S., 92, 144, 184

Cooper, Douglas H., 109, 119, 121, 123, 126, 128, 173

corn, 4, 17–18, 53, 54, 55. *See also* agricultural production and labor

cotton, 4, 47, 48. *See also* agricultural production and labor; slavery

Creek Constitution, 44

Creek language, 58

Creek Nation: alliances of, 80, 92, 95; maps, *6, 77, 183*

Creek people: as Confederate soldiers, 140; enslaved people of, 57; forced removal of, 37; land cessions of, 78; lighthorsemen of, 163; livestock cultivation by, 161, 162; on property, 23
criminality: on Choctaw Nation, 18–20, 32; in Indian Territory, 98. *See also* lighthorsemen
Curtis, William, 185–86, 187
Cushman, H. B., 15, 17, 39, 153, 155
Cutler, James Elbert, 196

Darnell, John W., 141
Davis, Harrison, 53
Davis, Jefferson, 80–81, 101, 104, 205
Davis, Lucinda, 57, 58, 60, 115, 132, 148
Dawson, Anthony, 186
Debo, Angie, 109
deerskin trade, 162
De Lusser, Joseph Christophe, 155
Deneale, George E., 137
Denson, Nelson, 63
DeRosier, Arthur H., Jr., 27
desertions, 133–34, 141–42, 149. *See also* Choctaw and Chickasaw Confederate soldiers
disabilities, 148
division of labor. *See* gender roles
Dixon, Emily, 52
Doaksville, 49, 84, 107, 123–24, 127, 136–37. *See also* Treaty of Doaksville (1837)
Dole, William P., 84
Douglass, Frederick, 63
Dowdy, Daniel, 55, 181
Draper, Joanna, 180–81

Eagleson, William, 195
Eaton, John, 30, 31
education: Aboha Kulla Humma on, 42; boarding schools, 33; of freedpeople, 195–96. *See also* literacy
Edwards, John, 84
Edwards, Whit, 133
election process, 41, 99–100, 166, 170, 174. *See also* voting rights

Emancipation Proclamation, 129–30, 179–82, 229n67. *See also* abolition; Reconstruction; slavery
enslaved people of African descent: abuse and killings of, 57–58; emancipation of, 180–87; gun and property ownership by, 63–64; on important crops, 53–54; labor routines of, 49–51; as language interpreters, 58–59; literacy of, 3, 61–63, 221n92; Lycurgus Pitchlynn on, 106–7; population statistics on, 3, 47, 228n26; as property of Cherokee, 62, 181, 182; as property of Chickasaw, 181, 219n14; as property of Choctaw, 2–3, 5, 19, 24, 48–60, 181; religious worship of, 52–53; WPA narratives of, 9–10, 220n77. *See also* Emancipation Proclamation; freedpeople of African descent; slavery
Evans, Eliza, 182, 184
Evans, William McKee, 7

Falconer, Henry I. and Ida L., 112
family organization, 13–16. *See also* matrilineality
farming. *See* agricultural production and labor
Fenderich, Charles, 100
First Choctaw and Chickasaw Mounted Rifles. *See* Choctaw and Chickasaw Confederate soldiers
First Kansas Colored Volunteers, 130, 132
Fite, Gilbert C., 53
Florida, 62, 179, 196. *See also* Confederate States of America
Floyd, Olivia, 149
Folsom, David, 35
Folsom, Edward, 132
Folsom, Israel, 39
Folsom, Jacob, 82–83
Folsom, J. P., 94, 107
Folsom, Peter, 79, 83
Folsom, Sampson, 84–85, 94, 104, 146–47, 189
food shortages, 9, 16, 59

INDEX

Foreman, Stephen, 126–27
Fort Arbuckle, 84, 123, 124
Fort Gibson, *37*, *77*, 130, 132–34, 143
Fort McCulloch, 124
Fortney, Jeff, 89
Fort Smith, 139
Fort Washita, *77*, 123, 124
Fox-Genovese, Elizabeth, 10, 50
Franklin, Thomas, 194
Freedman Bill. *See* Choctaw Freedman Bill (1883)
freedpeople of African descent: Black Codes on, 187–88; Choctaw citizenship of, 6, 68; Choctaw laws and treatment of, 65–67, 178–79, 188–98; on Choctaw Nation, 6, 64–65, 168; sharecropping system and, 191–92. *See also* Emancipation Proclamation; enslaved people of African descent; slavery
French traders, 162
Fugitive Slave Acts, 91, 168

Gabriel's rebellion, 221n106
Gaines, George S., 35
Galloway, Patricia, 40, 159
Gardner, J., 55
Garnes, Millie, 187
Gay, H. W., 71
gender roles: in agricultural production and labor, 16–18, 23–24, 43, 50–51, 54–56, 160–62; livestock production and, 23–24, 54–56, 161–62; in marriage, 70–72; in plantation agriculture, 50–51; in traditional Choctaw society, 16–17, 20–21, 41, 151–54, 205; work and, 29, 233n5. *See also* marriage; masculinity; two spirits
Georgia: forced Native removal from, 11, *37*, 91; landownership in, 195; literacy laws in, 62; marriage laws in, 185–86; on Native sovereignty, 2, 96, 97, 179, 216n103. *See also* Confederate States of America
Gerteis, Louis, 179
Gibson, Arrell M., 40, 139

Glenn, Jesse A., 138
Gold, Harriet, 22–23
Goode, William H., 49
Goodland Academy, 135
Grant, Ulysses S., 193
Graves, Edward, 141
Grayham, Nat, 105, 175
Grayson, Mary, 56–57, 148, 185
Great Depression, 9, 59, 184–85
Green, O. W., 52
Green Corn Dance, 18
Greenhow, Rose, 149
Grimes, William, 191
Guidon, 195
gun ownership, 63–64. *See also* property rights

Hall, Squire, 194
Harkins, George, 34, 77–78
Harkins, Richard, 58
Hauptman, Laurence M., 7
Havard, Gilles, 152
Hawkins, Annie, 185
Heald, John Hobart, 48
Henderson, Henry, 54
Henry, Ida, 183
Hicks, Durant, 143–44, 145–46
Hillyer, Morris, 55
Hindman, Thomas C., 139
Hitchcock, Ethan Allen, 56
Hogue, Erastus, 143–44, 145–46
Holmes, Theophilus, 139
Homa, Iskitini, 119, 173
Homastubbee (chief), 155
Honey Springs. *See* Battle of Honey Springs (1863)
horses, 141, 170–71, 174, 176
Howell, Sylvanus, 128
Hubbard, David, 86–87
Hudson, George (chief), 75, 78–79, 83, 90, 138
hunger, 9, 16, 59
Hunt, William, 226n104
Hunter, William L., 119, 226n104
hunting, 16, 17, 153–54, 161–62, 170, 235n55

Hutson, Hal, 238n42
Hutson, William, 186–87

Iholahata, 14
Imoklasha, 14
Indian Home Guard, 130, 131
Indian Pioneer History (IPH) Collection, 8, 9, 10, 69
Indian Removal Act (1830), 25, 26. *See also* removal
Indian Territory, overview, 4–5, 6, 49, 77, 125, 183. *See also* Cherokee Nation; Chickasaw Nation; Choctaw Nation; Creek Nation; Seminole Nation
Indian Trust Fund, 95
infanticide, 15–16, 20, 42
inheritance laws, 20–21, 42–43. *See also* property rights
Ishii, Izumi, 170–71
isuba, as term, 141

Jackson, Andrew, 4, 25, 30, 38
Jackson, George M., 196
Jackson, Lizzie, 60
John Brown's raid (1859), 65–66, 73
Johnson, Ben, 58, 181
Johnson, Robert, 77
Jones, Evan and John, 77
Jones, Robert M., 48, 54, 75, 89–90, 101, 167
Jones, Willis, 134
Jordan, Sam, 62

Kansas, 77–78, 240n99
Kansas Constitution, 77, 78
Kansas-Nebraska Act (1854), 77
Kemp, Ebenezer Cutnezer, 186
Kidwell, Clara Sue, 27
Kimball, Christopher, 130
Kingsbury, Cyrus, 20, 25, 29, 31
Krauthamer, Barbara, 52

Lafitau, Joseph-François, 152
Lahontan, Louis Armand, 152
Lakota, 180
Lambert, Valerie, 36

land cessions, 3, 4, 30–31, 44. *See also* removal
landownership, 23, 29, 178–79, 194–95, 206. *See also* communal landholding; property rights
language interpretation, 58–59. *See also names of specific languages*
Lause, Mark, 7, 130
LeClerk de Milford, Louis, 157
Lee, S. Orlando, 84
Leeper, Matthew, 128
LeFlore, Greenwood, 25–26, 34, 216n84
LeFlore, Mitchell, 140, 148
Lenoir, Mary Ann, 190
Lieber Code, 7
lighthorsemen: gender of, 41, 163; masculinity and, 163–70; payment for, 79, 102, 164–65; position responsibilities of, 19, 24, 63, 65, 66, 170, 172; as soldiers, 173–74, 176
Lincecum, Gordon, 39
Lincoln, Abraham, 75, 111, 179–80. *See also* Emancipation Proclamation
Lindsay, Mary, 181
literacy: of Choctaw, 164–65; of enslaved people, 3, 61–63, 221n92; missionaries and, 24–25. *See also* education
livestock: Choctaw management of, 28, 54–56; economic importance of, 160–61, 162; naming practices and, 158; as property, 23–24. *See also* agricultural production and labor
Louisiana, 9, 65, 179, 196–97. *See also* Confederate States of America
Love, Isaac, 49
Love, Isom, 57
Love, Kiziah, 50, 51, 52, 57, 59
Lucas, Daniel William, 187
lynchings, 196–97, 240n101

Mackey, M., 35
Makemson, W. K., 132
manumission laws, 67, 221n106. *See also* enslaved people of African descent; freedpeople of African descent; slavery

INDEX

marriage: Choctaw laws and practices on, 16, 21–23, 44, 60, 67–69, 72–73, 198–201; gender roles in, 70–72; naming practices and, 156–57. *See also* gender roles; polygamy

Marston, B. W., 119, 120

masculinity, 152, 175–76; alcohol use and, 165–66, 170, 171–72; Civil War military service and, 173–76, 205; horse raiding and, 170–71; naming practices and, 154–57, 174; red coats and, 158–59; warfare and, 151–56, 164, 172–73, 233n1. *See also* gender roles

matrilineality: of Chickasaw, 99, 102; of Choctaw, 14, 16–18, 44, 45, 69–70, 71, 99, 201, 204–5. *See also* clan organization; patrilineality

Maytubbie, Matthew, 194, 239n88

Maytubby, Peter, 135

McAfee, Abel, 134

McCabe, Edward P., 196

McCoy, Wesley, 68

McCulloch, Ben, 86, 103

McDermott, R., 132

McLoughlin, William, 170–71, 174

McPherson, James M., 7

Mead, Elizabeth Kemp, 14

men. *See* gender roles; masculinity; warriors

menstruation and naming practices, 157–58

Methodists, 25

migration of freedpeople, 196

migration of Native groups. *See* removal

mingoes, as term, 152. *See also* warriors

missionaries, 20–21, 31, 63, 135, 215n60, 216n103

Mississippi: Black Codes in, 187; Indian removal in, 25–37; lynchings in, 197; tribal sovereignty and, 25, 26–27, 216n103. *See also* Confederate States of America

Mississippian Mound Builders, 3

Mississippi River valley, 3–4, 13

Mixon, Eliza "Liza," 182, 237n18

Mobbly, J., 142–43

mob violence, 196–97

Moss, Sally Henderson, 182, 194

Mouse, Lacy, 105

Murrow, Joseph, 127

Muscogee. *See* Creek Nation; Creek people

Mushulatubbee (chief), 31, 34, 79, 155, 169

Muskogean language, 40

Nail, Joe, 35

Nairne, Thomas, 157

naming practices, 154–58, 174

Native military force. *See* Choctaw and Chickasaw Confederate soldiers; Confederate soldiers, overview

Native removal. *See* removal

Native sovereignty. *See* sovereignty

Nat Turner's revolt (1831), 64, 73, 221n106

Naylor, Celia E., 56

Nebraska, 77, 78

Neighbors, Lula, 194, 195

Nelson, Scott, 7

Neosho, 77

neutrality in Civil War: of Cherokee, 86–88, 92, 113; of Choctaw, 75, 76, 83–84, 89–90, 110–12

Ninth Kansas Cavalry, 130

Nitakechi, 31, 34, 35

North Carolina, 221n106. *See also* Confederate States of America

Northrup, Sarah, 22

Nunih Waiyah, 39

O'Brien, Greg, 155, 158–59

Oklahoma, 196, 206–7

Oklahoma Constitution, 204

Oklahoma Slave Narrative Project, 9

Oliver, Amanda, 53, 220n51

Osh Hochifoh Keyu, Chatah, 156–57

overhunting. *See* hunting

Pannell, Caroline, 68

patrilineality, 44, 45. *See also* clan organization; matrilineality

Pavao-Zuckerman, Barnet, 162
Pegg, Thomas, 105
Penicaut, Andre, 121
people of African descent. *See* enslaved people of African descent; freedpeople of African descent
Perkins, David, 129
Perryman, Mose, 56–57
Perryman, Patsy, 53, 58
Pesantubbee, Michelene E., 15
Petite, Phyllis, 181
Pierce, Louis, 68
Pike, Albert, 101, 103, 104, 112, 124, 127, 139–40, 146
Pitchlynn, John, 54, 105
Pitchlynn, Lycurgus, 104, 106–7, 134–35, 175
Pitchlynn, Peter P.: *Atlantic Monthly* piece on, 110–11; as chief, 34–35, 75; on Choctaw Confederate forces, 138–39; on Confederate alliance, 1, 109–10; on devastation of Civil War, 177; early life of, 54, 164; as federal delegate, 100, 226n86; on female prisoners, 149; historical papers by, 8; on labor of freedpeople, 189; on U.S. loyalty, 83
Pitchlynn, Thomas, 104–5
Poe, Matilda, 49–50, 51, 56, 184
police. *See* lighthorsemen
polygamy, 16, 40, 214n20. *See also* marriage
population statistics: of Choctaw and Chickasaw soldiers, 117, 118, 120; of Choctaw Nation, 3, 35, 239n74; of enslaved people, 3, 47, 228n26; of U.S. soldiers, 121; of white soldiers in Native troops, 119–20
poverty, 9, 59, 184–85
Prag, Edward Elmer, 118
prisoners of war, 142–46, 149
property rights, 20–24, 42–44, 63–64, 163–64, 215n79. *See also* landownership
Pushmataha (chief), 154, 155, 169, 234n23

Raboteau, Albert J., 52
ranching. *See* livestock
rape, 20, 42
Rawling, Alice, 181
Reconstruction, 111, 178–79, 188–98, 206. *See also* Emancipation Proclamation; freedpeople of African descent
Rector, Henry M., 85–86
red coats, 158–59
Red River, 48
religious worship, 52–53
removal, 37; of Cherokee, 26, 88–89; of Chickasaw, 4–5, 13, 27–28, 37–39; of Choctaw, 25–37. *See also* land cessions; sovereignty; *and names of specific tribes*
representation in Congress, of Native nations, 33–34, 99–100
retreat, as strategy, 153
revenge tradition, 14–15, 18, 20. *See also* warriors
Reynolds, James E., 200–201
rice, 48
Richardson, Red, 180
Ridge, John, 22
Robertson, Betty, 62
Robinson, Harriett, 238n42
Ross, Charley, 55
Ross, John, 85–88, 92, 105–6
Ross, Joshua, 105, 106
Rowe, Katie, 183, 185, 237n23

Saunt, Claudio, 23
scalping, 105, 213n13
Schermerhorn, John, 20
Scott, S. S., 75, 108, 128
Seddon, James A., 75
self-government. *See* sovereignty
Seminole Nation: alliances of, 80, 92, 95; maps, *6, 77, 183*; missionary work on, 195. *See also* Indian Territory, overview
Seminole people: citizenship rights of, 206; as Confederate soldiers, 140; removal of, 37
separation, 16. *See also* marriage

Seward, W. H., 78
sewing, 50, 220n51, 221n100
sexual violence. *See* rape
sharecropping system, 191–92
Shaw, Stephanie J., 9, 59
Shepherd, Robert, 55
Sheppard, Joe, 54
Sheppard, Morris, 54, 62
Sheriff, Carol, 7
Sherman, William Tecumseh, 192
Simms, Andrew, 62
Sixth Kansas Cavalry, 135
Slater, Sarah, 149
slave narratives project (WPA), 9–10, 59, 220n77
slavery: abolition, 129–30, 180–84, 229n67; among Cherokee, 62, 181, 182; among Chickasaw, 49, 181, 219n14; among Choctaw, 2–3, 5, 19, 24, 48–60, 181–83; Confederate soldier oath on, 144–45; Emancipation Proclamation on, 129–30, 179–82, 229n67; as institution, 5–6, 47–48, 177–78, 203–4; manumission laws, 67, 221n106; task system and, 63, 221n100; Thirteenth Amendment, 180, 182, 184, 229n64. *See also* enslaved people of African descent; freedpeople of African descent
Smallwood, Anna McClendon, 17
Smith, Lou, 185
Snyder, Christina, 164
social organization, 13–16. *See also* matrilineality; patrilineality
South Carolina, 197. *See also* Confederate States of America
sovereignty: of Cherokee, 179, 216n103; of Chickasaw, 27, 38–39; of Choctaw, 2–3, 10–11, 27, 39, 76; Lincoln on, 179–80; missionaries on, 31; slavery and, 176, 177–78, 203–4; states' rights and, 2, 26–27, 203, 216n103. *See also* citizenship, Choctaw; removal
sport. *See* ball playing
"squaw corn," 17–18
states' rights, 2, 26–27, 74, 203, 216n103. *See also* names of specific states

Stephenson, J. R., 35
Stewart, Charles, 94
stickball. *See* ball playing

Taaffe, Francis Desales, 35
task system, 63, 221n100
Taylor, Judy, 58
Tennessee, 6, 221n106. *See also* Confederate States of America
Terrell, Emmaline, 17
Texas, 81, 84, 109. *See also* Confederate States of America
Texas Road, 130, 133
textile production and sewing, 50, 220n51, 221n100
Thirteenth Amendment, 180, 182, 184, 229n64
Thomas, Ella Gertrude Clanton, 190
Thompson, Johnson, 185
Tonkawa Massacre (1862), 128–29
Tonkawa people, 128
trading and traded goods, 98, 159–60, 162
Treaty of Dancing Rabbit Creek (1830), 4, 30–35, 79, 80, 96, 99
Treaty of Doak's Stand (1820), 4, 96, 163, 169
Treaty of Doaksville (1837), 37, 40
Treaty of Fort Adams (1801), 4
Treaty of Hoe Buckintoopa (1803), 4
Treaty of Hopewell (1786), 171
Treaty of Mount Dexter (1805), 4, 79
Treaty of Washington City (1825), 79
Treaty with the Choctaw and Chickasaw (1866), 182–83, 184, 188, 192–94, 206
Tubbee, Ho, 137
Tulsa Race Massacre (1921), 206–7
Turner, Nat, 64, 73, 221n106
Tuskaya-hiniha, 115
Twentieth Texas Cavalry, 131–32
Twenty-Ninth Texas Cavalry, 131–32
two spirits, 17, 152–53, 233n10. *See also* gender roles

Underground Railroad, 65–66
Ural, Susannah J., 7

U.S. Constitution: loyalty oath to, 144; Native constitutions and, 92; Thirteenth Amendment to, 180, 182, 184, 229n64

violence against women, 20, 42, 106
Virginia, 221n106. *See also* Confederate States of America
voting rights, 99, 145, 197, 198. *See also* election process

Wade, Alfred, 94
Wagoner, Sweetie Ivory, 62–63
Wakatubbee, 161
Walker, L. P., 76
Walker, Robert J., 78
Walker, Tandy, 119, 127, 132
Walters, William, 59
Warde, Mary Jane, 8, 204
warriors: Civil War enlistment and, 172–73; naming practices of, 154–56; revenge tradition of, 14–15, 18, 20; in traditional Choctaw society, 151–53. *See also* Choctaw and Chickasaw Confederate soldiers; gender roles; lighthorsemen
Watie, Stand, 88
Watson, Molly, 221n92
weaving and spinning, 50. *See also* textile production and sewing
Webster, Wilson, 137
Wells, Samuel J., 26

White, Charlotte Johnson, 58, 182
White, Richard, 15, 18, 23, 160
white soldiers, 119–22, 137, 139–40
Wichita (tribe), 128
Wickett, Murray R., 196
Williams, James M., 130–31
Williams, Lizzie, 50
Williams, Robert, 181
Wilson, Sarah, 62, 181
Wofford, Acemy, 185
Wolfe, Patrick, 27
Wolfe, Thomas, 105
women: involvement and effects of war on, 148–49; matrilineality, 14, 16–18, 44; naming practices of, 157–58; traditional roles among Choctaw, 16–18, 20–21, 151; violence against, 20, 42, 106. *See also* gender roles
Worcester, Samuel, 216n103
Worcester v. Georgia, 179, 216n103
Word, Sam, 63
Work, Monroe, 196
work and gender roles, 29, 233n5. *See also* agricultural production and labor; hunting; warriors
WPA (Works Progress Administration): IPH Collection, 8; slave narratives project, 9–10, 59, 220n77
Wright, Robert, 194

Yahola, Opothle, 113, 124, 126–27, 149

www.ingramcontent.com/pod-product-compliance
Lightning Source LLC
Chambersburg PA
CBHW030734250426
43671CB00035B/356